D0911401

America's Pursuit of Precision Bombing, 1910-1945

Smithsonian History of Aviation Series
Von Hardesty, Series Editor

On December 17, 1903, on a windy beach in North Carolina, aviation became a reality. The development of aviation over the course of a little less than a century stands as an awe-inspiring accomplishment in both a civilian and military context. The airplane has brought whole continents closer together, at the same time it has been a lethal instrument of war.

This series of books is intended to contribute to the overall understanding of the history of aviation—its science and technology as well as the social, cultural, and political environment in which it developed and matured. Some publications help fill the many gaps that still exist in the literature of flight; others add new information and interpretation to current knowledge. While the series appeals to a broad audience of general readers and specialists in the field, its hallmark is strong scholarly content.

The series is international in scope and includes works in three major categories:

Smithsonian Studies in Aviation History: works that provide new and original knowledge.

Smithsonian Classics of Aviation History: carefully selected out-of-print works that are considered essential scholarship.

Smithsonian Contributions to Aviation History: previously unpublished documents, reports, symposia, and other materials.

Stephen L. McFarland

America's Pursuit of Precision Bombing, 1910–1945

Smithsonian Institution Press

Washington and London

Copyright © 1995 by the Smithsonian Institution.
All rights are reserved.
This book was edited by Initial Cap Editorial Services and designed
by Alan Carter.

Library of Congress Cataloging-in-Publication Data

McFarland, Stephen Lee, 1950–
　　America's pursuit of precision bombing, 1910–1945 / Stephen L. McFarland ;
　foreword by Richard P. Hallion.
　　　p.　cm. — (Smithsonian history of aviation series)
　　Includes bibliographical references and index.
　　ISBN 1-56098-407-4
　　　1. Precision bombing—United States—History.　2. World War,
　1939–1945—Aerial operations, American.　I. Title.　II. Series.
UG703.M376　1995
358.4′2′0973—dc20　　　　　　　　　　　　　94–21955
　　　　　　　　　　　　　　　　　　　　　　　　　CIP

Printed in the United States of America.
10 9 8 7 6 5 4 3 2 1 99 98 97 96 95

TO DR. WESLEY P. NEWTON,

who taught me there was a right way
and a wrong way to research and write,
and whose foot always found the appropriate place
when I did not remember the difference.

Contents

Foreword

In this often fascinating and always instructive book, Professor Stephen L. McFarland targets the entire notion of precision bombing as pursued by the United States from 1910 through 1945. "Precision," as the reader quickly learns, is a relative term: relative to the time in which it is used. In the First World War, airmen dropped bombs by hand or from crude racks, using equally crude sights that automatically built great imprecision into the whole process. In the post–"Great War" years it was this desire to ensure precision attack that drove development of the dive bomber—an ill-conceived vehicle that traded great accuracy for marginal survivability. American precision bombing in the Second World War, using optical sights even as sophisticated as the Norden sight that Professor McFarland discusses in detail, often meant bombs dropping an average of several thousand feet from their aiming points. Indeed, one study in 1944 concluded that only 7 percent of all American bombs fell within 1,000 feet of their aiming point. But, given the crude technology of the time, this was considered acceptable. (In fact, when the Royal Air Force learned that 90 percent of the bombs dropped against Pilsen in 1943 had fallen within 3½ *miles* of the aiming point, mission planners were overjoyed at the "accuracy" of the results.) Significantly, even these kinds of results often had a powerful and, at times, paralyzing effect upon a foe: consider, for example, the air–launched *Blitzkrieg* of 1939–40, or the Allied air campaign against German ground forces in France in 1944, or the success of the oil campaign against Hitler and the B-29 campaign against Japan. After the war, even the skeptical members of the U.S. Strategic Bombing Survey nevertheless were forced to conclude that air power had been "decisive in the war in Western Europe," while, in the Pacific, it had demonstrated that "no nation can long survive the free exploitation of air weapons over its homeland." Overall, the USSBS survey noted that, prior to the Second World War, the United States had "underestimated the predominant role that air power was to play" in the coming war.

To put a contemporary focus on the precision question, consider the following: During the Second World War, the Eighth Air Force found that it took two full combat wings—a force of 108 Boeing B-17 Flying Fortresses, crewed by 1,080 airmen and escorted by hundreds of fighters with hundreds of other pilots, supported by thousands of ground personnel—dropping a total of 648 bombs to guarantee a 96 percent chance of getting just two hits on a single Nazi power-generating plant measuring 400 by 500 feet. In the Gulf War of 1991, a *single* coalition strike airplane carrying two "smart" bombs functioned as effectively as this gaggle on similar strikes against Iraqi power-generation stations. Indeed, the average miss distance of a laser-guided bomb was less than *10 feet*, the average for a conventional "dumb" bomb about 300 feet. Both figures would have been greeted with incredulity by even the most ardent champion of "precision bombing" during the Second World War. For those reasons, then, one must be careful to note that the relativity of precision means that the "miss" of today is not typically the literal "mile" of yesterday. Further, in today's world, the effect of multiple hundreds or even thousands of pounds of high explosive from a "missed" conventional bomb detonating several hundred feet or so from a "soft" target is usually indistinguishable in its final, grim result from a "hit" bomb directly upon it.

But if precision is relative, it is nevertheless a quest that has occupied the American military—and other services in other nations as well—for a long time. It is tempting to state that the quest for precision is a peculiarly American one, traceable to the enshrinement of the frontier marksman and incorporating all the best elements of a New World desire to minimize the horror of war and the danger of the euphemistically named "collateral damage" to noncombatants. In fact, many of these elements are present in the history of the American quest for surgical strike. But the quest is primarily pragmatically rooted in the desire for strong, focused military effect, as reflected in the robust efforts other nations have made—particularly since the Second World War—to develop their own precision-attack capabilities. This subject—the post–Second World War development of the precision weapons and precision navigational technologies now embedded in the military capabilities of advanced nations—is one that richly deserves its own book, a "volume two" to the present work which, one hopes, Professor McFarland will write.

Just why is precision important? Is it just some shibboleth, some Holy Grail of war that lacks significance? Or is it the new face of war, an attribute of the combined aerospace and electronic revolutions of the past 50 years? In fact, precision has a profound influence on war. Hand in hand with precision weapons must be excellent intelligence and precision navigation, and the whole secured by reliable communications, and set in motion by military leaders operating to realistic doctrine.

Precision can offset the need for multiple strikes against the same target that characterized air operations in the Second World War, Korea, and Vietnam, and which resulted in literally thousands of aircraft falling victim to increasingly wary and prepared defenses. (Bridges are a notable example; bridge strikes often required dozens or even hundreds of sorties over several weeks or months to destroy a single bridge. In the Gulf War, forty-one bridges were dropped in two weeks by laser-guided munitions.) It also acts as a "force multiplier": it enables the attacker to do more with a lot less. A force of precision-strike airplanes, perhaps complemented by precision-guided "cruise" missiles, can attack simultaneously across an entire theater of conflict; these parallel attacks can undo in minutes an opponent well equipped to confront more traditional sequential attacks directed against difficult targets. In the modern world, coupled with stealth technology, it enables an attacker to slip undetected and unengaged into the very heart of an enemy's vital center, and deliver a decisive blow, no matter how prepared or otherwise alert the defender may be.

On the opening night of the Gulf War, for example, a small number of F-117 stealth fighters armed with laser-guided bombs shattered Iraq's air defense network, key command and control facilities, and key leadership targets, opening Iraq up to predatory follow-on conventional attackers. Within minutes of the opening of the war, then, the ultimate fate of Iraq's military machine had been cast. Such would have been unthinkable in previous conflicts. Finally, precision attack reduces to a great degree the traditional high "misery factor" present in previous wars. It reduces the human losses of both attacker and defender by targeting more precisely. (The reader may mentally compare, for example, the images of Berlin after V-E day and Baghdad after the ceasefire.)

Above all, and certainly since the advent of precision munitions, any nation contemplating aggression against a country possessing precision weapons now realizes that the results of a decision to go to war may be the utter destruction of its military machine. Thus, there is a deterrence value in precision attack that acts to constrain the impulses of would-be aggressors. This book is important because it traces the roots of the precision notion, when individuals of diverse motivation and background sought to ensure greater accuracy in air attack, typified by the "bomb in a pickle barrel" claims for the legendary Norden bombsight. If their vision far exceeded their grasp, it was their vision that helped generate the world in which we now live—a world characterized by precision in everything humanity does: from science and technology to, for both better and worse, the way wars of the late twentieth century are waged.

RICHARD P. HALLION

Acknowledgments

The general rule in historical writing is that publications are the product of many historians, as new works are based on what previous historians have written. In the current case, no body of secondary literature exists. This work is based on primary materials, necessitating a special acknowledgment of the custodians to those primary materials.

Special gratitude is therefore directed to Col. Elliott V. Converse III, director of the U.S. Air Force Historical Research Agency at Maxwell Air Force Base, Montgomery, Alabama, and his staff, including Capt. George W. Cully, Dr. James H. Kitchens III, and Archangelo Difante. At the National Archives, both in Washington, D.C., and Suitland, Maryland, Barry L. Zerby, Edward J. Reese, and Dave Giordano were especially dutiful in satisfying my requests for guidance and documentation. At the Hagley Museum and Library in Wilmington, Delaware, thanks to Dr. Glenn Porter, Carol Ressler Lockman, Michael H. Nash, and Barbara Hall. The staffs of the Library of Congress Manuscript Division in Washington and the Air University Library in Montgomery also deserve special mention.

A number of individuals provided assistance and guidance. Susan Moody at Norden Systems not only expedited access to the few resources her company retained from the early years but, more important, also provided a list of names of individuals who participated in many of the events included herein. Special among these was Ned Lawrence, who tirelessly provided his insight and memory of the war years.

The Auburn University Humanities Foundation, Dr. Paul Parks, Vice-President for Research at Auburn University, the U.S. Air Force Historical Research Agency, and the Hagley Museum and Library provided funding to make possible research trips to the primary materials on which this study is based.

At Auburn University Drs. Gordon C. Bond, Curtis T. Henson, Wesley P. Newton, and William F. Trimble provided assistance, consultations, support, and criticism.

Thanks also to Dr. Richard K. Smith, whose technical knowledge and keen critical eye made a special contribution, and to Therese D. Boyd of Initial Cap Editorial Services for the most essential of book publishing functions, copyediting.

I wish I could thank the staff of the Freedom of Information–Privacy Acts Section of the Federal Bureau of Investigation, but two and one-half years of waiting to access 1,000 pages of blacked-out 50-year-old files is hardly in keeping with the ideals of a government of the people, by the people, and for the people. Thanks to Congressman Glen Browder of Alabama for his attempts to break through the bureaucratic logjam of the Freedom of Information Act, that hoax perpetrated by official Washington on the American people in the name of democracy and open government.

Photographs are courtesy of Hagley Museum and Library, Library of Congress, U.S. Air Force Historical Research Agency, U.S. Air Force Air University Office of History, National Air and Space Museum of the Smithsonian Institution, Norden Systems Division of United Technologies, and the National Archives. Text selections are with permission as follows: selections from *The Fall of Fortresses: A Personal Account of the Most Daring—and Deadly—Air Battles of World War II* by Elmer Bendiner, publisher Putnam's Sons. Copyright © 1980. Reprinted by permission of the author. Selections from *Mission with LeMay* by Curtis E. LeMay and MacKinlay Kantor, copyright © 1965 by Curtis E. LeMay and MacKinlay Kantor. Reprinted by permission of Doubleday, a division of Bantam Doubleday, Dell Publishing Group. Selections from *High Honor*, edited by Stuart Leuthner and Oliver Jensen, copyright © 1989. Reprinted by permission of the Smithsonian Institution Press. Curtis LeMay quote from *The Making of the Atomic Bomb*, copyright © 1986 by Richard Rhodes. Reprinted by permission of Simon & Schuster, Inc. Selections from *The Price of Honor: The World War One Letters of Naval Aviator Kenneth Macleish*, edited by Geoffrey L. Rossano. Copyright © 1991 by the U.S. Naval Institute, Annapolis, Maryland. Selections from *Words on War* by Jay M. Shafritz. Copyright © 1990. Reprinted by permission of the publisher, Prentice Hall/A Division of Simon & Schuster, New York. Selections from *Voices from the Great War* by Peter Vansittart. Copyright © 1984. Used with permission of the publisher, Franklin Watts, Inc., New York.

Finally, my love, admiration, and apologies to my family for the seven years this effort required. This book belongs to them.

A Note on Terms

A major difficulty in writing a history covering three and a half decades of
the twentieth century is the changing spelling for new words created during the period and the changing names and designations of units, organizations, and equipments. In World War I the person dropping bombs from
an aircraft was generally referred to as a *bomber*. By the 1920s the term
bombardier had come into common use, though the U.S. Navy and the
British continued to use *air bomber* into the 1930s and World War II, respectively. Until World War II, *bombsight* was generally two words (*bomb
sight*). For simplicity in this history, bombardiers dropped bombs by aiming through bombsights.

In 1907 the air force of the U.S. Army was the Aeronautical Division of
the Signal Corps. In 1914 it became the Signal Corps Aviation Section. In
1918 it became the Air Service, though not officially until June 4, 1920.
In July 1926 it became the Army Air Corps (with an additional General
Headquarters Air Force in 1935) and in June 1941 the Army Air Forces.
Of greater potential confusion, in 1917 the Signal Corps established the
Equipment Division, later the Airplane Engineering Department, at
North Field, later McCook Field, Dayton, Ohio. In 1918 the new Air Ser-
vice changed the unit's name to the Airplane Engineering Division and

then the Engineering Division. In 1926 the leadership of the new Air Corps renamed it the Materiel Division, which moved to Wright Field close to Dayton in the spring of 1927. On April 1, 1942, the Division became the Air Corps Materiel Command and the Air Force Materiel Command on April 22, 1942. Then came the Materiel Command (April 15, 1943), the Army Air Forces Materiel Command (January 15, 1944), the Army Air Forces Materiel and Services (July 17, 1944), the Army Air Forces Technical Service Command (August 31, 1944), the Air Technical Service Command (July 1, 1945), and the Air Materiel Command (March 9, 1946). The Norden bombsight of World War II fame began as the Norden Mark XV bombsight with Roman numerals under Navy designation, changing to the Mark 15 bombsight with Arabic numbers in World War II. The Navy designated various versions of the Norden bombsight by adding Mod. numbers (e.g., Mark 15 Mod. 5). The Army preferred to call the Norden the M-series bombsight, with versions of it numbered sequentially (e.g., M-9). To keep it interesting, or at least confusing, the Navy chose to call its autopilots Stabilized Bombing Approach Equipment (SBAE), while the Army Air Corps/Army Air Forces preferred Automatic Flight Control Equipment (AFCE).

For historical accuracy, the titles of organizations and equipments will be the name used during the period under consideration, according to the service under consideration.

America's Pursuit of Precision Bombing, 1910–1945

Introduction

With any luck it would be the last bombing mission of the greatest war in human history. In a war of superlatives, of the most horrific weapons yet dredged from the human propensity for self-destruction, the mightiest bomber of the war carried one of the two most powerful bombs of the war to its target. In a war where mass slaughter of civilians had become commonplace, this would be total war with a vengeance. Here would be the climax to six years of strategic bombing aimed at bringing the war to the economies and civilians behind the soldiers on the front lines.

Hunched over in the nose of the B-29 *Enola Gay* on August 6, 1945, bombardier Maj. Thomas Ferebee of the 509th Composite Group followed a ritual performed hundreds of thousands of times during the war. In his hands was the most important secret project of the prewar era, the Norden bombsight,[1] there to drop the most important secret project of the war era, the atomic bomb. Over Hiroshima Ferebee located the target from 12 miles out. Uncharacteristically, clouds presented no obstacle on this day to his visual Norden bombsight. Taking control of the *Enola Gay*, he killed drift, the effects of wind, so that his aiming point, the Aioi Bridge over the Ota River, moved down the vertical cross hairs in his eyepiece.

Ferebee next killed rate, synchronizing the bombsight's mechanism to the B-29's movement over the target, so that the ground below seemed to freeze in the sight. Finally he positioned the bridge squarely on the sight's horizontal cross hair. With every adjustment of the bombsight's knobs, Ferebee moved the control surfaces of the B-29 through the Minneapolis-Honeywell C-1 autopilot linked to his bombsight. The bombardier had to direct the 55 tons of aircraft and bomb to intersect that one point in the sky from which the bomb, when dropped, could be expected to hit the target. The rest was up to the analog computer/bombsight this bombardier had come to know so intimately during the war. The dropping of the "Little Boy," atomic bomb was by machine, not human. When the *Enola Gay* reached that one point, the bomb would drop automatically.[2]

The approach to the target was routine, probably more routine than Ferebee's sixty-three missions in the European war. During the last two minutes of the bomb run, the autopilot controlled the *Enola Gay*, maintaining gyroscopically stabilized flight. The Norden bombsight's gears meshed, transforming Ferebee's manual adjustments into mechanical solutions to the geometric equations that represented the bomb release point. At 9:15 (8:15 Hiroshima time) the bombsight directed the bomb shackles of the B-29 to open while the *Enola Gay* flew at a ground speed of 328 MPH six miles up. In the 43 seconds it took for the bomb to drop to its detonation point at 1,890 feet, pilot Lt. Col. Paul W. Tibbets initiated his escape maneuver. The Norden bombsight, its job done, became dead weight.

Major Ferebee, despite using the most accurate optical bombsight ever developed, missed the aiming point by approximately 800 feet. Twelve and a half thousand tons of TNT-equivalent atomic explosion insured that accuracy was not critical. His inaccurate delivery meant little to those who waited for the holocaust on the ground. The detonator, which had caused so many problems for those involved in the Manhattan Project, worked to perfection. A city died.[3]

Three days later, the second atomic bomber, *Bock's Car*, flew first to Kokura, but haze and smoke from a burning steel mill bombed two days earlier concealed the target, the Kokura Arsenal. The great flaw of the optical Norden bombsight prevented Kokura's rendezvous with destruction—perhaps the greatest "close call" in history, especially because it had also been the back-up target for the Hiroshima mission. Clouds covered the primary Nagasaki target, the Mitsubishi Shipyards, but the pilot, Maj. Charles Sweeney, decided to make a radar bombing run because of fuel problems. A brief hole in the clouds three miles from the primary allowed the bombardier, Capt. Kermit Beahan, to lock his Norden sight on the secondary target, the Mitsubishi Steel and Arms Works. After 52 seconds of fall from 31,000 feet, the 22,000 tons of TNT-equivalent that was the "Fat Man" atomic bomb exploded at 1,650 feet above Nagasaki, nearly 1,500 feet from the aiming point.[4]

From direct causes and by 1950 from delayed causes, 200,000 had died in Hiroshima and 140,000 in Nagasaki from the two atomic bombs.[5] According to the prewar air power prophets, such attacks on civilians would bring a quick end to war. Forty-five months after the attack on Pearl Harbor, the Japanese surrendered. Was the surrender due to these terribly destructive attacks on civilians, or was Japan, nearly prostrate from blockade and conventional bombing, already prepared to surrender?

When humans fought with swords, lances, and pikes, accuracy was not a major concern. When humans first threw rocks, sharpened sticks, or spears, they quickly learned that the advantages of range were minimal without accuracy. David practiced with his sling to improve accuracy. The Romans wound cords around their javelins to give them spin and improve accuracy. In the age of gunpowder, gunsmiths added rifling to improve accuracy. Historians write about the importance of armor protection, mobility, range, and maneuver in achieving victory, but largely ignore the concern of accuracy.

The development of the airplane provided armies with increased range and speed, but with decreased accuracy. Two generations of airmen strove between the world wars to improve accuracy because World War I had demonstrated the potential of air power, but also its underlying weakness. Without accuracy, air power was more bluster than power.

In an atomic world, it seemed accurate bombing would never be the same. The awesome power of nuclear and thermonuclear bombs compensated for poor accuracy. In an earlier age the U.S. Army and Navy undertook bombsight research to make the airplane a weapon of war and developed aerial strategies for winning wars based on their experiences with bombing accuracy. Motivated by the horrors of trench warfare in World War I; repulsed by the thought of targeting civilian population centers through area bombing; inspired by organizational drives for independence, strategic bombing being the only function of air power not tied directly to the Army or Navy; in pursuit of the "economy of force" principle of war ("it is only the hits . . . that actually count"); and as historian Michael Sherry has shown, driven by a technological fanaticism, the services intended for precision bombing to sink ships and destroy an enemy's morale, not by terror, but by the cumulative effect of having its means of carrying on the conflict destroyed.[6]

For the Army this strategy evolved out of the antiwar atmosphere of the 1920s. From 1914 to 1918, 19 million human beings had died. The war killed 10 million soldiers and wounded 21 million, the majority in futile frontal charges against multiple layers of fetid trenches, "springy like a mattress because of all the bodies underneath,"[7] protected by barbed wire, machine guns, and rapid-firing artillery. Jacques Meyer described it as "a spectral semi-conscious life, interrupted only by the eruption of danger: sudden attacks, periodic bombardments, the insidious accumulation of gas in gullies and hollows, machine-guns discovered by surprise—everything overwhelmed the footsoldier . . . the eternal fame of Verdun—as hell, created as much by misery as by danger."[8] To military men the immediate postwar challenge was to insure the next war would not be a repeat of trench warfare. In Germany the answer was blitzkrieg. In the United States the Army's air arm proposed a revolutionary solution.

It seemed so simple—use aircraft to fly over an enemy's army and navy and strike directly at a nation's heart. It made sense—avoid a nation's strength and strike at the vulnerable industrial complexes at the center of modern warfare. It was a solution deceptively easy to advocate, but one that presented prodigious difficulties to those assigned to carry it out. Constructing a bomber to carry bombs to the targets was one major obstacle, another was developing a bombsight to aim the bombs to hit the targets.

The critical component of this new form of warfare was the Norden bombsight and associated equipment, with which the Army and Navy hoped to achieve the bombing accuracy necessary to destroy an enemy's industrial fabric and sink its ships. Accuracy was the key—achieving the desired results with the fewest wasted bombs. Sending bombers with their highly trained crews into the teeth of enemy defenses just to miss their targets made little economic sense when a B-17 cost $187,000 ($1.2 million in 1992 dollars), a B-24 $215,000 ($1.4 million in 1992 dollars), and a B-29 $509,000 ($3.3 million in 1992 dollars).[9] The Navy realized the cost was too great, the accuracy too poor, and abandoned the Norden bombsight in favor of dive bombing. Against Germany in World War II the U.S. Army Air Forces stayed with high-altitude Norden-directed bombing in the face of heavy losses, rarely resorting to area bombing. Against Japan, in the face of light losses but insufficient results, it rejected precision bombing in favor of area bombing, both to destroy the Japanese ability to resist and to terrorize the population, culminating in the atomic bombings.

The American experience against Germany proved the limitations of the Norden technology and the doctrine of war based on it. Such bombing could not win wars single-handedly, but could hasten their end. Against Japan the American experience proved that if a nation attacked population targets, killing enough civilians, then strategic bombing could end a war. Or so it seemed. The general in command of the bombing of Japan, Curtis LeMay, even with mass area fire-bombing raids and atomic weapons, still saw bombing as aimed at industrial targets. He struck Kyoto from the list of possible targets for an atomic bomb because it "wasn't much of a military target ... bombing people gets you nowhere—it's just not profitable."[10] One thing for sure—nuclear weapons destroyed the moral high ground of the American way of air war based on accurate, precision bombing. Army plans to attack the machines of war, not the people of war, gave way to killing the machines and the people of war. The ugliness, confusion, doubt, and discomfort of the Cold War and its nuclear bombs replaced the confidence, principles, and convictions of World War II and its precision bombing of the machines of war based on Norden bombsights.

The dead would not appreciate the tragic irony of what had happened at Hiroshima and Nagasaki. One nation, committed to the precision strategic bombing of the machines that produced the weapons of war when the war began and carried out at such great cost in Europe, had by the end of the war against Japan adopted the greatest weapons of mass destruction in the history of the world. Equally ironic, Ferebee and Beahan used the most accurate optical bombsight ever developed to drop weapons that needed the least precise aiming of any in the world until that time. Folk wisdom was that "close only counted with horseshoes and hand grenades." After Hiroshima and Nagasaki, pundits would add atomic bombs to that list.

Some public relations whiz once said that a Norden bombsight could drop a "bomb into a pickle barrel"—a phrase that stuck and still haunts the device.[11] It never could. One observer watched Norden bombsights in use at Monte Cassino. "I could see bombs bursting 10 miles behind American lines. They were dropping them all over the fucking landscape. Maybe it was true that they could hit a pickle barrel with that Norden bombsight, but there were no pickle barrels in the Liri Valley that day."[12] No matter. The phrase raised visions of frontier marksmen always hitting their mark—the guilty and never the innocent. It raised images of a special American way of war. It satisfied a deep-seated American need for the moral high ground in war while satisfying an American hunger for technological achievement. Until the arrival of laser- and television-guided conventional munitions during the conflict in Vietnam, there would be no more talk of hitting pickle barrels. In the Persian Gulf War, Americans seemed to gain special satisfaction from bombing marksmanship, again satisfying that especially American desire to kill only bad guys, not "innocent" civilians (in appearances, if not in fact), with "high tech" gadgetry.

Although nearly forgotten in the age of electronics and nuclear weapons, the Norden bombsight served an earlier generation as the ultimate technological wonder, the highest achievement of mechanical engineering. It was probably America's first top secret military project, a product of a company that represented the first hesitant step in the direction of what later became America's military-industrial complex, formed to develop a technology for which there was no commercial use. Shrouded in secrecy and myth until late in World War II, it was for Americans an example of good ol' Yankee ingenuity (actually a Dutch citizen living in Brooklyn invented it) and a weapon of democracy that would defeat the forces of totalitarian fascism. Maj. Gen. Benjamin D. Foulois, chief of the Army Air Corps from December 1931 to December 1935, called it "the most important *military secret project* under development by the Air Corps."[13]

In Europe American airmen called it the "football," in the Pacific the "Blue Ox," after Paul Bunyan's constant companion. Men and women went to jail or were court-martialed for revealing or trying to reveal its secrets. The U.S. Army and Navy almost went to war with each other over possession of it. Behind these headlines were the difficulties of protecting the security of the Norden bombsight, training some 50,000 young men to operate it, manufacturing 90,000 versions, and devising expensive programs to improve it and studies on how to use it. Army planners created a whole doctrine of warfare, one that continues to influence strategic planning today, based on its capabilities.[14] The United States spent approximately $1.5 billion (nearly $10 billion in 1992 dollars), 65 percent of the cost of the atomic bomb project,[15] to produce 90,000 Norden bombsights.[16] It was responsible for most of the destruction dropped on Germany and Japan from American aircraft during the war, and for killing over 400,000 human beings in pursuit of Allied victory.[17]

Exposed to the light of history, the Norden bombsight was just a mechanical device for dropping bombs. Although it did this better than any other similar device of its time, its achievements remain the stuff of mythology. Even today, nearly 60 years since its development, few know little more about the Norden bombsight than an earlier generation when the device was a military secret. One author described the B-17 Flying Fortress in World War II as old technology and the Norden bombsight as new technology—the Norden bombsight first flew in 1931, four years before the B-17. Another wrote that Carl L. Norden, Inc., produced 25,000 bombsights for the United States in World War II at a unit cost of $10,000—it produced over 34,000 and the price never reached $10,000. Another raised an old controversy about a Sperry bombsight being superior to the Norden bombsight, ignoring hundreds of thousands of test bombings that proved otherwise. Still another author of a detailed accounting of the atomic bombing of Nagasaki misidentified the Norden bombsight used on the mission as a Mark 15—one can only wonder how many Army airmen from the war might have become incensed at the use of the Navy designation for the Victor Adding Machine–produced M-9B Norden bombsight installed in *Bock's Car*. And there is the compelling story of Mary Babnick Brown, who has claimed for nearly 50 years that Carl Norden used her "blonde hair, never bleached or touched with a hot iron, 34″ long," to construct the cross hairs in his bombsight—Norden used etched glass.[18]

In the 1950s, at the height of the Cold War and with turbojets, radar, and nuclear weapons at the forefront of military technology, surplus Norden bombsights sold for as little as $24.50. Today, riding a wave of nostalgia, a Norden bombsight in good condition sells for $8,000. It is time to examine the reality. Curtis LeMay tried to put the Norden bombsight in proper perspective: "In war the main idea is to get the bombs on the targets."[19] Easier said than done.

1

Means for Dropping Projectiles from Aerial Crafts

When Lt. Franz Uchatius used some 200 unmanned balloons to carry small bombs over Venice in 1849, accuracy was not critical. The attacking Austrians aimed at the morale of the Venetians, not specific targets. Accuracy involved only the one-dimensional element of range error,[1] the distance from the target, the city of Venice, to the actual point of bomb impact, measured along the ground track of the balloon. Uchatius attached burning fuses to time the release of his bombs to solve the range problem, with most bombs falling short or long of the target. The wind determined the deflection error, or the distance from the target to the actual point of bomb impact, measured left or right of the track of the balloon on the ground. It was a simple, though not particularly accurate, bombsighting process. A few bombs fell on Venice, but most on the surrounding countryside. The Austrian army initiated a principle of air warfare that would guide air forces for the next 150 years: when the means and conditions for accurate bombing were unavailable, air forces would target easy-to-hit cities and the morale of the people who inhabited them.

Balloons gave way to powered, controlled, heavier-than-air flight in 1903 and the challenge of dropping a bomb accurately from the air became more complicated. Airplanes were faster and could overcome the influences of wind, forcing bombardiers to solve the two-dimensional problem of range and deflection. To regularize this task, they designed bombsights that treated the sighting problem as a line-of-sight concern, similar to aiming a rifle. The first bombsight was a line painted on the fuselage of an aircraft. When the target came into the pilot's line of sight along this painted line, he released his bombs. It worked at one altitude, at one speed, and with one type of bomb, depending more on luck than skill. At lower altitudes accuracy was better, but at the cost of greater exposure to defensive fire. The technological imperative so prevalent in flight soon led to a two-nail bombsight, permitting the movement of nails vertically to adjust for altitude and horizontally to adjust for ground speed, but did little to improve accuracy.[2]

In 1910 Riley E. Scott, a former soldier in the U.S. Army, constructed the world's first practical bombsight allowing different speeds and altitudes. Calling his device a "means for dropping projectiles from aerial crafts," Scott combined a telescope for measuring the speed of the aircraft with a table of figures and a barometer for incorporating speed and altitude into the sight. The bombardier pointed the telescope at a 45-degree angle in front of the aircraft and waited for an object on the ground to intersect the scope's cross wire. Starting a stopwatch, he pivoted the telescope to the vertical position, stopping the watch when the same ground object again intersected the cross wires, thus measuring his speed relative to the ground. After consulting the barometer for the altitude and a ballistics table for the bomb time of fall, the bombardier set the telescope at the proper forward angle. When the target appeared beneath the cross wires, the bombardier released his bomb.

The first timing bombsight, Scott's device measured the movement of a fixed point relative to the aircraft.[3] It depended on the ability of the pilot to maintain a constant speed and altitude during the timing process, but ignored the effects of wind and aircraft oscillation. According to Henry Arnold, commander of American air forces in World War II, Scott achieved "considerably more accuracy than was achieved by just tossing it [the bomb] overboard."[4]

The War Department expressed little interest in Scott's invention, costing the United States the world's lead in bombsight technology for 21 years. Lt. Paul Beck had to build his own bombsight when he dropped dummy bombs at a Los Angeles flying meet in early 1910. One year later Lt. Myron Crissy dropped America's first live bomb without an aiming

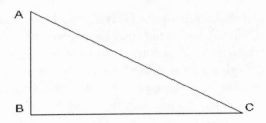

$$\overline{AC} = \sqrt{\overline{AB}^2 + \overline{BC}^2}$$

Figure 1.1

device. Crissy's achievement forced the Army to begin tests of Scott's bombsight in October 1911. When airmen accompanied Pershing's Punitive Expedition to Mexico in 1916, however, they dropped their small bombs by hand, over the side, with no aiming devices. Scott took his invention to France, where from 650 feet he dropped twelve out of fifteen bombs within 33 feet of the target at Villacoublay airdrome. His success won him a $27,500 Michelin prize and brought a bomb-aiming technology to Europe used by both sides in World War I.[5]

Scott's crude analog device provided a mechanical solution to the geometric problem of triangulation. The bombardier determined altitude, side $\overline{AB}$ of a right triangle, using an aneroid barometer marked in feet rather than in pounds of atmospheric pressure. He used a stopwatch to time the aircraft's movement over the ground during a period of time equal to the movement of the bombsight's telescope through a 45-degree arc. Next he determined ground speed and the distance on the ground, side $\overline{BC}$, covered during the bomb's time of fall. Side $\overline{AC}$, the line-of-sight distance from the point of bomb release to the target, was the square root of the sum of the squares of sides $\overline{AB}$ and $\overline{BC}$ (see Figure 1.1).

There were other factors Scott's bombsight did not consider. In a vacuum with no gravity, any bomb dropped would continue to travel with the dropping aircraft. Add gravity and the bomb would drop to earth on a parabolic, ballistic trajectory, at an acceleration of 32 feet per second per second. Add atmosphere and the bomb would fall short of the vacuum point

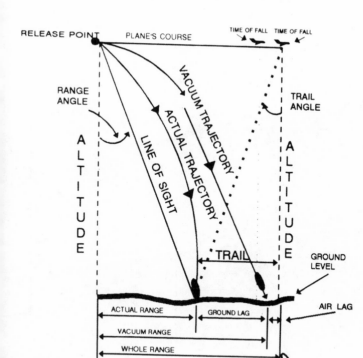

RELEASE POINT   PLANE'S COURSE   TIME OF FALL   TIME OF FALL

RANGE
ANGLE   TRAIL
                                                  ANGLE

VACUUM TRAJECTORY

ACTUAL TRAJECTORY

LINE OF SIGHT

A L T I T U D E   A L T I T U D E

TRAIL   GROUND
                                                  LEVEL

ACTUAL RANGE   GROUND LAG   AIR LAG

VACUUM RANGE

WHOLE RANGE

STILL AIR

Figure 1.2

of impact due to air resistance. The difference between the vacuum point of impact and the atmosphere point of impact was trail (see Figure 1.2).[6]

Wind, however, complicated the bombsighting problem, causing the bomb to fall to the side of the line of sight to the target or the track of the aircraft across the ground. This difference between the actual trajectory under the influence of wind and the projected or normal trajectory was crosstrail. Bombing tests revealed the importance of bomb ballistics and wind. Although gravity accelerated bombs toward the ground at a constant rate in a vacuum, in the atmosphere wind resistance and the size and aerodynamic design of the bomb contributed to varying bomb speeds and distances traveled during the time of fall. Wind affected bombing accuracy, changing the course of bombs after release, but also changing the speed of the bombing aircraft. Linearly, winds increased or decreased the bomber's speed, increasing the range error unless the crew had time to measure ground speed using Scott's timing technique.

With all factors calculated, the problem of accurate bombsighting grew

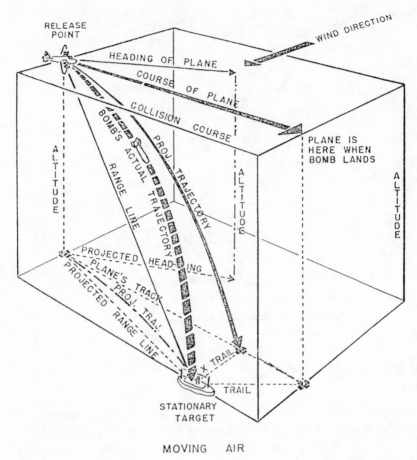

Figure 1.3

in complexity beyond Scott's simple triangle (see Figure 1.3). Even at low speeds and altitudes, his method was less than adequate. World War I–era altimeters were notoriously inaccurate and had no means of adjusting for temperature. His device measured ground speed with a greater degree of accuracy, but did not incorporate the influence of wind and only estimated the effects of gravity on the falling bomb. Scott did not consider aircraft oscillation about the vertical, longitudinal, and lateral axes of flight, which would distort the ABC triangle, altering the basic calculation. His primary consideration was range, calculated as the sum of the speed of the bomb at the point of release and its acceleration toward the ground due to gravity.

In World War I bombsighting calculations were primarily products of bombing tests and experience rather than mathematics. Training in the use of wartime bombsights for Americans consisted of direction from combat-experienced crews and practice near the front. Few cared for the technical aspects of bomb-aiming. Poet Gill Wilson wrote that

> Pilots get the credit
> but the gunner rings the bell
> When we go to bomb the columns
> on the road to Aix-la-Pelle! . . .
>
> Duck to set your bomb sight
> as the targets may unfold,
> Figure out your ground speed
> and compute your angles right
> For you pack a ton of shrapnel
> and you make report tonight! . . .
>
> Don't lie down you buzzard
> till you're God damn sure you're dead! . . .
> Gunners have no license
> just to crumple down and die
> While there's still a bit of team work
> to contribute in the sky![7]

Training manuals were largely nonexistent. After instruction bombardiers gained skill from flying missions and observing where certain adjustments of the bombsights caused bombs to fall. The Army established a bombardment training center at Clermont-Ferrand, France, in December 1917, but it prepared only 212 pilots and 262 observers before the armistice. Late in the war air forces offered ground bombing trainers. Originally, bombsights that were mounted on movable towers aimed at a board, trainees calling out when they believed they had aimed their sights correctly at a dot on the board. An advanced system by 1918 called for trainees to drop 40-gram dummy bombs from a fixed tower onto a simple conveyor belt moving painted targets past the view of a bombsight.[8]

With this preparation, airmen learned that a bomb took so many seconds to fall from a given altitude and traveled so many feet at a given speed. Flying by the "seat of their pants" solved any other aspects of the bomb-sighting problem. Simple observation revealed the relative impact of pilot errors, changes in altitude and speed, wind, and aircraft oscillations in reducing accuracy. An American aviator, Kenneth MacLeish, described his experience: "I sure am crazy about day bombing, because after having been up at Dunkirk during so many raids, I took a keen and personal interest in where my bombs went, and when I cut them loose I leaned over the side with a two-foot grin to watch them, and then I said to those below, Now, you run for a change!"[9]

The war brought quick lessons, the first of which was dropping bombs over the side of an airplane by hand was an inefficient and ineffective means of bomb delivery, despite MacLeish's grin.[10] But if bombing lacked accuracy, the danger of bombing missions was always there. Bruce Hopper of the 96th Bombardment Squadron "sat on a helmet filled with sand as protection" and "we had to look out for trees and German fighters, and we didn't have parachutes."[11] There was safety in altitude during bombing runs, though at the sacrifice of accuracy. German Gothas over England typically flew at 12,500 to 16,000 feet.[12] The U.S. Army's chief signal officer, in charge of the Air Service, told the Senate Committee on Military Affairs that the Germans had "small chance to hit what they are aiming at. They simply drop the bombs when and where they can." An American General Staff study of 1915 concluded that "at the height at which aeroplanes are required to fly it is extremely difficult to hit an object with any certainty" unless attacked with formations of thirty to sixty bombers.[13]

The first bombsight developed during the war to overcome these limitations was the British "pre-set vector" sight, consisting of a board with two wood sticks or nails, one for altitude and the other for ground speed, and a spirit level. The pilot or bombardier made all settings to this 1914 sight before reaching the target area, allowing the pilot to concentrate on the correct approach to the target. When the two nails or sticks came together in line as the pilot viewed through them at the target, the crew released the bombs. Easy to use and simple in design, its preset nature required the pilot to fly at a constant speed, height, and course, either directly into or with the wind. Smooth flying was essential. Training suggested an average circular error of 600 feet from 10,000 feet of altitude—an error that rose to 900 feet under the stress of combat. By 1918 the British had modified this sight to use a pivoted lever, allowing for different speeds and altitudes over the target area, found in a table of values carried aboard the aircraft.

Lt. Cdr. Harry E. Wimperis of the Royal Naval Air Service's Imperial College of Science developed the British Wimperis "drift setting bombsight," dependent on predetermined bombing tables. The bombardier adjusted several levers to reflect air speed, altitude, and the ballistics of the bombs being used. The pilot flew toward the target, directly with or against the wind, and when the front sight lined up with the rear sight, the bombardier released his bombs. Little more than two nails used in the same fashion as the sights on a rifle, the Wimperis differed only in allowing the nails to be adjusted to reflect different speeds, altitudes, and bombs.[14]

The Wimperis became the U.S. Army's choice to equip the DH-4 bombers American industry built during the war. The only Army modification was to install a windshield around the sight, which hung from outside the fuselage, requiring the observer to stand up to use it. In the U.S. Army the Wimperis was known as the Mark I, I-A, and I-B, or the Mark III, IIIA, or IIIB in Navy use, depending on the altitude bars used with the sight. When time was a limitation, the bombardier set the altitude of the aircraft over the target on the altitude scale, estimated the ground speed by adding or subtracting the wind speed to or from the air speed, lined up the rear sight and front sight, and released his bomb when his line of sight intersected the target.

When time and conditions allowed, the bombardier used the drift method, after which Wimperis named his bombsight, to measure the ground speed more accurately. The pilot flew at a 90-degree angle cross wind while the bombardier set the drift bar to find wind speed. For the bombing run, the pilot flew the aircraft directly up- or downwind and the bombardier set the air speed indicator, adding the drift setting if downwind or subtracting if upwind. After setting the altitude bar to match the time of bomb fall predetermined from charts, the bombardier attempted to line up the rear sight on the drift bar, the foresight on the altitude bar, and the target. When all three intersected, he dropped his bombs.[15]

Subject to the oscillations of the aircraft, requiring flying either directly with or against the wind, and with the sight settings based on assumptions of one type of bomb and one speed, the Wimperis represented only an estimated solution to the bombing problem. Inherent errors meant that it would have reasonable accuracy only at altitudes below 5,000 feet.

The Edison Photograph Works (Orange, N.J.), the Frederick Pierce Company (New York City), the H. W. Cotten Company (New York City), and the Gorham Manufacturing Company (Providence, R.I.) manufactured Wimperis bombsights in the United States. Unfortunately the copy of the Wimperis imported to the United States for use as a production pattern for the Mark I was defective and initial production proved unusable. The United States eventually procured over 12,000 Mark I/IIIs at $75.60 each before the armistice brought contract cancellation.[16]

The Michelin Company of Clermont, France, took Scott's ideas and adapted them to fit their own Michelin sight—the best of the war. Unlike the Wimperis, the Michelin Company manufactured all Michelin sights in American service during the war. The Michelin 7 AIC sight used charts developed at the Eiffel Aerodynamic Laboratory for the falling times of bombs. Using a stopwatch, the operator calculated his ground speed before arriving over the target, measuring the amount of time it took an object to intersect the front and back cross hairs on his bombsight, which subtended a distance of 600 meters on the ground. After setting the Michelin sight to the appropriate speed index, he also determined the approximate altitude, again adjusting the sight, which mechanically set the correct aiming angle. The bombardier aimed the front cross hair at the target and dropped his bombs when the target moved to intersect the rear cross hair.

The Michelin bombsight made only crude approximations of the calculations necessary for precision bombing and made no adjustments for the wind. For proper use the pilot had to fly either with or against the wind, exposing the aircraft to ground defensive fire for up to 1½ minutes. The bombardier yelled or pulled straps tied to the pilot's shoulders to inform the pilot of the correct target heading. Its major advantage over other bombsights was the French design's use of a pendulum with hydraulic shock absorbers (called "oil dash pots" at the time) to keep the sight mechanism level and stable despite the aircraft's changes in pitch and roll.[17]

Pitch was the deviation from level flight around the aircraft's lateral axis, causing the nose to rise or fall. Changes in pitch caused changes in altitude, making all bombing charts and bombsight adjustments incorrect. *Roll* was the deviation from level flight around the aircraft's longitudinal axis, tilting to the starboard or port. Roll disrupted the line of sight to the target and altered the vertical line from the aircraft to the ground representing altitude. Bombsights measured the sighting angle to the target based on this vertical reference line perpendicular to the ground. Any changes in the line away from true vertical increased inaccuracy (see figure 1.4).

The Michelin was the first bombsight to consider the problems of stabilization. The best line-of-sight bombsight, regardless of other factors, was subject to extreme bombing errors resulting from aircraft oscillation during the bombing run. From 6,000 feet, at a speed of 100 MPH, a pitch up or down of only two degrees from the direct line-of-sight aiming angle caused a bomb to land nearly 200 feet long or short in range, respectively.

Aircraft Attitudes

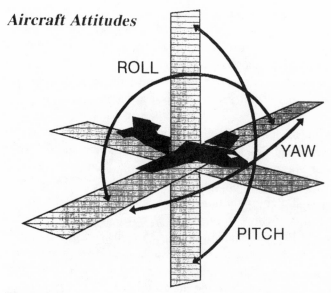

ROLL

YAW

PITCH

Figure 1.4

At higher speeds and altitudes, the errors grew proportionally. A roll of two degrees at 10,000 feet would cause a bomb to land nearly 350 feet left or right of the target.

Like other World War I bomb-aiming apparatuses, the Michelin did not compensate for wind-caused drift. Wind could change an aircraft's path or track on the ground. As an aircraft tacked into the wind, the heading of its flight changed to compensate for this drift effect. Called *yaw*, this deviation from straight flight around the aircraft's vertical axis changed the direction of flight, complicating the bombsighting problem, adding a third dimension of crosstrail (see figure 1.4). The aircraft's crosstrail was the distance between the true course of the airplane marked on the ground as affected by the wind and the collision course to the target. Without this drift, the true course and collision course were the same. The lack of proper stabilization to eliminate oscillation and proper drift determination to eliminate range and deflection errors formed the key remaining obstacles to finding a solution for the bombsighting problem.

By late 1915 the British had also developed a stabilized bombsight, but did so by using a large Sperry gyroscope to stabilize the entire aircraft, not just the bombsight. The pilot set his course on the directional gyroscope, compensated for drift, and dropped his bombs according to predetermined charts. The added weight of the gyroscope made the technique impractical, but the gain in bombing accuracy proved the importance of eliminating aircraft oscillation. The British reported average deflection bombing errors of only 65 feet in their stabilized aircraft from an altitude of 6,000 feet, compared to 567 feet of error for a bombsight on an unstabilized aircraft. Although the claims seemed excessive, bombsight stabilization had proved its worth.[18]

The U.S. Army made a greater effort to develop a suitable bomb release mechanism than it did developing bombsights, though in early 1918 it contacted Elmer Sperry Sr. at the Sperry Gyroscope Company about the production of a stabilized bombsight. Several months of fruitless correspondence followed. Bombsight procurement and development were under the control of the Army's Ordnance Department, out of step with the needs of airmen.[19] The availability of European sights also limited the effort. In addition to the Wimperis and Michelin, the Army procured the Type A-1 (Mark I), copied from a French design and produced in numbers less than 100 in the United States by the Gorham Manufacturing Company. The Type A-2 (Mark II) was a version of the Wimperis modified for high-altitude work. The Army ordered 1,000 copies from the Frederick Pierce Company. The Type A-3 (Mark I) was a Wimperis modified for low altitude, but was not procured.[20]

The U.S. Navy's first interest in bombsight development came from Sperry in mid-September 1915, concerning the need to stabilize aircraft, not bombsights, because of the greater inertia of the aircraft. In January 1916 the Office of Naval Aeronautics decided not to proceed with Sperry until all naval bureaus had thoroughly investigated the subject. Elmer Sperry began on his own, designing a gyroscopically stabilized bombsight weighing 60 pounds. In May 1916 the Bureau of Ordnance (BuOrd) gave the Sperry Gyroscopic Company $750 to design a "bomb dropping sight operated by a gyroscopic artificial horizon." Sperry submitted two prototypes to the Navy in 1918, but no quantity production resulted.[21]

In April 1918 the Navy contracted with the International Signal Company of Chicago to build a bombsight designed by three naval officers. This "Pilot Directing Bombsight" improved on the Wimperis, assigning the duty of bomb aiming to a spotter, freeing the pilot to concentrate on flying his aircraft. This feature was a matter of necessity, as pilots of Navy bombers flew from the middle of the aircraft and were usually unable to see their targets. The spotter, who sat in the front of the aircraft, aimed a sighting arm at the target, showing the pilot the proper course for flying over the target. The spotter dropped bombs by hand, with one arm strapped to the aircraft to prevent him from falling out.

The new bombsight never worked properly, so the Navy compromised by adding the pilot-directing device of the "Pilot Directing Bombsight" to the Wimperis "Course Setting Bombsight." Two months before the end of the war, it contracted with the International Register Company for the production of 3,500 of these modified sights, named the Mark III "Pilot Directing Bombsight." At a price of $120.62 each, International Register delivered 2,200 Mark IIIs before the armistice brought an end to the contract. The speed of manufacture was evidence of the simplicity of the design.[22]

The United States pursued another means of achieving accuracy in bombing as well. In 1909 Elmer A. Sperry Sr. first tried to stabilize an aircraft, installing a 22-pound gyroscope in a small aircraft belonging to Stanley Y. Beach, aeronautical editor of the *Scientific American*, because the craft had no ailerons for lateral control. Finding the device too heavy for the small monoplane, Sperry and his son, Lawrence B. Sperry, began a project to employ small gyroscopes to manipulate an aircraft's control surfaces rather than using the inherent stability of a larger gyroscope to provide stability by direct application. No one had yet thought of improving stability to increase bombing accuracy, only to increase crew comfort and safety. The first reference to stabilization to improve bombing accuracy came in a Sperry automatic pilot brochure from 1916, designed to interest customers in Sperry products.[23]

The gyroscope[24] was the key to stabilizing aircraft and bombsights because of two fundamental properties—rigidity in the plane of rotation and precession. The spinning wheel of the gyroscope resists any force acting to change the direction of its axis of rotation. This tendency allows the aircraft or bombsight to maintain a constant frame of reference, usually the true vertical line from the aircraft to the earth or a true horizontal line from the aircraft in the direction of flight. If large enough, this resistance would overcome any tendency of the aircraft to turn or oscillate, though at the penalty of stiffness of ride and weight. Sperry's stabilizer for Beach's aircraft operated according to this principle.

The second quality, precession, provided the key to stabilized flight through an autopilot. Precession refers to the spinning wheel's tendency to tilt about an axis perpendicular to the one acted upon by an outside force. Any oscillation of an aircraft moves the frame (cardan ring) inside which the gyroscope's wheel spins, causing the wheel to tilt to counteract the forces interfering with smooth and level flight. This tilt could be measured and transferred electrically or mechanically to the aircraft's control surfaces to bring the aircraft back into line with the gyroscope's original frame of reference.[25]

By 1912 Lawrence Sperry was using gyroscopes to direct servomotors operating the controls of test aircraft. The breakthrough came in 1913 when the younger Sperry realized that a turn was the result of a combination of the lateral and longitudinal controls of an aircraft. Although not technically an automatic pilot, Sperry's stabilizer used four gyroscopes to maintain level flight by linking the aircraft's control surfaces to the gyroscopes through a series of servomotors, drums, and cables. The unit maintained stability in two axes, controlling roll (lateral control about the longitudinal axis) and pitch (longitudinal control about the lateral axis) through the linkage of its four gyroscopes to the ailerons and elevators. It did not allow automatic control of direction or yaw (directional control about the normal axis) through the rudder. Electrical brushes mounted on the gyroscopes' gimbals made contact with brushes fixed to the frames when the aircraft moved away from the fixed axes of the gyroscopes. The resulting electrical flow engaged electromagnetic clutches mounted on a main power shaft, turning reduction gearing in servomotors. The shaft received its power mechanically from a propeller or electrically from a generator spun by a propeller, depending on the model used. Servomotors manipulated the aircraft's control surfaces to return the aircraft to the fixed reference planes established by the gyroscopes.

In 1914 Lawrence Sperry took his device to Paris to compete in the *Concourse par l'Union pour la Sécurité en Aeroplane.*[26] Sperry dazzled the judges by standing up and raising his hands from the controls, while his mechanic walked on the wing in an attempt to disturb the stability of the aircraft. The aircraft flew straight and level under the control of the Sperry automatic pilot, winning its designer the $10,000 grand prize.[27]

Lawrence continued to experiment with electrically driven servomotors to replace the 1914 version's air-driven motors, a single gyroscope to replace the earlier version's four, an electromechanical model with improved electrical contacts, and a single gyroscope model using all-electric servos. By 1915 the Sperry Company was selling commercial versions for $2,000 each and had completed military contracts with Great Britain and Italy. The project had cost the company $12,000.[28]

In April 1915 Elmer A. Sperry Sr. merged his son Lawrence's research into automatic flight control with his own work with sea torpedoes, initiating research into unmanned flying bombs. In September 1916 the Navy agreed to fund development. After American entry into World War I, the Naval Consulting Board, with Sperry as a member, recommended the accelerated development of the aerial torpedo or remote-controlled aircraft for use against submarines. Navy Secretary Josephus Daniels allocated $200,000 in funding. Although bombsighting technology was not yet sufficiently accurate to hit submarines, somehow the board decided that an automatically piloted flying bomb could.

The Navy provided Sperry with five N-9 seaplanes as testing platforms and contracted to buy six sets of automatic controls at $3,900 each. Curtiss Aircraft Company designed the aerial torpedo to carry a 1,000-pound bomb under the control of Sperry's mechanical pilot—a gyroscope connected to a servomotor to control the rudder and an aneroid barometer-servomotor combination to control the ailerons and horizontal rudder. A revolution counter connected to the propeller measured distance. Gyroscopic stabilization kept the aircraft flying level. The system was crude and could not counter the effects of winds that tended to drive the craft off course. Trouble with the launching system delayed progress and the Navy forced Sperry to hire a former employee, Carl L. Norden, as a consulting engineer to develop a large flywheel catapult.

By August 1917 the lateral and longitudinal controls worked, but the directional control was subject to "creep."[29] Four months later the aerial torpedo, with a human pilot to control drift, could fly 50 miles, landing within 580 yards of the target in range and 440 yards in deflection. On March 6, 1918, launched from the Norden catapult, the world's first cruise missile flew 1,000 yards without a human pilot. More aerial torpedoes crashed than flew, so Sperry considered adding radio control for correcting the directional problem. The Navy demurred because of security concerns over the large number of German immigrant workers at the Sperry factory. Sperry even considered having a gyroscope follow the sun at a certain angle to achieve directional control. Progress remained limited and in January 1919 the Navy canceled the Sperry project.

Carl Norden's catapult so impressed the Navy that it contracted for Norden to continue the aerial torpedo project separately, using new aircraft designed and built by the Witteman-Lewis Company. The Norden-modified Sperry autopilot design, constructed at the Ford Instrument Company, owned by another former Sperry engineer, Hannibal C. Ford, achieved its first success in March 1919. Ford built five experimental aerial torpedoes. Three crashed during testing and the Navy junked the remaining two before scrapping the project in mid-1921.[30]

The Navy also contracted with Cooper Hewitt in April 1917 to build an aerial torpedo based on five gyroscopes controlling flight through electromagnetic clutches. The effort failed, but in November 1917 the Army's chief signal officer decided to continue Hewitt's work at McCook Field under the direction of Charles F. Kettering of Delco. Unlike the Navy and Sperry beginning with controls and then designing an aircraft around them, the Army and Kettering began with a successful aircraft and then tried to build a control system for it. Using guidance systems provided by Sperry, Kettering designed a smaller, simpler aircraft, the "Liberty Eagle," built by Kettering's Dayton Wright Airplane Company, carrying a 185-pound bomb,[31] powered by a 37-hp Ford engine, costing about $400. The wings were doped muslin and paper, the fuselage cardboard, costing about $75. By the end of the war the "Kettering Bug," as it was popularly known, was flying nearly 40 miles, but the influence of wind and the continuing directional problem limited accuracy. By March 1920 the project had cost $275,000.[32]

Trouble with the launcher convinced the Air Service to contract with Lawrence Sperry in April 1920 to develop a larger aerial torpedo. The Army wanted a cruise missile and was willing to spend $66,000 for the contract, $3,000 per month for expenses, and up to $50,000 in performance bonuses. High technology was expensive.[33] Sperry used a new material, duralumin, and equipped his aircraft with air-powered automatic controls.[34] Problems with engines, duralumin construction techniques, sluggish controls, and vacuum leaks delayed progress. By March 1921 the torpedo was making successful flights, though the old problem of directional control forced Sperry to resort to radio control from an escorting aircraft. The Air Service objected, citing the contract wording that the device was to allow "automatic flight without manual control." An arbitration board ruled that radio control was not manual. In March 1922 a torpedo flew 63 miles and made a direct hit on its target, but required eighteen radio corrections from the chase aircraft. The Air Service certified Sperry's contract for payment in November 1922.[35]

Sperry shipped the completed aerial torpedoes to Langley Field for service testing, but the local commander refused to uncrate them, considering unpiloted aircraft a waste of money. Lawrence Sperry's death in December 1923 brought work to an end. In 1924 the Army lowered the priority of aerial torpedo work to concentrate on bombsight development. Insufficient funds encouraged Henry "Hap" Arnold to cancel the project on May 13, 1932, clearing the way for manned, heavy bombers equipped with precision bombsights to carry out the developing doctrine of daylight precision strategic bombing.[36] Ironically, the Army and Navy were then working to merge the two technologies of bombsights and automatic flight control to improve bombing accuracy.[37]

World War I created the weapons of air power, but the urgency of war left little time for considering how to employ it. Early bombing was entirely tactical, adding close air support and interdiction to trench warfare. Bombing missions rarely went beyond 15 kilometers behind the front lines. The Germans initially and later the British introduced strategic bombing in a desperate search for solutions to the stalemate on the Western Front, but these efforts amounted to little more than harassing raids.

Based in part on this limited precedent, the United States entered the war in 1917 with little idea of what air power could do in a war. The Air Service's Maj. Edgar S. Gorrell claimed 3,000 to 6,000 bombers could destroy German morale and bring surrender, but claims were not reality.[38] The single American bombardment manual available for use during the war already assigned bombardment aviation a unique role. Its authors initiated two decades of sometimes acrid debate on the role of air power: should bombing attack the morale of troops at the front or the morale of the civilian arms-builders behind them? If the latter, should the target be the civilian arms-builders themselves or the machines and factories used by the civilian arms-builders? The Army's wartime manual answered affirmatively to both of the first questions, but without specifying how to attack the morale of civilians: "The result of the battle depends a lot upon the moral of troops. The result of the war depends as much upon the moral of civilians. The aviation of bombardment allows to diminish the moral of the troops and the moral of civilians." The ratio of the effectiveness of bombing on morale to the effectiveness of mere physical destruction was 20:1.[39] The Air Service found that "while the material damage done by such bombing raids has been questioned, and while it has been proved that in many cases such damage was not great, there is absolutely no doubt that the moral effect of these operations is most considerable."[40]

The first written advocation of the bombing of the enemy's means of production came from then–Lieutenant Colonel Gorrell, head of the technical section of the Air Service, American Expeditionary Force, beginning three decades of a peculiarly American commitment to killing machines, not people, through aerial bombardment. Gorrell argued that ground warfare had reached a stalemate and the only solution was to bomb "manufacturing centers, commercial centers, and lines of communication" from the air. The only way "to affect the armies in the fields . . . was to affect the manufacturing output of the countries" by bombing choke-points. Destroying chemical factories would stop shell production and bombing engine and magneto factories would stop aircraft production. Concentrating all aerial forces on each target until destroyed would not only eliminate Germany's ability to wage war, but also crush the morale of German workers. Although Gen. John Pershing approved Gorrell's plan, opposition from Expeditionary Force headquarters, insufficient aircraft,[41] and inadequate accuracy thwarted Gorrell's plan. The tactical head of the Air Service in Europe, Brig. Gen. William "Billy" Mitchell, considered a modification of the plan, to employ incendiaries and poison gas against German forests and livestock.[42]

The one major American bombing campaign of the war was the Meuse-Argonne offensive, where American-manned Breguet 14 B-2 bombers attacked railroad stations, trains, troop concentrations, ammunition dumps, and airdromes. The intent was to disrupt the flow of enemy troops and supplies into the region. Although official American policy was precision bombing of individual targets, airmen made the "frank admission . . . that accuracy is limited and a given area is covered in the hope that enough bombs will strike the target proper to accomplish the mission." Commanders developed the technique of "drop-on-the-leader" bombing to improve accuracy, where the entire formation dropped its bombs when the leader fired the "six-green" signal and dropped his bombs. Flooding the target with bombs increased the otherwise small chances of achieving a hit. The largest American bombing mission of the war was against a railroad target at Montmedy on November 4, 1918, when thirty-seven aircraft dropped 8,500 pounds of bombs. The attackers achieved no hits on the target, but damaged a granary, a vegetable storehouse, two private houses, a repair shed, and a hospital. American airman Capt. Bruce Hopper claimed bombing accuracy was only "occasional."[43]

In all, American bombardment forces dropped only 138 tons of explosives on enemy targets during the war, losing thirty-three bombers in combat. The first American day bombardment raid did not come until June 12, 1918, only four months before the end of the war. The American bombing survey after the war determined the effort had killed 641 and wounded 1,262, damaged 35.4 million marks of enemy property, and caused the enemy 204.7 million marks in direct and indirect costs. Accuracy was so poor that the Army concluded "night bombing has usually been found to be more accurate than day bombing." The historian of the First Day Bombardment Group admitted its major contribution had been to serve as bait, keeping the Germans attacking group aircraft behind enemy lines and by that action not attacking American observation aircraft over the front lines. "Because of the very small weight of bombs dropped and the crude bombsights of the day, little damage could possibly have been done by these handfuls of aircraft."[44]

The major lesson to come out of bombsight development during World War I was the need for greater accuracy, largely dependent on stabilization, and a plan or doctrine for aerial bombing. Other lessons were the need for efficient instruments to insure more precise flying, more uniform bomb ballistics, drift compensation, simplified operation, and optical magnification to allow missions at altitudes sufficiently high to escape from the dangers of antiaircraft artillery. Air power had not been decisive in World War I, but after the war nations looked beyond the trenches, to the promise of airplanes and bombsights, for a means to overcome the quagmire of modern warfare.[45]

2

The Army's Pursuit
of Precision Bombing

The common and consistent goal of the Army's airmen in the 1920s was to develop an air force that could overcome the horrors of World War I's trench warfare. For some the solution was to return mobility to the battlefield, using aircraft as mobile artillery in close support of American ground forces fighting against enemy ground forces or to interdict the battlefield. A few dreamed of flying over the enemy's defending armies and navies, using aircraft to drop bombs on the sources of the enemy's war-making power. Improved bombing accuracy was the ingredient essential in both for the successful application of air power.

The Dickman Board, appointed to analyze the lessons of World War I, set the tone for the postwar development of air power in 1919, concluding "nothing so far brought out in the war shows that aerial activities can be carried on, independently of ground forces, to such an extent as to affect materially the conduct of the war as a whole."[1] Army field regulations made the air force subordinate to ground elements, assigning aerial bombardment the tactical duties of ground-strafing or close air support and of battlefield interdiction, striking at lines of communication, supply depots, bridges, and railroad facilities "beyond the effective range of artillery."[2]

The chief of the Air Service established the Field Officers School at Langley Field, Virginia, in 1920, renamed the Air Service Tactical School in 1922 and the Air Corps Tactical School in 1926, to formulate an air doctrine for the proper use of air power. That doctrine, the system of principles and ideas that would guide Air Service functions, made air power an auxiliary in support of infantry, the "Queen of Battles."[3] The Morrow Board, assembled in 1925 to study air power, also saw aircraft used in the role of low-altitude tactical ground support: "The next war may well start in the air but in all probability will wind up, as the last war did, in the mud."[4]

This direct, but restricted, role required bombsights of limited sophistication. Fluid battlefield conditions and the proximity of friendly forces dictated low-altitude daylight missions close to the front. Enemy defenses dictated night missions behind enemy lines. Both translated into an air force of light and medium bombers of limited range and bomb-carrying capacity flying at altitudes under 8,000 feet. The Tactical School taught that "bombardment never makes a diving attack" to remain above the danger of antiaircraft defenses.[5]

The Army's Bomb Board, in hearings held from August to November 1919, concluded that "the most important problem" in developing bombing was the acquisition of a good bombsight. It recommended the development of gyroscopic stabilization, because of the limited efficiency of pendulums damped by dash pots (shock absorbers), based on a 1916 Army research project that revealed the greatest single cause for bombing error to be the oscillation of airplanes in flight. The Army transferred responsibility for bombsight development from its Ordnance Department to the newly established Airplane Engineering Department at McCook Field, Dayton, Ohio (renamed the Engineering Division in 1918 and the Materiel Division in 1926). In 1927 bombsight research moved with the Materiel Division to a permanent home at Wright Field near Dayton.[6]

The starting point for the bombsight project was the World War I Wimperis. The Mark I Army Wimperis required different scales for each bomb, could not be used at night, was not stabilized, could not find ground speed, and could only be used flying directly with or against the wind. It was, according to legend, only better than nothing. Examining dozens of possible replacements, the Engineering Division appeared intent on stumbling onto the best available. As of June 26, 1922, the Air Service had 10,819 Mark I-As (Wimperis), 40 Mark Is (Wimperis), 1 "Course Setting" (modified Wimperis), 681 "Improved" Wimperises (Mark III), 14 Navy

Mark IVs (Norden stabilized Mark III-A), 1 Pioneer (D-1), 1 "gyroscopically stabilized test model," 1 Mark X sight designed and built by the Frankford Arsenal, and 9 improved Michelins. The Engineering Division had also examined the Barr, Loring, Ford, Duff Double Drift, Hathaway-Loring, Milne-Loring, Goerz-Boykow, Meijer, Beggs, Miller, Estoppey, Riley-Scott, Kimball, Hathaway, and Hatchett. A few sights introduced original ideas, such as the Estoppey, which used pendulum stabilization. The most revolutionary, though faulty in many respects, was the Kimball, which used a spoked wheel to synchronize the sight with the aircraft's ground speed. All had one common characteristic—they represented little or no improvement over existing Wimperis sights.[7]

These failures and a limited budget encouraged Army attempts to improve the Mark I-A (Army) and III (Navy) Wimperis bombsights. Sperry Gyroscope offered to stabilize the Mark III for $2,000 and the Mark I-A for $900. Sperry needed only one month to complete the stabilization of the Mark III, which the Army considered superior to the Mark I-A because of its drift compensation feature, but needed eight months to complete the Mark I-A, which required a telescope besides stabilization. Neither device met Army needs.[8]

In 1923 Wimperis offered a new bombsight to the U.S. government, promising it would allow bombing approaches from any direction, whatever the wind. He claimed to have sold it to the governments of Great Britain, Japan, Spain, Argentina, and Uruguay. The Air Service's Engineering Division concluded it offered nothing new over previous Wimperis sights. More important, in a sign that the United States had restored itself to the forefront of bombsight design, the Engineering Division concluded that current Army and Navy bombsights were superior to the new Wimperis. All new bombsights in American service would be American-designed and American-built.[9]

In the pursuit of simple low-altitude and complex high-altitude bombsights, the Air Service and its successor, the Air Corps, dealt mainly with three designers and one company: Alexander P. de Seversky, Georges Estoppey, Henry B. Inglis, and the Sperry Gyroscope Company. All stemmed from a March 1921 meeting in Washington between Brig. Gen. Billy Mitchell and Lawrence B. Sperry, father of stabilized flight and son of Elmer A. Sperry Sr. of the Sperry Gyroscope Company. Mitchell, preparing for ship-bombing tests scheduled to begin that summer, asked the Sperrys to undertake the development of a stabilized bombsight. Elmer Sperry judged the merits of the idea and invited the Engineering Division's chief bombsight engineer, Capt. Henry B. Inglis, to bring the division's resident bombsight expert, Alexander P. de Seversky, a World War I ace in the Russian air force, to Sperry's New York factory. Sperry, under an Army development contract, hired Seversky to turn his paper idea into a practical bombsight using Sperry equipment and employees.[10]

Seversky described his C-1 bombsight as highly accurate and completely automatic, with the exception of drift control. It employed a gyroscopic compass separate from the bombsight and a transmission system to pass compass data to the bombsight calculator. A gyroscope found the absolute vertical under the aircraft, but did not stabilize the device. Sperry had to use profits from his commercial ship stabilizer and gyrocompass business to pay for development in light of deep cuts in Army research funds.

The Army warned Sperry not to proceed because it had doubts about the Seversky design: "The price you have quoted is considered entirely unreasonable and it has been decided to test out the Seversky bomb sighting system in an airplane before proceeding with the expenditure of any more funds." After three years of work at Sperry, Seversky completed a working C-1 for Air Service testing in August 1924.[11] It required three crew members. The observer used a telescope and gyrocompass to transmit azimuth and elevation information to the bombardier. The bombardier operated the Seversky calculator to solve the bombing problem, combining ground speed (calculated using the timing technique), altitude, ballistics information from charts, and the gyroscope to determine the true vertical baseline. He plotted an interception course and transmitted flying instructions to the pilot. Although the Engineering Division deemed it better than any other available sight, mechanical failures caused "many wild errors." Maintenance problems with its fifty-five major subassemblies demanded "daily remedying." It also needed so much electricity that two propeller-driven generators had to be installed under the test aircraft's wings and two additional batteries installed in the fuselage. Extreme sensitivity to currency fluctuations meant the aircraft had to be flown at a precise speed to achieve the exact flow of current from the generators. Its many electrical connections tended to oxidize, causing further malfunctions.[12]

Sperry told Maj. Gen. Mason M. Patrick, chief of the Air Service, that the production of fifty would cost $12,500 each.[13] Patrick and the Engineering Division refused to standardize the C-1. In 1928 Seversky returned with a modified C-1, the C-3A, B, and C, with automatically orienting pilot direction indicators. By then, however, the Army had decided, after a decade of effort, that the Seversky C-series bombsights, in part because of their maintenance problems, were "a waste of time."[14] The Seversky bombsights were the first of several dead ends for the Army's air force in the interwar period.

The Engineering Division also sought bombsights from Georges Estoppey beginning in 1921. A naturalized citizen from Locle, Switzerland, Estoppey immigrated to the United States in 1916. During the war he formed the Musa-Estoppey Company of New York and produced a bombsight design for which he received three patents in March 1919. The company failed and in 1921 Estoppey went to work for the Air Service Engineering Division at McCook Field, where he turned his design into a practical bombsight, designated the D-1.[15]

Using a pendulum with dash pots for stabilization, the D-1 relied on a stopwatch to find ground speed. Tests at the Aberdeen Proving Ground impressed its examiners: "much greater accuracy than with the old Navy Mark III or Army Mark IA sights" and "twice as accurate as the Michelin," achieving an 80 percent hit average. The Navy agreed that "the D-1 sights are sufficiently superior to the Mark III sight to warrant the purchase of a limited number for use pending the development of the new Navy sight."[16] The Air Service ordered fourteen D-1s for itself and two for the Navy in 1922 from Eberhart Steel Products of Buffalo and stabilizers from the Pioneer Instrument Company of Brooklyn. They performed well in bombing tests against the USS *Virginia* and USS *New Jersey* in 1923 and the Air Service contracted for an additional one hundred, including fourteen for the Navy, at an average cost of $600 each. The Navy deferred making a larger purchase until the D-4, a modified D-1, was available in 1925.

In use, a D-1 bombardier aimed a direction wire at the target and determined the wind direction by noting which way the target drifted away from the wire. He directed the pilot to fly in the direction of the target's drift until the target remained steady along the direction wire. The bombardier then turned drums or pointers to settings for the correct type of bomb (representing terminal velocity from ballistic tests recorded on compact bomb charts), the approximate air speed, the altitude, and his personal time lag (determined by multiple practice bombings). When the target intersected the front cross wire, he cranked the cross wire until a white pointer appeared to set the correct timing (over a period of 15 seconds). When the target intersected the rear cross wire, he released his bomb.

The D-1 was no solution to the accuracy problem. Its dash pot–

dampened pendulum provided inadequate stabilization and was only useful at low speeds and for altitudes above 3,000 feet, while the preferred altitude was from 7,000 to 17,000 feet. Nevertheless, the D-1 represented state-of-the-art bombsight design, reducing the required time for straight and level flight from nearly a minute for other timing sights to only 20 seconds, minimizing exposure to ground fire. It also reduced the number of scale settings the bombardier was responsible for from four to one.[17]

At McCook Estoppey worked to improve the design. The D-2 was a D-1 with an automatic timing device. The Engineering Division paid $4,680 for an experimental model and $6,980 for two production models from the Pioneer Instrument Company of Brooklyn in 1925.[18] The D-3 was a D-2 with gyroscopic stabilization in place of the pendulum stabilization of the D-1 and D-2, designed at the Sperry Gyroscope Company in 1924 and 1925. The Army paid $9,000 for two prototypes plus $1,185 for Sperry's drawings. Although tests were successful, the D-3 was of insufficient value for standardization.[19]

More successful was the D-4, a D-1 with heavier construction and an improved internal timing mechanism. The stronger design was due to the Aberdeen tests of the D-1, which raised doubts about its durability "under exceptional rough usage in the hands of enlisted men who use the bomb sight bracket for a step in getting in and out of the cockpit." Still stabilized with a pendulum, it permitted the bombardier to preset the altitude and direct the pilot to fly straight over the target. Because it was so similar to the previous D-series sights, tools and dyes already existed and insured a price of only $1,100 for the first three prototypes from Gaertner Scientific Corporation of Chicago in 1925. Continued problems with the stabilizing system prevented standardization and the Air Corps deemed the sight too complex "to be worthwhile because D-4 soon to be replaced." The replacement was later than sooner, however, forcing the Army to purchase 230 D-4s for use in various aircraft over the next five years. Needing a low-altitude sight to replace the Mark III, the Navy purchased forty D-4s at the reduced price of $273 each. Gaertner also sold the D-4 to foreign governments.[20]

Wright Field tried to improve the Estoppey designs. The D-5 used different optics to eliminate parallax, an illuminated reticle for night bombing, and a synchronous target-following system. The Army's first true synchronous bombsight, the D-5 required the bombardier to rotate the sight's wheels and gears at a speed that matched the movement of the aircraft across a fixed point on the ground. Synchronizing the movement of the

D-5's internal mechanism with the ground speed of the aircraft held great promise, but provided worse accuracy than the D-4. The Air Corps recommended "that no further experimental work be done on the D-5 Sight" until other sights under development were tested.[21] The D-7[22] of 1931 was the most advanced of the Estoppey models, allowing the bombardier to signal the pilot to turn the aircraft during the bomb run by turning the bombsight. It incorporated an automatic bomb release, stabilization, and illuminated cross wires to allow use day and night. Although an excellent bomb-aiming device, it was superseded by a new generation of sights.[23]

Georges Estoppey provided the Army with several hundred bombsights of limited capabilities and with litigation covering nearly two decades. In 1924 Estoppey began demanding royalty payments for his inventions. Air Service chief Maj. Gen. Mason Patrick refused to pay royalties for devices designed while Estoppey was on the government payroll. His contract allowed him royalties of 7.5 percent up to a maximum of $7,500, but only after he left government service. This he did in July 1926, with the promise that royalties would be due him for any of his inventions procured after his separation. This agreement brought him $2,887 in 1927 and $2,600 in 1932.[24]

In 1932 Estoppey focused his litigious attentions on the Navy, claiming that the Navy's Norden Mark XI bombsights "clearly fall within the disclosures and scope of my patents." The Navy's BuOrd decided that the Mark XI employed "a means of operating a sighting member which appears to be similar to the means of sighting from a moving body, on a stationary target." The Navy had purchased the Norden Mark XI timing bombsight for sighting from a moving body on a *moving* target, but agreed to pay Estoppey $2,000 for patent 1,296,640. In violation of government procurement laws, the Navy had previously promised to protect the Carl L. Norden Company from such patent infringements.[25]

Estoppey was not finished with the Army. In the desperate period of America's entry into a new world war he would again call on Washington with an inexpensive, stopgap bombsight (the D-8).[26]

Capt. Henry B. Inglis left the Air Service in September 1920 to become an "aeronautical mechanical engineer" at McCook Field's Engineering Division in charge of bombsight development. The Engineering Division credited him with being "probably the best versed in the United States in this special field." Inglis claimed responsibility for recommending to Estoppey the timing method that the latter would use on the D-3 bombsight, which he also claimed to be a "joint invention of Mr. Estoppey and myself."[27]

With the limitations of the D-3 apparent from testing at McCook, Inglis initiated a program to develop a low-level ground-attack bombsight, the K-1, based on the designs to which he had been exposed in his position. In August 1926 Inglis applied for a patent for his low-altitude automatic bombsight, which he never received because the ideas contained in the K-1 were similar to previously awarded patents or were commonly known mechanical principles. The Air Corps never put the K-1 into production.

Inglis also worked on his L-1 high-altitude sight, based on the principles of the D-3 and C-1 bombsights, but equipped with the synchronous method of ground-speed determination and an automatic bomb release. In February 1928 the Air Corps Bombardment Board recommended the production of six L-1s for testing, approved by the chief of the Air Corps one month later. Before the L-1 contracts could be completed, however, Inglis resigned at Wright Field and went to work for the Sperry Company—a case of the "revolving door" in military procurement common in the history of bombsight development.[28]

Like Estoppey, Inglis hoped to profit from his inventions. At Sperry he helped Seversky with his C-type bombsight and worked on the engineering data and specifications for the L-1, to be delivered to the government at no cost in anticipation of an Air Corps order for mass production of the L-1 upon completion.[29] In April 1929 the Air Corps issued a contract to the Sperry Gyroscope Company for the construction of but five L-1 bombsights, at a cost of $40,000, with the Army providing optical systems and gyroscopes to Sperry at no charge.[30] Sperry delivered the first two sights to the Materiel Division for testing in September 1930. A "gyro-stabilized, vertical seeking, synchronous range determination, fixed telescope with a rotating prism, automatic electric and manual release" bombsight, it bore a resemblance to the Sperry C-4, but weighed 50 pounds less.[31]

After the Sperry Company completed its contract in July 1931, the Materiel Division reported "inferior accuracy" and an unsatisfactory "pilot directing system." Wright Field sent L-1s to Langley and March Fields for service testing, which involved the dropping of 108 bombs from different altitudes (6,000, 9,000, and 12,000 feet) using the Navy's Norden Mark XI, the Army's Estoppey D-7, and the Sperry/Inglis L-1. Crews judged the Norden as the best sight in terms of accuracy (331 feet average radial error) and general preference, though the most difficult to operate. The D-7 was the least accurate (459 feet average radial error), but the easiest to operate. The new L-1 came in second in accuracy (346 feet average radial error), general preference, and ease of operation. Lt. Col. R. C. Kirtland, commanding at Langley, concluded that "the procurement of a bomb sight which is considered inferior to another [the Norden XI] now in existence in this country cannot be recommended." With clearly no major improvement in accuracy or other advantages for the Sperry/Inglis sight, the Army Air Corps decided against recommending procurement of the L-1.[32]

Sperry delivered its own bombsight, the C-4, to Wright Field on March 12, 1931. Based on Seversky's C-1, C-2, and C-3, and Inglis's L-1 designs, the C-4 used a vertical-seeking gyroscope that made accurate leveling of the bombsight unnecessary at the time the sight's stabilizing gyroscope was unlocked. By this means the Sperry Corporation had solved one major problem facing bombsight development in the interwar era. The vertical-seeking gyroscope eliminated the "chasing the bubble" problem that forced a bombardier to attempt leveling his bombsight while the aircraft to which it was fastened knocked about in the air. The C-4 also used a rotating prism to synchronize the movement of the sight's cross wire with the target. Extremely effective in calculating the proper range for bomb dropping, the Sperry sight's "deflection errors are so large [averaging 352 feet] as to be unsuitable for service use." It was awkward in operation, requiring the bombardier to turn the entire sight to indicate to the aircraft's pilot the amount of turn needed to line up on the target. With a small open circle at the center of the cross wires for sighting that subtended an area of nearly 400 feet on the ground at an altitude of 20,000 feet, the C-4 did not meet Army Air Corps needs for an accurate high-altitude bombsight. The Air Corps nevertheless purchased twenty-eight for continued testing and installed some on service aircraft from 1933 to 1936.[33]

In an attempt to rescue the faltering Army bombsight program, Wright Field engineers pursued increased accuracy from a different angle. The minimizing of oscillation in yaw, pitch, and roll through gyroscopic stabilization had been the major achievement in bombsight development since World War I, but oscillation of the bomber aircraft had not been eliminated. Such movements would be the products of atmospheric effects or of human manipulation of the aircraft's control surfaces, as the pilot attempted to compensate for atmospheric conditions, for what might appear to be an incorrect bombing approach (a "gut" feeling or flying by the "seat of the pants"), or for survival instincts in the face of enemy defensive fire.

Additionally, the bombardier had to convey flight instructions to the pilot to achieve the proper approach path to the target. According to Ted Barth, president of Carl L. Norden, Inc., "perhaps the most important advance in the art of precision bombing will have been accomplished when, through the use of automatic flight control, the bombardier will no longer require, nor be dependent on, the pilot's assistance and ability to maintain a correct target course."[34]

During World War I research at the Royal Aircraft Factory in London revealed that aircraft oscillations were a primary factor influencing bombing accuracy. The factory concluded that the development of a mechanical pilot connected to a bombsight might eliminate human-caused oscillations.[35] Until automatic control could become reality, the key technology for improving bombsight accuracy in these bombers was the pilot direction indicator (PDI). Once a bombardier located a target, some means had to be found to inform the pilot of the correct course to fly so that the aircraft's ground track would intersect the aiming point. In World War I the common means was by hand signals if the bombardier sat in front of the pilot, by taps on the shoulder or tugs on strings attached to the arms of the pilot if behind. The most precise bombsight in the world was no more accurate than the communications taking place in these crude fashions. After the war the Air Service initiated an intensive program to improve the means of transferring directional information from the bombardier to the pilot.[36]

Products of this program included the B-1 turn indicator, which signaled the need for a turn to the pilot, but not the degree of turn. Others included the A-0, A-1, A-3, D-1, D-2, and D-3, developed by the Sperry Gyroscope Company, Pioneer Instrument Company, and others. By the late 1920s the D-1 PDI had become standardized for Army use. The bombardier manually turned a control knob while checking on the target's position through the bombsight and on the aircraft heading through a compass. A direct flexible coupling moved an arrow on the pilot's gauge, showing the direction of turn in 60-degree intervals, subtended at 30 degrees. A gyroscope stabilized the D-1 in azimuth so it also could be used as a navigational aid. The bombardier had to operate both the bombsight and PDI independently.[37]

Carl Norden designed an improved PDI for the Navy for use with his Mark XI bombsight. It used the "asymptotic" method, where the bombardier turned the bombsight on its mount, while a gyroscope held the mount stable. A voltmeter measured the amount and direction of the turn through an electrical current passed from a brush on a resistor coil in the bombsight. Being off course activated an electromagnet that caused the pilot's gauge to precess in the correct direction. The bombardier could concentrate on his bombsight, the pilot receiving constant course information automatically.[38]

Automatic PDIs represented a significant advance in technology, but still relied on communication between the bombardier and the pilot, with the pilot making course adjustments with little precision. Many pilots objected to PDIs because they interfered with their prerogatives—pilots wanted to fly by the seat of their pants. Some means had to be found for the bombardier to fly the aircraft directly through his bombsight. The PDI also did nothing to eliminate aircraft oscillation.

Lawrence Sperry's pioneering work in automatic flight control laid the groundwork for the development of a true automatic pilot capable of controlling pitch, roll, and yaw through a bombsight. Sperry Gyroscope of Brooklyn and General Electric of Schenectady, New York, administered the U.S. Army's development projects. General Electric's version first flew successfully in April 1929. Although the Air Corps judged its operation "quite satisfactory," the aircraft still needed a human pilot to maintain level flight, essential if it were to be used to increase bombing accuracy. The General Electric device remained little more than a rudder control, using the output from a magnetic compass to control a steering motor hooked to the rudder. As the aircraft deviated from a preset magnetic course, the compass generated electric signals. Vacuum tubes amplified the signals, driving a rotating drum to make corrections to the rudder. To distinguish it from the Sperry "automatic pilot" project, the Air Corps called the General Electric apparatus an "automatic steering control."[39]

Work on the General Electric project continued because Wright Field's Engineering Division felt "there is a great need in the Service for some means of automatic control of aircraft." The Air Corps was "particularly interested in" such a device for use in allowing "bombardment and long range observation airplanes" to "maintain a straight course for considerable periods of time." By 1932 the automatic steering control was flying a test airplane 100 miles with a course deviation no greater than 150 yards. Wright Field also modified it to be able to work with a radio compass, following a radio beam, though with little success. In October 1932 the Air Corps ordered two production versions for extensive testing, but on December 12, 1933, canceled the automatic steering control project because of the success of the Sperry project.[40]

Sperry Gyroscope entered Army autopilot research in February 1925 after an accidental meeting between the Engineering Division's Maj. Clinton W. Howard and Sperry vice-president Thomas A. Morgan.[41] Lack of funding and Air Service priorities prevented earlier action.[42] Morgan informed Howard of Sperry's continuing work on automatic flight control and announced his wish to "cooperate with you in every way possible." Shiras A. Blair, who in 1912 had flown with Lawrence Sperry in a Curtiss flying boat equipped with the world's first gyrostabilizer, also helped get the two sides together. During the period of the autopilot project he was an Air Corps captain stationed at the Engineering Division/Materiel Division first at McCook Field and then Wright Field.

Elmer A. Sperry Jr., brother of Lawrence Sperry, who had died in 1924, completed his work on the yaw or directional aspect of the autopilot problem in May 1926.[43] The Air Service began testing the prototype, the A-1, at McCook Field later that month. Three years of modification followed before final testing began in the summer of 1929.[44] Trouble with the Ford C-9 test-bed aircraft delayed work, but on October 4, 1929, under the careful supervision of Elmer Sperry Jr. and officials of the Stout Metal Company of Dearborn, Michigan, a division of the Ford Motor Company, the world's first successful fully automatic pilot flew through rough air "without anyone in the pilot's cockpit."[45]

Although Lawrence Sperry had understood how to control pitch and roll almost two decades earlier, Elmer Sperry Jr.'s contribution was connecting the rudder and ailerons to control yaw. In his patent Sperry explained:

> The importance of the aileron control has heretofore not been recognized because it has not been appreciated that the actuation of the ailerons is not merely for the purpose of imparting stability to the aircraft but that the ailerons play a very definite role also in controlling the direction of the aircraft. . . . I have recognized this situation and have provided an inter-connection between the aircraft wings and the rudder through the aileron control so that whenever the ailerons are actuated in response to the tilting of the wings there is also an actuation of the steering rudder so that any turning movement that has been introduced by the tilting of the wings will be at the same time counteracted by the actuation of the steering rudder.

Wright Field immediately ordered three A-1s at $5,400 each. In a "turnabout is fair play" arrangement, perhaps a reaction to the Navy-Norden connection, Sperry gave the Air Corps priority over all other purchasers, including commercial aircraft manufacturers clamoring for the device.[46]

The intent of the Air Corps all along had been to develop a bombing device. The final test report concluded that the device had "maintained the line of flight sufficiently accurate for bombing purposes over periods comparable to those required for approach." Upon receiving word of the autopilot test results, Chief of the Air Corps Benjamin Foulois ordered the A-1–equipped Ford C-9 flown to Washington for presentation to the media. He proclaimed, "The automatic pilot has arrived. Large airplanes may now be controlled by the untiring metallic arms of an ingenious mechanism—a mechanism which pilots transport airplanes straight and level and will hold them on a given course indefinitely." Foulois was enough of a politician to know that the antiwar atmosphere in the United States was still too strong to reveal the autopilot's original purpose—to guide a bomber aircraft through a smooth and straight approach to improve bombing accuracy.[47]

Sperry's device, weighing 50 pounds, was mounted beneath the copilot's seat, with 70 pounds of associated equipment mounted in the fuselage. Built around two gyroscopes[48] spinning at 15,000 revolutions per minute, one mounted vertically and one horizontally, any movement away from the gyroscopes' fixed planes made contact between the housing of the gyroscopes and electromagnets. The resulting electric current powered magnetic-clutch servomotors that engaged bevel gears mounted on a revolving shaft connected to a wind-driven propeller. The bevel gears rotated another shaft and pulley either clockwise or counterclockwise, pulling long cables linked directly to the aircraft's control surfaces: the rudder and ailerons for directional control (yaw), the elevators for up and down control (pitch), and the ailerons for lateral control (roll). Twelve-volt power came from a wind-driven generator.[49]

Proclamations of success were perhaps premature, as service testing of the Sperry automatic pilot showed it functioned well, but required "very frequent" adjustments and suffered from manufacturing defects. The main problem was with the long cables used to connect the central shafts to the control surfaces. Exposed to rapid drops in temperature at high altitudes, they constantly lost tension, making for increasingly "mushy" controls. Another problem was with irregular electrical production coming from the air-driven generators.[50]

Sperry focused on two improvements for the follow-up Army A-2 model automatic pilot. The major switch was from electrical controls and motors to pneumatic controls of hydraulic pistons for greater reliability and reduced maintenance. Hydraulics also gave a softer ride than the quicker responding mechanical linkages. An air pump drew air through two ports in the casing of the gyroscopes across vanes attacked to the gyroscope wheel, spinning it at high speeds. Deviation from level flight shut off the air flow through one port, increasing the pressure on one side of a diaphragm inside an air relay. The relay operated an oil valve that engaged a hydraulic servo and piston to adjust the aircraft control surfaces and return the airplane to level flight.

Sperry's second modification allowed the A-2 to maintain a constant altitude. An additional diaphragm remained open to atmospheric pressure until the aircraft reached its desired altitude. Any change in altitude after the inlet valve had been closed caused the diaphragm to expand or contract. Its movement changed the flow of air from the air pump across an attached disc, which adjusted the elevator control system of the automatic pilot through a bellows. This feature was critical for accurate bombing, because as a bomber dropped its first bombs, the lightened aircraft tended to leap upwards, upsetting the bombsighting solution for the remaining bombs.[51]

The success of the A-2 was solidified in 1933 when the famous aviation pioneer Wiley Post flew his *Winnie Mae* around the world, New York to New York, solo, in 115 hours, 36½ minutes. Post had paid Sperry $10,000 for an early model A-2, without which his flight would have been impossible. Elmer Sperry Jr. tore up the check when Post landed in New York. Weighing only 75 pounds, including a gallon of hydraulic fluid, the automatic pilot had arrived. It equipped the pioneering Boeing 247D commercial transport, ancestor to the B-17 Flying Fortress of World War II. A generation of wartime American airmen would know the A-2 by the affectionate nickname of "Elmer," the device that flew "more planes than any man who ever wore pilot's wings."[52]

The A-2 gave the Air Corps an automatic pilot, but the problem of bombardier-pilot communication remained. In 1926 McCook's Henry Inglis had suggested connecting a bombsight, in the fashion of the Norden Mark XI, to the PDI to allow the bombardier to signal the correct course directly to the pilot by adjusting the bombsight's controls. Although still relying on a human pilot, it was a step toward having the bombardier fly the aircraft. When Alexander de Seversky proposed to design and build a C-1 bombsight for the Air Corps in a letter of August 2, 1926, Inglis encouraged him to include an attachment to go one step further and allow the C-1 sight to detect and correct errors automatically by maneuvering the aircraft's control surfaces. Negotiations for this Seversky Automatic Azimuth Drift Control floundered, however, on Seversky's demand for a $10,000 payment for the idea. The Air Corps refused to pay for something its own Engineering Division had originated.[53]

Mortimer F. Bates of the Sperry Gyroscope Company sought patent protection in October 1929 for his design linking the A-1 autopilot to the C-series bombsights. His design put the steering of the aircraft "directly under the control of the bomber [bombardier] at the bomb sight [and] . . . to steer the dirigible craft in the act of sighting upon a target."[54] Turning the idea into a workable device proved difficult and by 1933 the lack of funds, the realization that the Sperry C-series bombsight project was going nowhere, and the rumored accuracy of a new Norden bombsight forced the Army to bring all bombsight development projects to a halt, including attempts to link bombsights and automatic pilots. Automatic pilot work continued, but mainly as a device for long-range navigation and safety in poor weather.

A decade of expensive research and development had left the Army's air force with many odds and ends, but no bombing equipment accurate enough to meet the goals of air power. This lack of success reached a crisis point in 1927 in a full-scale bombing exercise against the Pee Dee River Bridge near Albemarle, North Carolina. Although only two years old, this reinforced concrete bridge became a candidate for Army demolition tests when a dam under construction downstream threatened to submerge it. The Army divided the bridge into three sections, one each for use by the Field Artillery, the Corps of Engineers, and the Air Corps. Under Capt. Asa N. Duncan, a detachment of the 2nd Bombardment Group, designated the Provisional Bombardment Squadron and based at Pope Field, North Carolina, dropped sand-filled bombs from Keystone LB-5 bombers on the west span and its approaches from December 19 to 21, 1927. Two days of live bombings with 300- and 600-pound bombs with instantaneous fuzes followed, but did little damage to the reinforced concrete. On the 24th, attacks with 600- and 1,100-pound bombs, some with delayed fuzes, dropped multiple sections of the bridge. Of eighteen 1,100-pound bombs dropped from 6,000 feet, six were direct hits. Six days of generally inaccurate bombing in clear skies with little wind, from low altitude, by the most highly trained crews in the Air Corps did not speak well of Army bombsights.[55] To compensate for this limited accuracy, Duncan worked out a pattern-bombing tactic. Several aircraft flew in formation and all dropped their bombs when the lead bomber released its load, greatly improving the chances of getting a hit.[56]

The Pee Dee experiment escalated into a crisis because the Air Corps had just released Training Regulation 440-96 (December 12, 1927) with a section devoted to explaining the progress that had been made in bombsight designs since World War I. Average circular errors for the World War I Mark IA and Michelin bombsights had been 795 feet, dropping to 160 feet for the modern D-1 sight from 8,000 feet. An increase in accuracy of five times since the war convinced Chief of the Air Corps Maj. Gen. James E. Fechet that precision bombing was at hand, until the failures at the Pee Dee Bridge showed otherwise.[57]

Fechet responded to the report of Pee Dee results one day after he received it, probably spurred on by chiding from officers from the Corps of Engineers and the Field Artillery. His letter to the Materiel Division summed up the Army's frustration with the progress to date.

> Recent tests conducted by the War Department in the destruction of the Pee Dee River Bridge near Albemarle, North Carolina, and which were participated in by the Air Corps, demonstrated that the present bomb sight with which the Air Corps is equipped, falls far short of being the instrument of precision which is necessary in order to insure accurate bombing under service conditions from normal bombing altitudes. . . . It is most essential that the Air Corps have a bomb sight which reduces the possibility of personal error to a minimum. . . . I cannot too strongly emphasize the importance of a bomb sight of precision, since the ability of bombardment aviation to perform the mission of destruction is almost entirely dependent upon an accurate and practical bomb sight.[58]

The Materiel Division had spent the previous decade developing timing systems, synchronous systems, pilot direction indicators, pendulum stabilization, gyroscopic stabilization, and gyroscopically damped pendulum stabilization, but with no clear results. It had followed two lines of development, one for an inexpensive low-altitude sight and the other an expensive high-altitude device. The completion of the D-1, D-4, and D-5 Estoppey projects, the latter using the synchronous principle, fulfilled the requirement for a low-altitude bombsight, but a procurement decision had to await the testing of these sights against the Navy's Norden Mark XI, dismissed as a timing sight with little potential. Development of the high-altitude bombsight had "not progressed so rapidly." The Seversky/Sperry

C-1 was too complex and the C-2 too expensive at $30,000, while the Estoppey D-2 was too inaccurate and the D-3 required redesign. The hope was that the Inglis/Sperry L-1 would meet Fechet's need.[59]

Fechet wanted results, not excuses. The Air Corps chief demanded immediate action: "The question of expense to be incurred in this matter is decidedly of secondary consideration."[60] A bombardment board under the presidency of Maj. Hugh J. Knerr echoed Fechet's concerns.

It is the sense of the Board that the situation is exceeding acute, and demands prompt and positive action by all concerned in order to secure at once a precision sight for existing bombardment aviation and to provide for a development program that will insure keeping ahead of other nations. . . . [A] bombing formation is of no more value than the bomb sight installed therein. . . . The Board is of the belief that the question of cost should not be considered. . . . The effectiveness of bombardment cannot exceed that of the sight employed.[61]

Seversky would only sell for "large cash payments and royalties,"[62] challenging Fechet's words. The chief of the Air Corps concluded that the Air Corps would simply have to pay Seversky's price. Assuming personal charge of the deliberations, Fechet negotiated a $282,000 contract with Seversky (the designer) and Sperry (the manufacturer) for thirty-five C-4s (later reduced to twenty-eight), "embodying your latest ideas in a complete redesign," despite the opinion of the Materiel Division's experts that each bombsight would probably cost $34,500. Production would commence only if three prototypes won Air Corps approval. Delays forced money for the project to be carried over twice to new fiscal years by special acts of Congress. Fechet also authorized the immediate purchase of six L-1s from Sperry for $8,712.[63]

Despite the chief's attention, another crisis in Army bombing accuracy hit in August 1931, only three months before Fechet's retirement. The Navy made a surplus World War I cargo ship, the USS *Mount Shasta*,[64] available as a target for bombing in 1931. The 2nd Bombardment Group's Maj. Herbert A. Dargue, at the head of nine aircraft equipped with the Estoppey D-4, had great difficulty finding the target 60 miles off the North Carolina coast and achieved only two hits on the 400-foot cargo vessel with 300-pound bombs, one of which failed to explode. To the great chagrin of the Air Corps, the *Mount Shasta* had to be sunk by fire from nearby Coast Guard vessels to keep it from becoming a threat to maritime traffic.

The press had a field day: "Obsolete Vessel Takes Best That Army Can Offer" and "Buh-Lam! Missed Again." The Navy leaked the following poem to the press.

Oh Navy, take back your coast defense,
For we find that the sea is rough;
We thought on one hand it would help us expand—
We find we are not so tough.
The sea is your right, you hold it by might;
We would if we could, but we can't.
It seems that the sea is entirely Navy—
Army planes should remain o'er land, the land, the land
Army planes should remain o'er the land.

Lt. Col. Frank Andrews of the Office of the Chief of the Air Corps had been behind the idea for the *Shasta* bombing. When Benjamin Foulois took over as chief of the Air Corps in December 1931, one of his first actions was to replace Andrews.[65]

With the Great Depression and the penury that typified Depression-era military budgets, Air Corps leaders knew they were running out of time and money to equip Air Corps bombers with effective bombsights. In early 1932 Wright Field's 1st Lt. Clarence S. Thorpe toured Navy and Army production and testing facilities to judge the quality of American bombsight development and to find some ray of hope for improving bombing accuracy. Thorpe reported little progress, but with some chagrin "discovered" that the Carl L. Norden Company of New York was preparing an assembly line to manufacture a new and previously unknown (to the Army) Navy bombsight that promised a significant improvement in accuracy.[66]

Thorpe's Navy counterpart, Lt. Malcolm F. Schoeffel, also began an inspection of Air Corps facilities. His report revealed the poor state of Army bombsight development. The Sperry L-1 lacked accuracy. The Sperry C-4 was overweight, behind schedule, and its deflection error was "so large as to be unsuitable for service use." Schoeffel thought the Estoppey D-7 the best Army bombsight, but effective only at low altitudes. The Navy's bombsight expert concluded that the new Norden stabilization system was superior, had a better means for allowing the bombardier to direct the pilot to the target, and was mechanically simpler.[67]

Schoeffel convinced Thorpe that the new Norden bombsight was perhaps the most accurate bombsight in the world. It had "not been seen by any one at the [Materiel] Division, and, therefore, the comparative merits of the four sights [C-4, D-7A, C-5, and the new Norden] are not known."[68] Should the Air Corps rework the Estoppey D-7 into a refined D-7A, try to rescue the much-delayed Sperry C-5, go with the Sperry C-4s already contracted, or buy the Navy's new Norden bombsight?[69]

For fiscal year 1933 the Air Corps allocated $325,000 for bombsights to equip a new generation of bombers.[70] A decade of effort left it with only marginal capabilities, many untested. Chief of the Air Corps Benjamin Foulois had seen enough. He notified the division that he was diverting $223,000 for aircraft procurement, leaving just $102,000 for bombsights. That amount, he said, must be used to purchase *only* the new Norden bombsight.[71] Foulois' decision left no funds for examining any new Seversky, Estoppey, Inglis, or Sperry designs. On November 15, 1933, the Air Corps informed all four sources that it had "no expectation of procuring any quantity" of their bombsights other than those already contracted. Since Riley Scott's pioneering work in 1910, the Army's air force had managed to accumulate 12,124 World War I Mark I-As, which it could not discard because there was "no other available sight"; 68 D-1s and 107 D-4s in operational units; and 6 L-1s, 3 D-4As, 1 D-7, 3 C-4s, 1 C-5, and a Norden Mark XI undergoing testing. On order were 7 C-5s ($6,500 each), 26 C-4s ($5,500 each), and 25 new Norden bombsights ($4,500 each). The Materiel Division was also attempting to manufacture small numbers of D-7As ($2,500 each) for low-altitude use at Wright Field with Air Corps materials, tools, and employees.[72]

The bombsight development program had become an embarrassment. Henry H. Arnold, commander of the 7th Bombardment Group, complained that he had to throttle-back his B-12 bombers during bombing exercises because they were too fast for the D-1 and D-4 bombsights with which they were equipped. Sperry A-1 and A-2 automatic pilots were available to contribute to bombing accuracy, but the Air Corps was running out of bombsight options. Consecutive chiefs of the Air Service and Air Corps had extolled the accuracy of bombing to the public, to the Army, and to themselves, but inaccurate bombsights stood between the promise and the reality.[73]

Riley Scott preparing two 18-pound bombs for his "means for dropping projectiles from aerial crafts" and bombsight in 1911 to hit a practice target—"well, almost anyway." (*Source:* National Air and Space Museum.)

Elmer A. Sperry Sr. pioneered gyroscopic stabilization for aircraft and bombsights, founding the Sperry Gyroscope Company that became the Army's primary source of automatic pilots and bombsights until the Norden bombsight supplanted Sperry bombsights in the 1930s and '40s. (*Source:* Sperry Gyroscope Company Collection, Hagley Museum and Library.)

Elmer A. Sperry Jr., brother of Lawrence and son of Elmer Sperry, solved the yaw or directional aspect of the autopilot problem, making automatic flight control possible. (*Source:* Sperry Gyroscope Company Collection, Hagley Museum and Library.)

Lawrence B. Sperry, Elmer Sperry's daredevil son, dominated aircraft gyrostabilizer and automatic flight control development until his death in December 1923. (*Source:* Sperry Gyroscope Company Collection, Hagley Museum and Library.)

Headquarters of the Sperry Gyroscope Company, Brooklyn, New York, in 1935. (*Source:* Sperry Gyroscope Company Collection, Hagley Museum and Library.)

BOMB SIGHT MARK IA

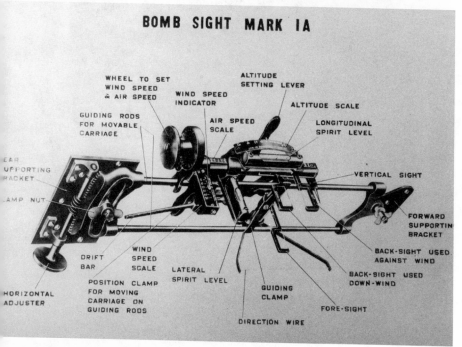

At $75.60 per copy, the Wimperis Mark I bombsight was developed to equip the 27,000 aircraft American industry was to build to darken the skies over Europe in World War I. With few exceptions, American airmen used European aircraft equipped with European bombsights in the war. (*Source:* USAF Historical Research Agency.)

Lawrence Sperry's 1914 autopilot, used to win $10,000 in the *Concourse par l'Union pour la Sécurité en Aeroplane*. (*Source:* Sperry Gyroscope Company Collection, Hagley Museum and Library.)

Lawrence Sperry's 1915 autopilot, with electrically driven servomotors, sold commercially at $2,000 apiece. (*Source:* Sperry Gyroscope Company Collection, Hagley Museum and Library.)

After World War I bombsight designers concentrated on stabilization as a means of improving bombsight accuracy. This Sperry-modified Wimperis Mark I bombsight connected to a Sperry gyroscope tried to make a silk purse out of a sow's ear in 1922. (*Source:* Sperry Gyroscope Company Collection, Hagley Museum and Library.)

The first attempt to link a bombsight and an automatic pilot to improve bombing accuracy, predecessor of the Norden and Sperry SBAE/AFCE, was this Sperry 1915 automatic pilot linked to a modified Wimperis Mark I bombsight from the early 1920s. (*Source:* Sperry Gyroscope Company Collection, Hagley Museum and Library.)

The Sperry A-1 mounted in place of the copilot's seat of a Ford transport, 1929. With electric motors and controls and two gyroscopes, the A-1 was the world's first successful automatic pilot. Development stretched from 1926 to 1929. (*Source:* USAF Historical Research Agency.)

Carl L. Norden, developer of the Mark XI and Mark XV/M-series bombsights and the associated stabilized bombing approach equipment, in a postwar photograph. He intended to shorten wars and reduce casualties by improved bombing accuracy, allowing airmen to target specific military and industrial targets. (*Source:* Norden Systems Division.)

Clown Emmett Kelly presented Ted Barth, Carl Norden's production manager, an oversized pickle at a Madison Square Garden circus performed exclusively for Norden employees in 1943 to celebrate winning an Army-Navy "E" award for production excellence. The pickle came from Barth's claim that a Norden bombsight could drop a bomb into a pickle barrel from 20,000 feet. (*Source:* Norden Systems Division.)

Carl L. Norden, Inc., at 80 Lafayette Street, New York City. Today it is the location of the New York City Consumer Protection Agency. (*Source:* Norden Systems Division.)

Wright Field, 1927, new home of the Materiel Division (formerly the Engineering Division, formerly of McCook Field), center of the Army Air Corps' bombsight and automatic pilot development programs. (*Source:* National Air and Space Museum.)

Navy Norden Mark XI bombsight installed in a Martin flying boat. (*Source:* National Archives.)

3

To Sink Ships

The U.S. Army and Navy faced different bombsighting problems. For the Navy, aircraft had to go to sea on the backs of expensive aircraft carriers with limited capacities. Land-based, long-range patrol bombers did not have the performance to follow the fleet to sea and were politically vulnerable to "turf" battles with the Army's air arm. Primary Navy targets were ships, difficult to hit because they could maneuver to avoid falling bombs. The Navy therefore committed itself to optimum accuracy against maneuvering targets by a few bombers. The Army could send dozens of aircraft to hit one unmoving target. For the Navy giant plumes of water caused by misses were beautiful but militarily useless.

Unlike the Army's Air Service/Air Corps Tactical School, the Navy did not establish a center for the preparation of doctrine for using the new air weapon. Alfred Thayer Mahan, the "high priest of American navalism," most clearly expressed existing Navy doctrine. Although it underwent no critical examination and by the 1920s had not been tested in war, Navy doctrine declared that the key to an industrial nation's power was economic expansion based on overseas trade. The U.S. Navy's objective was to keep open America's trading routes while cutting those of enemy nations. These sea routes were the choke-points of the enemy, vulnerable to attacks by the battleship, which could attack both commerce and defending enemy ships. The Navy's General Board believed that the function of the Navy was to use battleships to bring "pressure to bear on the enemy by injuring his commerce."[1]

The airplane encouraged the Naval War College to include studies of bombing accuracy and the damage effect of aerial bombing in its curriculum, but the key points of study remained battleship tactics. If the airplane were to assume a key position in Navy doctrine, it would do so because of the actions of generally young air officers. During exercises and tests they would force even the crustiest shellback to recognize the importance of air power.[2]

A series of ship-bombing tests that caught the attention of the American public, choreographed by Brig. Gen. Billy Mitchell, became the first postwar opportunity for naval air power. The Navy was in the midst of a series of ordnance tests against naval vessels and invited, under duress from Mitchell, the participation of the Air Service.[3] From the beginning, Mitchell and the Navy were at cross-purposes. Mitchell wanted a forum for his ideas while the Navy wanted to evaluate the effects of bombs on ships. The Navy also needed a means for testing the effectiveness of its own nascent air force. If any ships were to be sunk by aircraft, they would be Navy aircraft.[4]

Through June and July 1921 Army airmen and Navy aviators dropped bombs on various targets, including a German submarine, destroyer, and cruiser and an old American battleship. Although they sank all, the two aerial forces did not distinguish themselves with bombing accuracy.[5] The finale came on July 20 and 21 with strikes against the 546-foot German *Ostfriesland*. A modern dreadnought with watertight compartments (though anchored and with no defensive fire), bombing the former German battleship was a worthy test of the power of aerial bombardment. Bad weather and Navy and Air Service friction limited damage the first day. The Navy wanted to examine the ship after each attack, hoping to gather valuable data on the effects of aerial bombing on battleships. Mitchell wanted only to sink the German ship as fast as possible to prove the superiority of air power to sea power. On the first day the Navy dropped thirty-four 230-pound bombs, with six hits, and eight 550-pounders, achieving two hits. Mitchell's force added eleven 600-pounders with two hits. The *Ostfriesland* took on a slight list astern and had its port engine room flooded, but remained afloat at the end of the day.

On day 2 Mitchell was an irresistible force. Before the Navy could stop them to examine damage, Mitchell's crews dropped five 1,100-pound bombs, with three hits, holing the starboard side. Seven 2,000-pound bombs followed in quick order. At 12:25 one hit 25 feet from the port side. Three minutes later another hit five feet closer. The water-hammer effect split the *Ostfriesland*'s seams. Eight minutes later the stern was under water. By 12:40 the once great ship was gone.

The tests put to rest most doubts about whether an airplane could sink a ship.[6] There was, however, nothing especially profound about aircraft dropping hundreds of bombs to sink immobile ships unprotected by anti-aircraft artillery. Sixteen Navy and sixteen Air Service aircraft had dropped 38,320 pounds of explosives on a defenseless battleship and had sunk it. The Joint Army-Navy Board, with John J. Pershing as the senior member, drew wide-ranging conclusions from the tests. Most seemed to be a sop to the Navy—the battleship remained "the backbone of the fleet and the bulwark of the Nation's sea defense." Aircraft added to the dangers faced by battleships, but had "not made the battleship obsolete."[7]

It became an article of faith, though without serious examination until the 1930s, that bombing accuracy would be abysmal against a maneuvering ship, especially at the high altitudes from which antiaircraft fire would force airplanes to bomb. A report for the secretary of the Navy in December 1924 concluded that "it is absurd to contend that either the aerial bomb or the submarine torpedo has furnished the effectual answer to the capital ship." The Army came to the same conclusion: "from 10,000 feet the chance of hitting a moving ship with those instruments [current bombsights], is extremely remote." The Navy continued to develop an air force because of the obvious advantages in range and observation aircraft provided, but aircraft needed much improved bombing accuracy if they were to become an important weapon for commanding the seas.[8]

The Naval Bureau of Ordnance (BuOrd) held responsibility for developing bombsights. The challenge was clear. Against the *Ostfriesland*, from altitudes of less than 2,500 feet, Navy aircraft had achieved an accuracy rate of only 19 percent against a fixed target bigger than the broad side of a barn—546 feet long and 93 feet wide. At an accuracy of 30 percent, Mitchell's bombers, using World War I Michelins and the Navy's Mark III-A bombsights, did little better.[9] The Mark III-A performed adequately, but could be used only in calm weather because it suffered from excessive vibrations. Crews demanded "some sort of an automatic device to keep it [the Mark III-A] in a perpendicular at all times." Both the Navy and the

Army had to develop improved bombsights if air power were to achieve the role Mitchell and others had claimed for it.[10]

The Mark III was a low-altitude bombsight because it lacked a lens for improving the power of the human eye. Although it represented a technological dead end, a rapidly declining budget forced the Navy to refine this existing device rather than develop a new instrument. Tests revealed that without some means of stabilizing the Mark III in a bucking aircraft, little increase in accuracy would be possible. So limited in performance was the Mark III that pilots preferred using their "personal judgment" in bombing practice to aiming with the modified Wimperis device. On January 15, 1920, Cdr. Arthur C. Stott of BuOrd asked a Brooklyn-based engineer, Carl L. Norden, to investigate the possibility of gyroscopic stabilization for the Mark III. Norden had previously worked on ship stabilization and on the Navy's aerial torpedo project.[11]

Norden's first contact with the Navy had come indirectly in 1918 through the Sperry Company, which was working on an aerial torpedo catapult contract. Because of problems with the device, the Navy asked Sperry to consult an outside expert. Commander Stott, chief of the Aviation Ordnance Section of BuOrd, was impressed with the logic and clarity of comments appended to the outside expert's evaluation. It listed no author, but Stott saw the name "Norden" penciled in under several comments in the margins. A check of the Brooklyn telephone book and a telephone call began the contact that would prove so fruitful for the Navy and Norden over the next three decades.[12]

Stott and Norden continued to meet to discuss Navy technical problems, including the difficulties of bombing ships from altitude with any certainty of success. Stott wrote Norden on January 15, 1920, that the Navy was "extremely anxious" for Norden to initiate studies to improve the standard Navy bombsight, the Mark III, by adding stabilization, a telescope, and a pilot-directing mechanism. Reflecting the budget crunch, Stott asked that Norden incorporate as much of the Mark III in his design as possible. Norden intended to modify the Mark III to include automatic compass orientation and the precise automatic input of altitude and airspeed data. In subsequent correspondence, he refined his plans to include mounting the sight inside the airplane to reduce the effects of wind and weather on the bomb-aiming process and to build a stabilized base. Norden would work as a consulting engineer to the Witteman-Lewis Aircraft Company, which would build the bombsight Norden would design. Designated the Pilot Directing Bombsight Mark III-A (Mark IV Army designation), Norden would be paid on a cost plus percentage-of-cost basis.[13]

The first tests of the Mark III-A in October 1921 revealed basic difficulties. From 4,000 feet the Navy had only eleven hits out of 103 bombs dropped on the anchored USS *Indiana* and the USS *Smith*. Tests against the USS *Iowa* traveling at six knots on a straight course upwind achieved only two hits out of eighty-five bombs dropped. The testing authority concluded that the Army Estoppey D-1 was the "best sight available," simpler in design, with better stabilization (by pendulum) than the Norden-Wimperis hybrid design. Norden's first attempt to improve bombing accuracy was a failure.[14]

Carl Lukas Norden fit nearly all of the stereotypes associated with genius, though Norden preferred to think of himself as a person who worked harder than anyone else.[15] Sixteen-hour days were typical. Self-centered, impatient, domineering, driven, abrasive, and perfectionist, he was also a man of the highest ethical standards. Born on April 23, 1880, in Semarang, Java, Norden displayed as a youth the qualities that so typified his life. Although the middle child in a fatherless family of five children, Carl was his mother's choice to inspect the house and the surrounding grounds for trespassers before retiring at night. His strong will, absolute bravery, and trustworthiness made him the obvious preference for this task. His favored career was that of an artist, but his older brother's decision to pursue the life of a starving artist forced Carl to seek a money-making profession for the good of the family. He enrolled at the Federal Polytechnic Institute in Zurich, Switzerland, graduating in 1904 as a mechanical engineer. While at the institute he met a young Russian revolutionary, Vladimir Ilyich Ulyanov, known to history as Nikolai Lenin. According to Norden's son, both were "ruthlessly self-disciplined with outstanding powers of concentration" and a sense of destiny that drove them to great accomplishments. Both went on to find fame and fortune, one designing new technologies, the other leading revolutions.

Although Norden was a Dutch citizen by birth, his family ties were to Germany. His father was a Dutch-naturalized German, his wife Austrian-German. He saw the world in mechanical terms, everything fitting together in perfect harmony, like the gears of a watch. The greatest designs, he believed, were the products of mathematical formulas reflecting the natural workings of the universe. Norden typified the European tradition of skillful craftsmanship. During the 1930s and 1940s Norden always gave preference in his hiring practices to European emigré craftsmen and watchmakers, especially those from Germany. Despite this near reverence for German skills, Norden held Germans as a people untrustworthy. A great irony of the Norden story is the continuous theme of German involvement in developing and producing the bombsight that would contribute so mightily to Allied victory over Germany in World War II.

Norden emigrated to the United States in 1904, "because that's where the jobs were." An American uncle, Adolph Norden, a rich cotton merchant, got him his first job with the Worthington Hydraulic Company. Clearly Norden hated working for others—a prima donna, he in rapid succession worked for Vehicle Equipment Company, Lidgerwood Manufacturing Company, and finally Sperry Gyroscope Company in 1910. Elmer Sperry hired the Dutchman to solve problems associated with the gyroscopic stabilization of ships. Norden became acquainted with the U.S. Navy while at Sperry and acquired great practical knowledge of gyroscopes. He also learned to loathe Sperry's voracious appetite for patents. Sperry learned to loathe Norden's voracious appetite for "vile black cigars."[16] After receiving what he thought was an insulting $25-per-week raise for solving the tendency of Sperry's gyroscopes to oscillate, Norden quit to become a consulting engineer. Sperry took Norden's resignation as a personal affront, beginning a half century of conflict between the Sperry Company and Norden. Sperry felt he had taught Norden everything he knew about gyroscopes and therefore should share in any of Norden's future patents. Norden felt Sperry would have tried to patent gravity if the Patent Office had allowed his claim.

In 1913 Norden established an office as a consulting engineer in the shadow of the Brooklyn Naval Yard. He continued to work on Sperry's ship stabilization project for the Navy, attempting to substitute a small gyroscope with a movable counterweight for Sperry's unworkable giant gyroscope. While on one test voyage, Norden showed his nerve and resolve, performing a successful emergency appendectomy. The slow pace of the project and the absence of any clear successes encouraged the Navy to drop the stabilization project and transfer Norden to work on catapults for shipborne aircraft and aerial torpedoes with Hannibal Ford and Charles Kettering. After the war he also designed the hydraulic landing gear and restraining hooks for the aircraft carriers *Saratoga* and *Lexington*.

Although he lived in the United States for 43 years, Norden never became an American citizen. On three occasions he went to court to become a naturalized American citizen, but each time one or more of his witnesses failed to appear. On the third occasion an immigration judge gave him a severe dressing-down. For Norden, that ended the issue forever. In his mind, any country that would allow the dregs of the world to become citizens, but would deny him the same right, was not deserving of his allegiance. Later Norden would tell his few close acquaintants that his Dutch citizenship provided him with leverage in his dealings with the U.S. government, leverage he felt a citizen would not have. Before World War II, according to his family, the British government offered him a knighthood in return for emigrating to Great Britain to build bombsights and other instruments, which caused his American employers some anxious moments. There was no need for concern; Norden believed no respectable Dutchman could ever work for the British.

Norden held representative republican democracy as the most perfect form of government, but was, according to his son, "essentially an elitist who believed that human progress was the achievement of the lonely few guided by Divine Providence." The common people were not to be trusted, as they would follow anyone, but representative republican government best prevented tyrants who could suppress a people's creative abilities. Norden's thinking also reflected a touch of European ethnocentrism, or perhaps racism. The sun, he believed, was destructive of mental capabilities. Northern people, where the sun shown most obliquely, "were the most creative in science." A suntan was a symbol of mental weakness.

Although he was not a political man, Norden's three great hatreds were Hitler, Hirohito, and Franklin Roosevelt, the latter because he had defaulted on the gold clause in U.S. bonds and gold certificates. For Norden this was not a political but moral issue, for he believed in absolute integrity. Any man who did not keep his promises deserved no emotion but hatred.

On the outside and to those with whom he worked, Norden was a man of "immense nervous energy, excitable and volatile, with an unholy temper." The Navy referred to him as "Old Man Dynamite." He had a "pronounced disdain for lesser minds," to the extent that he was generally unsociable and reclusive. His "self-imposed obscurity" was so successful that Americans knew more of his secret bombsight than of him. One major reason for Norden's penchant for privacy was his exacting standards that few could meet. An incident that revealed this side of his character involved an autobiographical sketch he was to write for the man who was to award Norden the Holley Award for mechanical engineering in 1944. The presenter's instructions were for Norden to write "about 400 words." On a whim, the man counted the words in the autobiography when it arrived— exactly 400 words.

He was brutally direct in all his actions. According to his son, Carl Norden "laid down the law as though he were Moses descending the mountain." He established nonsmoking areas throughout his plant to maintain the dust-free conditions required for precision manufacturing, but constantly violated this restriction with his own cigars. Once an employee asked him why he had designed a part a certain way. Norden answered, "I had 10,000 reasons, none of which are any of your damn business." He rarely became directly involved with company projects during World War II, limiting himself to brief observations and to setting ground rules. His ground rules, however, became laws once uttered. One such law that caused difficulties for most of the company's wartime projects was "There shall be *no* AC motors used!" Norden always insisted that his products run on direct current, not alternating current. Unfortunately the Army Air Forces made a transformation during the war from direct current to alternating current. Norden's dictum forced his engineers to use relays and potentiometers rather than synchros and arbitrarily delayed the transition of Norden bombsights and equipments from mechanical to electronic engineering.[17]

This rough and exacting exterior, however, clashed dramatically with his inner self: "always religious, but never a churchgoer" and puritanical. He opposed established churches, especially the Catholic Church. Popes, he believed, belonged in the bottom level of Hell. Norden hated for anyone to speak of his "inventions," believing that only God could be responsible for inventions. Norden's achievements were "designs." He ate mostly steaks, drank great quantities of coffee, and lived comfortably. A devotee of the Christian theologian Emanuel Swedenborg, Norden committed himself to "being of use." His Swedenborgian Christianity allowed him to have all these characteristics, while being dedicated to charity and compassion for the disadvantaged. He despised taxes, preferring instead to give taxable profits to his employees as annual bonuses. This philosophy left no room for self-aggrandizement. Norden read Dickens avidly for revelations on the lives of the disadvantaged and Thoreau for the discussion of the simple life. In his will Norden left one-third of his wealth to the Swedenborgian Society to finance the publication of books.

Norden's genius expressed itself in the simple and systematic way in which he worked. He "liked always to start with a blank sheet of paper rather than first ascertaining what others had done. He was never satisfied with a solution, but tried to develop as many solutions as he could find and then chose the simplest and cleanest." Norden did all of his own drafting, with a skill and quality that over 50 years later still attracted admiration from his former employees. He had no extensive library, relying on his slide rule, a book of engineering tables, and a few basic manuals. He designed the *Saratoga* and *Lexington*'s arresting gear on a dining room table. Norden did much of the creative work for his famous bombsight during months spent in Zurich, Switzerland, at his mother's home.

His military employers never liked the threat to security that Norden's penchant for work at home and in Switzerland caused, but Norden told his son he had to go where the "Navy couldn't bother me." Although dedicated to his family, Norden also considered it a distraction, routinely shipping his wife and children to Switzerland while he worked in New York. His favorite place for creative thinking in the United States was the Netherlands Club in Brooklyn, where he would sit for hours staring into space, lost in thought. He was never absentminded; his prodigious powers of concentration allowed him to ignore everything around him in his endeavor to solve problems.

In Norden's view, security was not a consideration because so much of his work was mental. Norden recorded his ideas on paper and blueprints only to communicate with others. From Zurich these records traveled to New York by diplomatic courier, after the Navy asked the State Department to treat Norden with kid gloves because of "his work of the utmost value."[18] The Navy accepted this working arrangement because "Old Man Dynamite" left it no choice.

Henry Arnold, chief of the Army Air Corps, was aghast to learn of these working arrangements in the late 1930s. During a tour of the Brooklyn Norden plant in 1939, an Army inspector informed him of the Navy's arrangements and of Norden's continuing Dutch citizenship. Arnold fired off a letter to the chief of the Navy's Bureau of Aeronautics (BuAer): "It seems to me that it brings up what may prove a very serious situation. If Mr. Norden does consider himself at liberty to go to a foreign country and build equipment, some of our secret projects undoubtedly will be jeopardized." Arnold warned that Norden himself had told the Army inspector that he had sold out his interests in the company to his partner and had given the inspector "the impression that he considers himself now a free-will agent as regards the disposition of any brain children he has or may have had" and "that he could work for anyone." The Navy refused to change its obviously productive relationship with Norden, but did request the Federal Bureau of Investigation provide bodyguards for Norden and infiltrate the Norden plant to root out any threats to the facility's security.[19]

This was the man who recommended that the Navy drop the Mark III-A and contract with him to build an entirely new timing sight, using a clock to determine the closing speed between the aircraft and the target. Norden began work on the new sight in November 1921, without funding, while he worked on a pilot direction indicator (PDI) for the Mark III-A, completed in January 1922. The Navy ordered three of these devices, paying Norden $1,825, including $575 in negotiated profit.[20]

With this money, supplemented by family funds, Norden continued to work privately on a better bombsight. In June 1922, BuOrd, impressed with Norden's progress, issued a contract worth $10,700 for three experimental models of his timing bombsight, designated the Mark XI.[21] A year later, concerned that the project was too much for one man, especially a prima donna engineer who preferred to do most of his work in the abstract and was not the easiest person with whom to work, the Navy recommended that Norden link up with a more practical, more amenable engineer. The man they recommended was a former Army colonel who had made a name for himself as a man who could get things done.

Theodore H. Barth was the son of an Austrian immigrant plumber. A self-made man, he worked his way through Stevens Technical School lighting gas lamps at Union Square in New York. With his training as an engineer and a practical knowledge of plumbing from his father, Barth became one of the first plumbing contractors to specialize in the new skyscrapers sprouting in New York City. During World War I he joined the Army and at the rank of colonel was put in charge of gas-mask production.

When the Navy brought Norden and Barth together in 1923, Barth made the perfect counterpart to Norden's isolated and intense genius. "Infinitely patient, charming, and notably kind," Barth's "ingratiating manner was that of a born politician." According to Norden's son, Barth never had an original thought—that was Norden's job. Barth provided the practical engineering and business skills that almost immediately proved productive, channeling Norden's talents. Norden called Barth his "partner and friend" whom he esteemed "very highly as an engineer, and to whom I have given Power of Attorney signifying entire confidence on my part." Barth described himself as "just a lathe hand gone Hollywood," although a close friend and Air Corps officer, Herbert A. Dargue, called him a "composite of Albert Einstein, Henry Ford, and Mahatma Gandhi."[22] He was "as great a leader," in the opinion of those privileged to be employees, "as Mr. Norden was an inventor. Fun-loving, magnanimous and stable, he was a 'Prince of Light' during the difficult days of prodigious production." He gave away World Series tickets to his employees and rented Madison Square Garden for a private showing of the Ringling Brothers Circus for employees on the occasion of winning an "E" award for wartime production.[23]

Barth loved his role, his position, and his contacts. During World War II, at a time of rationing, he maintained a lunch room at the 80 Lafayette Street Norden building for the top thirty people at Norden, serving them lobster, suckling pig, and other gourmet delights. Calling it the "Pickle Barrel Conference Club," Barth also insured the club had well-hidden slot machines for the entertainment of his guests, programmed to always break even. Mayor Fiorello H. LaGuardia of New York was a common visitor, who, in keeping with his antigambling image, never played the slot machines.[24] Carl Norden's son recalled that Barth was more of a father to him than Norden himself, with a heart "as big as his body." After World War II Barth just "wanted to get out of business so he could concentrate on his philanthropic activities and so he could fish."[25]

Working out of his home and Barth's apartment, using the equipment and skilled labor of the Witteman-Lewis Aircraft Company, Norden delivered the three contracted PDIs and three experimental Mark XI bombsights to the Navy in the late winter of 1923 and spring of 1924, respectively. All were handmade. He described the bombsight as "a small, compact, optical, stabilized instrument for use on moving targets, with efficient pilot directing." An electrically driven gyroscope stabilized the sight on two axes. The bombardier would fix the foresight on the target and use the clock to time an interval equal to one-half the time of bomb fall, according to predetermined charts, at the current altitude, while adjusting the foresight to keep it fixed on the target. When the timing device reached the appropriate moment, the backsight automatically moved so that it was set at a distance proportional to the ground distance covered by the falling bomb. The backsight determined the range angle for that altitude, that type bomb, and that air speed. When the backsight cross hairs intersected the target, the bomb dropped. As the bombardier rotated the Mark XI around its mounting post, the PDI automatically pointed right or left to indicate the correct course for the pilot to fly to match the aircraft's path on the ground to the correct path needed to allow the bomb to hit its target under the influences of wind (drift).[26]

Under tests at the Dahlgren Naval Proving Ground in Virginia, the Mark XI proved "disappointing." Test bombs fell with "alarming irregularity." The Navy believed the sight to be too complicated, but Norden remained confident that he could correct the problems. Before the President's Aircraft Board (Morrow Board), BuAer chief Rear Adm. William A. Moffett claimed that the Navy had under development a bombsight that "is going to be extraordinarily acceptable, and we hope to have it in the near future."[27] In early 1925 BuOrd issued Norden a new contract for $3,400 to cover modifications to two of the original experimental sights. Norden added pendulum stabilization to one and made other adjustments, completing his work in June 1925. Tests that summer and fall at Dahlgren proved the improvements worthwhile. In the final test, eighteen bombs dropped from 3,000 feet achieved a mean point of impact only nine feet short in range, but 187 feet to the right (deflection) of the flight path. The test bombardier was impressed, but reported the sight was much too complex, requiring "both hands, both feet and the teeth" to operate. In an open cockpit, the cold and wind made fine adjustments to the sight nearly impossible.[28]

Norden viewed the basic design as good and the problems correctable. To facilitate the process, leaving Barth in New York to consult with the Navy and to supervise the machining of parts, Norden moved to Zurich and a year's isolation. The drawings he sent to Barth and the Navy offered sufficient promise for the Navy to issue a contract for $21,650 to cover two new models of Mark XI bombsights and three PDIs, delivered in the late summer and fall of 1926. Continued delays with development of the bombsights forced the Navy to order forty Army D-4 bombsights for $10,798 from the Gaertner Scientific Corporation of Chicago in 1926, with delivery in September 1927.[29]

In October 1927 the Navy completed testing of the Mark XI. Despite continuing problems with leveling, vibrations, and the PDI, the Navy began negotiations with Norden and Barth for the purchase of eighty sights, complete with PDIs.[30] Norden and Barth initially refused to negotiate, preferring to continue their relationship with the Navy as consulting engineers, not production contractors. Under encouragement and several unofficial promises, the bombsight designers gave in and agreed to form Carl L. Norden, Incorporated, to fulfill the Navy's orders. Barth and Norden each owned 50 percent of the stock, originally valued at $6,000. Barth would be president and Norden a consulting engineer. Verbal agreements required both to produce Navy bombsights, with no other stockholders than Barth and Norden, to do no business with foreign countries, and to do no commercial business, under the supervision and direction of BuOrd.[31] The Navy promised to provide the company with sufficient orders to keep it going.

The final obstacle was Norden's demand for patent violation indemnification. Carl Norden operated under the constant threat of legal action from the Sperry Gyroscope Company. Elmer Sperry Sr. felt Norden had betrayed him when the latter left the former's service and claimed rights over any Norden designs using gyroscopes. When Norden agreed to produce Mark XI bombsights for the Navy, the standardized military contract called for the contractor to "indemnify the United States and all officers and agents thereof, for all liability incurred of any nature or kind on account of the infringement of any copyright or patent rights." Remembering Sperry's unsuccessful lawsuit against him in 1919 for infringing on a Sperry patent in the development of his ship stabilizer, Norden wanted the Navy to assume liability. On April 14, 1928, the Navy's judge advocate general declared that the liability clause in Norden's contract could be omitted if Norden assigned the patent rights to the U.S. government through the secretary of the Navy.

The final contract of May 1928 called for the production of eighty Mark XI bombsights ($4,050 each) with PDIs, spare parts, and tool kits, for $384,800. Norden transferred all drawings, blueprints, vandykes, and patent rights to the Navy two years later.[32] Although Norden later claimed he had turned over all patent rights, models, and designs of his inventions to the government for $1 each, Navy records indicate the Navy paid him $250, still a paltry sum for what would evolve into a $1.5-billion project.[33]

Carl Norden's relationship with the Navy had been small-scale until the Mark XI contract of 1928. For 10 years he had served as a consultant to BuOrd, averaging $7,800 per year, working on catapults, arresting gear, PDIs, bombsight stabilizers, and the Mark XI out of loft space at 74 Lafayette Street, New York City. Until 1928, Norden's company consisted of just himself and Ted Barth. His preference had always been to remain a consultant and a designer, but the Navy contract for eighty Mark XIs forced him to incorporate and establish a small production facility on one floor of the Hallenback-Hungerford Building at 80 Lafayette Street in New York (see Table 3.1).[34]

Norden's relationship with BuOrd was irregular from the beginning. The Navy negotiated contracts with Norden that stretched or violated laws and regulations. Section 3709 of the Revised Statutes of the United

Table 3.1. Navy Contracts with Carl L. Norden, 1918–1928

Year	Amount	Contract
1918	$ 6,126	Consultation
1919	0	None
1920	0	None
1921	15,792	Consultation, PDI development
1922	15,970	Consultation, PDI purchase
1923	800	Consultation
1924	5,675	Consultation
1925	3,400	Mark XI development
1926	30,115	Mark XI/PDI development
1927	0	None
1928	348,700	80 Mark XI/spare parts purchase
1918–28	$426,578	

Source: Brown, "Navy's Mark 15 (Norden) Bombsight," Exhibit B1.

States, dating from the Civil War, required the military to advertise for all purchases and contracts and accept competitive bids. Congress added exceptions to the procurement law later, but none applied to the Norden case. In World War I purchasing officers could sign contracts without competitive bidding on a fixed-price or cost-plus basis. In a reaction against the debacle of World War I aircraft production, Congress required the Army and Navy to consider any design created under service contracts to be public property, not the proprietary right of the designer. The services were to announce specifications and design requirements. Companies or individuals submitted designs and the services signed contracts with several to produce experimental models. The completed prototypes became government property. Finally, the services advertised for bids on production models, with the contract going to the lowest bidder.[35]

Navy officers violated these procedures in their dealings with Carl Norden. The Navy did not announce specifications and design requirements, did not accept proposed designs, did not sign experimental contracts with several sources, did not accept completed prototypes from these sources, and did not allow other companies to bid on the production contract. BuOrd created a private bombsight factory, using claims of security to hide the fact from congressional oversight. According to Ted Barth,

The factory was to be a sort of under-cover plant for the development of our type of bombsight. Our business policy was to be controlled by the Bureau [BuOrd]. . . . The Bureau subsidized our output (both mental and mechanical), and we were to function as sort of subdivision of the Bureau as far as the bombsight problem was concerned. . . . In return, we were given assurances (unofficial, of course), that our outfit would be kept going with bombsight production . . . against any remote possibility of loss.[36]

Norden invested much time and money in his bombsight designs and would have never regained his investment without the Navy's special arrangement. The United States probably would have been denied the best bombsight in the world without it. That Norden and the United States benefited from the arrangement was beyond question. There were other bombsight manufacturers for the United States, but Norden had no other customers for his wares because he refused to sell to foreign governments. If Congress intended "to make the industry a model of traditional, laissez-faire capitalism," as historian Jacob Vander Meulen has asserted, then BuOrd exempted Carl L. Norden, Inc., from Congress' intent.[37]

While the Army sought bombsights through a multitude of sources, advertising for bids on projects in keeping with federal law, the Navy focused its efforts on Carl L. Norden exclusively. Congress clearly intended for the services to advertise for all purchases and contracts with a series of laws beginning in 1861. A series of amendments to the original law provided exceptions only in specific cases: the need for immediate delivery, if there were only one source, if a patent restricted production to the patent holder, if the contract covered replacement parts for items already in use, in an emergency, or when impractical. Contracts for experimental equipment were to be negotiated on a fixed-price or cost-plus basis, but all production contracts were to be through competitive bidding.[38]

Section 10(a) of the Air Corps Act of July 2, 1926, required the secretaries of war and the Navy to advertise for bids, but Section 10(k) allowed negotiated contracts for experimental development. The Navy's development contract with Norden was legal, but the production contracts were not. The Navy went around these restrictions by relying in part on Section 10(k), which allowed negotiated bids with developers if the experimental item was "considered to be the best kind." Section 10(q), however, limited such considerations to equipment designed before the passage of the act, which limited the use of 10(k) to justify the closed contracts with Carl L. Norden, Inc. Additionally, Section 10(t) required the services to award contracts to the "lowest responsible bidder" in all cases.[39]

Section 10(p) of the Air Corps Act stated that "any collusion, understanding, or arrangement to deprive the United States Government of the benefit of full and free competition . . . shall be unlawful [and punishable with] a fine of not exceeding $20,000, or to be imprisoned not exceeding five years, or both, at the discretion of the court." The secretary of the Navy went where the secretary of the Army feared to tread.

Another justification for the Navy's procurement policies was "national security." Besides Norden's patent liability problems, the Navy held the patent on the Mark XI because private individuals were unable to hold security-classified patents. The Navy refused to allow the U.S. Patent Office to release the Mark XI patent until 1947. This procedure gave Norden protection for his proprietary rights and, violating the will of Congress, protected Norden from liability, maintained the security of the device, and kept Norden and the Navy's procurement policies away from congressional eyes. The Navy classified the project "secret" and justified its procurement policies, its acceptance of liability, and its handling of the Norden patent by claiming "national security" concerns. Because no one could see the patent application or the contracts signed with Norden, no one could charge patent infringement or charge violation of procurement procedures, and Norden would be guaranteed proprietary rights to his invention. The arrangement raised the question as to whether the Navy was serving the nation or Carl L. Norden, Inc.

Carl Norden preferred this unusual arrangement because he hated the publicity and business competition that would come from the regular policies for procurement. He considered the Navy the "silent" service, while hating the Army's tendency to "ballyhoo" its actions. No doubt Billy Mitchell contributed to Norden's opinions. He felt Mitchell's grandstanding in the ship-bombing tests of the early 1920s denigrated his work. A man not to suffer fools, Norden believed Mitchell's bluster revealed an ignorance of the problems of bombing accuracy. After World War I the Army sent a colonel to New York to ask Norden to work on bombsights for the Army. He asked the colonel if he knew the Bible. Norden went on, "No man can serve the Lord and the Devil at the same time—and I work for the navy." A certain amount of snobbery added to his feelings, as he believed naval officers to be patrician gentleman and Army officers to be plebeians.[40]

Production of the Mark XI began slowly, allowing the Navy and Norden to continue testing and improving nearly each Mark XI as it was produced. Norden, the perfectionist, tried eight different metal alloys, 105 different levels, and 61 gyroscope armatures to find the best types for his bombsight. Nine years separated Stott's original request for Norden to examine the problem of precision bombing from the Navy's release of the first Norden sight for fleet use.

Were the results worth the wait? BuAer concluded that the Mark XI "lives up to all expectations reasonably held for it during the first year of its use," though nagging problems continued. Slippage of the "back sight" was never solved and leveling remained the operator's greatest challenge. The bombardier had to remove his eye from the sight's telescope to see the timing mechanism, thus losing sight of the target. Its complexity forced the need for continuous expensive overhauls after only several hours of operation. The cardan bearings of the gyroscope tended to bind at the cold temperatures of high-altitude flight. And most telling, the Mark XI still forced pilots to fly prolonged bombing runs at a constant altitude and speed to achieve decent results, dangerous in combat.[41]

The Navy was not so confident of the Mark XI to give Norden monopoly control over Navy bombsight development. In 1928 it paid General Electric of Schenectady, New York, $5,000 to study the feasibility of developing an advanced high-altitude bombsight, the Mark XIII. Intending to counterbalance Norden, the Navy called the program "Bombsight-Scheme B." BuOrd judged Norden "a handicap to the Bureau in that the subject could not be pursued as actively and from as many angles as might be possible if the ideas for this development came from several sources." Attempts to interest the Ford Instrument Company were unsuccessful.

General Electric initiated development in 1928. It built only one model, requiring $25,000 from the Navy and $53,000 from its own resources. After three years of development the Navy canceled the project because meanwhile Norden had developed a new bombsight so superior to the Mark XI that Navy concerns for an alternate source of bombsights withered away.[42]

Until this new bombsight was ready, the Mark XI would have to do. When compared to the Mark III, the Mark XI demonstrated a significant increase in accuracy. From an altitude of 6,500 feet, the Mark III averaged a circular error of 311 feet, while the Mark XI averaged 196 feet. Development costs had been nearly $75,000 and production costs $384,800.[43]

The Army expressed an interest in the Mark XI, but for several years received little more than vague Navy descriptions of its capabilities and promise. Army representatives did not observe testing until 1928. Wright Field's engineers deemed the Norden sight inferior to the Estoppey D-1, but superior to the Estoppey D-4. The Air Corps felt the Mark XI's biggest shortcoming was its utilization of the inferior timing method: "This sight, while an example of splendid workmanship, is a timing sight of extremely poor theoretical accuracy." When an Army representative asked if Norden was considering a synchronous sight, Barth replied: "He does not, at present, intend to develop a synchronous sight comparable to the L [Inglis/ Sperry] or C [Seversky/Sperry] series, but . . . after these sights are completed by the Sperry Company, he may take up such development along the lines studied by him some years ago." Barth probably lied, as Norden was already considering just such a sight. The Army, desperate for any decent bombsight, ordered fifteen Norden Mark XI bombsights in 1932 for $150,000, but switched the order to the new Norden synchronous Mark XV before production of the Mark XIs had begun.[44]

Norden did not ship the first three production Mark XIs to the Navy for testing until early 1929. Theodore Barth witnessed every aspect of tests at the Dahlgren Naval Proving Ground and had a hand in designing the tests.[45] While Dahlgren struggled with the complex sights, production of the essentially handmade Mark XI continued at a rate of only three per month. BuAer decided that the fleet's bombsight situation was so poor that even imperfect Nordens would be preferable to the Mark IIIs, by 1930 in use for seven years. BuOrd distributed the sights as they came out of the Norden workshop to torpedo and bombing plane squadrons of the Battle and Scouting Fleets. The fleet served as the primary testing unit, requiring all operating units to complete evaluation forms each time the sights were used.[46]

Although the Mark XI represented a substantial improvement over previous bombsights, it did not resolve the limitations of high-altitude horizontal bombing. Only mass bombing formations and bombing patterns could hope to hit a maneuvering target from high altitude. With the limited air force available to the fleet on the backs of its only carriers, the USS *Lexington* and *Saratoga* (1927), and later the *Ranger* (1934), and with each aircraft carrying only one bomb of limited size, effective bombing patterns would be difficult. The Navy gradually lost faith in the ability of an aircraft flying horizontally to drop bombs on maneuvering ships from high altitude.

The U.S. Navy therefore pursued two additional means for sinking ships from the air during the 1920s. The aerial torpedo was first considered in the United States in 1912. A Royal Naval Air Service Short floatplane became the first aircraft to drop an aerial torpedo in 1914. Actual testing in the United States began in 1918, spurred on by the success of other navies during World War I.[47] The torpedo allowed an aircraft to strike a ship at its most vulnerable point below the waterline. In 1920 the Navy formed its first aerial torpedo squadron based on land at Yorktown, equipped with the Martin MBT (later the TM-1). Other land-based torpedo bombers followed, including the Naval Aircraft Factory's PT-1 and PT-2, which launched the Navy's first torpedo against a moving ship in 1922; the DT-2, manufactured by various companies; Martin's SC-1 and SC-2; and Douglas' T2D-1. Beginning in 1926 torpedo bombers went to sea on aircraft carriers with the Martin T3M-1 and T4M-1, Great Lakes TG-2, and the Douglas TBD-1 of wartime fame.[48]

The Navy's first operational aerial torpedo was the Mark VII, developed in 1917, weighing 1,000 pounds with a 280-pound warhead. Development of a successor, the Mark XIII, began in 1925, but it did not become operational until 1936. An aerial torpedo weighing 2,200 pounds with a 600-pound TNT warhead (torpex in 1943), the Mark XIII routinely failed to detonate and had a restricted range of about 6,000 yards. Launching aircraft had to drop it from 80 feet of altitude at a speed of less than 100 knots within 1,000 yards of the target, requiring its crews to fly suicide missions. With a speed of 33.5 knots, the Mark XIIIs were barely able to catch the fast ships the world's navies were then building.[49]

The other means the Navy developed for sinking ships from the air was dive bombing. Its origins were more accidental than planned. Great Britain issued a patent for dive bombing to an inventor named Von Willisch in 1911. The first recorded instance of dive bombing in war was in Mexico from 1913 to 1915, where an American mercenary pilot, Leonard W. Bonney, used "spherical bombs of dynamite" dropped during dives. In World War I French pilots dove to bomb German zeppelin hangars in the first month of the war. Most probably these instances involved glide bombing (40 to 70 degrees from horizontal flight), not dive bombing (70 to 90 degrees from the horizontal).[50] Dive bombing provided answers to the Navy's twin concerns of aircraft survivability and bombing accuracy—high altitude during penetration to escape ship defenses and attain surprise, low altitude at the time of bomb release to maximize accuracy.

The Marine Corps initiated the systematic use of dive bombing. In 1919 Lt. Lawson H. Mc. Sanderson and his air group, using DH-4Bs, began experimenting with dive bombing in Haiti. Sanderson's tactic was to aim his aircraft at bandits at an angle of 45 degrees, which was a glide, not a dive, to improve bombing accuracy. Other pilots in his VO-9M squadron adopted the technique, later using "large canvas mail sacks" to carry the bombs for dropping. Sanderson's men released their bombs during descent by pulling a draw rope around the end of the sack.[51]

The first organized dive-bombing attack was the action of five Boeing O2B (DH-4M) aircraft of the VO-1M squadron under the command of marine Maj. Ross E. Rowell on July 17, 1927, against Sandino forces surrounding a marine garrison at Ocotal, Nicaragua.[52] The proximity of enemy forces forced the attacking aircraft to drop bombs while in steep, true dives to improve flying safety, not bombing accuracy. Against intense ground fire from Sandino riflemen, the marine aviators averaged only one rifle fire hit per sortie. Rowell claimed he learned the technique from Army Air Service pilots of the 3rd Attack Group at Kelly Field, Texas, in 1923, while the Air Service claimed the skill came from the British in World War I.[53]

Although the battle of Ocotal was important in the history of American air power, dive bombing did not impress those under the bombs. Augusto César Sandino, leader of the rebel forces, did not mention the marines' use of air power in his account of the battle. Later, at the battle of El Chipote, Sandino did recognize the repeated dive-bombing attacks of Marine aircraft, concluding, "In truth, those airplanes caused us very little personal injury, though it's a fact that in the beginning they shocked and worried us a great deal. But later we looked upon them as not much worse than a thunder storm, and we knew very well how to dig ourselves in. But they killed large numbers of cattle and horses." In November 1927 Sandino accused the marines of bombing peaceful villages, killing thirty-two women and eleven children. Carleton Beals, a reporter traveling with Sandino, recorded that Sandino's men overcame the bombings by traveling at night or in areas where the jungle blocked the view from above.[54]

While the marines perfected their technique in action, Navy aviators initiated their pursuit of dive bombing in exercises to achieve greater bombing accuracy. In 1925 Capt. Joseph M. Reeves worked with Lt. Frank W. Wead to develop bombing techniques for attacking beach defenses during amphibious assaults. At the low levels required to minimize the dangers of bombing to friendly forces, Reeves discovered antiaircraft fire from enemy defenses would ravage the assaulting aircraft. He ordered his pilots to approach the target at 10,000 feet, diving at up to 70 degrees to minimize exposure to ground fire. Working independently, Lt. Cdr. Osbourne B. Hardison led his fighter squadron, VF-2, in a series of dive-bombing attacks on anchored battleships. The squadron dropped no bombs, but

Hardison showed how difficult antiaircraft crews would find defending against dive-bombing attacks.[55]

On October 22, 1926, Squadron VF-2, then under Lt. Cdr. Frank D. Wagner, flying Curtiss F6C-2 fighters, simulated a dive-bombing attack on the Pacific Fleet in the first fleet demonstration of the technique. Diving from 12,000 feet at a nearly vertical angle, the squadron gained complete surprise and "so impressed fleet and ship commanders with the effectiveness of their spectacular approach that there was unanimous agreement that such an attack would succeed over any defense." Again the diving fighters dropped no bombs, so survivability, not accuracy, was the key factor in this demonstration.[56]

Two months later, Reeves, then a rear admiral and commanding Aircraft Squadrons, Battle Fleet, observed the first formal dive-bombing exercises during annual fleet gunnery competition. One marine and two Navy fighter squadrons and three Navy observation squadrons participated, making 45-degree dives (technically glides) from 2,500 feet and dropping 25-pound practice bombs at 400 feet. Lieutenant Commander Wagner's VF-2 squadron scored nineteen hits out of forty-five drops on a 100- by 45-foot target. Dive bombing was on its way to becoming the standard method of attack for the Navy's air force.[57]

A combination of bombing techniques, dive, torpedo, and horizontal, converted the U.S. Navy from a fleet built around battleships to one in which the aircraft carrier was the primary offensive weapon. These techniques developed in fleet exercises at sea. In Fleet Problem Number 2, held in the winter of 1923/24, the Black Fleet had four simulated carriers and deployed its 100 aircraft as scouts for the fleet. In Joint Army-Navy Problem No. 2, January 14–19, 1924, held in the Panama Canal Zone, each side had carrier-borne and land-based aircraft. Naval aircraft struck with torpedoes while Army Martin bombers attacked from 3,000 feet in level flight. Umpires credited aircraft with one destroyer sunk, two destroyers and a tender disabled, and one aircraft carrier damaged.[58]

By 1926 air power had become an essential ingredient in all Navy exercises. Joint Army-Navy Problem No. 3 of October 2, 1926, focused on the use of aircraft to defend the Hawaiian Islands. In May 1927 the Taylor Board, called to review the status of naval aviation, assigned aircraft to help the fleet's battle line, but also to undertake offensive operations away from the battle line. For the 1928 exercises, naval aircraft attacked both aircraft carriers and battleships.[59]

By the 1930s the aircraft had won a critical position in naval strategy, but the Navy was not yet sure how to sink enemy ships from the air. The torpedo bomber appeared to be the most deadly, but most vulnerable to defensive fire. The dive bomber was the most accurate with minimal vulnerability, but the least deadly. Horizontal bombers were the least vulnerable, but the most inaccurate, despite 10 years of bombsight research and development at a cost of $426,578.

Complicating these concerns was a technological revolution that promised geometric leaps in the capabilities of aircraft. A series of breakthroughs in aviation technology gave physical capability to what had begun as an idea. Initially the radial engine gave light weight with efficient cooling, the supercharger allowed greater altitude, flaps provided increased lift on takeoff without increased drag in flight, the variable pitch hydraulic propeller increased efficiency both on takeoff and in flight, and the National Advisory Committee for Aeronautics (NACA) cowling increased engine cooling while reducing drag. All-metal stressed-skin monocoque construction and the internally braced fully cantilevered single wing, designed after NACA airfoils, gave strength with reduced drag and made other developments cost effective. These included the enclosed cockpit, retractable landing gear, internal bomb bays, and flush rivets, all of which helped to reduce drag. Finally, 100-octane aviation gasoline based on tetraethyl lead and iso-octane allowed greater manifold pressures, giving more horsepower per pound of engine without knock, and allowed the supercharger to be used to boost power, not just altitude.[60]

These achievements allowed the Boeing B-9, at 188 mph, to fly as fast as most fighter aircraft of the time. Sixty percent faster than the Keystone bombers of the 1920s, the 207-mph Martin B-10 followed. Its major weakness, range, guaranteed a successor. And what a successor. The Boeing Model 299, designated the B-17 Flying Fortress by the Army, took advantage of the above technologies to become the preeminent platform for bombing of World War II. With turbosuperchargers and four Wright Cyclone radial engines rated at 775 hp, one version could fly 2,400 miles with 4,000 pounds of explosives at 291 mph, up to an altitude of 25,000 feet. The B-17's only apparent weakness was its cost, $99,000 each, which would limit Air Corps procurement until war opened congressional larders. For the Navy the results were the Martin BM-1 and BM-2 in 1931–32, which could carry 1,000-pound bombs and release them in dives, the Curtiss BF2C in 1933, the Northrop BT-1 in 1937–38, and the Douglas SBD in time for World War II.[61]

These gleaming, silver-winged bombers were but toothless marvels of American technological prowess without bombsights or tactics to aim their bombs accurately. Norden's expertise in the 1930s would be the key to solving the bombsighting problem for the Army and for Navy patrol bombers, while the early experiments with dive bombing promised a solution for the Navy's problem of sinking ships from the air.

4

The Norden Bombsight and Precision Bombing Doctrine

Carl Norden disliked the business end of bombsight production—that was Ted Barth's responsibility. With the completion of his Mark XI design, Norden shifted to other challenges. He originally intended to build a dive-bombing sight, but in March 1929 BuOrd directed him to design an inexpensive low-altitude horizontal flight bombsight to replace the Mark III. The Navy also wanted the General Electric Mark XIII, but lost interest because of its 200-pound weight, $10,000 per-item price, and promise of no major increase in accuracy over the Norden Mark XI. With the Mark XI under production, development priorities focused on Norden's low-altitude utility sight. For a unit price of $600, BuOrd wanted gyroscopic stabilization, simplicity, a weight of 10 pounds, one-fourth the number of parts used in the Mark XI, accuracy comparable to the Mark XI, a Mark XI-type pilot direction indicator, and gauges to display ground speed and drift. BuOrd and Norden signed a contract for $20,500 on August 15, 1928, to cover the development of two bombsights, one using the timing principle for determining ground speed, the other the synchronous method. Designated the Mark XV, the contract called for delivery in 1931.[1]

Three factors combined to make the Mark XV the most advanced of its age, despite the contract's call for a low-altitude utility sight. First, the specifications were unrealistic, considering the $600 unit-cost estimate. Second, desk officers could plan for low-level bombsights, but flying officers with the fleet were demanding high-altitude sights because improvements in antiaircraft artillery were forcing aircraft ever higher. Finally, the Navy failed to consider the character of Carl Norden. Here was an engineer who believed his destiny was to design the most advanced bombsight in the world, not a mechanic hired to design a simple, crude utility sight. It was a less-than-auspicious beginning for one of the most important weapons of World War II.

Lt. Frederick I. Entwistle, BuOrd's new chief of bombsight development, recognized these factors and encouraged Norden to pursue a sophisticated Mark XV with dispatch. Norden had designed his Mark XI bombsight on the timing method as potentially the most accurate means of bombsighting, even if the most complex. Navy criticism of the Mark XI's complexity encouraged Norden to try the synchronous technique as a means of simplifying the Mark XV.

In the synchronous method, the bombardier adjusted the speed of a wheel or gear in his bombsight mechanism to match the movement of the aircraft over a point on the ground. This technique synchronized the bombsight with the aircraft's ground speed, measuring the aircraft's movement at a particular moment relative to a fixed point on the ground. The timing method required a long bombing run because it measured a fixed point's movement relative to the aircraft as an average over an interval of time. The aircraft then had to fly at an unvarying speed, nearly impossible in combat, or the calculations of the timing technique would be thrown off. The synchronous bombsight precluded long bombing runs, measuring ground speed as an instantaneous rate, constantly updating the measurement. It also automated a critical portion of the bombsighting process—the determination of ground speed—eliminating human involvement and human errors in the timing procedure. In combat, under fire, bombardiers using the timing technique tended to rush the timing process, resulting in inaccurate ground-speed determination. In the synchronous technique, once the bombardier had synchronized the bombsight, no further human action was necessary. The bombsight, not subject to the errors and inconsistencies of human involvement, controlled the bombing process.[2]

Georges Estoppey, the Sperry Gyroscope Company, and the General Electric Company were experimenting with synchronous bombsighting, but as of 1929 no one had tested it in actual bombing. Georges Estoppey filed for a patent on his synchronous D-7 bombsight on January 7, 1925, but did not complete his design until 1932. Mortimer F. Bates, an employee of the Sperry Gyroscope Company, filed for a patent on his synchronous C-4 bombsight on June 1, 1926, but it, too, was not ready until 1932. Where Estoppey's device required the bombardier to crank the mechanism by hand, Bates's device used a motor to rotate a mirror or prism that synchronized the movement of the target with the movement of the aircraft. General Electric's Mark XIII never reached the operational level before cancellation in 1931.[3]

Carl Norden again retreated to his mother's home in Zurich in 1928, returning to New York in May 1930. Six months later, he presented an experimental model of his synchronous Mark XV to BuOrd's Entwistle at Norden's 80 Lafayette Street plant. The sight automatically provided the true air speed, ground speed, wind speed, wind direction, and angle of drift. So precise had Norden made it that the sight's complex gearing automatically compensated for forces such as the earth's rotation during the seconds a bomb was in flight. The bombardier adjusted the speed of a motor that moved the telescope to synchronize the speed of the target moving under the aircraft to the speed of the cross wires' movement over the ground. A motor displaced a roller inside the sight an amount equal to the speed of target relative to the aircraft multiplied by the time of bomb fall. The roller in turn moved a range bar on a graduated scale. When this bar lined up with the axis of the sighting scope fixed on the target, the Mark XV automatically dropped the bombs. The entire process took only 10 seconds. Although it was just a prototype on a test stand, Entwistle recognized Norden's device as a revolutionary bombsight design.[4]

Over the next year Norden technicians labored to turn the experimental design into a development prototype. BuOrd had such confidence in Carl Norden that it refused BuAer and Battle Force requests for overhauling existing or distributing new Mark XIs. It would be the Mark XV or nothing. The last Mark XI came out of the Norden shop in 1933 and remained in Navy inventory until 1938. After spending $316,000 for Norden's timing bombsight, the Navy was poised to begin a synchronous bombsight project that would in the end cost $1.5 billion.[5]

Norden delivered two development prototypes, one timing and the other synchronous, to the Dahlgren Naval Proving Ground in February 1931. Dahlgren would decide which worked best, also comparing both to the Mark XI. The experienced bombardiers at Dahlgren found they could adjust Norden's synchronous Mark XV in only 6 seconds compared to 50 seconds for the Mark XI. The Mark XV dropped bombs with twice the accuracy of the Mark XI, in large part due to an automatic bomb release feature that eliminated human variability in pushing the bomb release button. At 160 MPH, a bombardier dropping one second late would increase his bombing error by more than 200 feet. Dahlgren dropped eighty bombs using the Mark XV and forty landed within 75 feet of the target, achieving a circular error of less than 150 feet.[6] Operators reported the synchronous Mark XV to be small, simple to operate, dependable, and with an automatic crosstrail correction.[7]

Testing ended in August 1931, when BuOrd issued a contract to Carl L. Norden, Inc., for a production model Mark XV at a cost of $10,000. Delivered to Dahlgren for contract completion testing in the summer of 1932, it proved 60 percent more accurate in range and 69 percent more accurate in deflection than the original test model. The commander of the Navy's torpedo squadron VT-2B asked for permission to use this production model Mark XV in a bombing exercise against the USS *Utah* scheduled for October 1932. Curiously, BuOrd refused the request because "results from it would probably be very disappointing"—a peculiar answer coming from an agency that was preparing to order volume production with $235,125 of the taxpayers' money. BuOrd's denial of the Mark XV for the exercise was a harbinger of the Navy's eventual rejection of high-altitude horizontal bombing in favor of dive bombing as a means of attacking maneuvering ships.[8]

The Dahlgren Naval Proving Ground reported accuracies never reached in operational use. It advanced various explanations for such inconsistencies, not including what may have been a case of the "revolving door" in military procurement. Dr. L. T. E. Thompson was chief physicist/engineer at Dahlgren from 1923 to 1942 and tested and approved the Norden bombsight. His signature allowed BuOrd to pay Carl Norden for his work. In 1942 Thompson left Dahlgren and went to work for Norden as vice-president in charge of engineering at the Lukas-Harold Corporation, a Norden subsidiary responsible for the Naval Ordnance Plant at Indianapolis. In 1945, when Lukas-Harold completed its contract, Thompson became the technical director of the Naval Ordnance Test Station at Inyokern, California, responsible for testing Norden equipment competing for naval contracts. Several years later Thompson returned to Norden as vice-president of the Norden Laboratories Corporation, successor to Carl L. Norden, Inc., and then vice-president for research of the Norden-Ketay Corporation, which succeeded Norden Laboratories in

1955. In 1958 United Aircraft Corporation purchased Norden-Ketay and Thompson became a consultant for United's new Norden Division.

If Thompson had used his position to insure the Mark XV became the Navy's bombsight, he was handsomely rewarded. According to Donald Jacobs, a postwar competitor of the Norden Laboratories Corporation, Thompson excluded major bombing errors from his calculations on accuracy, using "trick tests and sympathetic mathematical treatment."[9] Jacobs claimed the Norden bombsight was capable of accuracy only one-sixth that reported by Dahlgren.

The wide difference between the bombing results of service units and Dahlgren provided Jacobs with supporting evidence. BuOrd's contract with Norden had specified a low-altitude bombsight, but Norden delivered a high-altitude sight incapable of low-altitude bombing. Such problems remained hidden behind the project's secrecy and the obvious superiority of the Norden over other bombsights.[10]

One of Entwistle's last actions before leaving his assignment as chief of bombsight research for BuOrd was scheduling a test of a production model Mark XI and the development prototype Mark XV against the anchored USS *Pittsburgh*. Ironically, the Navy intended to evaluate the effects of aerial bombs on a cruiser, not the effectiveness of bombsights. On October 6 and 7, 1931, in perfect bombing weather at an altitude of 5,000 feet, the Mark XI dropped fourteen bombs, achieving hits with three (21%). The Mark XV got four hits out of eight bombs (50%).

Until the *Pittsburgh* test, the Navy had kept Norden's development efforts secret from the Army. In July 1931, to comply with federal law requiring open bidding on military procurement projects, the Army Air Corps contacted the Norden company with specifications for a new high-altitude bombsight based on the synchronous method. Norden's president, Ted Barth, expressed an interest in bidding on the project. Not until September 1931, on a visit to Wright Field, did Barth inform the Air Corps of Norden's new Mark XV bombsight.[11]

On October 5, 1931, Brig. Gen. Benjamin D. Foulois, acting chief of the Air Corps, wrote Rear Adm. William A. Moffett, chief of BuAer, and expressed a deep interest in the Navy Mark XV project.

The Air Corps is experiencing considerable difficulty in developing a suitable bomb sight. . . . I have been informed that the Navy Bureau of Ordnance has undertaken a further confidential development, or improvement, of the Mk. XI sight—known as the Mk. XV. . . . I would appreciate receiving such technical details as would assist us in this parallel development and would also like to have two of my officers inspect the Mk. XV type sight and secure performance data in order that we may be in a position to more effectively determine our immediate and future procurements in bomb sights.[12]

Because of a recent exchange of information with the Army on bombsight development, BuOrd's Entwistle meanwhile had invited two Materiel Division officers, Maj. Willis H. Hale and Lt. Clarence S. Thorpe, to observe the *Pittsburgh* test. In their report, Hale and Thorpe judged the Norden bombsight clearly superior to all Army sights and recommended the cancellation of Inglis/Sperry L-1 procurement. On April 18, 1932, BuOrd placed its first order for the new bombsight: thirty-two for the Navy and twenty-three for the Army, at a unit cost of $4,275. Following the procedure begun for the Mark XI, the Navy assumed responsibility for patent infringements.[13]

All concerned wanted to protect the security of the sight, but patents issued to private individuals could not carry a security classification. Secretary of the Navy Charles F. Adams therefore requested patent protection in the name of the Navy. Fortuitously, such confidentiality also met Norden's personal demands for anonymity and made the U.S. government legally responsible for any patent infringement suits. Such protection was crucial because the Sperry Company regarded Norden's work with gyroscopes as knowledge gained from Sperry patents.[14] BuOrd filed the patent request on September 28, 1932, under Ted Barth's name, to provide Carl Norden with the anonymity he preferred, as "assignor to the United States of America as represented by the Secretary of the Navy."[15] The security classification kept the patent concealed until March 30, 1948.

The 50-pound Mark XV had thirty-five patentable features, including provisions for automatic crosstrail, ground speed–indicating scale, automatic bomb release, trail angle setting, tangent scale setting, and "a movably mounted sighting telescope." Carl Norden had designed an analog computer, so-called because the device was a physical or mechanical analog of the mathematical equations used to solve the bombing problem.[16] Each turn of the gears in the Norden bombsight represented or was analogous to the number quantities of these equations, including air speed, ground speed, time of fall, and so on. For example, taken from the patent,

An extension of screw **27** carries a pinion **42** that is meshed with the teeth of rack **43** on range bar **44** to which is attached a pin **45** that slides in a radially extending slot **46** in range quadrant **47**; it is obvious that rotation of screw **27** will shift rack **43** and so turn quadrant **47** through an **angle α** which is

$$\tan^{-1}\frac{S}{b^2}$$

which is readily seen to be equal to

$$\tan^{-1}\frac{R}{H}$$

where R is the range and H the altitude of the trunnions of telescope **40**, which is shown as being on the target and inclined at the range angle, i.e., in the position it has at the time the bomb is dropped.

So much for patents and descriptions of analog computers.

Although Norden's mathematical equations were exact, the mechanical components that represented them in physical form were subject to manufacturing errors, friction, slippage, wear, and other limiting factors. The accuracy, or rather inaccuracy, of the bombsight was the sum of its manufacturing tolerances. The Norden Company performed eighty-four different tests on its antifriction ball bearings before accepting them for use. Craftsmen then hand-polished each bearing to fit into the bearing seat. In theory the bombsight was capable of perfect accuracy, but the reality of manufacturing created an inherent inaccuracy.

In the wartime version, the optical system was a one-piece refracting telescope with an 18-degree field and 2.2 magnifying power, motor-driven to follow the target. Cross hairs etched on the lens transected the target, reflected into the telescope by a moving mirror.[17] The mirror was "driven continuously by a constant speed electric motor coupled through a suitable tangent motion in such fashion that if the mirror speed is once adjusted to match the apparent motion of the target (ground speed of the bomber) the target will remain stationary on the cross-hairs." Light from a small electric bulb entered the telescope through a narrow slit to illuminate the cross hairs for night operation.

In the Mod. 1 (Navy)/M-1 through 3 (Army) versions, the bombardier "flew" the aircraft through an associated pilot direction indicator (PDI) transmitting signals to the pilot through a brush riding on a resistance coil. In all later versions the bombardier accomplished this step directly through the aircraft's automatic pilot. First the bombardier had to level his gyroscopes, because a tilt of only one degree toward the aircraft's rear from the true vertical could cause a bomb to fall over 400 feet short of its target from 20,000 feet (called "bubble error" because bubble levels were used to level the sight). In the second step the bombardier entered the bombing altitude, bomb ballistics, air speed, air temperature, and barometric pressure into the bombsight, thereby setting the speed of a disc so that it revolved 88⅓ times during the time required for the bomb to fall to the ground.[18] This adjustment partially synchronized the movement of the telescope's mirror with the aircraft's movement over the ground. Next the bombardier "killed" drift caused by the wind, using the turn and drift knobs to fly the aircraft so that the target appeared to float down the vertical cross hair on the telescope lens. He "killed" rate by adjusting the rate knob to complete the synchronization of the telescope mirror and the movement of the aircraft relative to the target. This made the target appear motionless when viewed through the telescope.[19] Finally, using the displacement knob, the bombardier adjusted the telescope to place the target squarely on the horizontal cross hair. The bombsight automatically calculated the ground speed and the proper range angle, flew the aircraft directly to the correct release point, and released the aircraft's bombs.[20]

Once the bombardier had synchronized the bombsight, stability was essential. Any deviation of the sight from the true vertical or horizontal broke the synchronized lock among the bombsight disc speed, the telescope mirror, and the ground speed of the aircraft. The vertical gyroscope in the bombsight head stabilized the optics against roll and pitch movement and the directional gyroscope in a stabilizer assembly, on which the bombsight itself was mounted, counteracted any motion in yaw.

Eleven years separated the delivery of the Mark XV test model to Dahlgren from Cdr. Arthur C. Stott's contact with Carl Norden about Mark III stabilization. While America entertained itself with the Jazz Age, gorged itself on the stock market, and separated itself from international responsibilities, Carl Norden, a Dutch citizen, using his mind, a slide rule, a book of engineering tables, and a few basic manuals, designed the most sophisticated and most secret military weapon in American history to that time. It was the weapon, born in a time of isolation and pacifism, that later would add teeth to a worldwide crusade to crush fascism.

Carl L. Norden, Inc., delivered its production model Mark XV to the Navy in September 1932. The Army received its first Norden, Army designation M-1, in April 1933. Not including production, the Navy had paid between $30,000 and $40,000 to develop the Mark XV. It was clearly superior to any bombsight in the world. Although the Navy was already moving toward dive bombing as the primary means of sinking ships, the arrival of the Norden Mark XV bombsight was especially fortuitous for the Army. While Norden did his mental calculations in Switzerland, Army airmen were slowly leading the Army Air Corps away from a close air support doctrine to one of strategic bombing. Technology would be wasted without a doctrine for using it, while doctrine would be empty thought without the technology to give it life. Ironically, those responsible for developing aerial doctrine between the wars did so based on inaccurate Mark I, D-4, and D-4B bombsights. The Norden bombsight was not available until after the doctrine based on accurate bombing was well on the way to formulation.

The struggle to determine the proper use for the aerial weapon in war centered on Brig. Gen. Billy Mitchell, war hero and tempestuous prophet of air power. He saw civilians as "manufacturers of munitions" and therefore the legitimate targets of bombing. Mitchell's belief that air power was the only military force capable of carrying war to the assembly lines, behind defending field armies and fleets, brought him into direct conflict with the Army and Navy. Initially Mitchell limited himself to an air strategy based on his wartime experiences, claiming as air power's primary objective the "destruction of the hostile air force." In his 1921 book, *Our Air Force: The Keystone of National Defense*, he admitted that "whatever the future might hold, war was still a matter of defeating the enemy's armed forces." For the immediate future he saw the airplane in a tactical role, serving as America's "first line of defense."[21]

Mitchell's 1923 "Notes on the Multi-Motored Bombardment Group Day and Night" marked a transition in his thinking, completed in his 1925 book *Winged Defense*. A powerful, independent strategic air force must strike at an enemy's vitals. "Offensive aviation," he wrote, could "force a decision before the ground troops or sea forces could join in battle." For Mitchell "the hostile main army in the field is a false objective and the real objectives are the vital centers." He saw nothing wrong with attacking cities, the "vital centers," because wars would be completed more quickly and democratically (attacks on the people in common), which would be for the benefit of all—"more humane than the present methods of blowing up people to bits by cannon projectiles or butchering them with bayonets."

By attacking an enemy's "centers of production of all kinds, means of transportation, agricultural areas, ports and shipping," American air power could destroy the enemy's "means of making war" and paralyze governmental and industrial functions. Losses would decrease not only because of immediate civilian demands for peace, but because war would again become a battle between small forces of professional military men instead of the mass civilian-soldier armies of modern times.[22]

Mitchell recognized the need for precision bombing, identifying ships, railroad centers, canals, forts, and supply dumps as targets. Bombers would not need precision, however, to attack cities "to intimidate the civilian population" and "to act as an arm of reprisal." He expected international conferences to outlaw the bombing of cities, but argued that "the destruction of manufacturing centers and material brings the conflict to a quicker termination. Thus, manufacturing centers become military objects, even though they house non-combatant personnel." The purpose of strategic bombing was to interfere "with the manufacture of military equipment [by] hitting and destroying the factories, and . . . causing . . . such a nervous condition to obtain among the workers that their efficiency of production would be curtailed."[23]

Mitchell had little confidence in contemporary bomb-aiming technology. His solution was to organize bombers into formations, dropping on the command of the leader to achieve a "heavy collective effort." Mitchell was the best-known advocate of air power in the United States between the wars, but he was the champion of bombing in general, not precision bombing. He wrote of using poison gas, the penultimate area weapon, against cities and of poisoning water supplies from the air. For Mitchell, cities, not individual industries, were the vital centers.[24]

Also contributing to the debate over air power were various European strategists. The Italian Giulio Douhet saw trench warfare and the slaughter of World War I as a "colossal tragedy, with the whole world for its theater and humanity for its protagonist," resulting from the ineptness of military leadership. In two books, *Command of the Air,* first published in 1921 and revised in 1927, and *The War of 19—,* published in 1930, Douhet offered strategic bombardment from airplanes as the solution to the extended slaughter of modern war. Attacks on military forces, the focus of pre-airplane warfare, achieved nothing but an intensification of the carnage in the trenches. The key, he argued, was to target civilians, who lacked the iron will of military men and were much more vulnerable to the will-destroying power of aerial bombardment. No longer was the destruction of armed forces the objective of war. Now the target was "the enemy's will to resist."[25]

Although he did not specify area bombing, Douhet intimated that population centers were the targets of choice, with communications, factories, airfields, arsenals, and ships as secondary targets. Bombing would wreck civilian morale and prevent industry from supporting armies in the field and navies at sea. After a few days, without the need for long, drawn-out conflict, the enemy would feel "definitely that they had been defeated in the air and that they were hopelessly at the enemy's mercy." Like Mitchell, Douhet justified attacking civilians because it would end war quickly.[26]

Douhet's faith in the war-winning power of the bomber mirrored an earlier generation's faith in the "unsinkable" dreadnought battleship. He had unlimited confidence in bombing. Bombers would always hit their targets and achieve a uniform distribution of bombs—250 tons per square mile of urban area—to achieve absolute destruction.[27]

> Aerial bombs have only to fall on their target to accomplish their purpose. Aerial bombardment can certainly never hope to attain the accuracy of artillery fire; but this is an unimportant point because such accuracy is unnecessary. Except in unusual cases, the targets of artillery fire are designed to withstand just such fire; but the targets of aerial bombardment are ill-prepared to endure such onslaught. Bombing objectives should always be large; small targets are unimportant and do not merit our attention here.[28]

Douhet misunderstood even the most basic elements of air power. He assumed that once command of the air had been established, the destruction of an enemy's industries and civil centers would automatically follow. He grossly overestimated the power of bombs and the accuracy of bombsights. In his defense, when Douhet wrote of the capabilities of bombing, he was thinking of chemical and bacteriological warfare, making bombing accuracy less critical. He never considered, however, that a bomber might miss its target. For Douhet, air war was simply substituting technological fanaticism for the ideological or nationalistic fanaticism behind war. American airmen read and appreciated his views as early as 1923.[29]

British strategists reinforced the views of Mitchell and Douhet. Jan Smuts, whose report paved the way for the creation of the independent Royal Air Force (RAF) in World War I, believed that bombing cities would win wars. Basil H. Lidell-Hart compared the bombing of civilians to Paris killing Achilles with a blow to his vulnerable heel. Another observer called civilians the "nerve ganglia of national morale." Stanley Baldwin said in Parliament that "the only defence is in offence, which means that you have to kill more women and children more quickly than the enemy if you want to save yourself."[30]

Hugh Trenchard, the "father" of the RAF, also thought terrorizing workers could achieve victory without the need to defeat an enemy's armed forces. Britain's World War I experience convinced him that "the home front was, in modern warfare, both a great deal more important and a great deal more vulnerable than the front line." Trenchard argued that the morale effect of strategic bombing was greater than the material effect by the proportion of 20 to 1. This made precision unnecessary. Although he thought the enemy's will to resist was the proper target of strategic bombing, he never determined whether this should be done through attacks on civilians or on industry.[31]

Another Briton argued against this mainstream, fearing that area attacks on cities might be adopted as the proper use of air power: "Widespread is the idea that a feature of the next war will be the raining of high explosives and poison gas upon the great cities." Civilian workers were proper targets of war, James M. Spaight admitted, but "their dwellings cannot be regarded as a legitimate objective." War industries were where "victory and defeat will be achieved and suffered." He appealed to British air planners:

> Make machinery and not mankind the mark of your attack. Concentrate on the killing of machines rather than of men, and above all on killing them at source. Smash the machines and the machines which make the machines. Smash them—or silence them. Smash the turbines, the dynamos, the mighty steam presses, the mammoth steel hammers, which forge and fashion the instruments of destruction. Smash the whole metallic substructure of armed strength. Make the war of machinery impossible. Air power can do that and air power can do it alone.

Despite his pleas, Spaight believed that the precision necessary to attack these targets was not possible.[32]

The official doctrine of the RAF in 1928 was "to break down the enemy's means of resistance by attacks on objectives selected as most likely to achieve this end." The targets included centers of production, transportation, and communication. Destroying industries would not bring success, this doctrine surmised, but such bombing would crush the will of the workers. Any incidental loss of civilian life and property was acceptable, but the "indiscriminate bombing of a city for the sole purpose of terrorizing the civilian population" was "illegitimate." Bombing exercises in the 1930s forced Air Chief Marshal Edgar Ludlow-Hewitt to conclude that the RAF was incapable of achieving precision high-altitude bombing, which made targeting industrial targets unlikely. That left cities as targets, but Director of Plans Air Commodore John C. Slessor rejected "indiscriminate attacks on civilian populations." When the British entered the war, the RAF officially clung to daylight precision bombing,[33] while considering night precision and area bombing. The RAF had not prepared a precision bombing force, however, making the issue academic.[34]

Germany produced no prophets or strategic-bombing doctrine equal to Britain and the United States. Douhet's *Command of the Air* appeared in Germany in 1929, but had no significant impact on German military thinking. As a continental nation surrounded by enemies, German strategists looked to blitzkrieg warfare, which would leave the industries and resources of surrounding nations intact for German conquest and exploitation. In 1936 the Luftwaffe had two designs for heavy bombers, the Junkers (Ju) 89 and Dornier (Do) 19, but in 1937 Hermann Göring, commander of the Luftwaffe, canceled both. For a nation with limited aircraft manufacturing capabilities and requiring an air force to support the army, he determined that Germany needed medium bombers, not heavy bombers. The death of Luftwaffe Chief of Staff Gen. Walther Wever in 1936 removed the last important German advocate of strategic bombing.

Supporting this movement away from strategic bombing, trials in 1938 pitted the Heinkel (He) 111 and Do 17 bombers in level flight at 13,000 feet against Ju 87 Stuka dive bombers. The former dropped 2 percent of their bombs within a 330-foot circle, the latter 25 percent within a 165-foot circle. The Luftwaffe Operations Staff issued a "Statement of Technical-Tactical Requirements" in 1939 giving preference to "the development of bombsights specifically for dive-bombing operations over the development of multi-purpose bomb aiming devices." German strategic bombing doctrine for World War II was therefore to drop a few large bombs with great accuracy through dive bombing. The primary bomb was a 2,200-pounder with a thin, high-grade weldless casing and a TNT filling that made up 74 percent of the total weight. This contrasted with the American doctrine of dropping large numbers of smaller bombs, 500-pounders with a thicker, low-grade steel roller–produced tube casing and a TNT filling that made up 50 percent of the total weight.[35]

European air forces evolved bombing doctrines uniquely different from the daylight precision strategic bombing doctrine of the United States. According to the Air Corps' Herbert A. Dargue, a major factor behind these differences was the unavailability in Europe of a precision bombsight similar to the Norden. Dargue made eight trips to Europe during the 1920s and 1930s to check on "whisperings" that the British, French, and Germans had developed super-accurate bombsights. Each time he discovered that the bombsights were only Wimperis, Michelin, or Estoppey sights. On a trip in 1936 the British showed Dargue their newest type—a modified World War I Wimperis similar to the U.S. Navy's Mark III, obsolete in the United States for more than a decade. Because of inadequate bombsights, Dargue reported, the British were "resigned to the fact that horizontal bombing will be effective only against area targets." The French and Germans, because of the closeness of continental targets, were concentrating on dive bombing.[36]

These European views stood in stark contrast to a strong American conviction against bombing civilians or civilian targets. During World War I Billy Mitchell of the Air Service planned to initiate long-range bombing attacks on Germany, but Secretary of War Newton D. Baker ruled that the United States would not begin "promiscuous bombing upon industry, commerce or population, in enemy countries disassociated from obvious military needs."[37] Baker set the tone for the postwar debate in 1919 when he declared that bombing attacks on civilians "constituted an abandonment of the time-honored practice among civilized people of restricting bombardment to fortified places or to places from which the civilian population had an opportunity to be removed." Bombing civilians would be counterproductive, he said, because it would encourage others to unite against those who bombed civilians. Americans would not undertake such terror raids on "most elemental ethical and humanitarian grounds." Total war would be limited to soldiers at the front.[38]

Will Irwin, in *"The Next War": An Appeal to Common Sense* (1921), reinforced Baker's pronouncements in arguing that bombers could turn metropolises into "necropolises" unless restricted. A Navy captain echoed these convictions before the Morrow Board in 1925 when he objected to the United States becoming a nation of "baby killers."[39]

These men reflected the sentiments of many Americans in opposing the mass bombing of civilians. They seized the moral high ground, intending to limit the Air Service to tactical strikes against enemy armed forces. Ironically, prohibiting the Army Air Service from bombing civilians unintentionally opened the way for the development of precision strategic bombing because American airmen proposed to bomb machines, not people.

These declarations aside, Americans had a "traditional reverence for marksmanship" and a deep-rooted opposition to making civilians targets in war. Opponents of strategic bombing argued the waste and inefficiency of bombing cities. A *Harper's* magazine article concluded that war could not "be won by attacking civil populations in cities," citing as evidence the German experience in World War I. Losing 350 airmen, Germany launched a bombing campaign against England, costing Germany $20,000 for each of the 1,200 English killed in the bombing. Despite Sherman's "March to the Sea" and America's war against Philippine insurgents, the men responsible for creating bombing doctrine never wavered from their conviction that civilians should not be the targets of strategic bombing.[40]

Perhaps the most significant obstacle to the development of a strategic bombing doctrine, however, was American isolationism. Strategic bombing, whether of civilians or factories, was inherently offensive, which had no place in this climate. The purpose of the Army and the Navy, and any fledgling air force, was national defense. The Pratt-MacArthur Agreement of January 1931 assigned the Air Corps the responsibility for all coastal defense aircraft.[41] When Congress established General Headquarters Air Force in 1935, it directed that the new organization concentrate on the defense of the United States, not offensive warfare. Airmen set their sights on offensive strategic bombing, but operated under the umbrella of defense for the remainder of the interwar period.

While thinking about strategic bombing, airmen still had to heed the Army's official doctrine of close air support in the 1920s. Training Regulation 440-15 of 1926 identified close air support and the destruction of the enemy's armed forces as the primary responsibility of the Army's air force, but envisioned bombing attacks on targets beyond the battlefield as contributing to victory by damaging enemy morale. These included troop concentrations away from the battlefield; efforts to "hamper the manufacturing of war materiel"; "industrial centers, especially those devoted to the manufacture of war materiel"; and "attacks on centers of population" to "weaken the morale of the enemy people." The laws of war prohibited the latter, but the Air Service foresaw the need for such bombing in reprisal, while doubting the effect on morale. The Morrow Board was more certain: "Man can not make a machine stronger than the spirit of man."[42]

The Air Service's officer training school "Bombardment" text saw value in strategic missions to "hamper the manufacturing of war materiel" and "weaken the morale of the enemy people by attacks on centers of population." These strikes against morale would not be terror attacks, however. Morale would decline under aerial bombardment because bombing destroyed jobs and the amenities of urban living. The 1924–25 text demanded precision, concluding that sending out airplanes to drop their bombs over large areas was wrong. Within each major target, bombers should strike at specific points, including individual buildings, warehouses, offices, water plants, power plants, and aircraft, not residential areas. The text argued against bombing political centers because the laws of warfare prohibited it except in reprisal and because it would have a "doubtful" influence on morale.[43]

Central to the development of a strategic bombing doctrine in which the Norden Mark XV/M-series bombsight would play such a critical role was the Air Corps Tactical School (ACTS). Set up originally as the Field Officers School at Langley Field, Virginia, on November 1, 1920, with seven students, it was the first professional military school for aviators in the world. Its assignment was to prepare competent commanders and staff officers in tactical, technical, and administrative fields and to prepare air force doctrine. On July 15, 1931, ACTS moved to Maxwell Field, Montgomery, Alabama. By the late 1920s and early 1930s the thinking of the ACTS faculty began to reflect a deeper analysis based less on wartime experience but more on theoretical study. Technology followed doctrine because the backbone of the air fleet at the genesis of the daylight precision strategic bombing idea was the B-3A Keystone Panther, a twin-engine biplane with a skin of doped-fabric stretched over steel tubing. The Keystone had an open cockpit, struts and wires between the wings, fixed landing gear, and could carry only 2,500 pounds of bombs 363 miles at 103 MPH up to a service ceiling of 12,000 feet. It lacked the range, speed, bomb load, altitude, and dependability to carry out a strategic bombing doctrine. Bombsights in service at the time, including the Estoppey D-1 and D-4 and the Norden-modified Mark III, offered accuracy considerably short of the demands of this fledgling doctrine. When modern bombers equipped with Norden M-series bombsights began to appear in Air Corps inventories, the doctrine was already at the core of the ACTS curriculum.[44]

Doctrine therefore evolved in a technological vacuum. Despite limited capabilities, the Army's air force developed a doctrine of strategic bombing based on precision, in keeping with its need to bomb attacking ships in the defensive role and to target individual industries, not civilians, in the offensive role. Maj. Gen. James E. Fechet, chief of the Air Corps, encouraged his airmen to look beyond the battlefield when he criticized them in 1928 for their conservative thinking in developing air doctrine limited to supporting the Army. Fechet wanted a doctrine that would give his air force the responsibility of winning wars independently.[45]

1st Lt. Kenneth N. Walker answered Fechet's call. After serving in the 2nd Bombardment Group at Langley Field, Walker attended the ACTS in 1929 and, upon graduation, became an instructor there. While Fechet wanted wide-ranging theoretical thinking on the role of the Army's air arm, Walker preferred to consider the practical problems of aerial bombing. Working systematically, he developed a mathematical approach for calculating probable error in bombing. Field tests using 329 practice bombs dropped on a 100-foot circle from 5,000 feet showed him that the Air Corps could expect between 25 and 31 percent to hit the target. Using his mathematical method, this translated into a circular error probable of 147 feet, meaning that from 5,000 feet the Air Corps could plan on getting at least 50 percent of their bombs to fall within 147 feet of the target.[46]

In late 1929 Walker switched his attention to a decade-old Air Service Bomb Board recommendation that the United States develop delayed nose and tail fuzes for use in low-altitude bombing. The board's thinking was that low-altitude bombing was the most accurate, but detonation would have to be delayed to allow bombing aircraft to escape. The immediate cause for his action was Fechet's decision in 1928 to cancel the fuze development project. Airmen had always accepted low-altitude bombing as superior in accuracy and destructiveness, though less safe than high-altitude bombing. Walker intended to test the validity of this truism. Writing the Materiel Division at Wright Field, he requested information on current bombsight development. The answer, penned by Capt. Clarence F. Hofstetter, was more optimistic than the actual state of bombsight affairs. Hofstetter reported that significant progress had been achieved since World War I. The 1918 Mark I Wimperis sight gave an average error of 790 feet from an altitude of 8,000 feet, the 1925 D-4 160 feet, and a planned new model (the C-3) 80 feet. Hofstetter attributed this progress to gyroscopic stabilization, improved optical sights, refined mechanical components, and continuous synchronous sighting.

"However," the bombsight expert concluded, "if the Air Corps expects to take up extremely low-altitude bombing, there is no doubt but that much more accurate results could be expected than from high altitudes."[47]

Hofstetter's contradictory reply raised an interesting question for

Walker. If Army bombsights were as effective as the Materiel Division reported (and they were not), was low-altitude bombing necessarily superior to high-altitude bombing? Common sense dictated it was, but Walker wanted proof. In a series of letters from 1929 to 1931, Walker put the question to operational units and ordnance men. Maj. Ralph Royce, commanding the 1st Pursuit Group at Selfridge Field, Michigan, wrote back that it made no difference. At high altitudes, navigation was easier, and with accurate bombsights targets could be destroyed. At low altitudes, navigation was still possible and, again, targets could be destroyed. The commander of the Air Corps Advanced Flying School, Bombardment Section, at Kelly Field, Texas, responded that he was "absolute against" low-altitude bombing. Because of bombs ricocheting at low altitudes, "the bombing would always be very inaccurate" while "losses would be terrible." The Air Corps, he said, needed a high-altitude heavy bomber.[48]

Lt. Muir S. Fairchild at the Procurement Section of the Supply Division at Santa Monica, California, wrote that he opposed any consideration of low-altitude bombing because survival meant high speeds, which required unsafe landing speeds. He therefore suggested the Air Corps pursue high-altitude bombing. Maj. Gen. Henry D. Todd Jr., commandant of the Army's Coast Artillery School at Fort Monroe, Virginia, reported that anti-aircraft artillery would be more effective against low-altitude bombers. The commander of the 11th Bombing Squadron at Rockwell Field, California, pointed out that any bomb dropped at low altitude must have a 20-second delay fuze to allow the aircraft to escape from the blast, which would make bombs more complicated and more expensive.

Most critically, the commander of the 3rd Attack Group at Fort Crockett, Texas, responsible for low-altitude bombers, complained that training showed low-altitude bombing to be more inaccurate than high-altitude bombing because bombs tended to bounce and roll on impact and navigation was more difficult. He concluded that the Air Corps could achieve "more accurate performance of missions" with "high flying than with low flying."[49]

Walker had audaciously challenged common wisdom and discovered that the obvious answer to his question was incorrect. Because of Walker's actions and test results, Chief of the Air Corps James E. Fechet made the achievement of accurate bombing from high altitudes the priority of the Air Corps on January 2, 1931. This action inspired a series of tests at the Aberdeen Proving Ground in July, September, October, and November of 1931 to test the effectiveness of low-altitude bombing. Using B-2 and B-5 bombers flying at 120 to 180 MPH at an altitude of 150 feet, these tests proved "extremely high accuracy" could be achieved at low altitudes only if the bombs penetrated a building and came to a stop before exploding. Maj. Fred H. Coleman, the Air Corps representative at Aberdeen, identified many problems with low-altitude delivery. If they landed on hard surfaces, the bombs tended to roll, skid, or tumble an average of 141 feet in range and 25 feet in deflection. The small angle of impact made fuzes more liable to fail. Bombs tended to detonate on their sides, reducing the effects of both the explosion and resulting fragmentation. "In short, a decision to go in for low-altitude bombing as a standard practice is liable to be very defective."

Coleman, with remarkable foresight as to the need for air superiority to carry on any strategic bombing campaign, continued,

> On the offensive in a major war we would probably most need planes capable of high altitude and long radius. This for the reason that we having air superiority could by operating above 14,000 feet force out and destroy enemy pursuit (his principal protection at such altitude)—thus leaving our bombardment completely free. Besides, at low altitude one of our bombers would probably face up to fifteen thousand rounds of machine gun ammunition from the defenses, while a high altitude bomber would face a maximum of twenty-five rounds of artillery fire.

The Air Corps assistant chief of ordnance endorsed Coleman's study. A low-altitude bomb was "not as effective as one dropped from high altitudes. . . . The best destructive action of demolition bombs is due to the mining effect" achieved when a bomb buried itself in the earth. Bombs had higher terminal velocity and therefore greater kinetic energy when dropped from high altitude. A 500-pound bomb dropped from 20,000 feet reached a speed of about 880 feet per second. Walker's calculations showed that the kinetic energy of a bomb was equal to one-half of the mass of the bomb times the square of the velocity. The key to increasing the power of the bomb was to increase its speed through the air by dropping from a higher altitude, not simply increasing its mass.[50]

Walker wrote a series of studies on the issues of low- and high-altitude bombing. Because when released at 160 MPH a bomb traveled 235 feet per second, rolling was a serious problem. Against a bridge, a bomb would have to be dropped to come to rest on the bridge, where it would do only superficial damage. Attempts to navigate at low altitudes added to inaccuracy. Walker knew that the RAF had proved low-altitude bombing was more dangerous than high. Defenses could locate their guns along the best avenues of low-altitude approach and erect barrage balloons, making successful bombing improbable. His own research showed that in the 12⅗ seconds necessary for an antiaircraft artillery shell to reach 15,000 feet, a bomber at 160 MPH would move 2,957 feet to safety.

Testing showed that because of reduced angular error at higher altitudes, bombing accuracy decreased only by the *square root* of the quotient of the change in altitude, while the accuracy of antiaircraft fire decreased by the *square* of the quotient. Up was clearly the way to go. Walker concluded that low-altitude bombing had its uses, especially against targets requiring a high degree of accuracy: trucks, tanks, parked aircraft, ammunition dumps, railroad rolling stock, and roadbeds. The inability to produce the mining effect for a low-altitude release, however, reduced the explosive power of bombs by four and a half times.[51]

For proof, Walker examined the Army's tests against the Pee Dee bridge in late 1927. Engineers used both static charges and bombs dropped from 6,000 feet to compare the efficiency of tamping, or burying bombs beneath the surface of the earth, to intensify the effect of the explosives. Both static charges and bombs with instantaneous fuzes caused little damage to the bridge. Delay-fuzed bombs and static charges buried in the sand near bridge beams "completely destroyed" them and caused spans to fall. Surface blasts shattered the concrete surfaces of the supporting beams, but tamped bombs completely shattered the girders, exposing and bending the reinforcing bars. A 2,000-pound bomb, for example, displaced 12¾ times more dirt if a delayed fuze permitted tamping than if an instantaneous fuze gave a surface detonation.[52]

These tests proved bombs gave an extremely localized "shattering effect," but the "lifting effect" resulting from the expansion of gases after detonation caused the greatest damage. Nothing could enhance the former, but tamping by burying the bomb in the earth increased the latter by a factor of four and a half times. Walker argued that bombs dropped from low altitude carried insufficient inertia to bury themselves. High-altitude releases were essential. Tests at Aberdeen revealed that buildings were also "best destroyed by mined charges." Tests against armor plate showed that "even a moderate degree of penetration of the target before explosion will produce a considerably greater demolition effect"—gained only from bombs dropped from a great height. The increased destructive force gained by the bombs from their velocity added to the effect. Even instantaneous-fuzed bombs did greater damage when the force of their impact was added to their explosive force.[53]

Walker's 1931 ACTS pamphlet, "Bombardment Aviation," concluded that "bombardment missions are carried out at high altitudes, to reduce the possibilities of interception by hostile pursuit and the effectiveness of anti-aircraft gun fire" and to increase the explosive effect of the bombs. Walker's conclusions had justified the value of high-altitude bombing, but high-altitude bombing was inherently inaccurate. His logic could not overcome the obstacle of bombing accuracy not yet achieved by Air Corps bombsights. The Norden-aimed bombing of the USS *Pittsburgh* in October 1931 was too late to support Walker during the formulation and promulgation stages of his ideas. Walker initiated the doctrine of high-altitude daylight precision strategic bombing based on a confidence in bomb-sighting technology that had not yet been achieved. He would have been the fool if Carl Norden's bombsight had not pushed that technology to a higher level. The idea gave purpose to the means and the means gave life to the idea.[54]

The Victor Adding Machine–manufactured Norden M-9 bombsight, mounted on top of stabilizer. (*Source:* USAF Historical Research Agency.)

The Army's line of Estoppey bombsights: (a) D-1 of 1922; (b) D-2 of 1925; (c) D-4 of 1926; and (d) D-7 of 1932. (*Sources:* [a] and [d] USAF Historical Research Agency; [b] National Air and Space Museum; [c] National Archives.)

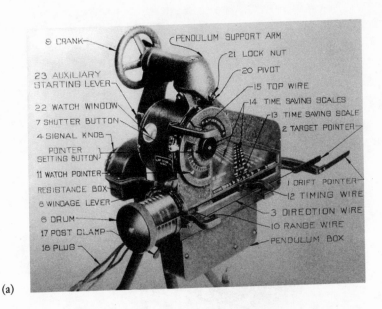

(a)

(b)

(c)

(d)

The Army's line of Sperry bombsights: (a) C-1 Seversky of 1921; (b) C-4 of 1932; (c) L-1 Inglis of 1932; (d) N-1 of 1938; (e) O-1 of 1939; (f) S-1 of 1940. (*Sources:* [a] National Air and Space Museum; [b] National Archives; [c] and [f] USAF Historical Research Agency; [d] and [e] Sperry Gyroscope Company Collection, Hagley Museum and Library.)

(a)

(b)

(c)

(d)

(f)

Calculator for Seversky C-1 bombsight. The gears, arms, motors, and disks of this device demonstrate the analog nature of bombsights before the development of electronics. Each component as it moved or rotated represented the analog of one of the mathematical formulas in the bombsighting equation. (*Source:* Sperry Gyroscope Company Collection, Hagley Museum and Library.)

The 1933 Sperry A-2 automatic pilot that allowed Wiley Post in the *Winnie Mae* to fly around the world, solo, in just over 115 hours. In World War II "Elmer," as the A-2 was affectionately known, flew "more planes than any man who ever wore pilot's wings." (*Source:* Sperry Gyroscope Company Collection, Hagley Museum and Library.)

The Norden bombsighting system, including the Norden Mark 15/M-series bombsight (*A*) and Norden stabilizer (*B*) and the C-1 Automatic Flight Control Equipment/automatic pilot, consisting of a Norden flight gyroscope (*C*), electrically driven servomotors and pulleys for driving control surfaces (*D* for ailerons, *E* for elevators, and *F* for rudder), and the Minneapolis-Honeywell Regulator Company electronic automatic pilot adapter (*G*). (*Source:* Norden Systems Division.)

One of Billy Mitchell's bombs registers a near-miss on the *Ostfriesland*, July 21, 1921. Mitchell proved airplanes could sink ships if they could be hit, intensifying the effort to improve bombing precision in both the Army and Navy. (*Source:* USAF Historical Research Agency.)

The first 600-pounder dropped on the Pee Dee River Bridge missed by several hundred feet on December 22, 1927. Poor bombing accuracy sparked a crisis in the Air Corps, prompting Air Corps Chief Maj. Gen. James Fechet to admonish the Materiel Division: "I cannot too strongly emphasize the importance of a bomb sight of precision, since the ability of bombardment aviation to perform the mission of destruction is almost entirely dependent upon an accurate and practical bomb sight." (*Source:* USAF Historical Research Agency.)

"Buh-Lam! Missed Again." The nadir of interwar efforts to achieve precision bombing was the August 1931 training mission against the 400-foot USS *Mount Shasta*. Two bomb hits, only one exploding, forced the Coast Guard to rescue the Army Air Corps and sink the derelict vessel. (*Source:* USAF Historical Research Agency.)

(*Upper left*) Maj. Donald Wilson contributed the idea of bombing an enemy's industrial fabric, 1934. (*Upper right*) Capt. Kenneth Walker justified high-altitude bombing at the Air Corps Tactical School, 1930. (*Below*) Air Corps Tactical School from the front, 1934. (*Sources:* [upper left and right] Air University Office of History; [below] USAF Historical Research Agency.)

In the 1930s Air Corps Tactical School faculty searched the American industrial web for choke-points, photographing them as course materials. On the back of this photograph of the Philadelphia railroad and port facility, Col. Herbert Dargue, the director of instruction at the school, wrote, "Is it hard to see the bottleneck here? The airman could hardly mistake the place to put his bomb to accomplish the greatest inconvenience to rail facilities here." (*Source:* USAF Historical Research Agency.)

With a touch of sarcasm, Dargue chose this complex as an example of a choke-point in the "industrial fabric" that would be a perfect target for Army bombers in carrying out the doctrine of daylight precision strategic bombing. The site is the U.S. Naval Academy at Annapolis, 1932. (*Source:* USAF Historical Research Agency.)

Adm. William A. Moffett (*right*) greeted Marine aviators Maj. Thomas C. Turner (*left*) and 2d Lt. Lawson H. Mc. Sanderson (*center*) at Bolling Field upon their return from a flight from Washington, D.C., to Santo Domingo in April 1921. In 1919 Sanderson started the U.S. Navy in the direction of dive bombing using "large canvas mail sacks" to drop bombs on Haitian bandits. (*Source:* National Air and Space Museum.)

Sperry Mark I Aiming Angle Sight for dive bombing, canceled by Adm. John H. Towers because it was difficult to use and represented only a "slight improvement" over eye-balling. (*Source:* Sperry Gyroscope Company Collection, Hagley Museum and Library.)

Douglas TBD Devastator torpedo bomber from USS *Enterprise* dropping Mark XIII torpedo, October 20, 1941. The Mark XIII forced the TBD to fly at 80 feet, 80 knots, and within 1,000 yards of the target at the point of release, leading to nearly suicidal attacks at Midway. (*Source:* National Archives.)

Douglas SBD Dauntless dive bombers attack the Japanese cruiser *Mikuma* at Midway on June 6, 1942. (*Source:* National Archives.)

America's bombsights for World War II: (*left*) the Norden Mark 15/M-series (nearly 90,000 produced); (*center*) the Sperry S-1 (over 5,000 produced); (*right*) the Estoppey D-8 (over 10,000 produced). (*Source:* USAF Historical Research Agency.)

5

The Air Corps Adopts a Bombing Strategy for World War II

n the 1930s U.S. Army airmen prepared to look beyond mere tactical uses for the airplane. They began to see air power for what it could do to win wars independent of conventional ground and sea forces. Through a lawn-watering analogy, tactical air power would provide close air support at the sprinkler and interdiction at the hose. Strategic air power would strike at the spigot. Antoine Henri Jomini had issued principles of war in the nineteenth century based on lines of communication and trade,[1] but these American airmen aimed to go beyond Jomini to strike directly at the sources of these lines of communication and trade—if their bombs hit the targets.

1st Lt. Kenneth N. Walker's work at the 2nd Bombardment Group and at the Air Corps Tactical School (ACTS) had justified high-altitude bombing for the U.S. Army Air Corps. His conclusions created the potential for long-range missions by large bomber aircraft able to escape defensive fire by flying at high altitude, exposing the enemy to bombing attack. Walker established how bombs would be dropped, but left the question of targets to another generation of ACTS officers.

William C. Sherman, an instructor at the Air Service Tactical School in the early 1920s, began the process in his 1926 book *Air Warfare*, identifying industry as the proper target of aerial warfare.[2] He argued that an air force need not destroy all industry to be successful. "Industry consists rather of a complex system of interlocking factories, each of which makes only its allotted part of the whole." In launching an air attack, Sherman believed it "necessary to destroy certain elements of the industry only, in order to cripple the whole." He also argued, inconsistently, that nations won wars by destroying an enemy's "belief in ultimate victory and its will to win," by attacking large population centers, supply systems, fortifications, and seacraft. *Air Warfare* did not attract great interest because the technology of bombing was not yet sufficiently advanced. The controversy and publicity surrounding Billy Mitchell also obscured Sherman's message.[3]

Other instructors helped make the ACTS the breeding ground for the evolving doctrine of daylight precision strategic bombing. They contributed an analysis of the best targets for the high-altitude bombs of Kenneth Walker, based on little practical experience. ACTS instructors developed the doctrine of precision bombing without knowledge of the Norden bombsight, assuming "that if the advantages of precision bombing could be established in theory, American ingenuity and inventiveness would provide the means for making such bombing possible in practice." Laurence S. Kuter recalled that he had based his thinking on the promised accuracy of a future bombsight that was only rumor at the time. Donald Wilson remembered that he "started teaching the theory . . . even before you had the means to do such a thing." Haywood S. Hansell Jr. reported that none of the theorists knew of the Norden bombsight and its capabilities until after they had left Maxwell's ACTS and returned to flying units. The commander of the 1st Bombardment Wing, Henry Arnold, did not report test results with the new Norden bombsight until late 1935, several years after these men had begun teaching their doctrine.[4]

Joining Walker in the formulation phase were Harold L. George, Muir S. Fairchild, Robert M. Webster, and Donald Wilson.[5] According to Wilson, no one had the freedom to change the old curriculum that taught that air power was auxiliary to ground forces until the arrival in 1934 of another key individual, the ACTS's new assistant commander, Herbert A. Dargue. Because the commander of the ACTS was the post commander, Dargue served as the head of instruction. The first man to transmit a radio message from an aircraft to the ground and to receive a radio message from the ground, he led the Pan-American Flight of 1926–27 and the Good Will Tour of seventy American cities in 1927. He came to the ACTS from a tour as commander of the Air Corps' premier bombardment group, the 2nd, at Langley Field. Perhaps most important, Dargue brought to Maxwell Field a knowledge of and conviction in the value of the new Norden bombsight, based on a long and close personal relationship with Theodore H. Barth, president of Carl L. Norden, Inc.[6]

Together these men strove to perfect the doctrine of daylight precision strategic bombing. Where Mitchell had emphasized the morale effects of bombing, ACTS concentrated on the material effects. Both agreed that the specific objective of bombing was to destroy an enemy's will to resist. Mitchell believed this could be accomplished by intimidation through the threat of bombing or of direct attacks on civilians. The young ACTS officers believed they could destroy the enemy's ability to resist by attacking the "vital objects of a nation's economic structure that will tend to paralyze the nation's ability to wage war and . . . the hostile will to resist."[7]

According to Donald Wilson, critical in this "fundamental change in military strategy; perhaps unique for modern times," was "fear and ignorance." Wilson's lack of higher education and ignorance of proper research allowed him to "avoid a great waste of time in looking for material expounding the new idea." Out of this difficulty came the "excitement and the zeal" that made his efforts a "crusade." For Wilson the lesson was clear—because of the nature of modern warfare, so dependent on industrial production, the target for strategic bombing must be the industrial ability of an enemy to wage war. Because of the traditional American opposition to attacking civilians or nonmilitary targets, this bombing would be aimed not directly at the enemy's will, but at the machines and industries that supported both that will and its military defenses. The destruction of an enemy's industries would destroy an enemy's will to resist because the enemy would no longer be capable of resisting.[8]

Like Sherman, Wilson believed air forces would not have to attack all of an enemy's industries because every industrial economy had certain chokepoints, the destruction of which would cause the economic system, and therefore the nation, to break down. These critical industries produced materials needed by most other industries. Wilson contributed this theory of "industrial fabric,"[9] which came "out of nowhere," whereby "future wars for survival would be between industrial nations; continuation of the war would depend upon maintaining intact a closely-knit and interdependent industrial fabric." Wilson viewed precision bombing as "an instrument which could cause collapse of this industrial fabric by depriving the web of certain essential elements—as few as three main systems such as transportation, electrical power and steel manufacture would suffice." He developed the phrase "industrial fabric" to identify the interrelationship and interdependency between components of a nation's industrial capabilities. An example would be the importance of oil to a mobile society dependent on the internal combustion engine, or of antifriction bearings to an industrial society.[10]

The Great Depression had a significant influence on ACTS thinking. It revealed the world's great industrial economies vulnerable to the collapse of a few key industries. Everyday newspapers carried reports of the ripple effect, as plant closings in one industry seemed to lead to closings in another industry. If the collapse of a paper stock market could devastate an economy as strong as the American economy, what would well-placed bombs and the physical destruction of key industries accomplish? In a more direct sense the Depression also forced ACTS planners toward winning wars with the greatest economy of forces because of declining budgetary support. Attacks on industries promised results with limited efforts, especially if launched with precision. Political factors encouraged them to avoid attacks on cities, but economy of force required it.

At this time, the Air Corps was struggling for identity and fighting for a military role. The only part of war the Corps could claim as its own, free from connection to the other military branches, was strategic bombing. Donald Wilson said the "Air Corps was . . . really struggling for an excuse for existence." He discovered that 75 percent of American industry was located in the Maine–Chicago–St. Louis–Norfolk rectangle. Such a concentration was vulnerable to long-range bombers with accurate bombsights. The spark for Wilson came from reading that floods had washed out two railroad bridges and that one had to be repaired before repair equipment could be brought to the second. Much of this was what Wilson called "guess work," because the ACTS had no means for testing these ideas.[11]

Key to convincing others of the correctness of his theory was flood damage on St. Patrick's Day, 1936, to a Pittsburgh factory. Water delayed aircraft production throughout the United States because the factory produced a spring necessary to the manufacture of controllable pitch propellers. Attacks on such critical choke-points in an enemy's industrial fabric would eliminate its war-making capabilities without requiring the destruction of every enemy industry or of an enemy's civilians. In Wilson's words, "This industrial fabric was the thing that could bring about defeat of an enemy not because of lack of morale or killing people, but that they would be removing the capability of conducting military operations."[12]

The 1931 ACTS texts "Bombardment Aviation" and "The Air Force" were the last before Walker and Wilson's influence became dominant. "Bombardment Aviation" identified the French and German night strategic bombardment of World War I as generally ineffective, largely because of bombing inaccuracy, but emphasized the success of British day bombing. "The Air Force" identified winning control of the air over the battlefield as air power's primary function.[13]

The 1934 ACTS text was the first to emphasize daylight precision strategic bombing, ranking the national will and industrial economy as more important targets than the enemy's armies. The 1936 ACTS text "Air Force, Part I, Air Warfare" asserted that the target of warfare was no longer just the Army, but the nation and its "vital centers": production centers, communication, and power plants, attacks on which would damage a nation's war potential and will to resist. In 1939 ACTS lecturers were telling their students that bombardment should be aimed at vital centers,[14] not people, because attacks on civilians would have only "temporary effects" on a nation.[15]

School instructors directed their students to study the American industrial fabric to identify choke-points, the kinds of attacks necessary to destroy them, and the effect their destruction would have on the American economy. In the early 1930s, before Walker and Wilson's influence, assigned targets for study were bridges, railroads, roads, docks, and ships. After their influence students studied various targets in the industrial fabric of Pennsylvania, including rail terminals, electrical power plants, oil refineries, bridges, steel mills, dams, and the Philadelphia Naval Yard. Laurence Kuter and Harold George assigned students to look for the sensitive elements in New York City's infrastructure that could make the city unlivable—water, electricity, and transportation. Research included aerial photographs added by Herbert Dargue, a pioneer in aerial reconnaissance. Students learned that choke-points could be physically apparent, such as tunnels or bridges critical to transportation systems, or not physically apparent, such as ball bearings at the foundation of an industrial economy.[16]

ACTS instructors classified targets into two categories, area and precision, and developed separate tactics for each. A precision target was a bridge, ship, or similar compact aiming point to be attacked by individual bombers each aiming separately. In the words of Field Manual 1-10 (1932),

"Tactics and Techniques of Air Attack," "precision targets are those, which
. . . require either a direct hit by a bomb of the proper size or a hit within
a limited distance therefrom." The choice of the term "area" was unfortunate, because planners had in mind the precision bombing of a large target.
FM 1-10 defined area targets as "those which require a distribution of
bombs of the proper size throughout the area in which the definite targets
lie." In 1938 the Air Corps conducted area bombing exercises at Lake
Muroc in California. The target was 900 by 2,400 feet, representing large
targets such as harbors, airfields, or factories. A lead aircraft signaled other
aircraft in the formation when to bomb, later known as "dropping on
leader." Each bomber released its bombs at regular intervals, "in train," to
achieve a sufficiently wide distribution of explosions to destroy the entire
area.[17]

The doctrine of daylight precision strategic bombing evolved at the
ACTS without challenge.[18] No one stepped forward to question whether
bomb-aiming was sufficiently accurate to destroy precision targets. These
targets of the industrial fabric seemed large and easy to hit, covering tens
of thousands of square feet, easily distinguishable from surrounding structures. Air Corps annual bombing and machine gun matches at Langley
Field in the 1920s should have given the theorists pause to reflect on
bombing accuracy. With newer sights considered "about five times as accurate as those in use during the world war," and even at low altitudes, the
results hardly justified the Tactical School's faith in strategic bombing. The
average radial error from 5,000 feet was 173.8 feet, 282.6 feet from 8,000
feet.[19] The largest bomb in the Army inventory, 2,000 pounds, could cause
a crater no larger than 22 feet in diameter with an instantaneous fuze and
50 feet with a delayed fuze. The maximum effective range of fragmentation was 110 feet. At the lower altitude of 5,000 feet at the annual matches,
even this largest bomb would be ineffective.

In July 1926 the Air Corps received a firsthand lesson in the importance
of accuracy when lightning struck the Naval Ammunition Depot at Lake
Denmark, New Jersey. Exploding shells struck the nearby Army Picatinny
Arsenal. A watchman 1,500 feet from the arsenal was only slightly
wounded when 775,000 tons of TNT exploded. Accuracy was clearly more
important than the size of the bomb. Tests done in the late 1930s convinced planners that "it is better to attack more objectives or to obtain a
better chance of hitting by dropping a larger number of the proper size
bombs than it is to drop fewer bombs of a size larger than necessary." Before the war the Air Corps determined that the 500-pound bomb was the

Table 5.1. Air Corps Tactical School Summary of Bombing Accuracy

Year	Bomber	Speed (mph)	Bombsight	Altitude (feet)	Radial Error (feet)
1930	B-3	75	D-4	5,000	135
	B-3	75	D-4	8,000	173
1934	B-4	85	D-4	5,000	120
	B-4	85	D-4	8,000	174
1935	B-4/6	100	D-4	5,000	130
	B-12	100	Norden	5,000	130
	B-4/6	100	D-4	8,000	181
	B-12	100	Norden	8,000	181
1936	B-10/12	125	Norden	5,000	145
	B-10/12	125	Norden	8,000	159
	B-10/12	125	Norden	15,000	410
1937	B-10/17	130	Norden	7,000	144
	B-10/17	130	Norden	10,000	202
	B-10/17	130	Norden	15,000	258
1938	B-10/17/18	135	Norden	7,000	107
	B-10/17/18	135	Norden	10,000	144
	B-10/17/18	135	Norden	15,000	235

Source: Kuter to Arnold, n.d. (1939?), File 168.7012-23, HRA.

optimum-sized bomb for most industrial targets. Wartime experience would prove it too small, but that was in the future.[20]

How many bombs were needed? One study evaluated the requirements for destroying the Sault Ste. Marie locks between Michigan and Ontario. Engineers reported nine 300-pound bombs, carried by one medium bomber, would do the job—if bombing was accurate. Such studies reinforced the Air Corps' commitment to daylight precision strategic bombing.[21]

From 1930 to 1938 the Air Corps dropped over 200,000 bombs in training. The overwhelming majority of these drops came from 4,000 to 11,000 feet, dictated by prevailing tactics and gasoline shortages. Less than 3 percent came from above 16,000 feet. This data provided Laurence S. Kuter, an instructor at the ACTS, the information for creating the probability studies on which the bombing doctrine was based (see Table 5.1).[22]

Although impressive, these results showed that bombing was accurate only in excellent weather against a clearly outlined, undefended target in the middle of wide-open terrain. New technology obscured these limitations and continuing accuracy problems. From 1934 to 1936 Henry H. Arnold and his 7th Bomb Group and later his 1st Wing put this technology and high-altitude bombing to the test with Norden-equipped Keystone, B-9, and B-10 bombers at California's Muroc Dry Lake Bed. The speeds of the new bombers blinded airmen to difficulties with accuracy. The B-9 was the first of several bombers that could outrun Air Corps fighters. In Arnold's mind, enemy defenses could not stop bombers, reinforcing the conviction that strategic bombing was possible. In 1932 England's Stanley Baldwin said "the bomber will always get through." A year later the assistant chief of the Air Corps, Brig. Gen. Oscar Westover, echoed Baldwin: "No known agency can frustrate the accomplishment of a bombardment mission." He was wrong—inaccuracy still stood between the Army Air Corps and its doctrine of daylight precision strategic bombing, despite the Norden bombsight.[23]

Arnold did make one concession to bombing inaccuracy and the power of defensive weapons. He realized that pinpoint "pickle barrel" accuracy would be difficult at the high altitudes and speeds enemy defenses would force his bombers to fly. To compensate, the future Air Corps' chief organized his forces into forty-bomber formations. All would drop their bombs in a single salvo, overcoming inaccuracy with overwhelming firepower. Tests against outlines of battleships drawn in the desert proved the efficiency of this "shotgun" approach. With considerable practice Arnold's crews achieved improved accuracy, though without having to confront the heavy cloud covers that would later prove to be the Norden bombsight's greatest enemy.[24]

An air leader who did have to face weather problems was Robert Olds, commander of the 2nd Bombardment Group at Langley Field, previously of the ACTS. His group was the first to fly the B-17 Flying Fortress equipped with the Norden bombsight. Olds's group experimented with blind bombing techniques to overcome the detrimental effect of clouds on the visual Norden bombsight. Called "bombing through overcast," Olds and his bombardiers flew by dead reckoning from a visible initial point to the obscured target. Measuring the distance from the initial point to the target on maps, the bombardiers calibrated their sights and used stopwatches to determine the time needed to fly the appropriate distance. The 2nd Bombardment Group achieved reasonable accuracy by this method, with errors of 1,200 to 1,800 feet in range and 500 to 700 feet in deflection common. Olds discovered, like Arnold before him, that strategic bombing

Table 5.2. Army Air Corps Bombing Accuracy, 1936–1940 (average circular error from 15,000 feet)

Year	All Bombings (feet)	Record Bombing (feet)
1936	442	320
1937	360	275
1938	300	240
1939	254	215
1940	400	280

Note: These averages were the product of nearly 115,000 practice bombs, though misses of over 1,000 feet were eliminated from consideration. See Sorenson lecture, July 14, 1939, File 248.2208A-1, HRA.

Source: Experimental Engineering Section to Materiel Division, April 24, 1941, File 471.6-F, Box 299, Central Decimal Files, 1939–42, Series II, RG18.

would require large formations of bombers dropping bombs in salvo to achieve strikes on the target.[25]

Further practice and testing under the pressure of approaching war revealed only greater problems. In the six months before Pearl Harbor, bombardiers dropped nearly 50,000 bombs on practice targets. At an average speed of 170 mph and with no drops from above 20,000 feet, not one group, on average, could achieve the standards set in Training Manual 1-250 for first-, second-, or third-class bombardiers. This was in perfect weather against no enemy defenses. The Army Air Forces Board concluded in its report to Arnold, now chief of the Army Air Forces, that "mean points of impact of Air Forces bombing and training school bombing continued to fall short of the target." The reality of bombing inaccuracy collided with the doctrine-makers' theories.[26]

A founder of the doctrine, Laurence S. Kuter, began to have doubts. His continuing analysis of bombing probable errors, based on thousands of actual bombings against isolated targets in the middle of empty deserts in clear weather, under ideal conditions, at low speeds, against no enemy opposition, revealed the strategic bombing doctrine's vulnerability to bombing inaccuracy (see Table 5.2).

Kuter reevaluated his earlier calculations on the force needed to destroy the Sault Ste. Marie Canal locks. Yes, strategic bombing would work, but he would need more than 120 bombers dropping over 1,000 bombs to get the nine hits to do the job. "Such a mission," he wrote, "is beyond the capability of all of our bomb groups today." Lt. Col. Edgar P. Sorenson, another instructor at ACTS, analyzed 40,000 bomb drops and concluded that "any categorical answer to the question how many airplanes must be dispatched to obtain a reasonable chance of destroying an objective is of no practical value because of the many factors that must be considered in each case." Another ACTS critic, Capt. Matthew K. Deichelmann, wrote that many more bombs were going to be necessary to insure the destruction of the industrial fabric.

Kuter considered the options. The Air Corps could reduce altitude to increase accuracy, but "it is manifestly not a practicable method" because of modern antiaircraft artillery. It could reduce the expectations of success on individual missions. Lowering expectations from a 98 percent chance of success to 90 percent would reduce the number of bombs required by 55 percent, but the purpose of air power was to destroy targets. The odds of success would have to remain high or costly repeat missions would be necessary. Kuter concluded that the only practical solution was to increase bombing accuracy. Minor increases would not help. "Arbitrarily reducing the errors would be a neat but not effective method of talking ourselves out of the hole this [mean probable bombing error] table has placed us in. This table is the Air Corps' story and we are stuck with it."

The doctrine of daylight precision strategic bombing had major holes. Theorists had based their thinking on the results of the Langley annual bombing competitions, recorded by the best bombardiers in the entire Air Corps, flying old, slow Keystone bombers at 10,000 feet with inadequate D-4 bombsights. Now crews were flying Martin B-10s and Boeing B-17s with Norden bombsights at higher speeds and altitudes and had reduced bombing errors, adjusted to 8,000 feet of altitude, from 238 feet to 28 feet. A target requiring ninety-nine bombs for destruction with the D-4 needed only twenty-five bombs with the M-1 Norden, but only under artificial "laboratory" conditions. Obviously the Norden bombsight was critical, but in the field among the crews and bombardiers who would fight the war from above 20,000 feet, would it be enough? When the war began bombardiers still practiced for high-altitude missions at 12,000 feet.[27]

The greatest single cause for error continued to be bombardier error. The Army Air Forces Board "acknowledged faulty technique" for one out of three bomb drops.[28] Because short-range dive bombing was not practical for the Air Corps' strategic bombing role, Arnold ordered the Air Corps Board to consider glide and low-altitude bombing to increase accuracy. Glide bombing meant losing altitude during bombing to increase speed and complicate the task of defending ground fire. Low-altitude strategic bombing was below 5,000 feet. By 1940 it was too late. The Norden bombsight could not be synchronized at high speeds and low altitudes and did not allow range synchronization in glide bombing because of constantly changing altitude and angle of glide data. Tests showed that from 13,000 feet, the bombing error was 2.2 times greater in glide bombing than in level bombing. High-altitude daylight precision strategic bombing may not have been that accurate, but it was all the Air Corps had.[29]

One spectacular success at the expense of the Navy restored Air Corps faith in its doctrine of precision bombing. In August 1937 Lt. Col. Robert Olds's 2nd Bombardment Group and Lt. Col. George C. Stratemeyer's 7th Bombardment Group, with thirty-four B-10s, seven B-17s, and three B-18s, participated in Joint Air Exercise No. 4, calling for Navy patrol bombers to locate and Army land-based bombers to bomb the USS *Utah* with Navy water-filled practice bombs off the coast of California.

At 1557 hours on August 12 the Navy found the battleship, but signaled the Army an incorrect location. The Army launched forty-one bombers that never found the *Utah*. The next day, commanding general Delos C. Emmons refused to wait for Navy trackers to locate the *Utah* again and launched his B-17s and B-18s for a long-range search. The formation's navigator, Curtis LeMay, headed for the ship's last known position, after adjusting for another erroneous position report from the Navy. With only 12 minutes left before the 1200 hours deadline for the exercise, the B-17s dropped below the overcast at 400 feet to bomb a *Utah* caught unawares. The Navy reported "at least one and not more than two hits per plane as they dropped in train" with several more near misses.

On August 14, the Navy demanded another effort, insisting the *Utah* could have evaded the bombs if it had seen the B-17s in clearer weather. This time the entire Air Corps bomber force found the maneuvering *Utah* and bombed from 8,000 to 18,000 feet, achieving thirty-seven direct hits, spread along the battleship's entire 500-foot length, 23 percent of all bombs dropped. Forty-seven more fell within 50 feet of the ship, close enough to have a water-hammer effect. In two days of bombing, the Air Corps, using the Navy's Norden bombsight, had achieved a hit rate on a ship underway at sea of 11.9 percent.[30]

Bombing tests revealed the operational limitations of the technology and doctrine. The Air Corps believed improved training, salvo bombing, and blind-bombing techniques would make daylight precision strategic bombing possible. On the eve of World War II, however, official doctrine in the Army's air force continued to emphasize defense and close air support. The official doctrinal statement of the Air Corps was Training Regulation 440-15, dated October 15, 1935. Entitled "The Employment of the Air Forces of the Army," it was still in force at the outbreak of World War II. TR 440-15 placed all air forces under the control of the field commander and assigned them tactical duties "in direct or indirect support of other components of the Nation's armed forces." Specific functions were reconnaissance, interdiction, air superiority over the battlefield, and attacks on ammunition dumps, supply centers, and troop concentrations. Similarly the Joint Army-Navy Board of 1935 saw the Air Corps as an "arm of the mobile Army, both in conduct of air operations over the land in support of land operations and in the conduct of air operations over the sea in direct defense of the coast." The Air Corps Board of 1936 reflected this view, writing that "the diversion of effort incident to preparations for strategically offensive operations is not justified."

Army Field Manuals 1-5, "Employment of Aviation of the Army," and 1–10, "Tactics and Techniques of Air Attack," made no significant changes to the planned employment of American air forces when they appeared in 1940. The mission of the Air Corps was to defend the United States and its overseas possessions, support the Army, and be prepared to deal with "other situations" that might arise. The offensive use of air power was in counterair operations and in support of ground and naval forces, including attacks on supply and repair depots. Committed to tactical twin-engine bombers, the Army's General Staff restricted the Air Corps to thirteen new B-17s for 1939.[31]

Working against official doctrine, airmen still believed strategic bombing would work. The Air Corps Board changed its views in 1940, assigning the Air Corps the primary mission of hemispheric defense and a secondary mission of "offensive strategic bombardment." Ted Barth, ever the salesman/promoter, expressed the confidence of many in the Norden's capabilities on the eve of America's entry into World War II: "We do not regard a fifteen foot square . . . as being a very difficult target to hit from an altitude of 30,000 feet, provided the new Army M-4 Bombsight, together with the Stabilized Bombing Approach Equipment [automatic bombing pilot], is used."[32] It was equivalent, in the idiom of the day, to dropping a bomb into a pickle barrel from six miles up.

This feeling that daylight precision strategic bombing would work carried over to Pres. Franklin Roosevelt. After Hitler used the threat of his air force to bully Britain and France into consenting to his takeover of the Sudetenland and eventually all of Czechoslovakia at Munich in September 1938,[33] Roosevelt ordered the capacity of America's aircraft industry expanded to 10,000 per year. The Army's General Staff refused to alter its commitment to close air support, allowing the Air Corps to order only 206 B-17s. Two years later, with the German invasion of France, Roosevelt raised the expansion to 50,000 per year, sweeping away the General Staff's attempts to limit heavy bomber production. The president had decided to allow the Air Corps to try defeating America's enemies through daylight precision strategic bombing, which complied with his call on all nations not to "undertake the bombardment from the air of civilian populations." By the time of the Anglo-American ABC-1 agreement of March 27, 1941, the U.S. Army had agreed to an Air Corps strategic bombing attack "primarily against German military power at its source."[34]

Commander of the new Army Air Forces, Maj. Gen. Henry H. Arnold reinforced this role with a plan for fighting the air war, Air War Plans Division/1 or AWPD/1, in the fall of 1941. On July 9, 1941, President Roosevelt asked his armed services to project their weapons requirements for winning a possible war against "our potential enemies." Although the Army War Plans Division would handle the Army's projection, the newly established AWPD of the Army Air Forces was to present the Army Air Forces's requirements—an early sign of the independence Gen. George Marshall would grant the Army's air force during the war.

Arnold's team—Lt. Col. Kenneth N. Walker, Maj. Haywood S. Hansell Jr., Maj. Laurence S. Kuter, and headed by Lt. Col. Harold L. George— met to decide what role the newly formed Army Air Forces would play in the war. They were in Washington precisely because they were of one mind with Arnold about the value of daylight strategic precision bombing. All had extensive contacts with ACTS, both as students and instructors.[35] All had been critical to the formulation, testing, and teaching of the bombing doctrine. All were opposed to attacks on morale: "Area bombing of cities may actually stiffen the resistance of the population." Hansell recruited captains Richard Hughes and Malcolm Moss, former businessmen with ties to Wall Street, to identify the industries of Germany and Japan that, if destroyed, would make "these two countries incapable of continuing to fight a war."

Hughes and Moss chose 154 German targets for precision bombing, including eighteen aircraft production plants (the Luftwaffe was considered an "intermediate objective"), fifty electrical power plants, forty-seven transportation centers, twenty-seven oil plants, six aluminum plants, and six magnesium plants. Much of the information on which Hughes and Moss based their selection came from New York financial institutions investing in or lending money to German enterprises. They extrapolated additional information from American industry, though the two industrial economies were significantly different. Germany placed greater emphasis on machine tools and lesser emphasis on large assembly-line manufacturing processes. Hughes and Moss avoided detailed targeting for Japan because of a near-total ignorance of Japanese industry.

Hughes described what happened next. Using the "accuracy probabilities of the Norden Bomb Sight, they calculated the tonnage of bombs which would need to be dropped on each target to destroy it, and, from that, the numbers and types of bombing planes which would be necessary." Data from bombing groups, based on training and practice bombings, showed that one heavy bomber from 20,000 feet had a 1.2 percent probability of hitting a 100-foot by 100-foot target, with an average circular bombing error of 555 feet. Using Kuter's probability tables, the group calculated that 220 aircraft would be necessary to raise to 90 percent the probability of destroying a target. The AWPD group multiplied this figure by the square of 2.25 to reflect the influences enemy defenses, weather, and combat conditions might have on accuracy. These calculations gave the planners the requirement for 1,100 aircraft or thirty group missions to destroy a target. They assumed each group of thirty-six bombers could mount eight missions per month. "To wage a sustained air offensive against German military power" was a matter for the adding machines.[36]

From these calculations the planners determined the number of bombardiers, pilots, navigators, mechanics, instructors, trainers, and aircraft that were needed to fight the war. Against Germany, this task required, by the AWPD's calculations, 98 groups (6,834) of heavy and medium bombers, backed by a reserve of 1,708 bombers and replacements of 1,245 each month. Given the weather in Europe, they estimated this force would require six months to do the job. The plan made no provision for an offensive against Japan. To man Norden bombsights, AWPD/1 required the training of 8,125 bombardiers. AWPD/1 would be the blueprint for America's air war. Product of this hurriedly assembled planning group, it was at once testimony to the American doctrine of daylight precision strategic bombing. In the minds of the writers of AWPD/1 and of the Army Air

Forces leadership, daylight precision strategic bombing could best defeat Germany and Japan, from high altitude, in level flight.[37]

The American air war in World War II was the fruit of six staff officers working with adding machines in extreme heat and humidity, largely without intelligence information, divorced from the exploding bombs, burning fuel, smoke, and torn flesh of war. They based their calculations on practice bombings flown in clear weather and at low altitudes. Practice bombings were one bomb at a time, making multiple passes to achieve higher accuracy. In wartime, enemy defenses would make such practices impossible.

AWPD/1 used no information from foreign agents and little knowledge of the structure of the German industrial economy other than what the British provided to Hansell during a trip to England in the summer of 1941. To provide a "sense of reality," the planners named specific industries, which, according to Hughes, was "unnecessary and impractical." The AWPD plan called for an all-out bomber offensive from April to September 1944, based on intelligence gathered before the war. George, Hansell, Hughes, Kuter, Moss, and Walker perceived an inflexible, unchanging industrial mesh incapable of repairing itself as its choke-points were destroyed. The German economy of 1944 would be dramatically different from this hypothetical German economy of 1941. It would prove throughout the war its ability to repair and expand itself under a barrage of Allied bombs. America's air war planners did not foresee dispersal, Minister for Armaments and Munitions Albert Speer's reforms, the incorporation of much of Western Europe's industrial might into the German war economy, the utilization of millions of contract and slave laborers, and the transformation of Germany from a predominately consumer economy with surplus capacity in 1941 to a primarily war economy in 1944. The plan had many faults, not the least of which was the way in which the AWPD had formed it. According to Hughes, "In retrospect it seems fantastic that the air power program for the United States of America for World War II should have been based on the arbitrary and hurried opinions of two junior reserve Captains."[38]

Carl Norden's bombsight had yet to drop a bomb in anger, but AWPD/1 would have to serve as America's blueprint for World War II until wartime experiences required its modification. For the doctrine to work, commanders had no choice but to send larger forces on each mission, flooding targets with bombers and bombs to insure their destruction. The gun of strategic bombing would still be aimed at specific targets of the "industrial fabric," "those vital objectives in a nation's economic structure which will tend to paralyze that nation's ability to wage war . . . [and] will to resist," but instead of a rifle, the Army Air Forces would use a shotgun. Four months after the submission of AWPD/1, the Japanese attacked Pearl Harbor.[39]

6

The Navy Adopts
Dive Bombing for World War II

Fleet Problem IX at Panama, January 23–27, 1929, under the command of Adm. William V. Pratt, established the aircraft and aircraft carrier in Navy plans. The USS *Saratoga* acted as an independent task force under Rear Adm. Joseph M. Reeves and successfully attacked the Panama Canal. The issue was basic—would the Navy's offensive capabilities focus on battleships firing large shells at targets up to 20 miles away or on bombers dropping large bombs on targets up to 200 miles away? Combat missions in Nicaragua and fleet exercises showed the potential of dive bombing, but the Navy had too much tradition and too many resources invested in battleships and torpedo and horizontal bombers to rely solely on still-unproven dive bombing.

Before the Navy could focus on dive bombing, it had to advance the technology of dive-bomb aiming beyond the "eye-balling" used with Lieutenant Sanderson's "large canvas mail sacks." In an early indication that it was gradually giving up on high-altitude horizontal bombing in favor of dive bombing, BuOrd directed Carl Norden away from efforts to improve the Norden Mark XV bombsight in favor of an "aiming angle sight," designated the Mark II, for dive bombers in July 1933. Encouragement came from the aircrew of the USS *Saratoga*, who experienced a "large percentage of misses," blamed on the lack of a proper bombsight. BuOrd contracted with the Sperry Gyroscope Company for a Mark I dive-bombing sight. The idea was to free the pilot from having to correct for dive angle, lift angle, release altitude, and diving speed.[1]

The Mark I was an extension of an earlier Sperry project to build an instrument that would indicate the proper diving angle. The Mark I would be a combination of the dive-angle indicator, a telescope, and an altimeter reading into the telescope. BuOrd did not specify a sight that would correct for wind and target motion because of the apparent complexity and greater size and weight such calculations would involve and because freeing the pilot of other responsibilities would allow him to concentrate on those two adjustments.[2]

Sperry delivered sixteen experimental Mark Is to BuOrd for testing in May 1935. The device consisted of an aircraft gun sight coupled to a gyroscope-driven computer and altimeter. The pilot preset the required altitude for bomb release, the expected air speed at the point of release, and the expected lift angle derived from tables based on the preset air speed. A gyroscope fed the dive angle to the computer, which automatically set the sighting arm in the gun sight. The pilot flew the aircraft at the preset speed, keeping the sighting arm fixed on the target while compensating for target motion, the effects of wind, and deflection. Squadron VB-4 tested the experimental Aiming Angle Sight, Mark I, against moving targets and concluded that it did "not afford a complete solution of the dive-bombing problem but it does correct for variations in angle of dive and incorporates a warning light to indicate when the proper release altitude is reached." The Mark I achieved 64 percent hits on a maneuvering target, only marginally more than the gun sight without the Sperry computer, gyroscope, and altimeter.[3]

Four years of modifications brought little progress and in April 1941 BuAer Chief Rear Adm. John H. Towers canceled the Mark I Aiming Angle Sight project. "In view of the slight improvement in bombing performance, the restrictions inherent in its use, and the installation difficulties involved, it is recommended that none of these sights be procured but that a more vigorous effort be made to perfect the Aiming Angle Sight Mark II."[4]

Using $32,000 of National Industrial Recovery Act funds, BuOrd contracted with Carl L. Norden, Inc., on January 2, 1934, for a stabilized dive-bombing sight, the Aiming Angle Sight, Mark II, in cooperation with the Army. Norden spent two years in Zurich working on the mathematical equations of dive bombing and their mechanical analogs, mailing blueprints to the New York Norden plant in the diplomatic pouches of America's Zurich embassy. His company delivered an experimental version to the Dahlgren Naval Proving Ground in late 1936.[5]

Testing revealed shortcomings: "Angles of vision are too small and the resulting steep angles of dive required did not give the pilot sufficient time in dives to compensate for the total amount of drift involved." The barometric altimeter gave readings that lagged considerably behind the actual altitude—a dangerous quality considering the speeds aircraft approached the ground in a dive. Norden's design had promise over the Sperry design because, after entering the dive, adjustments were automatic except for the pilot having to release the directional gyroscope. The Army and Navy agreed to fund four experimental models for $95,000, soon raised to $100,000.[6]

Continued development revealed a bombsight that was too complex, required too much of the pilot's attention, and allowed little variation from a constant speed and steady course. Norden made little progress because impending war brought an explosion of orders for his Mark XV/M-series bombsight and new Army demands for modifications to it. Work continued at a slow pace until the Army and Navy canceled the project in 1944.[7]

The failure of the Norden project ended Navy attempts to automate the dive-bombing technique. Navy dive bombers entered World War II equipped with the simple Mark III (Mark 3 in World War II) line-of-sight telescopic gun sight for aiming their bombs. Keeping the cross hairs on the target, the pilot used a turn-and-bank indicator to maintain level flight. Army dive bombing in support of ground forces used the N-3A gun sight equipped with an adjustable reflector (Model A-1) and a Norden-style gyroscopic stabilizer.[8]

For the remainder of the prewar period, the Navy continued using torpedo, dive, and horizontal bombing, though the importance of horizontal bombing declined. Exercises in May and June 1931 revealed an additional problem. Solid cloud cover off San Diego made high-altitude bombing "impracticable," allowing ship gunners to concentrate their fire on attacking torpedo bombers. In the opinion of the commander of the Battle Force, "it is not believed that these squadrons could have survived." BuAer questioned the continuation of the high-altitude horizontal bombing technique when "the average low cloud form ceiling throughout the world is approximately 4,000 feet." The commander-in-chief of the U.S. Fleet determined that even "at 10,000 feet [bombers] would have little chance against the anti-aircraft fire." Torpedo bomber units attempted to perfect night attacks to avoid ship defensive fire, but without success.[9]

In contrast, dive bombing continued to prove its merit. Adm. Joseph M. Reeves, commander-in-chief of the U.S. Fleet, wrote, "These dive bombers, equipped with 1,000-pound bombs, are probably the most deadly air weapon thus far devised." In exercises late in 1933, two squadrons made mock dive-bombing attacks on the USS *Lexington* and *Saratoga*, scoring sixty-eight hits according to umpires. Powerful opponents of air power still controlled the exercises, because the umpires ruled that sixty-eight hits failed to sink either carrier. Such rulings could not obscure the obvious—the Navy was moving away from Norden-equipped horizontal bombers in favor of dive bombers. Against the battle cruiser division, bombers diving out of the sun from 12,000 feet met what observers described as ineffective antiaircraft fire and pressed their attacks without opposition. Reeves judged associated torpedo bomber attacks to be ineffective: "Probably in all naval warfare there is nothing more difficult to deliver than a successful torpedo attack."[10]

In 1936 Reeves itemized the duties of carrier-borne aircraft,[11] limiting torpedo attack to "just prior to the main engagement," and assigning dive bombers the primary responsibility for the destruction of enemy capital ships. Each carrier's contingent would include four aircraft squadrons: one squadron of VBFs (fighters with dive-bombing capability), two squadrons of VSBs (scout bombers with dive-bombing capability), and one squadron of VBs (dive bombers) or VTBs (torpedo bombers). The VBs were to carry 1,000-pound bombs. The VTBs would be capable of carrying torpedoes or 1,000-pound bombs, to be dropped from high altitude using Norden bombsights.[12]

Fleet Exercise 74, April 1938, was the culmination of dive bombing in Navy plans. The *Lexington*'s dive bombers attacked three cruisers and the battleships *Tennessee* and *Oklahoma* with "nearly total surprise" and against ineffective antiaircraft fire. Five minutes later the *Lexington*'s torpedo bombers struck at the *Tennessee* and *Oklahoma* against "heavy and effective" return fire from the battleships. The *Saratoga*'s dive bombers attacked several cruisers and the battleship *California* with complete surprise. Torpedo bombers from the *Saratoga* confronted heavy antiaircraft fire. The *Ranger*'s aircraft attacked three cruisers, repeating the experiences of the two other strikes. Shore-based PBYs and VPBs bombed the *Tennessee* and *New Mexico* horizontally from above 10,000 feet against heavy fire.

In analyzing the exercise, the Navy expressed extreme concern about the survivability of horizontal and torpedo bombers. Without testing the accuracy of bombing, the fleet commander concluded that he would not be able to defend his ships against a dive-bombing attack. Together, survivability and accuracy spelled an end to the Navy's reliance on high-altitude horizontal bombing with the Norden bombsight.[13]

The Navy retained the Norden bombsight and a horizontal-bombing capability for its land-based patrol bombers because of the unsuitability of dive bombing for long-range aircraft of this type. Admirals could have less accurate long-range horizontal bombing from land or more accurate short-range dive bombing from carriers at sea, but not in the same aircraft. Also preserved was the capability in carrier-borne aircraft because occasional successes in exercises maintained hope that increased training could make the technique work. In 1932 Squadron VT-2B, using Norden Mark XI bombsights, hit a maneuvering USS *Utah* from 10,000 feet with five of thirty-one practice bombs. Adm. David F. Sellers, commander of the Battle Force, concluded that "further demonstrations of the accuracy of high-altitude bombing may change opinions as to the value of dive-bombing." Critics pointed out that the *Utah* was at reduced speed and the weather had been perfect.[14]

Horizontal bombing persisted, but changes in the rules of bombing practices in the nine years before World War II laid bare the weaknesses of level bombing. Antiaircraft artillery forced horizontal bombers ever higher. Each increase in altitude negatively affected bombing accuracy, despite what BuOrd's paper calculations claimed (see Table 6.1). The dive bomber continued its move to the forefront of naval aerial warfare.

Official Navy policy was to use high-altitude precision bombing or torpedo bombing first to surprise enemy ships and to divert attention from dive bombers that would carry out the main attack. Against maneuvering targets, BuOrd concluded, the dive bomber "held a practical monopoly on effective attacks."[15]

Dive bombing evolved in the 1920s and 1930s almost incidentally, implemented to overcome the accuracy limitations of horizontal bombing and the survivability limitations of torpedo bombing. It arose from below, from a handful of young men who knew nothing of doctrine and little of battle lines, but knew flying and knew bombing. A decade of tests and exercises proved them irrepressible and their tactic irresistible, though dive bombing never completely supplanted the other two bombing techniques in Navy use.

When the United States went to war in 1941, the Navy hedged its bets.

Table 6.1. Fleet Bombing Exercises, 1932–1940: Dive Bombing Versus High-Altitude Level Bombing

Year	Maneuvers by USS *Utah*	Hits by Dive Bombing (percentage)	Hits by Level Bombing (percentage)	Altitude of Level Bombing (feet)
1932	Simple	18.2	5.6	8,000
1933	Radical	20.0	0.0	8,000
1934	Radical	13.0	0.0	8,000
1935	Restricted	17.3	9.4	8,000
1936	Radical	23.7	8.3	10,000
1937	Steady	12.7	11.1	10,000
1937	Sharp turns	11.3	5.6	10,000
1938	Steady	13.9	4.1	12,000
1938	Sharp turns	14.5	2.4	12,000
1939	Zig zag	21.8	4.4	17,000
1939	Unrestricted	18.1	1.1	17,000
1940	Zig zag	19.1	1.9	17,000
1940	Unrestricted	23.1	1.9	17,000

Source: Army Air Corps Board, Report No. 4, Vol. 4, 1941, File 167.5-45, HRA; and Brown, "Navy's Mark 15 (Norden) Bombsight," 235–39.

It had spent two decades developing three techniques for sinking ships from the air and it was unwilling to give up on any of them. Navy carriers carried Douglas TBD Devastators, dual-purpose torpedo bombers equipped with Norden bombsights for horizontal bombing; Vought SB2U Vindicators, dual-purpose scout aircraft capable of dive bombing; Grumman F4F Wildcats, dual-purpose fighter aircraft capable of dive bombing; and Douglas SBD Dauntless dive bombers. The *Ranger*, because of its small size, was an all-dive bomber ship. At the Battle of the Coral Sea in May 1942, the *Lexington* and *Yorktown* together carried forty-two F4F Wildcat fighters, twenty-five TBD Devastator torpedo bombers, and seventy-four SBD Dauntless dive bombers.

Perhaps the origins of dive bombing prevented the Navy from adopting it exclusively. In the tradition-bound Navy, with a hierarchical rank structure that discouraged such innovation from below, especially in peacetime, this failure was not unusual. In the Air Corps, itself too young to be bound by traditions and a hierarchical rank structure, young lieutenants and captains forged the revolutionary doctrine of high-altitude daylight precision strategic bombing. The absence of a unified Navy doctrine left hundreds of torpedo bomber crewmen vulnerable and exposed to enemy defenses. It also caused the Navy to hold on to thousands of Norden bombsights when the Army Air Forces had a critical need for them. The irony was the failure of the U.S. Navy to use its own Norden bombsight, developed at great expense, in World War II. The U.S. Army, which did use the Norden bombsight, had to subordinate its needs for the device to those of the Navy for more than a decade.

7

Preparation for War

In April 1933 Chief of the Air Corps Benjamin D. Foulois secretly visited Norden president Ted Barth's New York apartment seeking a direct Army contract for Norden Mark XVs free of Navy involvement. Foulois objected to Norden as the sole source for this critical technology, the restricted size of the Norden operation, the "unusual amount" of handwork that went into the sight, and the requirement that the Army had to place its orders through BuOrd. Barth refused Foulois' request to modify the Navy-Norden arrangement, prompting Foulois to explode, claiming the patent for the bombsight "belonged to the U.S. Government and not to the Navy!" He threatened to go to BuOrd, the chief of naval operations, the secretary of war, and "to the committees of Congress." Barth still refused, claiming he was "morally bound" to sell all Norden bombsights to the Navy.[1]

Despite such difficulties, the shotgun of the Army Air Corps doctrine of daylight precision strategic bombing needed an aiming device. The Norden Mark XV/M-series bombsight was it, if it could be procured in quantities sufficient to equip the thousands of bombers required for a strategic bombing campaign. In the seven years from the beginning of production to the outbreak of World War II, Carl L. Norden, Inc., assembled 847

Mark XV bombsights for the Army and Navy, one at a time, at its 80 Lafayette Street, one-floor factory in New York. Carl Norden controlled every aspect of design and construction. Workers hand-tooled each part to his specifications. He inspected each piece, more often than not ordering a part "thrown out the window" if not perfect.[2] Workers had to grind and polish several hundred ball bearings for each bombsight by hand. The key to Norden's successful design was to produce each sight, one at a time, to minimize the friction between moving parts that represented the mathematical formulas, or analogs, of the bombsighting problem. In preparing for war, planners were looking for tens of thousands of Norden bombsights. Could they be mass-produced?

The Army would have to rely on the Navy, which had largely given up on the Norden bombsight, but was nevertheless responsible for producing it. Moreover, the Army had to rely on the Navy to upgrade and modify the Norden bombsight and associated equipment to meet Army needs. One service assigned the Norden bombsight its highest priority for wartime production, while the other gave it a lower priority. Only war against the Axis powers prevented war from breaking out between the two American services over the Norden bombsight.

Confusion reigned over exactly how many were needed. In November 1938 President Roosevelt told his military commanders to work toward an Air Corps of 20,000 aircraft, though before Congress in January 1939 he lowered the figure to 3,000. In April 1939 Congress raised that number to 6,000. With the German invasion of France in May 1940, Roosevelt set 50,000 aircraft as the annual goal of America's aircraft production. In the fall of 1941 the six officers of the Air War Plans Division required a bombsight for each of 10,837 heavy bombers, a monthly production of 1,260 for replacement bombers, and thousands more for medium bombers, for trainers, and to meet Navy requirements. Roosevelt raised production goals in January 1942 to 60,000 aircraft for 1942 and 125,000 for 1943. No one knew how many bombers would be needed, but the two government agencies charged with bombsight procurement, the Navy's BuOrd and the Army's Materiel Division, knew Carl L. Norden, Inc., producing an average of only 108 Mark XV Norden bombsights per year from 1931 through 1938, could not meet the demand (see Table 7.1).

One major obstacle to the incorporation of the Norden bombsight into the Air Corps was security. The Navy classified the bombsight and "all correspondence and conversation relating thereto" as secret, requiring "every precaution in order to prevent information regarding this develop-

Table 7.1. Carl L. Norden, Inc., Bombsight *Craftsmen* (Navy contracts, 1929–38)

Year	Amount	Contract
1929	$ 25,546	Mark XV development, 1 Mark XI
1930	27,739	Mark XI modernization, parts
1931	26,041	2 Mark XI, 1 Mark XV, parts, overhaul
1932	411,746	95 Mark XV, parts, overhaul
1933	686,352	162 Mark XV, parts, overhaul, SBAE development
1934	737,910	153 Mark XV, parts, overhaul
1935	145,182	22 Mark XV, parts, overhaul, instruments
1936	659,067	122 Mark XV, parts, overhaul
1937	293,352	50 Mark XV, 4 SBAE, parts, overhaul
1938	2,524,330	242 Mark XV, 225 SBAE, parts, overhaul
Total	$5,537,265	847 Mark XV, 3 Mark XI, 229 SBAE

Source: Brown, "Navy's Mark 15 (Norden) Bombsight," Exhibit B1.

ment from becoming available to any person who may utilize it in a manner contrary to the best interests of the United States." Especially stringent security restrictions surrounded the Norden bombsight because of experiences with the Norden Mark XI bombsight. The Navy discovered drawings and blueprints of the Mark XI in the hands of the Sperry Gyroscope Company, a commercial competitor of Norden. A livid Carl Norden demanded better security. BuOrd Chief Rear Adm. Edgar B. Larimer wrote the chief of BuAer on October 16, 1931, that he wished to prevent any unauthorized persons from securing information on the Mark XV, not because of national security, but because he wanted to "prevent anyone securing patents" and "to keep secret the manufacturing details."[3]

Until superseded by the Manhattan Project, the Norden bombsight was what General Foulois called "the most important *military secret project* under development." The Air Corps nevertheless asked the Navy in 1934 to reduce the secret classification to confidential to facilitate development and allow the acquisition of manufacturing information to plan for emergency production in case of war. Crews could not use Norden technical and instructional manuals or keep records of individual sights because of security restrictions. The Navy finally acceded to the request 18 months later, downgrading the Norden to confidential status. The reduction meant its unauthorized release would be "prejudicial" to the national security, not that it would "endanger" the national security as under the secret classification.[4]

The drop from secret to confidential did little to reduce friction among the Army, Navy, and Norden. Over the next three years Maj. Gen. Frank Andrews, commanding general of the General Headquarters Air Force, regularly accused Norden, Barth, and BuOrd of obstructing his efforts to integrate the Norden bombsight into Air Corps operations. Barth just as regularly accused Wright Field engineers of transferring Norden technology to the Sperry Corporation. Andrews believed Barth's policies had created a "know nothing" mentality among Materiel Division personnel, fearing they would be transferred or fired if they learned anything about the Norden bombsight.[5]

Army airmen, under attack for security leaks, bitterly challenged the Navy's policy of allowing Carl Norden to spend months in Switzerland working on bombsight-related projects. The Army secretly used Lt. Col. Herbert A. Dargue to spy on Norden's activities in Europe. Dargue disliked the lack of security, but admitted the Navy-Norden procedure of using American diplomatic pouches to transport drawings and correspondence worked "very satisfactorily."[6]

On occasion the Navy tried to restrict Norden, but "Old Man Dynamite" refused to budge. He needed the tranquility of Switzerland to do his work. Anything of value, Norden claimed, was in his head. As war in Europe threatened, the Army urged the Federal Bureau of Investigation to assign agents to follow Norden. Chief of the Air Corps Henry Arnold and FBI director J. Edgar Hoover were also concerned for Norden's continuing Dutch citizenship. The FBI investigation showed that Norden believed the United States was the only country "deserving his invention and the only country which he felt would use it with judgment and discretion."[7]

A series of public revelations in 1939 proved embarrassing. *Time* magazine carried a story about the sinking of the HMS *Ark Royal* and asserted that the American Army had a bombsight that would allow it to sink such ships from altitudes above 18,000 feet. *Collier's* reported that the Army's bombsight was the envy of the world, produced in a small factory in the east run by two civilian engineers. *Collier's* also claimed that the Japanese had recently requested a quotation on this company's bombsights in lots of 500.[8]

In 1940 both services received a momentary scare from an Englishman identified as Capt. E. W. Percival, who contacted the Air Corps about purchasing a Norden bombsight. He claimed the Germans had stolen one and transported it to Germany on the last trip of the steamship *Bremen*. Percival wanted a Norden bombsight so that England could prepare defenses against it. Enlisting the FBI again, the Air Corps inventoried its bombsights and demanded signed affidavits from bombsight equipment officers. No Nordens were missing.[9]

Carl Norden provided his own security scare in May 1940. He left New York aboard the USS *George Washington* intent on a trip to Switzerland to concentrate on an antiaircraft artillery fire-control system for the Navy and to be with his family in Zurich. The Army, fearing that the British might attempt to remove him from the ship at Gibraltar, requested intercession at the highest level. President Roosevelt ordered the FBI to assign an agent to act as a "chaperon to Norden, [and] serve as protection." Norden similarly worried that the British might try to detain him "permanently" and asked Adm. Harold R. Stark, the chief of naval operations, to send an American destroyer to Lisbon to transport him to Genoa, avoiding Gibraltar.[10]

The root of the problem was a Navy interception of a British wire identifying Norden as a "dangerous individual, destitute, and friendly with the Nazi Government in Germany." Norden, an Anglophobe, feared "those damn Britishers" might "execute" him. At Gibraltar on May 10 the British indeed intercepted him, but the intervention of the American consul prevented a crisis in Anglo-American relations. The British apologized for the incident, claiming Norden was not the man for whom they searched. Discovering that the Germans had invaded France on May 10, Norden wired his family in Zurich to meet him at Genoa, ordering them to destroy all of his papers and drawings before departing. Reunited with his family, Norden and his FBI escort left for New York on the *George Washington* on May 19.[11]

This incident spurred the Navy to increase security. FBI agents began examining the company's overseas mail for evidence of espionage. In June 1940 Naval Intelligence asked the FBI to plant an undercover agent at the Norden factory to check on the loyalties of the many Norden employees of German and Italian ancestry. FBI sources suggested that Germany knew the secrets of the Norden bombsight, though Norden and Barth insisted it did not. After seven months on the job, the agent uncovered no indications of espionage, but established a network of "twenty-six confidential informants and two sources of information" in the plant. He reported that assembly at Norden was so carefully supervised and so widely distributed and fragmented that espionage or sabotage would have been difficult. The

FBI withdrew its agent on May 16, 1941, most of his reports having dealt with union activities, not espionage.[12]

Germany had already acquired plans to the bombsight through the activities of Hermann Lang, who had begun working for Norden as a mechanic and draftsman in 1936. In July 1940 the FBI learned that the German Abwehr spy agency had contacted Lang and ordered him back to Germany to complete the basic plans he had stolen earlier. FBI activities included placing an agent in the apartment under Lang's but failed to uncover sufficient evidence to arrest him for espionage. The FBI prevented Lang from receiving a passport for a planned escape to Mexico, while deploying a double agent to gather evidence for prosecution. In June 1941 the FBI arrested Lang, Sperry engineer and designer Everett M. Roeder, and thirty-one others in the Kurt F. Ludwig spy network. The government charged Lang with conspiracy to transmit documents relating to the national defense of the United States. Seventeen of the conspirators pleaded guilty, including Roeder, damaging Lang's defense. Lang and fifteen others went on trial at the Brooklyn U.S. District Court on September 3, 1941.[13]

Court testimony revealed that drawings of the Norden bombsight had been in German hands since 1938, carried to Germany by Lang, in return for $1,500 in cash and an additional RM 10,000 deposited in a German bank account. The key witness for the government was double-agent William C. Sebold, who produced a film recording of several meetings between Lang and himself. Ludwig's network planned to steal or buy a Sperry bombsight, but not the Norden bombsight, because "they already had that."[14]

Federal Judge Mortimer W. Byers imposed 310 years of sentences on the thirty-three defendants convicted of violating the Espionage Act in January 1942. Lang's sentence was eighteen years in a federal penitentiary for espionage and two years for failing to register as a foreign agent. In response to pleas for clemency, Judge Byers said, "He of all men knew to what use it might be put by the chivalrous powers of the Axis in waging their war against civilization."[15]

Another embarrassing revelation came from Wythe Williams of the Mutual Broadcasting System in 1940. Soviet agents had stolen a Norden bombsight, he reported, but, unable to manufacture it in their "poorly equipped factories," had shipped the device to the German Zeiss Works in Jena in compliance with the Hitler-Stalin Pact. Williams also claimed that the United States had passed the sight, its most critical military technology, to the British. Chief of Staff George Marshall sent Brig. Gen. Sherman Miles to question Williams on the story. His source had been an informant claiming to be in contact with a German officer in Berlin. No Nordens were missing.[16]

The Navy-Norden prohibition against Army contacts with Carl L. Norden, Inc., violated section 10(l) of the Air Corps Act of 1926 that "the manufacturing plant, and books, of any contractor for furnishing or constructing aircraft, aircraft parts, or aeronautical accessories, for the War Department or the Navy Department . . . shall at all times be subject to inspection and audit by any person designated by the head of any executive department of the Government." The Navy argued that unrestricted access would cause chaos, waste Norden's time, "embarrass" the Navy, and threaten secrecy. That unrestricted Army access might also reveal the Navy's less-than-legal arrangement with Norden went unsaid. BuOrd's chief bombsight officer warned the Navy that "unless we . . . convince the Air Corps that their needs are fairly considered and met, I believe they will carry a fight for direct dealings with Norden to higher authority." Assistant Secretary of War for Air Robert A. Lovett requested fair consideration, but Undersecretary of the Navy James Forrestal refused. The Navy, he said, paid for the bombsight, needed it, and believed the company should not have to deal with more than one department of government.[17]

The Navy also fought against Air Corps efforts to modify the Norden bombsight. Of all the changes made to the basic Norden design, for only one, automatic flight control through the bombsight, did the Navy provide unrestricted support. Eliminating the human factor in piloting the aircraft over the target promised to make the most accurate bombsight in the world even more accurate.

By 1933 the Sperry Company had replaced the mechanical linkages of the younger Elmer A. Sperry's A-1 autopilot with hydraulic hoses and the electrical gyroscopes with rotors driven by air. The momentary lag that was typical of hydraulic drives made the new A-2 autopilot perfect for commercial passenger-carrying aircraft, but less than perfect as a precision bombing device.[18] Sperry also produced an A-3 autopilot in the late 1930s, similar to the A-2, but smaller, lighter, and with a magnetic compass for maintaining a magnetic heading. The A-2 and the A-3 could not be used with the Norden bombsight without the penalty of extra weight, complexity, and cost because the Sperry autopilot employed air-driven gyroscopes while the Norden bombsight used electrically driven gyroscopes and because the Norden bombsight provided directional signals incompatible with Sperry autopilots.[19]

The Air Corps and Sperry had taken the lead in autopilot development, but the Navy and Norden were at the front of bombsight development. Distrust between the two sides prevented any cooperation to merge the two technologies. The Air Corps therefore worked to link Sperry bombsights and autopilots through the Sperry Gyroscope Company and one of its engineers. Mortimer F. Bates's 1926 bombsight and his bombsight-autopilot combination of 1929 were the first successes of the Army program. The device

> distinguishes from all previous arrangements wherein the bomber operated an indicator near the pilot of the craft to indicate to the latter the desired direction, and the pilot then steered the craft accordingly. By this invention the pilot is relieved of the duty of steering the craft during the time of sighting and alignment on the target, and the alignment is accomplished more quickly and more effectively.

Although Bates's bombsight was inferior to the Norden Mark XV, he had pioneered the incorporation of the autopilot into the bombing process.[20]

The Navy's program grew out of a visit of BuOrd's Lt. Arnold J. Isbell to Wright Field in February 1932 to examine the Army's D-7, L-1, and C-4 bombsights. He discovered the Army was working to link the Sperry A-1 autopilot and the General Electric automatic steering control to bombsights, based on Bates's design. BuOrd received Isbell's report on Wright Field's work and Lt. Cdr. Malcolm F. Schoeffel immediately contacted Carl Norden about developing what the Navy called the stabilized bombing approach equipment, or SBAE, to improve the accuracy of the Norden Mark XV bombsight.[21] Sperry patents already covered aspects of autopilots and bombsight-autopilot combinations, restricting Norden's options. Because Sperry and the Army had given up on the A-1 autopilot with its mechanical linkages in favor of the A-2's hydraulics, Norden had free rein to install mechanical linkages in his SBAE. Fortuitously strong-willed Carl Norden had a predilection for the quicker and more accurate responses of mechanical devices.[22]

Norden pursued "automatic flight control in connection with bombing approaches" as a private venture because the Navy had no available funds. In December 1933 he received $5,000 for the development of one prototype, the patent for which would go to the government. Carl Norden at this time perceived the device as a joint SBAE/autopilot, to be used for bombing and for general navigation. Lt. Cdr. Forrest P. Sherman, BuOrd's head of Aviation Ordnance, told Norden on August 11, 1933, that "in order to keep Bureau cognizance straight on this feature, we will probably have to justify the contract on a basis of improved bombing accuracy and leave the sea-going navigational value more or less to be read between the lines for the present."[23]

Carl Norden again isolated himself in Switzerland to work on the SBAE while his business partner, Ted Barth, strove to head off the Army's rush to buy Sperry autopilots. Barth wrote his contact in the Air Corps, Col. Herbert Dargue, in charge of instruction at the Air Corps Tactical School, expressing the hope that the Air Corps would await the completion of the Norden SBAE because it would be the "simplest, and the most complete system ever developed." Capable of reducing errors in bombing by one-third and the length of the bombing run from 50 to 20 seconds, Barth claimed, he felt it would be a duplication of effort for the Air Corps to equip its aircraft with Sperry autopilots and Norden SBAEs when the latter also could serve as an autopilot.[24]

Barth should have talked to his partner, who was purposefully avoiding work on an automatic pilot under BuOrd direction. In 1935 BuOrd changed its policy and suggested to Norden that at some point in the future he might modify his SBAE to allow its use as an autopilot for long-range navigation. By then it was too late. Carl Norden was a man who saw suggestions as criticisms. An engineer of single-minded purpose, he dismissed BuOrd's proposal in typical fashion: "The trouble with your ideas is that they are primarily intended to relieve the pilot while with mine, that feature is merely incidental, for I am only concerned with *precision* flight regardless of weather conditions and *only* for the purpose of improving bombsight performance" by "stabilizing the flight of the airplane." The intent was clear: "It may be that it will prove to have value in connection with blind flying or long distance overseas flying but it has been developed primarily as ordnance equipment for the purpose of improving bombing accuracy."[25]

Norden delivered his SBAE to the Navy on February 14, 1935, after three years of work, warning BuOrd that his experimental prototype had problems. Proposals to fix them, however, "would probably run afoul of a bunch of Sperry patents, which, as you know, cover a wide range of claims including the law of gravity and centrifugal force." Norden could not use "electrically operated oil valves" (hydraulics) because of Sperry patents on the A-2 autopilot and because he disliked the slow action they provided.[26]

Tests at the Dahlgren Proving Ground showed "that the Norden equipment . . . is at least the equal of if not superior to the Sperry gyro-pilot," especially the quality of its gyroscopes, though it was not as simple to operate. Norden's SBAE still had trouble controlling the rudder—the same problem that had vexed Elmer Sperry Jr. Barth and Naval Testing Ground personnel could not get the proportional banking/roll feature to function, but BuOrd's bombsight officer, Lt. Cdr. Forrest Sherman, ordered Dahlgren to ignore these problems and press on. Bombing tests proved a 30 percent improvement in the Mark XV's accuracy with the SBAE in smooth air, 39 percent in bumpy air. In very rough air Dahlgren bombardiers had not released bombs manually for fear of the bombs landing outside the target area. With the SBAE, they not only bombed, but achieved accuracy close to what an aircraft under manual control had achieved in smooth air.[27]

Although it lacked the means for maintaining a steady altitude and was too complex and too heavy (126 pounds), production nevertheless began in late 1936, entering service in 1938. Installed with the Mark XV Mod. 2 bombsight, the Norden bombing system weighed 178 pounds. Barth filed for patent protection in April 1940. As with his bombsight, Carl Norden's penchant for anonymity kept his name off the patent. Barth again assigned the classified patent to the United States of America as represented by the secretary of the Navy. The Navy did not declassify the SBAE until 1947 and the U.S. Patent Office did not award a patent to Barth on the device until October 25, 1949.[28]

The SBAE operated with two gyroscopes. Deviations in roll, yaw, and pitch moved the gyroscopes' cardans or frames, fixed to the aircraft, while the axis of the azimuth gyroscope remained horizontal and the axis of the flight gyroscope remained vertical. This movement established an electrical contact, starting rudder, aileron, and elevator servomotors. Pulleys mounted on the centrally located servomotors pulled long wire cables connected to the aircraft's control surfaces until the gyroscopes precessed back to their horizontal or vertical positions.

As a bombing device, the SBAE transferred any adjustment of the bombsight's controls through mechanical linkages to the azimuth gyroscope, establishing the electrical currents necessary to initiate the ailerons and rudder, allowing the bombardier to fly the aircraft in roll and yaw. No connection between the bombsight and the flight gyroscope was necessary because the bombardier did not alter the pitch of the aircraft, which was automatically kept in level flight by the flight gyroscope.

To encourage the services to buy the SBAE, then undergoing tests, Norden offered the Air Corps and the Navy the option of buying future SBAEs for the 153 Norden Mark XV bombsights then under order for $2,400 each. BuOrd agreed to the option in June 1935, despite reports from Dahlgren questioning the device's complexity, failure to operate the rudder properly, defective proportional banking feature, ruggedness, and dependability. By the time BuOrd allowed the Air Corps to test the SBAE, the option had run out and the Air Corps had to pay more than $3,000 per SBAE. Norden completed two production models in late 1936, one for the Army and one for the Navy, but BuOrd decided to keep both for Navy use, concluding that it was not in the Navy's interests "to let the Air Corps have one of the production models."[29] After production began in June 1937 at a rate of seven to ten per month, BuOrd agreed to release one for Army testing. Ted Barth decided, however, that the action would interfere with production for the Navy and the Army's first acquisition was postponed for another year.[30]

Security restrictions interfered with incorporation of the SBAE into Air Corps use as they did with the Norden bombsight. The Navy classified not only the device but the name "SBAE" confidential, interfering with such everyday Air Corps activities as advertising for bids on aircraft. To escape these restrictions, the Air Corps adopted the unclassified name "automatic flight control equipment" (AFCE) when referring to the Navy SBAE. It took the Navy four years to accept the Air Corps' argument that security restrictions were inhibiting aircraft manufacturing plans. In April 1941 the Navy reluctantly downgraded the SBAE from confidential to restricted. An observer could only wonder if both services were serving the same country.[31]

By 1937 Wright Field's efforts to connect the Norden bombsight with the Sperry A-2 autopilot had gone nowhere. Efforts to connect Sperry bombsights to the Sperry A-2 autopilot were more successful, but left the Air Corps with inferior bombsights. The Air Corps had little choice but to go with the Norden SBAE, to decrease bombing errors, decrease the length of bombing runs, allow the bombardier to undertake evasive maneuvers to the target, and reduce the training required for novice bombardiers. It also had to continue to purchase Sperry autopilots because of the SBAE's inadequacies in directional control and because of the jarring ride the SBAE's mechanical linkages provided. The first SBAE-equipped Norden Mark XV bombsight appeared on an Air Corps aircraft (the B-18 bomber), also equipped with a Sperry A-2 autopilot, in June 1938.[32]

Adding 126 pounds of SBAE to allow an aircraft to serve as a bomber was wasteful and inefficient when the autopilot could perform the same functions as the SBAE, though perhaps not as effectively.[33] Even Navy units complained. Patrol Squadrons 7 and 43 built their own adapters to allow the Sperry autopilot to be used with the Norden bombsight, though the commander of the Aircraft Scouting Force expressed concern that bombing accuracy would deteriorate if the Sperry autopilot replaced the Norden SBAE. Patrol Wing One wanted the Sperry autopilot because it was more rugged and reliable, less expensive (in 1940, $3,000 compared to $4,200 for the Norden SBAE), more amenable to quantity production, lighter by 50 pounds, created no security problem, and required less maintenance.[34]

BuAer ruled that twin-engine patrol aircraft only had room for one and they would get the SBAE. Four-engine aircraft could carry both and would get both. Chief of Naval Operations Stark ordered the fleet to use the SBAE, asserting that the "effectiveness of the SBAE is solely a matter of *proper adjustment* and *intelligent use.*" Dictums from on high could not correct the problems users experienced, however. The Navy had temporarily solved the problem by deciding to do nothing.[35]

The Army could not equivocate. It needed an autopilot that could serve both functions. Every pound of extra equipment meant one less pound of explosives in Air Corps bombers. Operational units and Wright Field engineers spoke with one voice in their dislike for the Norden SBAE. The complaints were constant: the SBAE caused skidding in turns, gave a ride too rough for the crews, and failed to work effectively at high altitudes and at low speeds. The SBAE's "very high" maintenance and training requirements caused nightmares among Air Corps planners. Requests that the Navy and Norden modify it to meet Air Corps needs went unanswered, largely because "Old Man Dynamite," according to BuOrd's Cdr. Malcolm Schoeffel, would never agree to change it.[36]

One problem with the SBAE proved unsolvable and insured the Air Corps would pursue a replacement. Norden had designed the SBAE with long steel cables connecting servomotor drums to aircraft control surfaces. Cables could experience a 140-degree drop in temperature at altitudes above 20,000 feet, where 60 degrees below zero was common, resulting in a complete loss of tension and, therefore, control. The temperature inside an aircraft could also vary, with cables in the wings being cooler than cables inside the cabin. The differing thermal expansion of aluminum, the main metal component of aircraft, and steel, from which the cables were constructed, caused additional tension problems.[37]

Three years of work by Wright Field's Special Design Unit of the Aircraft Laboratory failed to solve the tension problem. This, plus BuOrd and Norden's refusal to pursue a solution, forced the Air Corps' hand. On January 6, 1940, it formally informed the Navy that it intended to replace the Norden SBAE with a new Sperry A-5 AFCE, to be designed with electrical controls, servomotors located near the aircraft's control surfaces, and electrically operated gyroscopes compatible with the Norden bombsight. Although the project proved a failure,[38] it pressured the Navy into action. In December 1940 BuAer ordered the Naval Aircraft Factory in Philadelphia to create a "highest priority" device that would allow the Norden bombsight to be connected to the ubiquitous Sperry A-3 autopilot. The Naval Aircraft Factory had a prototype adapter ready and installed in an XPBY-1 test-bed aircraft at Dahlgren two weeks later. Weighing 35 pounds, it provided a savings of 91 pounds for an aircraft that formerly had to carry both the SBAE and Sperry autopilot.[39]

Dahlgren finished testing of the Naval Aircraft Factory adapter in April 1941, but could not make it work. Sperry designed its autopilots to receive direction instructions by rate signal, while Norden designed its bombsights to send direction instructions to the SBAE by displacement signal. BuOrd again tried to scuttle the project, claiming that the results did "not indicate the need to replace the Norden SBAE with the Sperry automatic pilot at this time," but in a major policy reversal decided not to object to the adapter. The Naval Aircraft Factory in Philadelphia solved the signals problem and reported excellent results from the revised adapter, though a human pilot had to control the ailerons because of the absence of a proportional banking feature. Dahlgren completed bombing tests in late August 1941 and the Naval Aircraft Factory began construction of forty adapters for service testing in September, completed in December, at approximately $750 each.[40]

In January 1942 BuAer recommended to the chief of naval operations that the SBAE be eliminated in favor of the A-3 autopilot and Naval Aircraft Factory adapter, judging the SBAE "superfluous." BuOrd disagreed but did not block the measure. The Bureau of Supplies and Accounts notified Norden in May 1942 that all remaining SBAE contracts would be for skeletonized units only, still needed to connect the Norden bombsight to the new Naval Aircraft Factory adapter and Sperry A-3 autopilot. The complete Norden SBAE served into 1944, however, because of A-3 shortages.[41]

While the Navy pursued the Naval Aircraft Factory's adapter, the Air Corps sought a different solution. Carl Norden, "adamantly a mechanical engineer," refused to consider electronic components to correct the SBAE. In mid-1941 the Army Air Forces asked the Minneapolis-Honeywell Regulator Company of Minneapolis to design a new AFCE with electronic parts to link the A-3 autopilot and the Norden bombsight without the need for the Naval Aircraft Factory's mechanical-electrical adapter. In a rush to complete the project, engineers removed the gyroscope from a Norden SBAE and installed it in a reworked A-3 autopilot, replacing the hydraulic units with electrical drive. Wright Field found the results sufficiently impressive ("installed easily, turned perfectly, useful for both bombing and navigation, and didn't require large numbers of skilled personnel") to order preparations for mass production of the hybrid system in October 1941, designated the C-1.[42]

Wright Field ordered 9,000 AFCEs equipped with Minneapolis-Honeywell electronics in May 1942. The C-1 became the standard bomber autopilot/AFCE/SBAE for the remainder of World War II, consisting of Minneapolis-Honeywell's new electronic adapter combined with the flight gyroscope and stabilizer of the Norden SBAE—what the services called a "skeletonized SBAE."[43] It had at least three other advantages over the Norden SBAE. Norden had designed his SBAE with motors having a maximum pull of 350 pounds. The Army Air Forces's larger bombers, including the B-29, B-32, and B-36, needed 600 pounds of pull to move their rudders—a power built into the C-1. Its electronic components operated much faster than the mechanical components of the Norden, providing up to 300 flight corrections per minute. Finally, its electrical cables connecting the central unit to the servomotors at the control surfaces were less vulnerable to enemy fire than the SBAE's long cables. More than a few bomber crews owed their lives to pilots able to fly their aircraft home by the C-1's controls after their regular aircraft control cables had been shot out.[44]

BuOrd was not finished with its obstructionism. Robbins and Meyers, a subcontractor to Carl L. Norden, Inc., and a significant beneficiary of Navy contracts, filed a complaint with the Army-Navy Munitions Board, reporting that it already had sufficient facilities to meet the Army's C-1 needs. The Army Air Forces told the board that it had evidence that the complaint originated at BuOrd, which wanted all production of the Norden bombsight and associated SBAE/AFCEs to be under Navy control. In the end the Army Air Forces retained the "right to take all of the Minneapolis-Honeywell production regardless of Navy commitments if and when it should be necessary." Turnabout must have been fair play.[45]

BuOrd's actions had delayed the C-1's development and hindered the initial bombing efforts of the Army Air Forces. Only a crash development program and the emergency transport of Minneapolis-Honeywell technicians and advanced bombardier instructors to England allowed the C-1 to enter the air war on May 18, 1943, for a mission to Vegesack. A technological revolution was underway during World War II, marking a shift from mechanical to electronic equipment. Carl Norden represented the best of the mechanical world, but rejected the new electronic engineering.[46]

The SBAE/AFCE imbroglio was one of several points of contention between the Army and Navy in preparing bomb-aiming equipment. The Air Corps needed an improved Norden Mark XV bombsight. New Army four-engine bombers flew at twice the speed and altitude of the Navy aircraft for which the Norden bombsight had been designed. Only a major redesign would allow its use up to 300 MPH and 30,000 feet. The Air Corps wanted a glide bombing attachment (GBA) to allow changes in altitude during the bombing run to confuse antiaircraft artillery gunners; an automatic erection system (AES) that would automatically level the bombsight's gyroscopes instead of forcing the bombardier to level them manually using bubble levels; a low-altitude bombing attachment (LABA) for bombing runs below the standard minimum altitude for the Norden bombsight; an improved stabilization system to allow greater evasive maneuvers during the bombing run; an increase in voltage from 12, the Navy standard, to 24, the Air Corps standard; and a change from direct to alternating current.[47] These requests created six additional opportunities for strife between the Army and Navy.

The Navy was de-emphasizing the technique of dropping bombs on maneuvering ships from high-altitude horizontal flight and saw no need for expensive improvements that would interfere with Carl Norden's other projects for the Navy. Although Norden believed the GBA and AES were possible, BuOrd informed the Army that development would be at the expense of bombsight production.[48] That Norden went ahead with the requested improvements was testimony to the tenacity of Air Corps officers, especially Henry Arnold. When the Army asked for more sensitive altimeters, air speed indicators, thermometers, and especially an electrically operated automatic bomb release assembly, the Navy responded with delays and obstructions. Not until February 1937, five years after the Army first requested changes, did the two services agree to consolidate performance requirements.

Barth's plan was to make only minor adjustments to the Norden bombsight, what Barth called "band aids," while Carl Norden worked on a "Universal Bombsight," Navy designation Mark XVII, that would meet all Army needs. Norden never completed his "Universal Bombsight," leaving improvements in the accuracy of daylight precision strategic bombing to come from band-aids for the Norden Mark XV.[49]

The first band-aid was the Mark XV Mod. 2 (Navy)/M-4 (Army) Norden bombsight with a new pilot direction indicator and two attachments not completed in time: the LABA and the SBAE/AFCE. The Mod. 3/M-5 had an improved tachometer. Norden added improved optics (increasing magnification from 1.4× to 3× for altitudes up to 30,000 feet), and improved forward vision for low altitudes to the Mod. 4/M-6 model, raising the unit cost to $6,010, up from $4,993 for the Mod. 3/M-5 version. The SBAE/AFCE added $3,890 to the cost.[50]

The next improvement was the Mod. 5/M-7, the last Navy model. With the GBA, LABA, and AES, the Mod. 5/M-7 was the most complicated Norden bombsight ever built. The LABA allowed greater disc speeds for low-altitude bomb deliveries.[51] After two years of development and two and one-half years of testing and modification, Carl Norden produced the add-on LABA too late to be included on the Mod. 2/M-4 as planned. Production of the LABA-equipped Mod. 5/M-7 began in 1938 at the increased price of $7,100, $10,990 with the SBAE. Navy units reported the attachment to be "additional gear and served no useful purpose." In 1941 Chief of Naval Operations Adm. Harold Stark declared the LABA not practical for use, but BuOrd continued production because it had no other bombsights for use at low altitudes.[52]

The Air Corps used the LABA because it had no other "means for readily indicating to the bombardier a solution of dropping angles" for low-altitude bombing. By 1942 Wright Field had modified the Type E-6B computer, essentially a circular slide rule, to allow it to calculate dropping angles for low-altitude missions, making Norden's LABA superfluous. The Materiel Division requested it deleted at a "considerable savings of material and skilled labor." BuOrd notified all concerned that it had stopped production of the LABA on December 16, 1942, by which time Norden had completed 3,797 attachments.[53]

The AES had a similar history. The Norden bombsight required the bombardier to level the stabilizer gyroscope manually—no small task under combat conditions. Most Army Air Forces units called it "bubble chasing" or "chasing the bubble." Fifteenth Air Force called it "bubble, bubble, toil and trouble," and the Navy called it "the curse of the Mark XV bombsight." A good level eliminated the need to make large corrections during the bomb run; a bad level required a prolonged straight and level bomb run under enemy fire. The Air Corps insisted on the AES because Sperry had successfully built such a capability into its bombsights, beginning with the N-1.

Carl Norden completed his AES in mid-1938 for the Mod. 4/M-6 Norden bombsight. Testing and modification took two years, by which time the Navy had redesignated it the Mod. 5/M-7, the first Norden bombsight to operate on 24 volts. The Army and Navy procured 16,725 of the Mod. 5/M-7, the first wartime version of the Norden bombsight. Service use revealed Norden's AES too delicate and complicated and in August 1942 BuOrd stopped production.[54]

Still wanting a solution to "bubble chasing," the Army Air Forces pursued development of an AES with the Minneapolis-Honeywell Regulator Company of Minneapolis, Delco Products of Dayton, Alcon Specialties Company of Locust Valley on Long Island, and the Victor Adding Machine Company of Chicago. Renamed the automatic gyro leveling device (AGLD) to avoid conflict with Norden and BuOrd, none proved effective.[55]

Carl Norden completed his design for the GBA in February 1941, but admitted that it increased the bombsight's inherent errors because of the difficulty of accurate altitude determination. Tests at Dahlgren and Wright Field proved him wrong, though the GBA had a maximum ceiling of 15,000 feet, well below the 20,000 feet that the British experience in Europe dictated for safety from antiaircraft fire. Pearl Harbor interrupted development, but the services ordered it included on Mod. 5/M-7s previously ordered. The GBA added $2,500 to the price of the Norden Mark 15 (the Navy switched to Arabic numbers in World War II) bombsight, nearly 60 percent of the price of the original Norden Mark XV. An Army-Navy disagreement over the maximum altitude of the GBA delayed production until August 1943, when reports from Europe on the effectiveness of German antiaircraft fire forced a compromise.[56]

The production-model GBA allowed glides of up to 150 feet per second and climbs up to 45 feet per second at altitudes up to 20,000 feet. Norden completed only 107 units before Arnold froze procurement until Carl Norden could modify the GBA to work up to 25,000 feet. Production began again in August 1944, but the GBA did not appear in sufficient numbers to have a significant impact before the end of the war.[57]

Combat conditions caused other problems with the Norden bombsight, including congealed lubricating oils caused by the extreme temperatures found at high altitudes. A General Electric–designed heating cover and improved lubricants solved the problem. Low temperatures and clear air at high altitudes also intensified a problem known as "bombardier's eye," caused by rough air banging the Norden's hard rubber eyepiece against the bombardier's eye socket and by harsh glare from the sun. B. F. Goodrich of Akron, Ohio, manufactured a soft "free resisting" neoprene eyepiece and various firms produced treated optics to reduce glare.[58]

The last models of the Norden bombsight, the M-9, M-9A, and M-9B, included increased trail (M-9A) and disc speed (M-9B) for bombing up to 50,000 feet and over 400 MPH, and a "trail spotting device which permits the dropping of bombs 30 mils short of or over the target." The M-9 was the only Norden bombsight designed primarily by non-Norden sources. Continued advances in technology caused the Army to ask in July 1941 for increased performance in a new Norden. Norden and the Navy claimed to be too busy with other projects "to consider any additional developments of the Mark 15 bombsight at this time." Using its own production facilities, the Army deleted the AES and incorporated an external X-1 reflex sight for the M-9B, manufactured by the W. L. Maxon Corporation of New York, to allow quick approaches and facilitate target acquisition at high altitudes. Coated optics improved bombing under low light conditions. The reflex optics involved adding an uncovered, movable plate glass reflector. A light bulb projected a reticle for sighting on this glass, tilted by the range mechanism of the bombsight in the same manner as the prism of the standard bombsight.[59]

Combined with several flight instruments, the Norden bombsight created the world's most accurate bombing system. Especially critical to its success were the intervalometer and salvo switch. The intervalometer was a device for achieving train bombing, the release of bombs at precise intervals with a single sighting operation. Bombardiers used intervalometers against area targets and "against precision targets to obtain a higher probability of getting a hit on a single attack." In operation the intervalometer was a simple electrical timer that opened the bomb shackles at timed intervals. The standard intervalometer until 1943 was the B-2A and after 1943 the AN-B-3, produced primarily by the J. P. Seeburg and P. R. Malloy companies, capable of twenty-one settings between one-twentieth and one-half a second. On the B-17 Flying Fortress these devices allowed the bombardier to drop up to fifty bombs, at ground speeds from 100 to 500 MPH. Ground intervals could be from 7 to 750 feet.

More important, because many wartime missions required carpet bombing or the instantaneous release of all bombs, these intervalometers had salvo switches to achieve a concentrated pattern on the ground. The A-2 salvo switch was mechanical-electrical and the A-4 all-electrical. On the B-17 and B-29 bombers these switches were on the control panel next to the bombardier. On the B-24 the salvo switch was on a panel behind the bombardier, as part of the control stand containing a handle for opening the bomb-bay doors. These salvo-switch arrangements eased the task of B-17 and B-29 crews in dropping at the formation leader's direction, but caused some difficulty for B-24 crews.

Before procurement, however, all other problems were minor difficulties. The Navy had promised to share production equally, but instead satisfied its own requirements before sending any to the Army. Because the Navy and Norden refused to establish a definite procurement schedule, the Army never knew when to expect a bombsight delivery. Before the war Martin B-10B bomber production surged ahead of bombsight production, leaving the chief of the Air Corps pessimistic: "It is the opinion of this Headquarters that it is improbable that a satisfactory solution will ever be accomplished." By March 1937 the Air Corps had 200 bombers without bombsights.[60]

Norden's manufacturing process was inadequate for Air Corps and Navy needs in the 1930s, but struck a careful balance between his Old World craftsmanship and the demands of a military preparing for war. The order for 242 Mark XVs in 1938 was a harbinger of production requirements that would dwarf even the most radical estimates. Carl Norden withdrew from "all active participation as an officer" and sold his stock, preferring employment as a consulting engineer. Barth was then free to expand the facility on Lafayette Street and adopt mass-production techniques based on interchangeable parts to keep up with demand. To produce components for the Norden bombsight, he convinced a long-time friend, Paul Berger, to move Berger's Manufacturers Machine and Tool Company to the seventeenth floor of the 80 Lafayette Street building. Barth's company also contracted with the Robbins and Meyers Company of Springfield, Ohio, and International Projector Corporation of New

York for additional parts. By 1940 Manufacturers Machine and Tool Company produced about 60 percent of the parts for the bombsight and its stabilizer, with Robbins and Meyers and International Projector producing the other 40 percent. Norden workers produced no parts, but did subassembly on the sixth floor and final assembly on the sixteenth at 80 Lafayette Street, adding the third and fourth floors to expand production in February 1941.[61]

Production remained snail-like in the eyes of Air Corps Chief Arnold, despite the changes. One year before American entry into the war, with Allied fortunes at a nadir, the Norden plant still closed for holidays and every weekend, operating on a peacetime schedule of five days a week, 8:00 to 5:30. Not until February 1941 did it consider extending the work week. That month it also granted raises to most employees, not to encourage increased production, but to forestall union activity. Accuracy still counted more than speed of manufacture.[62]

The chief of the Materiel Division at Wright Field summed up the Air Corps' frustrations with the Navy-Norden arrangement: "The procurement situation, boiled down, amounts to the fact that the Navy takes Air Corps money and delivers a bombsight which may or may not be satisfactory to the Air Corps at such time as it is convenient for the Navy to deliver same."[63] Prompted by the SBAE snafu, Maj. Gen. Frank Andrews, commanding general of GHQAF, threatened to go to the secretary of war, or higher if necessary, to get a meeting with Norden to present the Army's case and "break down the wall of secrecy around the Norden Company." BuOrd reluctantly agreed to a meeting on July 29, 1937. Andrews represented the Air Corps, supported by four colonels, two lieutenant colonels, and a major. Barth and Norden attended for Carl L. Norden, Inc. BuOrd expressed its disregard for the proceedings, sending only Cdr. Malcolm Schoeffel. Andrews identified the many technologies the Air Corps was making available to the Navy, including aircraft engines, automatic gun turrets, fire control systems, aircraft, and navigation equipment. Other than the Norden bombsight, he argued, the Navy was giving the Army nothing in return. The Air Corps wanted modifications to the Norden bombsight allowing greater speeds, glide bombing, and higher and lower altitudes; greater access to Carl L. Norden, Inc.; complete design information; and the SBAE. Lt. Col. Oliver Echols, chief of the Materiel Division, expressed disbelief that the Navy, "by means unknown to me," could contract for Norden bombsights without advertising for bids—actions the War Department would not allow.

Barth criticized the Air Corps for failing to participate in the development of the SBAE, for not ordering enough bombsights, for wasting $1 million of the taxpayers' money on Sperry bombsights, and for "peddling" Sperry's bombsights abroad.[64] Echols blamed Congress for the lack of funds to buy bombsights and Navy and Norden obstruction and secrecy for the SBAE situation. Carl Norden limited his comments to assurances to the Air Corps that he was modifying the Mark XV to meet Air Corps needs. BuOrd's Schoeffel opposed any attempts to improve the Mark XV Mod. 1 bombsight, believing it to be perfect for Navy needs, but promised that the Navy would "assure an adequate supply for both services in an emergency." Andrews had to accept what Norden and BuOrd offered, because they were the Air Corps' sole source of bombsights at the time.[65]

Brig. Gen. Henry Arnold, acting chief of the Air Corps, expressed the bottom line to the chief of the Materiel Division: "The M-1 sight still appears to be superior to any other now available." The only way to get the Navy or Norden to increase production would be to declare a national emergency. Like it or not, the Army was stuck with the Navy and Norden. A lack of funds forced the Air Corps to halt all other bombsight projects and limit procurement to Norden bombsights.[66]

When Germany invaded Poland on September 1, 1939, Norden had just started production of the new Mark XV Mod. 4. One day later BuOrd Chief Rear Adm. William R. Furlong called Ted Barth and ordered him to increase the level of production immediately. Unfortunately it was too late. The Navy had eighty Mod. 4s on order and the Army 469, and it would be months before these prewar orders were ready. In Norden's defense, it made little economic sense to expand production to hundreds of bombsights per month when the company had orders for only 549. The Phony War in Europe after the conquest of Poland encouraged BuOrd to drop production from a planned 120 per month to 100 per month.[67]

Germany's invasion of France in May 1940 exposed this lack of preparation, especially after Roosevelt announced his 50,000-aircraft plan. Brig. Gen. George Brett, chief of the Materiel Division, notified BuOrd that the Air Corps would need 316 bombsight/SBAE combinations in 1941, 3,645 in 1942, 5,000 in 1943, and 5,115 in 1944, plus 10 percent in spares and parts each year. Brett recommended that BuOrd establish new plants in more secure locations. This BuOrd refused to do, but Norden agreed to raise production back to 120 per month. Two months later Barth agreed to increase production to 400 per month, but only after BuOrd provided a letter of intent to purchase 4,800 bombsights.[68]

As war raged in Europe and the Pacific, a shortage of machine tools, caused by America's rearmament effort, thwarted BuOrd and Norden expansion plans. Barth blamed the Army for failing to provide his company with adequate orders to justify expanding productive capacity. BuOrd blamed Barth's "complacency," dictatorial air, and poor management. The Air Corps blamed Barth and BuOrd. In March 1941 BuOrd took charge and forced an expansion program, intended eventually to produce 800 bombsights and SBAEs per month. This included $8,525,000 for a new U.S. Naval Ordnance Plant at Indianapolis, to begin production in September 1942. The Army thanked the Navy for its efforts, but pointed out that it needed 4,513 M-7 bombsights. Production would lag behind needs until April 1942 if the Navy's expansion worked according to plans. In April 1941 the Army exacerbated the problem with an order for 5,420 additional sights and 5,185 SBAEs, making the Navy's expansion plans inadequate until March 1943.[69]

BuOrd contracted with Carl L. Norden, Inc., to operate the Indianapolis plant when completed. Barth and Norden organized a subsidiary holding company, the Lukas-Harold Corporation (Lukas was Carl Norden's middle name, Harold was Ted Barth's), as primary contractor. The plant became operational in May 1942. Carl L. Norden, Inc., for its part, rented four new floors for tools and machinery and one new floor for assembly at 80 Lafayette Street. Lukas-Harold occupied an additional floor, until the Indianapolis plant was ready for production, giving Norden a total of nine floors. The Navy also contracted with Remington Rand, Inc., to produce Norden bombsights at the new "N" Division bombsight factory at Elmira, New York. The Navy spent $1,902,903 to finance the expansion of Robbins and Myers to produce 800 SBAE subsystems per month. Finally, International Projector Corporation of New York prepared to construct low-altitude bombing attachments, SBAE sector panels, and subcomponents. Total Navy investment in manufacturing facilities for the Norden bombsight and the SBAE during the war came to $34 million.[70]

It would not be enough. The Army Air Forces was beginning the largest buildup in the nation's history and the promise of thousands of bombers pouring off assembly lines without bombsights threatened to derail the effort. The United States was the leading capitalist democracy in the world between the two world wars, with strong traditions of competition; of open government "of the people, by the people, for the people"; and of soldiers in service to the nation. By 1939 this nation led the world in bombsight development, the product of a government contract not open to competitive bidding, behind a wall of official secrecy designed in part to protect the patent rights of its developer, from the fertile mind of a Dutch citizen. In 1941 this nation went to war with a bombsight program under the direction of a department of the U.S. government not operating in the best interests of the United States, for another department of the U.S. government not acting in the best interests of the United States. The history of the bombsight/SBAE development program in the United States between the two world wars was fraught with secrecy, interservice rivalry, waste, and self-serving motives that spoke poorly of the officers and men assigned the responsibility of administering it.

8

Procurement for War

The Japanese attack on Pearl Harbor laid bare America's lack of preparation for the mass production of bombsights. Eleven days later the Army Air Forces notified the Navy of its new bombsight requirements. According to Navy production estimates there would be a cumulative shortage of over 3,000 bombsights for the Army Air Forces by June 1943 (see Table 8.1). The lack of that 50-pound assemblage of screws, bolts, gears, springs, and assorted parts threatened to derail the Army Air Forces's strategy for winning World War II. For the want of a nail . . .

Assistant Chief of the Materiel Division Brig. Gen. George C. Kenney did not mince words: "It is believed that continuance of the present Army-Navy policy relative to the manufacture of bombsights by the C. L. Norden Company is injurious to the interests of National Defense." As evidence of Navy-Norden negligence, he cited the Air Corps' request for price quotations on 319 bombsights submitted on January 30, 1939. The Navy returned the quotation on May 8. Eight days later the Army ordered the sights, but BuOrd failed to present the contract to Norden until August 13, 1939, eight months after initiation. Kenney refuted Norden's defense that it could not expand production because of the lack of contracts.

Table 8.1. Army Air Forces Bombsight Procurement Requirements and
Navy Planned Production (set on December 13, 1941)

Period	AAF Requirements	Planned Production for Army	Shortage
1941			
December	730	381	349
1942			
January	498	200	298
February	533	270	263
March	609	370	239
April	685	365	320
May	645	360	285
June	576	350	226
July	436	300	136
August	300	300	0
September	349	300	49
October	469	300	169
November	440	375	65
December	527	416	111
1943			
January	608	430	178
February	642	465	177
March	667	505	162
April	626	525	101
May	640	575	65

Source: Production Engineering Section to Chief of Army Air Corps Forces, December 13,
1941, and BuOrd to Chief of Air Corps, December 23, 1941, Folder—Norden, File 471.63,
Box 1893, RD-2451.

As funds became available, in 1941 the Army ordered 4,065 bombsights
on March 5, 520 on March 14, 273 on May 21, 4,513 on July 23, 2,374 on
September 4, 80 on December 12, 664 on December 18, and 1,405 on
January 1, 1942.[1]

Surging production of lend-lease bombers for America's allies and medium bombers for the Army Air Forces left the Materiel Division desperate for bombsights. The Norden production shortage plus the Navy's refusal to allow Allied nations access to the Norden bombsight forced it to
contract with the Gaertner Scientific Corporation of Chicago for eighty
redesigned Estoppey D-4s. Lacking a pilot direction indicator and an
AFCE (automatic flight control equipment) link, the D-4B proved inadequate for modern aircraft. Gaertner modified it to handle faster speeds and

higher altitudes and the Army Air Forces contracted with the National Cash Register Company of Dayton, Ohio, to manufacture 15,000 of the newly designated D-8s at $200 each immediately after Pearl Harbor. In head-to-head tests the D-8 achieved three hits out of fifty bombs dropped, compared to forty-eight out of fifty for the Norden bombsight. With production running at 2,000 per month, but aware of its limitations, the Army Air Forces ordered it installed only "in airplanes for which no other sight is available."[2]

The British-designed Mark XIV (T-1 in American use) was another interim bombsight. Developed by the Royal Air Force, the stabilized vector sight minimized bombardier adjustments and allowed evasive action during the bombing run. The *New York Times* called it a "shotgun" sight, as opposed to the American Norden "rifle" sight. The Royal Air Force sought Mark XIV manufacturing support from Canada and the United States and asked that the Army Air Forces equip all lend-lease aircraft destined for Great Britain with American-built Mark XIVs. AC Spark Plug Division of General Motors, Flint, Michigan, began production in May 1942 and by war's end had manufactured 23,000. The Mark XIV/T-1 equipped British Wellingtons, Lancasters, Mosquitoes, and Halifaxes and American B-25s, B-26s, B-17s, B-24s, PBYs, and A-20s in British use.[3]

The D-8 and T-1 bombsights were stopgap solutions. Unable to meet Army Air Forces needs, the Navy finally but only momentarily agreed to allow the Army to seek its own sources for Norden bombsight production at a Washington meeting on January 8, 1942. Navy Secretary Frank Knox certified the agreement in a letter to Secretary of War Henry Stimson on January 18, 1942, and promised to divide Navy production with the Army on a 50/50 basis. BuOrd withdrew its permission on February 24, 1942, however, fearing that competition for scarce resources would create chaos. Mindful of Norden and Barth's opposition, and wanting to maintain control over all production, the Navy met with Army Air Forces and Norden representatives to hammer out an arrangement on February 27, 1942. Wright Field would continue to submit all requests to BuOrd, which would place orders with Carl L. Norden, Inc. Norden would then farm out the contracts. The Cardanic Corporation, a Norden subsidiary, would handle Army Air Forces orders, produce bombsights for the Army Air Forces, and act as a communication channel between the Army Air Forces and Norden. The Army Air Forces would also seek its own source for bombsight production, coordinated through Cardanic. Meanwhile, General Arnold ordered an allocation program to provide the best equipment

Table 8.2. Army Air Forces Bombsight and Autopilot Allocation Program
(January 31, 1942)

Aircraft	Bombsight	Autopilot
B-17E and B-17F	Nordens	AFCEs
B-29	Nordens	AFCEs
A-26	Nordens	AFCEs
B-26, 139 B-26A, and 791 B-26B	Nordens	AFCEs
Remaining B-26s	50% Nordens	100% AFCEs
B-25B	Nordens	AFCEs
B-25C	71 Nordens, 1,254 D-8s	71 AFCEs, 1,254 A-3s
B-25D	200 Nordens, 1,000 D-8s	200 AFCEs, 1,000 A-3s
B-28	Nordens	AFCEs
F-3	Nordens	AFCEs
AT-11	50% Nordens, 50% no bombsight	50% AFCEs, 50% no autopilot
AT-13	None	None
B-24	Sperry S-1s	A-5s
B-32	Sperry S-1s	A-5s
B-33	Sperry S-1s	A-5s
B-35	Sperry S-1s	A-5s
AT-15	Sperry S-1s	A-5s
All others	D-8s	None

Source: Assistant Chief of Material Division to Chief of Materiel Division, January 31, 1942, File 471.63, Folder—Bomb Sights, Box 2893, RD-2885, RG342.

for bombers assigned the most critical missions. American lend-lease bombers for Great Britain would get the Mark XIV/T-1, the Soviets the D-8 (see Table 8.2).[4]

Norden's Cardanic Corporation, named after the cardan ring around a gyroscope, allowed the Army Air Forces more direct contacts with Norden, while keeping it at the arm's length Norden and BuOrd wanted. The Army Air Forces negotiated all technical and engineering matters with Cardanic, while all contracts went through BuOrd. Plans called for Cardanic to set up an assembly line and produce 700 bombsights, AFCEs, and glide bombing attachments per month beginning in February 1943. The February 27, 1942, agreement also allowed the Army Air Forces to seek an independent source of Norden bombsights, coordinated through Cardanic. Wright Field representatives contracted for the Burroughs Adding Machine Company of Detroit to produce 1,000 Norden bombsights per month at approximately $5,000 each as a Cardanic subcontractor. Problems in collecting the necessary machinery delayed production until late 1942, despite the intervention of Gen. William S. Knudsen of the War Production Board. Once production began, the unit price exceeded $7,000.[5]

Because Burroughs had more machines and a trained workforce, it received priority over Cardanic in starting production. Mismanagement and Norden's weak commitment to its subsidiary caused the War Production Board to judge the Cardanic situation "well nigh hopeless" in April 1943. Cardanic had fewer than one-third of the machines it needed for meeting production goals and operated only one shift of 100 workers. Worse, the management had not yet placed orders for many machines it needed. According to an Army Air Forces investigative team, the president of the Cardanic Corporation had never even visited his bombsight plant. It was supposed to represent Army Air Forces's interests, but when Cardanic contracted with Robbins and Myers for 1,000 bombsight stabilizers and 2,500 servomotor sets, BuOrd canceled the order. The Navy would allow the Army Air Forces and Cardanic only what was left over after Robbins and Myers had satisfied Navy contracts.[6]

In May 1943 the Army Air Forces decided that "Cardanic's usefulness in the present picture is purely that of being a vehicle through which engineering information, designs, and subcontracting on certain facilities is made easier." Cardanic had served as little more than a paper corporation responsible for diverting Army Air Forces complaints and for providing technical representatives to help units in combat zones. In the summer of 1943 the Army transferred the Burroughs plant to Navy control and disbanded Cardanic under orders from the War Production Board to eliminate excess facilities.[7]

The Army Air Forces continued searching for an independent manufacturer capable of producing Norden bombsights for the Army free of BuOrd obstruction. After investigating four other companies,[8] the Army selected the Victor Adding Machine Company of Chicago, with plans to begin production in November 1942. Victor, the Navy complained, would interfere with production by competing with Norden for parts, but the Army Air Forces refused to back down. The Navy also claimed that Army production plans for Burroughs and Victor, 5,700 per month, were in excess of needs, especially because Norden had set up additional production lines at 50 Varick Street in New York, Lukas-Harold in Indianapolis, and Remington Rand in Elmira, New York.[9]

The development of the Minneapolis-Honeywell C-1 automatic pilot had freed the Army Air Forces from Navy-Norden control, but still required Norden to produce the flight gyroscopes and stabilizers ("skeletonized AFCEs") needed by the C-1. The Navy tried to take over C-1 AFCE production, arguing before the Army-Navy Munitions Board that Minneapolis-Honeywell's effort duplicated work and facilities the Navy already possessed for SBAE manufacture. Learning from a decade of experience with BuOrd and Norden to defend its use of independent manufacturers of AFCEs, Wright Field allowed the Navy to talk directly to Minneapolis-Honeywell. "All Army Air Forces requirements," however, would be "met first, and the Army Air Forces reserve the right to take all of the Minneapolis-Honeywell production regardless of Navy commitments if and when it should be necessary."[10]

BuOrd was too busy expanding Norden production to do much about the AFCE situation. In addition to the six companies involved in assembling bombsights, it had to coordinate three dozen additional firms producing parts and components, including everything from wire, ball bearings, washers, screws, and cotter pins to commutators, resistors, and Alemite fittings. The Norden bombsight, born of construction by Old World craftsmen to destroy the industrial fabrics of enemy nations, became itself the product of the American mass-production industrial fabric.[11]

Despite this impressive expansion, Army Air Forces's frustration with the Navy's handling of Norden bombsight production grew. Airmen generally accepted BuOrd's explanations of sluggish expansion, but could not accept the Navy's continued hogging of available production. At a meeting with the Navy on November 11, 1942, the Army Air Forces presented two major complaints. First, the Army was using every Norden it could get on a daily basis, while the Navy was putting its Nordens on the shelf as spares. Second, inconsistent deliveries were playing havoc with aircraft delivery schedules. If BuOrd told the Army Air Forces to expect 250 bombsights in one month, then Wright Field ordered that many bombers for that month. When the Navy then delivered 400 bombsights, the effect was to cause the Army to lose 150 aircraft. The Navy representative at the meeting replied that additional production would not be possible until the Army placed more orders. Army Air Forces representatives argued that they had ordered more than 10,000 in 1942, but were scheduled to receive only 4,473 in 1943 and the remainder in 1944. One protested, "We've got boys all out all over the world right now without any true precision bombsights in their planes and they've got this damn D-8 sight that I would just as soon have a couple of nails and a wire." The Navy representative ended the meeting with a flippant answer to Army objections: "We just thought we were being good to you."[12]

Chief of Naval Operations Ernest J. King inflamed matters in late November 1942, notifying the Army that the Navy intended to break Secretary of Navy Knox's 50/50 production-split promise of January 1942. King justified his actions on the grounds that the Army had other bombsights it could use, while the Navy had only the Norden bombsight. Secretary of War Stimson wrote Knox and Army Chief of Staff George C. Marshall wrote King that the Navy had never lived up to the agreement and that planned allocations to the Army were insufficient to meet minimum needs. Arnold, tired of Navy obstruction, presented the issue to the Joint Aircraft Committee. One week later BuOrd requested that the committee stop its consideration of the matter, promising to expand production and increase allocations to the Army Air Forces. In Arnold's view, correct as it turned out, the Navy was not using the Norden bombsight and yet was gobbling up a major share of production. Twenty percent of these ended up on naval depot shelves as spares while Army Air Forces bombers flew into combat with lesser bombsights. A Navy reliant on dive bombing was keeping 54 percent of the bombsights designed for horizontal bombing, leaving Arnold with only half an air force (see Table 8.3).[13]

Arnold went back to the Joint Aircraft Committee in September 1943, intent on demanding that the Army Air Forces take over all M-series bombsight production. He backed off only on the advice of his top procurement man, Maj. Gen. Oliver P. Echols, who told him that legal and personnel problems would probably delay production. Before the Joint Aircraft Committee could take action, the Navy again promised increased production and allocations to the Army.[14]

Plant expansion promised an adequate supply in the future, but production bottlenecks dimmed short-term prospects. A shortage of machine tools and difficulty with Norden specifications kept Lukas-Harold, Victor, Cardanic, Remington Rand, and Burroughs from getting into production on time. In early 1942 optical lenses were in short supply. In early 1943 a shortage of precision antifriction ball bearings froze assembly lines.[15] To allow mass production, Barth purchased more ball bearings than needed, to be picked through to find the right fit, rather than fine-machining and hand-polishing each ball bearing to insure the right fit, as in the 1930s. This simple change in procedure eliminated a time-consuming step and was critical to meeting the Army Air Forces's growing appetite for Norden

Table 8.3. Navy Production Plans for the Norden Bombsight (as of January 30, 1943)

| Period | Total Production | Allocation | |
		Navy	Army
1943			
January	575	245	330
February	625	212	413
March	700	494	206
April	830	540	290
May	910	602	308
June	1,008	652	356
July	1,240	635	605
August	1,520	669	851
September	1,630	724	906
October	1,800	733	1,067
November	1,800	707	1,093
December	1,800	689	1,111
1944			
January	1,800	651	1,149
February	1,267	694	573
March	1,200	721	479
April	972	761	211
May	600	463	137
June	600	253	347
July	600	600	—
August	600	600	—
September	562	562	—
Unscheduled	175	175	—
Total	22,814	12,382	10,432

Source: "Schedule of Bombsight Procurement," January 30, 1943, File 202.2-35, HRA.

bombsights, but at the cost of a ball-bearing shortage. The only source for precision ball bearings was the Atlas Ball Bearing Company of SKF Industries, New York City, which was overwhelmed with orders in 1942. Norden and Barth established the Barden Precision Bearing Company (named from the first three letters of Barth's last name and the last three of Norden's) in Danbury, Connecticut, but the shortage continued until April 1943.[16]

The Army Air Forces pursued an additional source of bearings for its Victor bombsight factory through the New Departure Division of General Motors, Bristol, Connecticut. In a repetition of the obstruction Wright

Field met at every stage of bombsight procurement, SKF refused to discuss specifications with General Motors without BuOrd's permission. BuOrd delayed two months before approving the transfer of manufacturing data. SKF then provided inadequate information, making initial New Departure production unsatisfactory. The Army Air Forces had to order Victor to produce its bombsights with greater tolerances than stated in Norden specifications to allow it to use New Departure Division bearings. Greater tolerances had a negative impact on the inherent accuracy of Victor-produced Norden bombsights. By mid-1943 Barden and SKF production, including a new SKF plant at Gwynnedd, Pennsylvania, overcame the shortage.[17]

One year after Pearl Harbor the Army Air Forces faced a bleak situation. In the first year of war American industry had produced only 6,900 Norden bombsights, of which 75 percent had gone to the Navy. Too many Army bombers were flying without precision bombsights. As a stopgap measure the Army Air Forces accelerated the procurement of the Sperry S-1 bombsight, development of which Wright Field had stopped in the 1930s as a cost-cutting measure. In 1936 Maj. Gen. Frank Andrews, commanding general of GHQAF, wrote Acting Chief of the Air Corps Brig. Gen. Henry Arnold to request the Air Corps attempt to develop and acquire Sperry bombsights as a solution to continuing problems with Norden-Navy production. The Air Corps saw Sperry as a means to force Norden to "move it" with the increased production of bombsights modified to fit Air Corps needs. According to the chief of the Materiel Division, Brig. Gen. Augustine W. Robins, the intent was to create another source of bombsight supply to force Norden to cut costs, make improvements to the M-series bombsight, and increase production, even if the Army had to make "some concessions" as to quality.[18]

Ted Barth saw the Air Corps' decision as a threat that would "tend to undermine confidence as well as interest in the M-1 [Norden] sight" though Sperry bombsights were "inferior . . . as to accuracy but also as to tactical value." The S-1 would be a new bombsight, but Barth believed any Sperry design to be little more than a "slightly modified L-1 with perhaps a different coat of paint." Barth sought the assistance of his old friend, Air Corps colonel Herbert Dargue, to fight off the Sperry challenge and get "Air Corps Bombardment Activities on a clean, wholesome basis . . . through the use of the best available equipment, the maximum proficiency and efficiency in the art of bombing."[19]

So desperate was the Air Corps that it ordered 295 S-1s at $20,000 each in 1940 before Sperry had delivered prototypes for testing. Derived from the Sperry N-1 and O-1 bombsights, the S-1 was a gyroscopically stabilized synchronous bombsight with an associated Sperry A-5 AFCE. The chief of the Production Engineering Section at Wright Field predicted that if tests were successful, "it is likely that the shift to exclusive use of the Sperry bombsight and pilot equipment on all future bombardment type aircraft . . . will be made."[20] Needing bombsights and frustrated with the slow pace of Norden production, Wright Field ordered 930 additional S-1s in January 1941 for $5 million and 105 in July 1941 for free in exchange for twenty N-1s and fifty-nine O-1s in storage.[21] The Army Air Forces went ahead with Sperry production despite tests revealing optical vibrations and sensitivity to power fluctuations, critical in a bomber with power turrets.

In June 1941 the Air Corps authorized Sperry to construct a 186,000-square-meter factory at Great Neck, New York, to manufacture 5,500 S-1s plus spares for $45 million. Because Sperry was occupied with other military projects, Wright Field arranged in 1942 for International Business Machines of Endicott, New York, to manufacture 3,725 S-1s and for National Cash Register of Dayton, Ohio, to manufacture 6,000 S-1s—contracts worth $33 million and $49 million respectively. It also contracted with Sperry, AC Spark Plug of Flint, Michigan, and Electric Auto-Lite of Toledo, Ohio, to build nearly 36,000 A-5 automatic pilots to serve as AFCEs to the S-1. The contracted price varied from $16,000 to $18,000 for each S-1/A-5 combination.[22]

The S-1 left a mixed record after two years of use in training and combat units. Training units liked the S-1 because its automatic erection system (AES) relieved bombardier students of the need to level the bombsight.[23] Combat units found the S-1 bombsight/A-5 AFCE combination never worked properly. After an examination of Norden production and a comparison of all data on the Norden M-series and the Sperry S-1, an Army Air Forces Board of Officers recommended in September 1943 the standardization of the M-series bombsight and cancellation of all Sperry S-1/A-5 combination contracts. The board found the Norden superior in accuracy, more dependable, and "far superior" in operational design. Arnold approved and the Army Air Forces so notified Sperry in November 1943, after having invested over $100 million in S-1 production.[24] When production ended in February 1944, contractors had produced 5,563 S-1/A-5 combinations, installed primarily in B-24 Liberator bombers. Sperry

S-1s helped fill the gap left by the Norden production predicament, but complicated maintenance, inferior accuracy, and supply concerns left it the bombsight of second choice. When America went to war, the Norden bombsight was a known quantity and tested in hundreds of thousands of bombings—the S-1 was not.[25]

Norden production began to catch up with demand by late 1943, but declining quality resulting from the mass-production techniques adopted for the Norden bombsight in wartime threatened to become a scandal. In December Wright Field tested 200 M-9 model Norden bombsights produced by Norden, Remington Rand, Burroughs, Lukas-Harold, and Victor, finding "them to be inferior to those sights which were being produced about two years ago." The Army Air Forces asked for a conference with BuOrd and Norden to discuss the problem, but Norden engineers dismissed Wright Field representatives with a curt "there are only two ways to produce bombsights, the Norden way and the wrong way." The Army Air Forces believed the biggest problem was the "incomplete, inaccurate and obsolete" engineering data Norden provided to the other plants, which forced, for example, the recall of the first 600 sights produced at Victor. Col. R. E. Jarman, technical executive of the Armament Laboratory at Wright Field, concluded: "I have been in this Norden-Navy-Army Air Forces scramble for the past three years, and as a result of this last trip, insofar as I am concerned, if I never enter the Norden factory again and deal with their high executive personnel, it will be too soon."[26]

Quality did not improve. In late 1944 Wright Field was still reporting 75 to 80 percent of all bombsights did not meet specifications. The average inherent error of the 1944 Norden bombsights was 14 mils, considerably over the 2.5 mils called for in Navy specifications. In operation this difference meant missing a target from 20,000 feet by 50 feet with a bombsight meeting specifications, compared to 280 feet with a 1944 bombsight. Materiel Division testing showed Norden-produced bombsights remained the best, with Burroughs second, and sights from Remington Rand, Lukas-Harold, and Victor the worst. Wright Field concluded that the Norden bombsights produced in 1944 were "not sufficiently accurate to hit the pickle barrel."[27]

Greater manufacturing tolerances and resulting inaccuracy, however, meant expanded production. The break-even point came in April 1944, when U.S. Strategic Air Forces in Europe notified Wright Field that it had a large inventory of bombsights and therefore wanted the next 1,000 replacement heavy bombers sent to Europe without Norden bombsights, with only one bombsight for every two bombers after that. Ninth Air Force began sending its B-26s on missions with only six Norden bombsights for every eighteen aircraft to save weight.[28]

Another sign that the production crisis was over was the decision to allow the shipment of Norden bombsights to Allied countries. Thousands of American bombers went to Great Britain and other Allied nations under the Lend-Lease Act of 1941, but the Navy opposed any release "of this country's most prized possessions" to foreign nations for security reasons. The Navy claimed "the Norden bombsight is superior to the best bombsight available to the unfriendly nations in the ratio of 5 to 2 . . . and is considered to be the principal single factor of superiority which the air forces of this country possess over those of potential enemy countries." But when the Norden bombsight became "compromised because of loss in action," the Navy decided in January 1942 that Allied nations except for the Soviet Union could buy Norden bombsights. Two months later the secretary of the Navy altered the policy to exclude purchases until after production had met American needs, delaying foreign sales until 1944. By then shipments to the Soviet Union were also authorized. With the exception of confidential transfers to the Soviet Union, no foreign governments placed orders for the Norden bombsight.[29]

Almost as production caught up with demand, overproduction became a problem. In June 1944 the Army Air Forces concluded that production facilities were in "excess of requirements," canceled 2,375 bombsights on order from the Navy, and reduced production at Victor from 500 to 250 per month. Which of five plants to reduce or eliminate first would be the next struggle. The Army Air Forces was in no mood to return to the BuOrd-Norden monopoly situation. The chief of the Materiel Division declared "this reduction will not be made at the expense of wholly controlled Army facilities."[30] Although Remington Rand closed its assembly line on October 1, 1944,[31] and Burroughs on December 31, 1944, production was still twice the number needed. AFCE/SBAE production exceeded demand in November 1943.[32]

With Norden bombsights plentiful, the Navy finally admitted it had little use for high-altitude horizontal bombing in a Navy wedded to dive bombing. In July 1944 the Pacific Fleet authorized its torpedo bomber squadrons to remove their Norden bombsights, maintaining in reserve only one per three aircraft. BuOrd stopped equipping replacement aircraft

Table 8.4 Comparative Costs of Bombsights and SBAE Combinations

Model	Year	Bombsight	SBAE	Total
Estoppey D-4	1926	$ 286	None	$ 286
Norden XI	1929	4,500	None	4,500
Norden XV-1	1934	4,275	None	4,275
Norden XV-1	1934	4,725	$2,375	7,100
Norden XV-2	1934	5,145	2,375	7,520
Norden XV-3	1937	4,993	2,375	7,368
Norden XV-4	1939	5,845	3,560	9,405
Sperry O-1	1939	9,480	None	9,480
Norden M-6	1940	6,442	3,992	10,434
Sperry S-1	1942	8,103	9,426	17,529
Norden M-9	1944	8,800	3,559	12,359

with Norden bombsights. In March 1945 Chief of Naval Operations Adm. Ernest J. King ordered all horizontal bombing training terminated and the removal of Norden bombsights from all aircraft except multiengined photographic aircraft (PB4Y) and VT (torpedo) Squadrons 17 and 83. All units were to return their Navy Mark XV Mod. 5 bombsights for reconditioning to Army M-9B standards and transfer to the Army.[33]

In January 1945, reacting to the shock of the Battle of the Bulge, the Army Air Forces reordered 4,000 M-9B Nordens from the Navy. Most came from Navy stocks, reworked to M-9B standards. The Navy offered the Army Air Forces directorship of the Norden facility at 80 Lafayette Street in another indication of its rejection of high-altitude horizontal bombing. The Army had its own production line at Victor and wanted nothing to do with Carl L. Norden, Inc.[34] All production ended on V-J Day.

From 1932 to the end of World War II, the Army procured 81,537 Norden bombsights, the Navy 8,353, at a cost of nearly $1.1 billion (see Table 8.4). In addition the Army produced, procured, and sold 40,723 Sperry S-1s, T-1/Mark XIVs, and Estoppey D-4Bs and D-8s (see Table 8.5). Directly in support of these devices, American industry produced 90,000 SBAE/AFCEs, 35,000 glide bombing attachments, 55,000 bombsight disc speed tachometers, 3,500 rotor speed tachometers, 52,000 pilot direction indicators, 9,000 reflex sight kits, 16,000 low-altitude attachments, 10,500 tangent scale kits, 15,500 formation sticks, and 1,000 rate end computers. It was a prodigious, expensive, controversial, and dilatory achievement, re-

Table 8.5. Service Production of Bombsights

Item	AAF	Navy
Mark XV Mod. 1/M-1, 2, 3	100	179
Mark XV Mod. 2/M-4	81	72
Mark XV Mod. 3/M-5	82	102
Mark XV Mod. 4/M-6	469	80
Mark 15 Mod. 5/M-7	8,805	7,920
M-9	27,500	—
M-9A	1,500	—
M-9B	43,000	—
Norden total	81,537	8,353
Sperry S-1	5,563	—
T-1/Mark XIV	23,000	—
Estoppey D-4B	2,080	—
Estoppey D-8	10,080	—
Other total	40,723	
Total	122,260	8,353

sulting in an Army-Navy imbroglio kept from public eyes by security restrictions.

For the Army Air Forces the issue had been simple. It had built an air force based on a doctrine dependent on the Norden bombsight and yet was unable to procure the necessary numbers to fight a war because of Navy and Norden obstruction and covetousness. Wright Field believed "in every incident of improved design in this equipment, including both the basic bombsight and related automatic flight control equipment, design modifications essential to the Army Air Forces's use of the equipment have been obtained from sources other than the C. L. Norden Company," though Norden and the Navy still controlled production and distribution. For the Navy, the issue was not simple. It had to confront shortages of precision ball bearings, stringent inspection standards, challenges to security, and the thankless task of producing bombsights for the Army. Not until after the war did the Navy admit that it had not really needed the Norden bombsight: "Naval missions were not suited for the use of high altitude horizontal bombing techniques—the only type of attack for which the Norden Bombsight was useful." Nevertheless, the Navy felt robbed by the general perception of the American public that the Norden bombsight was an Army achievement. BuOrd claimed it was "a natural irritant to the service which had fostered its development since the end of World War I, then guided the half-billion dollar procurement program through World War II." As Army Air Forces colonel J. T. Murtha Jr. said concerning Navy bombsight policies, "We're both working for the same Government; we're both fighting the same war." Perhaps. Perhaps not.[35]

9

The Young Men behind Plexiglas

The Norden Mark 15/M-series bombsight may have been a marvel of precision mechanical engineering, but without well-trained bombardiers it was but an expensive gadget. Before the war, hundreds of regular Army bombardiers trained at the leisure of peacetime, but the coming of war demanded the quick conversion of thousands of civilians to combat-ready bombardiers.

Prewar training relied primarily on individual study. Bombardiers read all the available information on the bombsight they were using, studied the bomb ballistic tables, and then "went out and practiced bombing." Until July 1940, each bombing group was responsible for training its own bombardiers, who came primarily from the ranks of enlisted men. The Air Corps also held annual bombing and gunnery matches at Langley Field to encourage greater proficiency. Harold L. George, an originator of the doctrine of daylight precision strategic bombing, won the first of the annual matches in 1924. Bombardiers dropped bombs from 300, 5,000, and 8,000 feet. With improved bombsights and training, the average circular error dropped as low as 150 feet in 1931.[1]

Regulations required each bombardier to drop twelve bombs from 5,000 feet and twelve from 8,000 feet in proficiency training. Training

Table 9.1. Anticipated Bombardier Requirements

Number of Groups	Number of Bombardiers Required
25	1,093
41	1,800
54	2,500
84	5,590
115	11,016
224	14,000
273	19,400

Source: "Individual Training of Bombardiers," AAF Historical Study No. 5, May 1944, File 101-5, HRA.

Regulation 440-40 of 1929 allowed crews to drop a sighting bomb to check for bombsight leveling, altitude settings, disk speed, wind, and other variables before beginning official bombing for record, though a revised regulation prohibited such aids in 1935. General Headquarters Air Force (GHQAF) pushed the high-altitude drops to 15,000 feet in 1936, but limited fuel and aircraft forced units to drop most practice bombs between 8,000 and 12,000 feet. Targets were generally circles marked on the ground in the middle of wide-open bombing ranges, though the Air Corps did simulate attacks on industries, bridges, locks, and cities.[2]

The outbreak of war in Europe in September 1939 encouraged Chief of the Air Corps Henry H. Arnold to establish a 16-week program in bombardier training at Lowry Field, Denver, to meet anticipated needs (see Table 9.1). Arnold clashed with Maj. Gen. Delos C. Emmons, commanding general of GHQAF, over which office would bear responsibility for this training, delaying Lowry's opening by nine months. In July 1940 Arnold, with the support of Chief of Staff George C. Marshall, assumed responsibility for the bombardier training program and pushed ahead with Lowry training. He appointed Fred L. Anderson, who would later lead American bombers against Germany, commander of the school. The first class consisted of pilot-training washouts, with eighteen graduating in October 1940. Fifty-two in November 1940 and fifty in January 1941 followed, before all began a 10-week "service test class" to prepare them as bombardier instructors for the thousands of civilians then beginning to pour into the Air Corps' training program.[3]

In 1941 Arnold expanded the successful Lowry program to Barksdale Field, Louisiana, and Ellington Field, Texas. Arnold's decisions to use the first three classes of Lowry graduates as instructors for bombardier schools and to increase the 10-week instructor course to 12 weeks in March 1941 delayed progress, but set the basis for future expansion of the program. By the end of 1941 these schools had graduated only 206 bombardiers, far short of the 1,367 planned and the 8,100 needed. The first Lowry class trained for combat bombing was not ready until May 3, 1941.[4]

The expanding Air Corps, Army Air Forces after June 1941, needed Ellington and Barksdale fields for bombardment group training and formation. In December 1941 and February 1942 it therefore opened fields at Albuquerque, New Mexico, and Midland, Texas, for bombardier training. Arnold's 30,000-pilot program called for 5,590 bombardiers, but the 50,000-pilot program that followed in March 1942 called for 14,000 bombardiers. By July 1942 the 70,000-pilot program raised the requirement to 22,400 bombardiers and to 24,640 soon after that.[5]

On January 23, 1942, Arnold established the Flying Training Command (FTC) to regularize this chaos. FTC opened new bombardier schools at Victorville, California, in March 1942; Roswell, New Mexico, and Higley, Arizona, in June 1942; Big Spring, Texas, San Angelo, Texas, and Hobbs, New Mexico, in September 1942; Carlsbad, New Mexico, in October 1942; Deming, New Mexico, in December 1942; and Childress, Texas, in February 1943. The Carlsbad school joined Lowry in training bombardier instructors in January 1943, but the instructor program moved to Midland in August 1943.[6]

First in a trickle, but eventually in a flood, these schools mass-produced standardized bombardiers. In 1940 there were no bombardier school graduates. In 1941 there were 224, by June 1942 a cumulative 1,407, by December 1942 4,748, and by the end of the war 52,495. The new Army Air Forces Training Command, formed on July 7, 1943, did not catch up with demand until January 1944, but by then possessed sufficient Norden bombsights and aircraft to meet training quotas. Its teacher-to-student ratio of 1:3.7 would have been the envy of any air force, especially because many of its instructors were combat veterans. By January 1945 the Army Air Forces could trim the bombardier training system to four fields: Big Spring, Carlsbad, Childress, and San Angelo.[7]

At maximum output, the average Army Air Forces training field dropped 55,000 practice bombs per month and used 2,000 rolls of film to score them. In 12 weeks these bombardiers received 32 hours of bombardment theory, 16 hours of gyroscope training, 8 hours in a ground trainer, 32 hours of instruction in bombs, 128 hours in bombsight operation, 16 hours in the operation of the automatic flight control equipment (AFCE), and 8 weeks of flying training, involving 34 missions of at least three hours' duration.[8] Training Manual 1–250 required each student to drop 188 bombs with a circular error of less than 230 feet from 12,000 feet to graduate.[9] Training dropped to 10 weeks because of war needs in January 1942 and to 9 weeks in February 1942, but by 1943 had risen to 12 weeks and 18 weeks in 1944. When it appeared in late 1944 that there would be a surplus of bombardiers for the remainder of the war, the Army Air Forces ordered a 24-week program, requiring 471 hours of ground school, 150 flying hours, and 300 practice bombings.[10]

When time permitted, bombardiers received five to six weeks of gunnery training, because combat units expected them also to be responsible for firing defensive machine guns, coordinating defensive fire, administering first aid, and managing the oxygen supply. Some also attended a ten-week "bombing through overcast" course to train for radar bombing.[11]

Entry requirements for bombardier school included a high school diploma and successful completion of the General Classification, Physics, and Mechanical Aptitude Tests, taken at one of three replacement training centers, later called preflight schools. A wartime book identified a bombardier as "cool-headed, a deft and expert mathematician, capable of split-second reactions and complete concentration." At preflight school aviation cadets received basic military instruction, including physical training, academic instruction, map reading, aircraft recognition, radio instruction, drill, and military courtesy. This program required four weeks until March 1942, nine weeks until May 1944, and then ten weeks.[12]

Training was rigorous. In five classes at Childress Army Air Field, 647 graduated from 777 entering, or an 83 percent graduation rate. The elimination rate was significantly higher than the 3 percent at the Eagle Pass advanced single-engine fighter pilot training program, though ironically pilot training washouts were a primary source for bombardiers during the war.[13]

The United States needed one bombardier for every five pilots, but only one out of eighteen cadets in training requested bombardier school. As one bombardier put it, "When you're only one of the hired hands, who's being carried along to do the dirty work, to drop the bombs and do the killing, you don't feel so good about it." The Army Air Forces always had a hard time finding volunteers for bombardier training because the lot of the bombardier in the war was not good. Sitting in the nose of a bomber, surrounded by clear plexiglas, he was the most exposed of all crewmen. Wartime statistics showed that of the positions in a heavy bomber, bombardiers experienced the greatest number of casualties.[14]

A major obstacle to efficient bombardier training was the security surrounding the Norden bombsight. Trainees spent hours both learning the proper procedures for guarding it and being indoctrinated with its capabilities. A wartime article in the *New Yorker* revealed the feelings of many young Americans exposed to America's greatest secret weapon before the appearance of the atomic bomb.

> The more I found out about the bomb sight, the more ingenious and inhuman it seemed. It was something bigger, I kept thinking, than any one man was intended to comprehend. I ended up with a conviction, which I still have, that a bombardier can't help feeling inferior to his bomb sight.[15]

Another bombardier spoke of the Norden bombsight as a

> collection of knobs and setscrews, lenses, and cross hairs. . . . It was all right, no more. But, Oh, God, it was magic. . . . This . . . is the Norden Bombsight. You will use it. You will guard its central component with your life and destroy it if your plane was hit. It is the chief secret apparatus of this government—no this nation. It will wipe out Nazi and Japanese expansionism and clean the world of dictators. In your hands, it will do miracles. From thirty thousand feet you can obliterate anything you can see. Your training has equipped you for no earthly purpose but to handle this weapon.[16]

Secrecy and such mystical views continued as obstacles to training until the secretary of war declared on November 18, 1942, an easing of security restrictions because the Norden bombsight had fallen into enemy hands. Before the war, with access to the device limited to several hundred career officers, security was mainly a matter of good paperwork. When tens of thousands of civilians rushed into bombardier and bombsight maintenance training beginning in 1940, security became a nightmare.

The Army Air Forces assigned local commanders responsibility for insuring all personnel granted access receive instruction in the importance of security. Local rules were to "insure an unusual degree of secrecy." Shipping was to be done under a code system, substituting the words "siding, latent, telescope, mickey, dusty, external, and talon" for "bombsight." If shipped by Army truck or aircraft, the bombsight and SBAE/AFCE required an armed guard. If threatened with enemy capture, the device was to be destroyed.[17]

To impress young trainees with the seriousness of security, some commanders required their charges to take a bombardier's oath.

In the presence of Almighty God, I do solemnly swear and affirm that I will accept the sacred trust placed in me by my Commander in Chief, the President of the United States of America, by whose direction I have been chosen for bombardier training.

I pledge myself to live and act according to the code of honor of the bombardiers of the Army Air Forces. I solemnly swear that I will keep inviolate the secrecy of any and all confidential information revealed to me, and in full knowledge that I am a guardian of one of my country's most priceless military assets, do further swear to protect the secrecy of the American Bombsight, if need be, with my life itself.[18]

Stateside, bombardiers in training learned the routine: trips to the bombsight vault with an armed escort, the long walk with a heavy metal bombsight box to the airplane, the metal covers and stowage boxes on the aircraft for hiding and securing the SBAE/AFCE and bombsight, and the hours spent under arms guarding the instruments on the aircraft. Not until August 29, 1942, did General Arnold retreat from the absolute commitment to security he had made to the Navy, allowing canvas covers and canvas carrying cases to be used, under the justification that the metal boxes and cases were too heavy, built of strategic materials, too bulky, and required too many keys. Security overseas was less stringent. One crewman remembered when his B-17 group landed in England, the local commander told the crews to leave their Norden bombsights lying on the edge of the runway.[19]

Regulations specified the means for destroying the bombsight to prevent its capture. "Two rounds with a .45 caliber service pistol into the rate end mechanism . . . and one round through the telescope," and (if possible) throwing it overboard were acceptable means of destruction, though manuals explaining this technique failed to consider the possibility of ricocheting bullets. Navy personnel had the Mark 15 Mod. 1 demolition unit. The Army developed a bombsight destroyer device that might have served double duty as an aircraft destroyer device, consisting of an 18-inch cylinder of steel, 5½ inches in diameter, packed with 15 pounds of magnesium and an oxygen compound. Ignited by fuse, it acted as a blow torch focused on the bombsight. Perhaps effective, it was certainly hazardous.[20]

While thousands of citizen-soldiers worked their way through the Army Air Forces's bombardier training program, with all its security checks, the American public remained largely ignorant of the Norden bombsight until 1944. In 1942, when John Steinbeck wrote his propaganda piece *Bombs Away: The Story of a Bomber Team*, he made no reference to the Norden or any specific bombsight. Later the military allowed vague references to it. Henry B. Lent, in his book *Bombardier: Tom Dixon Wins His Wings with the Bomber Command* (1944), typified the obscurant treatment the Norden bombsight received for most of the war. It was "Uncle Sam's Number One military secret," kept in a vault and only removed under armed guard. Such printed information was hardly grist for espionage.[21]

Some journalists wrote with apparent inside information or at least misinformation. Stanley Johnstone revealed in the *Chicago Sunday Tribune* in July 1941 that the Norden bombsight was a timing device connected to a Sperry automatic pilot similar to the German Lotfe 7B used over England. The secrets of the Norden's synchronous operation and of Carl Norden's SBAE/AFCE were safe. The wall of secrecy surrounding the Norden bombsight began to crack after the American entry into the war. These cracks presented no threat to national security, but they served to intensify the aura surrounding Carl Norden's invention. *Newsweek* told its readers in April 1942 that "the most discussed American military secret is undoubtedly the Norden bombsight."[22]

The Navy, with authority over security policies, did not begin to ease up on the secrecy surrounding the Norden bombsight until October 1942, when the need for production efficiency overcame security obstructions. BuOrd that month lowered the security classification of the Mark 15/M-series bombsight from confidential to restricted, including the bombsight stabilizer, the glide bombing attachment, and the low-altitude bombing attachment.[23] BuOrd still required bombardiers to destroy the equipment to prevent it from falling intact into enemy hands. Bombers had gone down in enemy territory, but officials presumed the crashes had destroyed the bombsights. On February 25, 1942, however, an Army Air Forces B-24 Liberator flying from Tobruk to Oran with personnel due leave in England ran low on fuel and landed in Spanish Morocco. The bombardier failed to destroy the aircraft's Norden bombsight. Franco's officials allowed the German consul to inspect the airplane and its contents before permitting it to leave. The secret was out.[24] Although the American military made an enormous effort to keep the secret, the German acquisition should have raised few fears. Germany would not only have great difficulty reproducing it, but would have to change its air power doctrine, its training system, and the type of aircraft its industries were producing to take advantage of the Norden bombsight.

Information began to flow more freely. *Newsweek* claimed Col. John P. Kenny, commandant of the Army Air Forces Bombardier School at Midland, Texas, first released the secret details of the Norden bombsight to John M. Mecklin of United Press International. *Stars and Stripes* told its readers that "there was no cause for alarm if the Axis captured some of the bombsights, because Axis scientists would require at least two years to duplicate the device." *Science News Letter* described the special qualifications for Norden bombardier training in April 1943. *Flying* magazine revealed in July 1943 "one of the ancient but favorite jokes" about America's high-tech wonder: "Any time now, the Army is going to start giving commissions to the bombsights and leave the bombardiers at home." *Flying*, without mentioning the Norden bombsight, also described in great detail the bombsighting problem and compared the merits of the timing and synchronous methods. Keith Ayling, in *Bombardment Aviation*, revealed that the Sperry and Norden bombsights were America's best and had to be destroyed when ditching.[25]

This secrecy extended especially to photographs. A generation of Americans could be forgiven for believing that American bombers went to war carrying canvas sacks in their plexiglas noses. Even in 1943, when the secret was out, photographs of bombardier positions still showed the bombsights covered. The public received its first look at America's most secret military device in 1944. In November Norden bombsights went on public display. Despite these revelations, the Navy did not remove its restricted classification on the Norden bombsight until May 5, 1947.[26]

Bombardiers had to learn to use the precision Norden M-series and Sperry S-1 and the nonprecision Estoppey D-8 and British T-1 bombsights, and several manual computing devices as part of their trade. Thousands of bombardier trainees found little excitement in learning to use the E-6B aerial computer (also known as the E-6B aerial "confuser") for determining ground speed, fuel consumption, altitude, and air speed; a Weems plotter for navigation; an AB computer for drift angle and drop angle; a C-2 or AN computer for altitude; a G-1 computer for air speed; a J-1 sighting angle computer to provide time of run; and free air temperature gauges, air speed indicators, altimeters, magnetic compasses, astro compasses, gyro-stabilized flux gate computers, drift meters, and radio compasses. There was nothing easy about the training process, nor about the instructor's responsibility for insuring the crew of a bomber did not waste seven hours of flying time, exposed to enemy fire, just to miss its target.[27]

FTC's aim was to produce five types of bombardiers. Of highest priority were the precision bombardiers slated for heavy bombers using Nordens and Sperrys. Next came the precision bombardiers–celestial navigators for manning B-29s. Due to the navigator shortage early in the war, General Arnold in 1940 ordered the training of a third type, bombardier-navigators, but after Pearl Harbor canceled the program, with the exception of the joint-training of crewmen for medium bombers. The fourth type were D-8 bombardier-gunners, trained for bombing and shooting from medium bombers. Finally, the training establishment turned out D-8 bombardiers-navigators, prepared for bombing and navigating on medium bombers.[28]

America's primary bombing trainer was the Beech AT-11, a version of the C-45 Expediter. Developed from the Beechcraft Model 18 commercial aircraft, the Army purchased over 5,000 of the twin-engine, all-metal monoplanes. Training for the Sperry S-1 bombsight usually occurred in the Lockheed-Vega B-34 Ventura, procured in numbers fewer than 200. A mid-wing medium bomber with twin rudders, the B-34 was a modification of the Lockheed Hudson built for the British in 1938. It was a less-than-satisfactory training platform because its engines required 100-octane fuel, expensive and scarce.

From a beginning of only seventy-six aircraft in the first three months after Pearl Harbor, the Army Air Forces by October 1942 had 3,578 students sharing 577 aircraft, a ratio of 6.2 students per aircraft. By February 1943 the ratio had dropped to 4.3. Aircraft were available, but a shortage of bombsights forced trainees to use mockups and defective bombsights to fill the gap left by bombsight production problems. The Training Division of the Air Service Command estimated its needs at 1,320 Nordens in late 1941, revised upward to 3,453 in February 1942, for deployment by May 1943. By October 1943 the Army Air Forces Training Command held 1,953 Norden bombsights, only 57 percent of needs. Almost half these were obsolescent M-1 through M-6 models. The Training Command also used 917 Sperry S-1 bombsights to supplement its training quotas, but still fell 583 sights below anticipated needs.[29]

To fill the gap in aircraft and bombsights, the Army Air Forces used large numbers of ground bombing trainers. In the 1930s the Air Corps used models built at Wright Field, but had to equip them with D-4 bombsights because Air Corps Chief Benjamin Foulois refused to use his few Norden bombsights in ground trainers. The D-4 had no pilot direction indicator or provision for an automatic pilot, limiting its usefulness. For World War II the Army Air Forces used the A-2 trainer. A pilot steered a three-wheeled, 10-foot-high, electrically driven platform in response to the trainee's signals through a pilot direction indicator. The trainee aimed his Norden bombsight at an electrically driven box on the ground, decorated with a photograph of an actual target, moving at a uniform rate. A solenoid marked the point of impact. The A-2 could simulate drift and air speeds up to 284 MPH.

The Link A-6 Bombing Trainer, which better simulated bombing missions, improved training beginning in the fall of 1944. In the A-6 a projector beamed the image of the terrain onto a mirror mounted on the ceiling of the forty-foot, silo-shaped trainer. The mirror reflected the image back to a photographic plate on the floor. Another beam of light indicated the bomb impact point based on the manipulation of the Norden bombsight. Unfortunately, it could only simulate missions to 18,000 feet, below most combat altitudes. By May 1945 the Army had 350 A-6 trainers in operation. With a unit cost of $2,800, the A-6 saved FTC $150 per hour for training a bombardier in the air.[30]

After graduation, bombardiers joined bombardment groups at one of four numbered air forces (First, Third, or Fourth, but mainly the Second) located in the United States, for crew and unit training, including formation bombing. Here the various components of a bombardment group merged to train as a team. From December 1942 to August 1945 nearly 30,000 heavy (B-17 and -24) and super-heavy (B-29) bombardment crews received such training. Bombing accuracy was generally worse than under Training Command because bombers now flew in formation. For the first six months of 1942, these units dropped 46,493 bombs. The best group, the 25th, needed four aircraft to achieve a 70 percent assurance of a hit, the worst group, the 309th, forty-three—hardly what AWPD/1 planners had anticipated. What did not vary was low altitudes for training missions. In the first six months of 1944, the four stateside numbered air forces dropped 678,190 practice bombs, but more than half were from below 10,000 feet. Bombardiers dropped only 12,000 bombs from above 20,000 feet due to shortages of aviation fuel. Accuracy as a result remained high, with B-17 units achieving mean circular errors of 282 feet and B-24 units 304 feet when adjusted to an altitude of 12,000 feet.[31]

In addition to training bombardiers in the use of the Norden bombsight and associated equipment, the Army Air Forces had to provide for three echelons of bombsight and autopilot maintenance during the war. Wartime precision bombsights and their associated automatic pilots depended on the smooth interaction and movement of gears, hydraulic cylinders, gyroscopes, and discs for accuracy. The smallest particles of dust or dirt, worn lubrication oil, or worn-out parts would have a detrimental effect on bombing accuracy. The prevailing shortage of bombsights through 1944 also meant bombing equipment had to be used repeatedly, relying on maintenance and repair rather than replacement to maintain accuracy.

First-echelon maintenance at the squadron level, done generally by bombardiers, involved preflight checks, cleaning, oiling, and simple parts replacement. More sophisticated maintenance, including calibration and replacement of most parts, came at the group level or second echelon. Each major numbered air force also had a third, depot-level maintenance program carried out by a service command. Responsible for diagnosing problems, maintaining spare parts, and everything short of manufacturing a new sight or autopilot, this echelon was generally the highest level of Army Air Forces bombsight maintenance. A fourth level of maintenance involved the factories producing the bombsights and autopilots, responsible for upgrades, remanufacturing, and spare parts.[32]

From 1928 to 1938, 140 airmen graduated from bombsight maintenance training in the Air Corps. Minimum qualifications for officer and enlisted candidates were mechanical proficiency, color vision, and until June 1943, a special security clearance. The security clearance was generally stricter than for bombardiers because of the special knowledge mechanics would have of the bombsight's operation and composition. Before 1941 a trainee had to have at least three years in service, to establish his reliability, before acceptance into bombsight maintenance training. Initially tactical units provided first- and second-echelon maintenance training, while the Norden factory held responsibility for all third- and fourth-level maintenance. In May 1936, to bring order to this process in hopes that improved maintenance would bring better accuracy, Chief of the Air Corps Maj. Gen. Oscar Westover ordered Chanute Field in Illinois to begin a formal training course of eight weeks' duration for third-echelon bombsight maintenance officers. Wright Field in Ohio assumed responsibility for training enlisted mechanics for the third echelon of maintenance. In February 1938 the Air Corps moved these courses to Lowry Field in Denver, where officers received 135 hours of specialized instruction added on to the general maintenance engineering course. Enlisted men received an expanded 12 weeks of training with the move to Lowry.

These original classes at Lowry were spartan. No textbooks existed because of security restrictions and few aircraft were available to allow maintenance trainees experience in actual bombsight operation. Tactical units complained about the quality of the maintenance personnel sent to them and continued to offer informal training to all bombsight and autopilot maintenance officers and enlisted men. While the Navy provided its personnel with four months of training, the Air Corps was providing only three months. By the beginning of World War II in Europe, the Air Corps had only seventy-five qualified bombsight repairmen. The "Augmentation Program" of 1939 required Lowry to boost its training program to twelve new graduates each month. The 1940 program called for class sizes increased to forty-eight students, training two shifts per day.

Pressures from the Norden Company changed the program even more. In May 1940 a trip by a Norden Company representative to inspect bombsight operations at Barksdale Field resulted in a scathing report to the chief of the Air Corps. Of the training maintenance men received, he said, "half of what they were taught at Lowry Field is wrong." The Air Corps responded by raising the formal maintenance program at Lowry on July 1, 1940, to 16 weeks, sending Lowry instructors to special courses at the Norden plant in New York, and inviting Norden officials to visit Lowry regularly. With war approaching, the Air Corps reduced the training program to 12 weeks later that year. Three weeks later, after protests from Norden and the Navy, it extended the course to 14 weeks, adding two weeks of training specifically for the Norden SBAE/AFCE. To produce more qualified enlisted technicians, the Air Corps also canceled officer training at the Lowry training facility for several months. When officer training was restored in March of 1941, 16 weeks of the 30-week armaments officer course were devoted to bombsight maintenance.

Training at the Norden plant in New York became an official operation in May 1940, though not without the controversy that so typified the Army-Navy-Norden relationship. For the first class the Army sent fourteen enlisted men, but the Norden Company would train but five, refusing entry to the other nine. When the Army tried to get fifteen students into the second class in September 1940, BuOrd interfered and limited the enrollment to ten. Norden wanted the course to be of three to four months' duration, while the Army insisted on six weeks. Similar to the problems facing the conversion of Norden to mass-production techniques in manufacturing, Carl Norden and his craftsmen fought against the "mass production" of bombsight maintenance.[33]

The Japanese attack on Pearl Harbor forced a complete revision of the maintenance training program. The Air Staff called for 3,480 mechanics to be trained in 1942, but later raised the quota to 4,160. Lowry went to a six-day work week, two shifts per day, to provide training for what was now a 12-week course for 110 students at a time. Yale University assumed responsibility for training additional mechanics for the first and second echelons of maintenance, while Minneapolis-Honeywell began a 28-day training program for its new C-1 automatic flight control equipment at the University of Minnesota.[34] In September 1943, because of continuing complaints about Lowry-trained mechanics, the Army Air Forces adopted an extended training program, following the course at Lowry with an eight-week internship at a bombardier school. The Navy refused to expand the training program at Norden until March 1942 and then within the year stopped all such training, claiming it interfered with plant production. The decision to discontinue Sperry S-1 bombsights and A-5 autopilots relieved pressure on the program in late 1943 and the quality of instruction increased.

Bombardier training and bombsight and autopilot maintenance training formed key components in the struggle for precision bombing during the war. Carl Norden had designed a device so complex that proper operation and maintenance had a significant impact on bombing accuracy. Ultimately the Army Air Forces training program met its goals. Bombardier and bombsight technician shortages were only temporary and combat groups did not have to reduce operations because of them. But quantity did not necessarily mean quality.

The training schools ranked their graduates at one of three levels. The highest rank was Distinguished Bombardier, signifying a graduate who had attained an average circular error in training of less than 106 feet. Next was the Master Bombardier, with an average circular error of less than 136 feet. The lowest rank was Bombardier, with a circular error of less than 185 feet. Although impressive, these achievements were for low-speed training missions with bombing runs of two minutes or more in ideal weather

163 The Young Men behind Plexiglas

against clearly marked circles surrounded by miles of open terrain. At cruising speeds in average weather with only 45-second bomb runs, the average circular errors for these three bombardier ranks rose to 172, 221, and 300 feet, respectively.[35]

A bomb landing over 200 feet from an industrial target did no damage. What results could be expected from these same bombardiers in combat conditions? Where bombing altitudes under 20,000 feet were rare? Where targets were surrounded by urban clutter and hidden by camouflage, clouds, industrial haze, and the smoke and dust of exploding bombs? Where enemy defenders used ground-fired artillery shells, air-fired machine gun bullets and cannon shells, air-fired rockets, and even aerial bombs dropped from higher altitudes?

Stateside training could do little to duplicate wartime conditions. Training flights were too short and too low. Shortages of aircraft, bombsights, equipment, and facilities were constant until the last year of the war. Shortages of oxygen and 91-octane fuel kept training flights at low altitudes. Trainees dropped bombs individually rather than in salvo. They did not fly formation bombing missions until the operational training unit stage. Training did little to prepare bombardiers for nonvisual or partially visual bombing. Some instructors had never seen combat. The AT-11 bombardier trainer could not reach the combat altitudes of heavy bombers and handled so differently through the SBAE/AFCE systems that significant retraining had to accompany any transfer to a combat unit.

For all its faults, the training program produced the most qualified personnel of any air force in the world, in larger numbers and faster. The greatest weakness of American bombsight training was in expectation, not quality, numbers, or speed. The Army Air Forces had adopted a strategic doctrine based on high-altitude daylight precision bombing, which severely complicated the training process. In too little time, men had to learn to drop bombs into "pickle barrels," to use the idiom of the time, from over four miles up and to maintain and repair the most complicated pieces of mechanical technology yet designed.

The training program's greatest weakness was the failure to reproduce warlike conditions during training. According to Curtis LeMay,

Anybody could bomb a friendly distinct white circle, there on the ground. No smog, no industrial haze, no seven-tenths cloud. The area wasn't built up. No floundering mass of rail lines, canals, bridges, factories, docks, civilian residential areas, hospitals, oil tanks, prisoner-of-war concentrations—no mangled puzzle of things to be attacked and things to be missed at all hazards.[36]

And there could be no training for the threat of enemy defenses—flak thick enough to walk on and fighters with guns blazing, closing at speeds over 500 MPH, heading right for the bombardier in his plexiglas position. Such training, if such training were possible, would have to come from war.

World War I belt-driven bombing trainer in France. The "bomber" or bomb-aimer sighted his Michelin bombsight onto a canvas belt containing terrain features. Support personnel simulated flight by cranking the belt. (*Source:* USAF Historical Research Agency.)

World War II powered bombing trainer. The bombardier sighted his Norden bombsight on a powered "crab" target. The movement of the trainer across the ground simulated the movement of the aircraft and the movement of the "crab" target simulated the effect of wind causing the aircraft to "crab" or drift relative to the target. (*Source:* USAF Historical Research Agency.)

Midland Army Air Field Bombing Range. Bombing such targets as this trained thousands of bombardiers for combat and continually proved the capabilities of the Norden and Sperry bombsights. No such targets, so clearly marked, isolated, and defenseless, existed in Germany, Japan, or Italy. (*Source:* USAF Historical Research Agency.)

Beechcraft AT-11 bombing trainer. The Norden stabilizer mount is protected from prying eyes in the nose, while trainees stand ready to board, two carrying the Norden bombsight from its protective vault. (*Source:* National Air and Space Museum.)

...he unveiling of "Uncle Sam's Number One military secret." By 1943 combat losses made certain that the Axis nations had captured the Norden bombsight, freeing the American public and 100,000 American bombardiers from security restrictions. (*Source: Norden Systems Division.*)

Americans could not read about the Norden bombsight, but they could sing about how bombardiers would make the world free (lyric by Lorenz Hart, music by Richard Rodgers, 1942) and chuckle with glee at its fabled accuracy (*Collier's*, September 26, 1942).

"Was that address 106 Leipzigerstrasse, or 107?"

Air Corps problem No. 1—bombing through overcast: "One place was about as good as another." B-17s dropping four-pound incendiaries through 10/10 overcast/undercast on Kiel, December 13, 1943. (*Source:* National Air and Space Museum.)

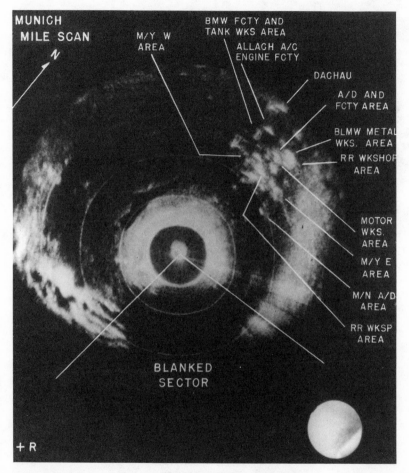

H₂X airborne radar helped some, but involved much guesswork and no pickle barrels. A Fifteenth Air Force H₂X radar screen representation of Munich. (*Source:* National Air and Space Museum.)

The electronic revolution—a harbinger of future wars. This B-17's NOSMO (*Norden Sight Modification*) attachment, under the lamp, fed radar data directly and continually into the Norden bombsight. (*Source:* Courtesy of the Library of Congress.)

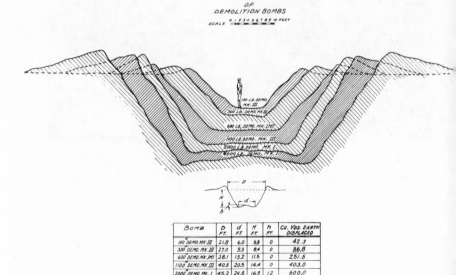

CRATERS
OF
DEMOLITION BOMBS
SCALE 0 1 2 3 4 5 6 7 8 9 10 FEET

BOMB	D FT.	d FT.	H FT.	h FT.	CU. YDS. EARTH DISPLACED
100 DEMO. MK. III	21.8	6.0	6.8	0	42.3
300 DEMO. MK. III	27.0	9.3	8.4	0	86.8
600 DEMO. MK. IMI	38.1	15.2	11.5	0	251.5
1100 DEMO. MK. III	40.5	20.5	14.4	0	403.0
2000 DEMO. MK. I	45.2	24.5	16.5	1.2	600.0
4000 DEMO. MK. I	57.7	29.0	19.0	2.0	1078.0

Varying sizes of craters—the source for all calculations on the number of bombs required to destroy a target, if they hit their target. (*Source:* National Air and Space Museum.)

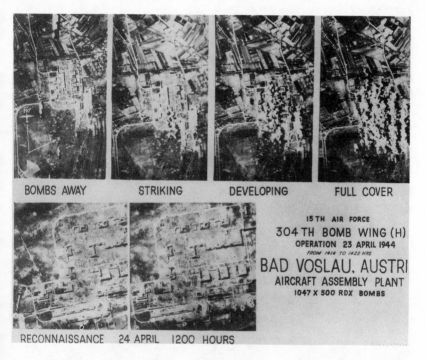

BOMBS AWAY   STRIKING   DEVELOPING   FULL COVER

15 TH AIR FORCE
304 TH BOMB WING (H)
OPERATION 23 APRIL 1944
FROM 1414 TO 1422 HRS.
BAD VOSLAU, AUSTRI
AIRCRAFT ASSEMBLY PLANT
1047 X 500 RDX BOMBS

RECONNAISSANCE   24 APRIL   1200 HOURS

Precision carpet bombing when it worked—Fifteenth Air Force attack on Bad Voslau, April 23, 1944. (*Source:* Sperry Gyroscope Company Collection, Hagley Museum and Library.)

How choke-point bombing was supposed to work—Eighth Air Force attack on the I. G. Farbenindustrie synthetic rubber plant at Hüls, June 22, 1943, before and after bombing. Circle around three storage tanks is to provide a reference point between the two photographs. (*Source:* National Air and Space Museum.)

What it looked like on the ground—German salvage attempts at the VKF#2 ball-bearing factory, Schweinfurt. (*Source:* National Air and Space Museum.)

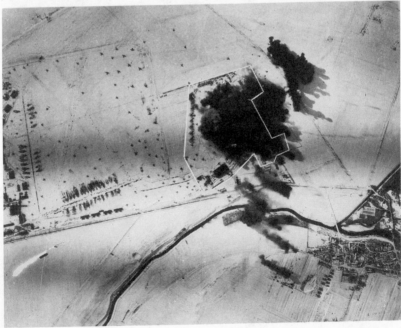

Not all choke-points were this isolated, this discernible, and this unobscured by clouds—the Ju 88 aircraft plant at Bernburg, February 20, 1944, before and during bombing. (*Source:* National Air and Space Museum.)

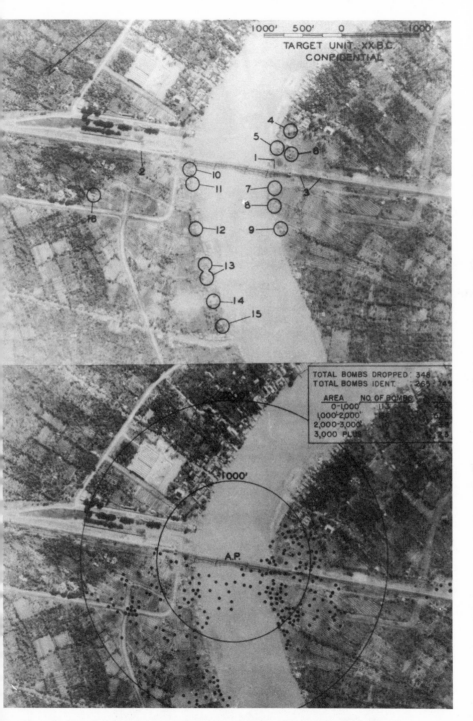

The Norden "shotgun sight"—XX Bomber Command B-29s dropped 348 bombs on the 1,456-foot Rama VI railroad bridge over the Chao Phraya River on January 3, 1945, in clear weather, to get one hit on the bridge, four hits on the bridge abutments, and ten near-misses. (*Source:* USAF Historical Research Agency.)

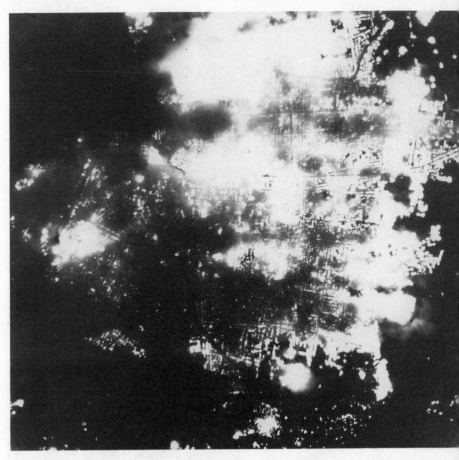

Japan's "congested and highly inflammable cities" when precision bombing failed—XXI Bomber Command firebombing of Toyama on August 1, 1945, destroying 98.6% of the urban built-up area. (*Source:* National Air and Space Museum.)

(a)

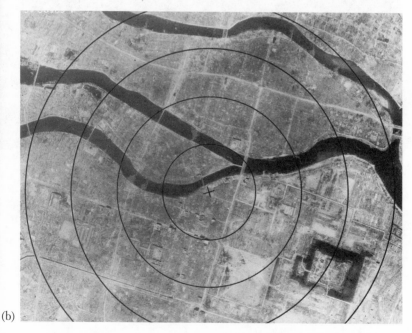

(b)

Hiroshima, (a) before and (b) after. The circles indicate radii of 1,000-foot intervals from ground zero, which was 800 feet from the aiming point. With atomic bombs, accuracy was no longer critical. (*Source:* National Air and Space Museum.)

The ultimate area weapon and antithesis of precision bombing—the "Fat Man" atomic bomb mushroom cloud at Nagasaki, August 9, 1945. (*Source:* National Archives.)

10

Daylight Precision Strategic Bombing against Germany

itler's declaration of war on the United States transformed the industrial complexes of Germany and German-occupied countries into targets for a new type of warfare. The U.S. Army Air Forces had a doctrine of high-altitude daylight precision strategic bombing, a war plan (AWPD/1), the support of Pres. Franklin Roosevelt, and a technology based on the Boeing B-17 Flying Fortress, Norden bombsight, and Norden SBAE/Minneapolis-Honeywell AFCE (stabilized bombing approach equipment/automatic flight control equipment). With two decades of peace and fewer than 100 heavy bombers behind it, the Army Air Forces lacked only the experience and muscle that war could provide.

Some experience could be gained from the British after three years of war, which did not bode well for the teachings of the Air Corps Tactical School. Initially committed to daylight precision strategic bombing, the Royal Air Force's Bomber Command struck at oil, electrical power, coke plants, gas works, and aircraft factories. Two factors, however, pushed it toward area bombing. First, German attacks on British urban areas in late 1940 encouraged a partial switch to "large towns and centres of industry, with the primary aim of causing very heavy material destruction which will demonstrate to the enemy the power and severity of air bombardment and the hardship and dislocation which will result from it."[1]

The second factor was German defenses. Losses of up to 50 percent drove Bomber Command to seek the cover of darkness. The strategy remained attacks on industrial targets until the Butt Report of August 1941 revealed how inaccurate night bombing was. One-third of all sorties never bombed their primary targets. Only two crews in five came within five miles of their targets on full-moon nights, but only one in fifteen on the moonless nights that the Royal Air Force preferred because of the protection such nights provided. A five-mile circular error meant Bomber Command was scattering a few bombs over 78 square miles of German territory. Hugh Trenchard, "father" of the Royal Air Force, came out of retirement to argue that ninety-nine out of one hundred bombs aimed at precision targets would miss, but if dropped on a city, all would do damage.[2]

Chief of the Air Staff Sir Charles Portal identified forty-three German cities for destruction. If Bomber Command could not hit precision targets, then it would bomb what it could—cities. Secretary of State for Air Sir Archibald Sinclair and the British Defence Committee ordered the switch to night area bombing on February 14, 1942, eight days before Sir Arthur Harris assumed command of Bomber Command. "The primary objective should now be focussed on the morale of the enemy civil population and, in particular, of the industrial workers." Harris aimed not at morale, but at the German capacity for war by reducing the number of industrial man-hours available to war production. Reductions in industrial production would be "at least as much by the indirect effect of damage to services, housing, and amenities, as by any direct damage to the factories." Industrial destruction would be "regarded as a bonus." This "city-busting" or "de-housing" campaign, according to the official history of the British bombing effort, was based on the "principle that in order to destroy anything it is necessary to destroy everything."[3]

The baptism of fire for the American Norden bombsight and daylight precision strategic bombing was the England-based Army Air Forces's Eighth Air Force campaign against Germany. Based in Italy, the Fifteenth Air Force joined the endeavor in late 1943. Equipment shortages, diversions, German defenses, and other problems interfered with the strategic bombing effort, but throughout, bombing accuracy remained the key consideration and determinant of success. With suitable conditions, the proper adjustments, and a well-trained bombardier, a generation of Americans believed the Norden bombsight would hit its target. Analyses of bombing errors focused on other causes, rarely questioning the basic design of Carl Norden's mechanical marvel—known affectionately in Europe as the "football" because of its size and shape.[4]

Wartime experience forced a wholesale reevaluation of bomb-aiming techniques developed before the war. Antiaircraft artillery fire forced bombers to fly higher. Ground fire plus German fighter attacks forced shortened bomb runs, interfering with the Norden aiming procedure. By far the greatest obstacle to precision bombing proved to be obstacles to the Norden's visual aiming: clouds, smoke, dust, and debris.

The most immediate problem was building a force for the job. AWPD/1 had assumed an air force of 6,834 medium and heavy bombers requiring six months to defeat Germany. While Maj. Gen. Carl Spaatz organized Eighth Air Force in the United States, Brig. Gen. Ira Eaker went to England in February 1942 to pave the way for units to follow. Preparing bases in England and problems putting the American economy onto a war footing, not the least of which was Norden bombsight production, delayed the first B-17 bombing raid until August 17, 1942. Eaker's twelve Flying Fortresses attacking the Rouen/Sotteville marshalling yard in France represented less than two-thousandths of the force called for in AWPD/1. It was only a beginning—day one of 973 days of American strategic bombing to destroy the German ability to wage war.

After the first five missions, one of which dropped no bombs, Eaker reported 10 percent of bombs dropped landed on the targets and 25 percent fell within 750 feet of the aiming points. Although the targets were large marshalling yards and an airfield, the Americans proved more accurate than the British, who were getting 10 percent within one mile of the aiming point at night. With ten groups, Eaker told Spaatz, he could destroy Germany's aircraft and submarine industries.[5]

While the buildup continued, Eaker and Spaatz struck mainly at submarine installations and shipyards. Not until January 27, 1943, did Eighth Air Force attack a target inside Germany. Not until May 1943 was it able to launch missions of 250 bombers. But what to attack? Wartime experience revealed AWPD/1's target list to be obsolete. According to Elihu Root Jr., special advisor to Army Air Forces's chief Henry Arnold, "The enemy economy was too large—thousands of times too large—to blast it all. We had to choose vital points where small physical damage would cause great industrial disruption." The German machine-tool industry, for example, consisted of over 6,000 small firms. The colonels and captains of AWPD/1 had identified the Luftwaffe, electrical power, transportation centers, oil, and morale as targets. Lt. Gen. Dwight Eisenhower, as commanding general of American forces in Europe, assigned Eighth Air Force the tactical task of "obtaining and maintaining domination of the air over Western France." Eighth Air Force commander Spaatz assigned aircraft factories, marshalling yards, and submarine installations as targets for fulfilling Eisenhower's directive. In 1943 Eighth Air Force was ready to begin a limited offensive, but no one could agree on the choke-points that would strangle the German economy. One thing was for sure—the United States would not target civilians. Ira Eaker said later that "we should never allow the history of this war to convict us of throwing the strategic bomber at the man in the street."[6]

Arnold's Committee of Operations Analysts, committed to selective, precision bombing, believed it "better to use a high degree of destruction in a few really essential industries or services than to cause a small degree of destruction in many industries." The committee recommended six industries for destruction, in order of priority: submarines, aircraft, ball bearings, oil, synthetic rubber, and military transport. Under the direction of Col. Richard D'O. Hughes, formerly of the AWPD/1 unit, the Enemy Objectives Unit of the American embassy in London selected seventy-six targets in these industries, the destruction of which "would have the greatest, most prompt, and most long-lasting direct military effect on the battlefield." Incorporated into a Combined Bomber Offensive in June 1943, code-named POINTBLANK, all that remained was to destroy the targets.[7]

Eighth Air Force strength slowly rose to fifteen groups in June 1943 and twenty-six in December. Fifteenth Air Force added nine more, enabling the Army Air Forces to launch missions of 750 bombers by January 1944, 1,000 bombers by February. It would need them all because of poor bombing accuracy. Against Amiens/Longeau, the circular error was 3,550 feet. At Lille the circular error was 5,000 feet, achieved at a cost of four bombers. According to the official history of the Army Air Forces in the war, the results were "disappointing to all those . . . trained in the pickle-barrel school of bombing." If not corrected, the "Norden bombsight . . . would be valueless" and "the ideal of precision which underlay the American bombardment theory" would have been "compromised." Eighth Air Force blamed mechanical errors, target misidentification, poor formation flying, improper aiming procedures, and enemy defenses.[8]

Rather than dropping bombs into pickle barrels, Eighth Air Force bombardiers were having trouble hitting the broad side of a barn. The Army

Air Forces Bombing Board and the Operational Research Section of VIII Bomber Command, Eighth Air Force's operational command, evaluated American efforts and determined daylight precision strategic bombing would work, if training and maintenance improved.[9] Missions to Germany were too costly in aircrews and aircraft just to miss the target. In the first five months of bombing the average circular error was 900 feet, twice the prewar average.[10] The preferred American bomb until April 1943, the 1,000-pound M-44, packed with 547 pounds of TNT (trinitrotoluene), created a crater 13 feet deep and 45 feet in diameter in sandy loam with a delayed fuze. Even such big bombs required at least a near-miss to destroy a target—hard to achieve with an average circular error of 900 feet. Brig. Gen. Newton Longfellow, commanding general of VIII Bomber Command, was the foremost advocate of big bombs with delayed fuzes, arguing that the bigger the explosion and the larger the mining effect, the greater the damage.

The Bombs and Fuzes Subsection of the Operational Research Section of Eighth Air Force used actual bombings to prove, however, that many smaller bombs had a better chance of achieving a hit. Shorter fuzes would cause explosions in the structural members of a building, increasing fragmentation and causing greater damage to machinery. Section studies showed four bombs with delayed fuzes of 0.25 seconds could produce about 6,400 square feet of damage. With 0.01-second delays, the bombs produced about 16,000 square feet of damage. The short-delay 500-pound M-43 and M-64 bombs therefore became the standard weapons for the daylight precision strategic bombing campaign against Germany for the remainder of the war, combined with the M-47 incendiary bomb preferred by Longfellow's successor, Maj. Gen. Fred Anderson.[11]

The 500-pound M-43 with 267 pounds of TNT created a crater two feet deep and nine feet in diameter in sandy loam with an instantaneous fuze.[12] If the calculations of the Bombs and Fuzes Subsection were correct, and they were too optimistic, the eight M-43s carried by a B-17 would damage 32,000 square feet. Eighth Air Force's average circular error of 900 feet was an area 79 times greater.

Richard Hughes, then head of Eighth Air Force's Operational Planning Section, concluded:

The pre-war myth of a bomb in an apple barrel from 20,000 feet was quickly exploded, and, to the intense disappointment of the regulars, it became apparent quickly that to destroy, or even to hit, a given target was going to call for a vastly greater weight of attack than had been dreamed of in a pre-war doctrine. Contrary to all expectations, with a few notable exceptions, the strategic bombers of the 8th and 15th Air Forces seldom succeeded in achieving real precision bombing.[13]

The Norden rifle would have to become more of a shotgun.

Carl Norden's bombsight did not receive a fair trial in the first several months of operations. Commanders decided that a B-17 force could not fly straight and level for more than ten seconds without getting shot down. Ten seconds or more gave antiaircraft gunners time to determine the elevation, slant range, and azimuth of a bomber. Norden had not designed his bombsight for such a short bombing run.

Commander of the 305th Bombardment Group Curtis E. LeMay refused to accept the inaccuracy evasive action over the target brought. He felt that "the only point in flying a bomber in this war . . . was to drop bombs where they would do the most harm to the enemy." Analysis of poststrike photographs revealed that American bombing was far from precision; LeMay called it "stinko." But what to do?

After several frustrating missions, the answer came to him in bed. Using an old ROTC artillery manual, he calculated the chances of a flak gun hitting a target the size of a B-17 at a distance of 25,000 feet. Guessing that it would take 372 shells to down an American bomber over the target, he determined that the chances of getting shot down while in level flight "didn't look too bad." Because the German 8.8-cm cannon had an operational ceiling of about 20,000 feet, LeMay decided to substitute altitude for evasive maneuvers. Flying above 20,000 feet would reduce the threat, but could bombardiers still hit pickle barrels at that altitude?

LeMay had to balance accuracy against the impulse for self-preservation. He ordered his group to ignore the threat of flak and approach the target straight and level in a group formation. Staggering his aircraft in a tight "combat box" or "Javelin Down formation" uncovered the maximum number of defensive machine guns for protection against German fighters. Brig. Gen. Laurence S. Kuter, commanding general of the 1st Bomb Wing, organized LeMay's combat box of eighteen to twenty-one bombers into a combat wing of two or three combat boxes. These formations were "force multipliers," giving B-17s and B-24s a degree of protection from German fighters because of their overlapping fields of fire. Each formation would fly straight to their targets from the initial point, approximately 10 minutes, rather than maneuvering to avoid flak, giving bombardiers plenty of time to synchronize their bombsights. The arrival of the C-1 automatic flight control equipment (AFCE) in early 1943 insured a straight and level approach.[14]

With all aircraft flying in a fixed formation, however, bombardiers were unable to aim their loads individually. LeMay's solution was "dropping-on-the-leader," by which a lead bombardier aimed the bombs of the entire formation. The combat box maintained proper positioning, following the leader to the target. The other bombardiers released their bombs either after receiving a radio cue from the lead bombardier or a visual cue from a flare or from seeing the lead's bombs drop.[15] In larger formations the lead bombardier maneuvered to bring the formation over the target, but deputy lead bombardiers determined the proper drop point. Eighth Air Force's Operational Research Section recommended that one bombardier should calculate both, leaving individual bombardiers to serve as "toggliers," flicking the bomb-release toggle switch upon signal from the leader.[16]

Carl Norden had designed his bombsight to minimize human involvement and human error, but dropping-on-the-leader forced the human back into the procedure. Eighth Air Force discovered that the technique caused combat boxes to overshoot the target, especially when tail winds increased ground speeds. Larger formations of several combat boxes tended to undershoot. At 185 MPH, a delay of one second caused a bomb to drop 270 feet beyond the target. The lead bombardier therefore had to override his Norden bombsight and drop early or late to compensate. Guesswork had replaced the mechanical precision of Norden's analog computer in daylight precision strategic bombing. Bombing patterns on the ground took on the look of the aircraft formation. Only a few of these bombs could hit small targets. According to the Strategic Bombing Survey, "The rest spilled over on adjacent plants, or built-up areas, or in open fields."[17]

LeMay chose his lead crews based on experience and past performance—the best bombardiers aimed for all others. An Army Air Forces study supported his methods, finding that only one in ten bombardiers had the aptitude and ability to become a lead bombardier. Each lead crew became responsible for studying a separate target folder, making them experts in locating landmarks and finding the target in the chaos of the run over the target. Eighth Air Force launched its first mission using the tactic to Vegesack, Germany, on March 18, 1943. By July 1943 drop-on-the-leader was standard procedure in Eighth Air Force operations. Group formations dropping-on-the-leader achieved 24.6 percent of all bombs within

1,000 feet of the aiming point through October 1943, while those dropping on individual sightings achieved only 8.3 percent. Fifteenth Air Force believed individual aiming to be more accurate.[18]

The irony here was each group only needed one Norden bombsight, plus backups. General Arnold was fighting a procurement war with the Navy and Carl L. Norden, Inc., to acquire them by the thousands and was training tens of thousands of bombardiers to operate them, yet LeMay's tactic meant most bombers carried Nordens into combat as dead weight and bombardiers as gunners. The drop-on-the-leader technique eliminated bombsight shortages in Eighth Air Force. In March 1944 it asked that the next 1,000 bombers sent to England come without bombsights because it held 366 excess Nordens and 1,351 excess Sperrys.[19]

The drop-on-the-leader technique also raised the question about whether the formation should drop its bombs by intervalometer or by salvo (instantaneous release) technique. Intervalometer bombing appeared more efficient, flooding the target area with bombs at regular intervals and guaranteeing a higher probability of a hit. Studies by the Eighth Air Force Operational Analysis Section, however, showed "the probability of missing altogether small or medium size targets is not greater with salvo release than with intervalometer release; indeed, on small targets it is substantially less." Roughly twice as many bombs fell within 500 feet of the target with instantaneous salvoing. Too many malfunctions and the difficulty of holding formation for the seconds required for a bombing run by intervalometer encouraged Eighth Air Force to de-emphasize the intervalometer in 1943 and to give up on it in 1944, except especially large targets. The Army Air Forces was moving away from "pickle-barrel" precision bombing to highly concentrated, but not precision, overwhelming force. Several hundred bombs would now cancel the errors of high-altitude bombing.[20]

These changes forced a revision in the procedure for scoring accuracy. For nearly three decades American airmen had determined accuracy by measuring the distance from the point of impact to the aiming point. Now they were aiming hundreds and thousands of bombs at one target, making circular error measurement difficult and misleading. Dropping-on-the-leader, formation bombing, and saturation or carpet bombing forced the move away from circular error to "mean point of impact." Photo interpreters drew a circle of 1,000-feet radius around the greatest concentration of bombs. The distance from the assigned aiming point to the center of the 1,000-foot circle became the new circular error, measured as the percentage of bombs falling within the 1,000-foot circle. Eighth Air Force consid-

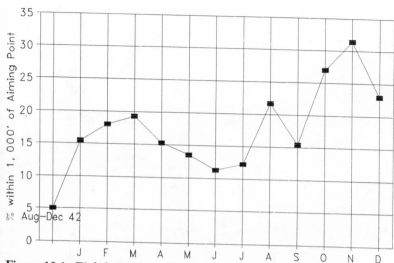

Figure 10.1. Eighth Air Force Bombing Accuracy (August 1942–December 1943)

Source: Eighth Air Force, "Bombing Accuracy," n.d., Folder—Bombing Accuracy, Box 76, Subject File, Spaatz Papers.

ered any errors greater than 3,000 feet "gross errors" and excluded them from accuracy calculations.[21]

LeMay's tactics, combined with the new C-1 AFCE, tripled Eighth Air Force bombing accuracy in the first months of 1943. Training and experience raised accuracy through the remainder of the year (see Figure 10.1).

The average circular error nevertheless remained an abysmal 1,200 feet. Put another way, out of every 100 bombers flying into harm's way, sixteen dropped bombs within 1,000 feet of the aiming point. Eighty-four missed. With bomber losses averaging 7 percent in May and 10 percent during the Blitz Week of July 24–30, the United States was paying a high price for daylight precision strategic bombing. Every B-17 or B-24 downed meant the Army Air Forces lost ten men and a $187,742 or $215,516 airplane ($1.2 million and $1.388 million in 1992 dollars). Despite the public relations blitz that accompanied daylight precision strategic bombing, these figures were the reality of high-altitude bombing under wartime conditions.[22]

A major cause of bombing error was the increased altitude bombers sought to escape German flak. The B-17 proved more survivable in the skies over Germany largely because it could fly higher than the B-24. Ev-

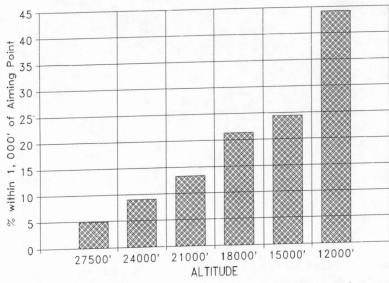

Figure 10.2. Effects of Altitude on Bombing Accuracy (January 1– November 16, 1943)

Source: VIII Bomber Command Operational Research Section, "Effect of Altitude on Bombing Accuracy," November 24, 1943, Folder—Bombing Accuracy Analytical Studies I, Box 76, Subject File, Spaatz Papers.

ery foot of extra altitude, however, increased the variables Norden's analog computer had to solve. It was a problem the Army Air Forces never resolved (see Figure 10.2).

Also affecting accuracy was the size of bombing formations, the order of arrival over the target, and the number of aiming points. The more aircraft, the greater was the chaos, causing the wartime average circular error to increase from 945 feet with three groups to 1,095 feet with nine and 1,140 feet with fifteen or more. Until late 1943 the tactic was to get as many groups over the target as quickly as possible, but bombing analysis showed accuracy declined precipitously based on the order of arrival over the target. Smoke, debris, dust, and exploding bombs obscured the visual aiming of trailing formations. By extending the time over target to intervals from two to twenty-five minutes, the second unit saw a 32 percent improvement in accuracy, the third 58 percent, the fourth 105 percent, and the fifth 178 percent. Although the improvement was impressive, the first three groups still averaged over twice as many bombs within 1,000 feet of the target as all other following groups. Finally, based on prewar practice, individual bombardiers aimed for different spots on larger targets to achieve a better distribution of bombs. Again bombing analysis showed better results when all bombardiers aimed at one point.[23]

By mid-1943 these lessons and techniques were ready for the strategic bombing campaign. An initial choke-point target was the I. G. Farbenindustrie synthetic rubber plant at Hüls on June 22. The 541-acre site was Germany's largest producer of synthetic rubber (30 percent of wartime production) and also produced diethyl benzene for aviation gas. The Norden "rifle" sight failed to work that day, but 1,780 bombs aimed by the Norden "shotgun" sight shut the facility down for one month and restricted production for six, creating a serious rubber shortage. Craters covered over 12 square miles, with 20 percent landing inside the plant area. A participant summed up daylight precision strategic bombing that day: "We had dropped 422 tons of bombs and, according to the reconnaissance photos, only 333.4 tons had been wasted on homes, streets, public parks, zoos, department stores and air-raid shelters. This passed for precision."[24]

Famous among these early bombing efforts was the second attack against the Schweinfurt ball-bearing factories on October 14, 1943. Sixteen bomb groups flew over 500 miles into Germany, without escorting fighters, in pursuit of the elusive choke-point in the German economy. The cost was high—60 out of 229 B-17s bombing that day and 138 more damaged, and 599 crewmen dead or missing in action. First and Third Bomb Division aircraft dropped 459 1,000-pound and 663 500-pound high-explosive bombs and 1,751 100-pound incendiary bombs (482.8 tons).[25] Three groups missed the targets and five more dropped fewer than 10 percent of their bombs within 500 feet. Most accurate was the 351st, with 29 percent hits. Overall, one bomb out of ten hit within 500 feet of the targets and there were sixty-three direct hits. Three bearings plants lost 10 percent of their machines damaged or destroyed.[26]

In early 1944 the Army Air Forces won air superiority over Europe and bombing accuracy increased. Eighth Air Force commander Jimmy Doolittle believed "there was no real improvement in the bombing equipment. The improvement was in the environment in which the bombing took place."[27] Bombing accuracy also improved as the Army Air Forces began to focus its efforts against specific industries, most well defined and generally clear of urban congestion: the aircraft industry in early 1944, oil in mid-1944, and oil and the transportation network in late 1944 and 1945, with occasional forays against jet aircraft production and urban areas. The February and April 1945 averages of 49.3 and 59 percent within 1,000 feet

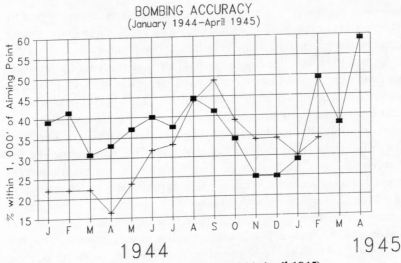

Figure 10.3. **Bombing Accuracy (January 1944–April 1945)**

Sources: Eighth Air Force reports on bombing accuracy for January 1944 through March 1945, File 520.547A, HRA; and USSBS, "Daylight Bombing Accuracy of the Eighth, Ninth, and Fifteenth Air Forces," August 24, 1945, File 137.306-6, HRA.

of the aiming point for Eighth Air Force were the highest of the war. Average bombing altitudes for those two months were 16,500 feet compared to a wartime average of 24,500 feet. The effect of lower altitudes on bombing accuracy, especially in conditions of near-total air superiority, was dramatic (see Figure 10.3).[28]

Accuracy was especially critical when Army commanders called on the strategic bombers to provide close air support for troops on the ground. Twenty-five missions in Italy, mainly around the Anzio beachhead, resulted in seven total misses, one achieving over 50 percent hits within 1,000 feet of the aiming point, and the remainder between 20 and 50 percent of bombs within 1,000 feet of the aiming point. In all, the effort caused "relatively few casualties" among enemy units. At Monte Cassino on February 15, 1944, bombers dropped 576 tons of explosives with poor accuracy from 15,000 feet, largely due to smoke and dust obscuring bombardiers' aim.[29]

The most famous use of strategic bombers from high altitude in the close air support role was the COBRA carpet bombing at Saint-Lô on July 24 and 25, 1944. Over 2,000 bombers attacked a target one mile deep by five miles long, some dropping early by accident and others because dust, smoke, and debris near the target area obscured the aiming points. In a tragic example of how the drop-on-the-leader technique could magnify one bombardier's mistake, an early release by one leader caused his formation to bomb the American 30th Infantry Division, killing more than 100 soldiers. Nearly 50 percent of the bombs fell on target, 30 to 35 percent fell beyond the target area, and 5 to 10 percent fell short. The attack helped Lt. Gen. Omar Bradley's forces to break out of the Bocage country of Normandy, but the massive effort killed only 3 percent of the German soldiers facing Bradley's command.[30]

In 1944 and 1945 Eighth Air Force identified the synthetic oil industry as the most vulnerable choke-point in the German industrial fabric. With production concentrated at fifty-four sites, planners saw oil as the Achilles' heel of the motorized German military machine. The targets were relatively easy to locate and highly concentrated—the perfect target of daylight precision strategic bombing and the Norden precision bombsight.

The Ammoniakwerke Merseburg GmbH at Leuna, Germany, was particularly important for producing fuel, ammonia, and nitrogen for explosives from coal. Minister of Armaments and Munitions Albert Speer ordered it defended by 506 antiaircraft guns. Covering a rectangle 11,600 feet long by 3,500 feet wide, it received eighteen American day and four British night attacks. Bombing statistics did not speak well for daylight precision strategic bombing. Of 85,074 bombs dropped, only 10 percent landed inside the plant's perimeter fence covering 757 acres. Of these, 16 percent failed to explode. Few hit critical components and the damage was quickly repaired.

Forty-five B-17s dropped 1,383 bombs on Leuna under good visual conditions on the most accurate mission. Excluding unexploded bombs, 33 percent hit the target. On the worst day 574 bombers dropped 8,000 bombs by blind-bombing techniques because of a total cloud cover. Only six bombs hit the target, at a cost of 27 bombers and their crews. A nearby decoy plant attracted more than half the bombs aimed at Leuna.

Leuna was not the exception. The U.S. Strategic Bombing Survey closely examined the results of dropping 146,000 high-explosive bombs on Leuna and two other oil targets (Ludwigshafen-Opau and Zeitz) during fifty-seven raids. Only one bomb in twenty-nine hit the targets and did any damage. For the entire oil offensive, the Army Air Forces dropped 123,586 tons of bombs to get 19,029 tons inside the fences of the synthetic fuel plants, only 4,326 tons of which hit anything significant. The Bombing Survey concluded that it was "easier to hit an elephant with a shotgun" than a rifle.[31]

Table 10.1. Effects of Clouds on Bombardment Operations

Period	Total Number of Days	Number of Visual Days
Jan.–March 1944	91	14
April–June 1944	91	38
July–Sept. 1944	92	42
Oct.–Dec. 1944	92	10
Jan.–March 1945	90	28
Total	456	132

Source: USSBS, Report No. 62, Weather Factors in Combat Bombardment Operations in the European Theater (Washington, D.C.: Government Printing Office, 1947), 29.

Speer's army of several hundred thousand laborers repaired damage within days of a strike, forcing costly return missions. Production at Leuna resumed on May 22, 1944, after the attack of May 12, June 3 after the May 28 attack, July 9 after the July 7 attack, and so on. After nine strikes, it still produced at 28 percent its normal level.[32]

One reason for the lack of accuracy during the oil campaign was clouds and smoke obscuring the targets. Throughout the strategic air campaign against Germany, according to the Eighth Air Force Operational Analysis Section, "the most pressing problem of daylight formation bombing from the point of view of bombing accuracy is the development of more effective techniques for bombing under conditions of poor visibility." Cloud cover, generally measured in tenths, blocked the view of the bombardier. The great weakness of the Norden bombsight was that it required visual contact between the bombardier's eye and the target. Solid cloud cover was an obvious barrier, but any stray cloud blocking the bombardier's vision between the bomb release point and the target was equally obstructive. "Now you see it, now you don't" allowed bombardiers too little time to operate the Norden bombsight. So critical was the problem that Arnold authorized Eighth Air Force to area-bomb the built-up areas of German cities when the weather made precision bombing impossible.[33]

In the 456 days from January 1944 to March 1945, visual bombing with the Norden bombsight was possible only 132 days (see Table 10.1). Based on data from 723 missions, the Strategic Bombing Survey concluded that circular error nearly doubled when clouds blocked the aiming point. Daylight precision strategic bombing would fail unless bombardiers could find a means for seeing through clouds (see Figure 10.4).

Until late 1943, clouds generally meant aborted missions or a timed

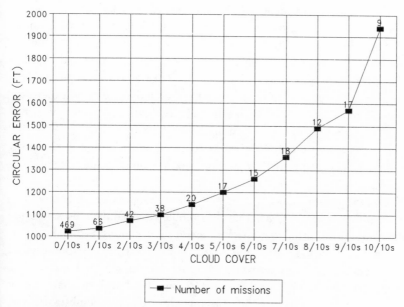

Figure 10.4. Effects of Cloud Cover on Bombing Accuracy

Source: USSBS, "Daylight Bombing Accuracy of the Eighth, Ninth, and Fifteenth Air Forces," August 24, 1945, File 137.306-6, HRA.

bomb approach by dead reckoning. In a maneuver developed by Asa Duncan in 1927 at the Pee Dee River Bridge and Robert Olds in the 1930s at Langley Field, the bombardier would lock a visible initial point into the Norden bombsight and use a map to measure the time necessary to fly to the target. The navigator was responsible for flying the correct heading. The 464th Bomb Group used a timed run of 50 miles against Oberweissenfeld in September 1944, socked in with 10/10 clouds, and dropped its bombs 3,000 feet left of target. A month later the 97th Bomb Group attacked Pilsen Skoda after a 40-mile timed run and missed by 10 miles.[34] The Army Air Forces needed a better solution.

The search for solutions to the problem of clouds, dust, or smoke obscuring the line-of-sight view of the Norden bombsight began on November 4, 1939, when Major General Arnold directed the Materiel Division to investigate bombing through overcast. Researchers examined optical filters for conventional bombsights and the use of a pilot aircraft flying below the overcast, controlling a bomb-carrying aircraft flying in or above the overcast. Research into radio waves suggested two other solutions. The first was radio ranging dependent on ground beacons. The second was self-contained systems in which the radio transmissions came from the bomber.

The United States did little research into ground beacons during the war, relying instead on British systems. *Gee* used one master and two subordinate stations transmitting radio pulses. The bomber's equipment measured the differences in time between the arrival of the different transmissions. The intersection of the beams and *Gee* charts allowed the navigator to determine the aircraft's location. *Gee* had a range of only 300 to 400 miles, was accurate only to within five miles, and was subject to enemy jamming. The Army Air Forces employed it primarily for general navigation.

Oboe used two ground stations transmitting radio pulses to bomber aircraft. It differed from *Gee* in that the bomber received the pulses, boosted them, and transmitted them back to the ground stations. Ground stations timed the pulses to measure the range to the aircraft. One station tracked the aircraft over the target while the other determined the bomb release point. *Oboe* had shorter range than *Gee*, but could achieve accuracies of several hundred yards. Neither *Gee* nor *Oboe* required bombsights. The Army Air Forces used *Oboe* rarely because of range limitations.

Gee-H was *Gee* plus *Oboe* in reverse, but required a bombsight. An aircraft carried a transmitter and a receiver, bouncing signals off two ground stations to determine range, which appeared on a scope in the aircraft. Accuracy was similar to *Oboe*, but with greater range due to a longer radio beam. The operator fed rate information to the bombardier, who used visual sightings when possible to improve accuracy. When this was first used on January 28, 1944, Eighth Air Force achieved an average circular error of 1,864 feet on *Gee-H* missions.[35]

Micro-H triggered *Gee-H* ground beacons, whose signals appeared on a radar screen in the aircraft, adding *Gee-H* range information to the ground returns of the radar equipment. The radar operator called out predetermined check points, allowing the bombardier to synchronize his bombsight. *Micro-H* improved ground-beacon accuracy to around 1,500 feet and entered combat for Eighth Air Force on August 5, 1944.[36]

A second means of blind bombing, self-contained radar systems, were products of General Arnold's decision in 1940 to name "bombing through overcast" as the Air Corps' "problem No. 1" for the consideration of the newly established National Defense Research Committee.[37] By the American entry into the war, Western Electric and Sperry Gyroscope had connected an ASV-10 submarine searching radar to a Sperry S-1 bombsight. Out of this research came the AN/APQ-13, a modification of the British H_2S radar; the AN/APS-15, the American H_2X, popularly known as "Mickey"; the AN/APQ-7, with greater range and higher resolution; and the AN/APQ-10, which allowed evasive maneuvers at a constant altitude.[38]

These devices measured reflections of radio transmissions off terrain features. H_2S and H_2X were primarily for high-altitude aerial navigation, most useful when land/water contrasts were present. H_2S used the S band (10 cm) and had poor resolution, making identification of ground features difficult. H_2X used the X band (3 cm) and had better resolution from its higher frequency and a range advantage over the H_2S radar of 30 to 50 miles, reaching out as far as 90 miles. Army Air Forces units first used the H_2S operationally in September 1943, the H_2X in November 1943.

H_2S and H_2X were not radar bombsights, only assisting the bombing operation by replacing the optical telescope. With the Norden bombsight alone, the bombardier killed drift by turning the drift and turn knobs to fly the aircraft so that the target appeared to move down the vertical reticle in the scope. He then killed rate by turning the rate knob to synchronize the bombsight so that the ground appeared motionless in the scope. Finally, he placed the target at the intersection of the horizontal and vertical reticles using the displacement knob.

In H_2X synchronous bombing, the H_2X operator killed drift by directing the pilot to fly the aircraft over the target. He then notified the bombardier of several angle measurements between the vertical and a line from the aircraft to the target, allowing the bombardier to determine the ground speed of the aircraft, killing rate by turning the rate knob and fixing the unseen target on the horizontal reticle. The radar set measured altitude and ground range. If a break occurred in the undercast, the bombardier could optically adjust any of the three steps to improve accuracy. An in-the-field modification synchronized the H_2X set with the Norden bombsight,[39] using the radar to fix the cross wires on the target directly. If visual corrections were not possible, the bombardier dropped his bombs when the target touched bomb-release circles on the radar scope that matched dropping angles for various speeds and altitudes.[40]

Radar-assisted bombing was inherently inaccurate. Operator error contributed from 1,000 to 3,000 feet of inaccuracy, beam width up to 1,500 feet, data transmission 250 feet, and the spot size of the target on the radar screen 200 feet. If all factors involved in the radar sighting method worked perfectly, inherent uncertainties in the radar system could cause errors up to 2,750 feet. Because the radar received information from other instruments, additional errors in the determination of air speed, wind speed, altitude, and roll rate could account for another 3,700 feet of error. When dropped by radar alone, circular errors of two miles were average. With Norden visual assistance, errors below one mile were common.[41]

The capricious nature of European weather guaranteed adequate opportunities to use H_2X in combat. With visual bombing, Eighth Air Force achieved an accuracy of 33 percent of its bombs dropping within 1,000 feet of the target in the first half of 1944, 45 percent by the summer of 1944. During the last eight months of the war, on missions with the ground obscured by clouds, Eighth Air Force bombardiers relying on H_2X achieved hits within two or three miles of the target. On missions specifically chosen for H_2X bombing because of excellent land-water contrasts, getting 25 percent of bombs within 1,000 feet of the target was not unusual, however.[42]

Late in the war the Army Air Forces deployed the NOSMO system (*Norden Sight Modification*) that fed radar data directly and continually into the Norden bombsight rather than having the H_2X operator transfer the information to the bombardier verbally. Allowing continuous synchronous range tracking and visual-radar coordination, it was most effective with the higher resolution Bell Telephone Laboratories X-band Eagle (AN/APQ-7) radar. Known as NOSMEAGLE, this first true radar bombsight proved twice as accurate as H_2X. The Eagle radar determined ground speed, wind speed and direction, and altitude. The bombardier set the disc speed on the Norden bombsight according to this information, while the radar operator killed drift and synchronized the sight with the target. In test bombings near Orlando, Florida, NOSMEAGLE achieved a circular error of 800 feet from an altitude of 20,000 feet with the Norden bombsight. War in Europe ended before it could be tested in combat.[43]

Despite the limitations of radar and beacon bombing, these technologies allowed the Army Air Forces to bomb when weather otherwise would have prevented it. Crews especially appreciated "electronic" attacks; protected by clouds, the chances of getting home safely from a blind-bombing mission were nearly six times greater than from a visual-bombing mission. If the Allies had been forced to await weather conditions conducive to visual bombing, the number of bombs dropped on Germany would have declined by 52 percent in 1944 and 1945. These additional 195,000 tons of bombs, nearly 20 percent of all bombs dropped by the Army Air Forces on

Table 10.2. Eighth Air Force Bomb-aiming Techniques (percentage of total bombing effort)

Year	Visual	H_2X	H_2X with Visual Assist	Gee-H	Gee-H with Visual Assist	Micro-H
1942	100%	—	—	—	—	—
1943	73%	25%	2%	—	—	—
1944	51%	34%	5%	7%	2%	1%
1945	41%	35%	8%	9%	2%	5%
1942–45	50%	33%	6%	7%	2%	2%

Source: Odishaw, "Radar Bombing."

Table 10.3. Accuracy of Eighth Air Force Blind-bombing Techniques

Aiming Means	Weather	Percentage within 1,000 ft.	Percentage over 5 miles
H_2X only	10/10 clouds	0.2%	41%
H_2X + visual	8-9/10 clouds	1.0	18
H_2X + visual	6-7/10 clouds	2.0	9
H_2X + visual	4-5/10 clouds	4.4	4
Gee-H	Various	5.0	6
Micro-H	Various	5.0	11
Visual	Good	30.0	8
Visual	Poor	9.4	9

Source: "Eighth Air Force—Tactical Development, August 1942–May 1945," August 1942–June 1945, File 520.057-1, HRA.

Germany during the war, were an integral part of the bombing campaign to destroy the German war economy (see Table 10.2).

Beacon aids and radar allowed American bombardiers to aim their bombs at specific targets in the German industrial web through clouds and smoke, though bombing inaccuracy made such missions area attacks in effect (see Table 10.3). These techniques meant that Eighth Air Force dropped 3.7 bombs on clear days to achieve one hit within 1,000 feet of the target, 13.4 on days of poor visibility, 23.2 with *Gee-H*, 24.1 with *Micro-H*, and 567.4 with H_2X in total cloud cover. Missions relying on blind-bombing aids remained officially "last resort attacks."[44]

The doctrine of daylight precision strategic bombing still depended on the Norden optical bombsight operating in clear weather. Bombing through overcast made targets out of urban areas, despite official and unofficial policies against terror bombing. For bombardiers, the difference between precision and urban area bombing was not always significant. Directed to bomb the Fredrichstrasse Station in Berlin, Charles "One Shot" Hudson of the 91st Bomb Group said, "No one expected me to hit it. Anyplace in the center of the city would do just as well. This is total war, and I feel not the least reluctant about bombing this city." Phillip Ardery believed he was there to bomb Berlin, "and one place was about as good as another." Another aimed for a hole in the clouds, hitting "whatever part of the city happened to be underneath."[45]

Air Corps Tactical School doctrine had foreseen the bombing of enemy urban areas to destroy morale, but had restricted such strikes to the latter stages of a war after the industrial infrastructure had been destroyed and the enemy people were susceptible to the effects of morale bombing. World War II reached that point in its last winter. In late October 1944 Eighth Air Force widened its definition of precision bombing, allowing its aircraft to attack towns and cities as "secondary and last resort targets" if they contained or were adjacent to "one or more military objectives." On January 31, 1945, the Malta Conference directed American air commander Carl Spaatz to bomb urban areas and cause confusion among civilians evacuating the east. Eighth Air Force commander Jimmy Doolittle saw this as violating "the basic American principle of precision bombing of targets of strictly military significance for which our tactics were designed and our crews trained and indoctrinated."[46]

Despite protests, 932 B-17s dropped nearly 2,300 tons of bombs on the center of Berlin on February 3, 1945. Even at this point, however, the influence of the precision bombing doctrine was apparent. The official targets for that day were the Anhalter, Tempelhof, and Schlesischer railroad stations (marshalling yards) and government offices along Wilhelmstrasse. Although Germany claimed 25,000 civilian dead, more probably 1,000 died.[47] Eighth Air Force also participated in the Allied bombing of Dresden on February 14 and 15—a city of little military significance. One week later nearly 1,400 heavy bombers struck at transportation targets in forty small cities and towns yet untouched by bombing. Ironically, this time the intent was morale bombing, though the chosen targets were consistent with the strategy of daylight precision strategic bombing.

Returning to Berlin on March 18, 1945, 1,251 B-17s and B-24s attacked precision targets (two railroad stations, a locomotive works, and an armored vehicle plant), but clouds and the resulting need to use H_2X turned the mission into area bombing. Eighth Air Force's three air divisions averaged circular errors of 2.46, 0.73, and 2.27 *miles*. In urban, congested Berlin, any bomb missing by these distances would invariably land on civilian areas. The intent was precision bombing, the effect terror bombing.[48]

Initiating area attacks late in the war was not evidence of the failure of precision strategic bombing. Billy Mitchell and the faculty of the Air Corps Tactical School wrote that civilian morale might become a target when it was most vulnerable after a daylight precision strategic bombing campaign. Beginning in February 1945, civilian morale had become the chokepoint in the German war effort. The limits of technology often turned precision bombing into area bombing, but the Army Air Forces remained committed to the doctrine of daylight precision strategic bombing until the end. American airmen intentionally aimed fewer than 4 percent of their bombs at German civilians.[49]

A combination of factors contributed to the lack of accuracy in daylight precision strategic bombing. The Air Corps Tactical School faculty could not have foreseen the quality or quantity of German defenses. According to the Strategic Bombing Survey, enemy opposition required an "increase in altitude, size of attacking force, and size of box," all contributing to inaccurate bombing. Crews misidentified targets, improperly leveled their gyroscopes, and cut bomb runs short. On visual missions, each additional 100 feet of altitude caused an increase in circular error of 6.1 feet, the result of increased atmospheric influences and the effect of additional pure oxygen use by the crew. Each additional flak gun caused 4.5 feet more error. A smoke screen added 281.9 feet.[50]

Human error in the use of the Norden technology similarly contributed to inaccuracy. The Norden M-series bombsight was a precision bombing device, but only as accurate as the information the bombardier fed it. An altitude miscalculation of 250 feet resulted in an error of 136 feet in range and deflection. An error in wind speed determination of 20 MPH added 120 feet of error. One Army Air Forces study estimated that human errors contributed 1,277 feet of error to an average bombing mission.[51]

The inherent limits of the Norden technology also affected accuracy. The key to the Norden bombsight's accuracy was the precision of its manufacturing process in eliminating friction between the moving parts. Excessive friction changed the analogs representing the mathematical formulas solved by the relative movements of the bombsight's discs, gears, and cogs. Wartime demands forced Carl Norden, his company, and other manufacturers to adopt mass-production techniques that gave average inherent inaccuracies 5.6 times greater than specifications. Wright Field's Materiel

Command reported in August 1944 that a major factor behind bombing inaccuracy was the

> fact that the majority of the [Norden] bombsights in use by the combat forces and training organizations have errors in excess of the specification. When the service, as a whole, realizes the sights they are now using are not sufficiently accurate to hit the pickle barrel, the question immediately arises as to what will happen and what effect this will have on morale. . . . Air Service Command feel that this is of sufficient importance and is so susceptible to criticism by the public with a morale factor also involved that they desire a headquarters decision on their future action in this matter.

The only feasible solution was to overhaul all Norden bombsights then in service, which would take "at least, one to two years." By August 1944 the Army Air Forces had acquired over 40,000 bombers and trainers using these inferior Norden bombsights. It was too late to make changes.[52]

Despite two decades of research and development, the United States discovered in the skies over Europe that the precision bombing often compared to a surgeon's keen scalpel[53] was in fact a bludgeon.[54] The 85,074 bombs dropped on the Leuna synthetic oil facility were a far cry from the nine bombs prewar planners assumed would destroy the Sault Ste. Marie locks between Michigan and Ontario.[55] There was nothing surgical or precise about dropping 158 4,500-pound bombs, 48,575 2,000-pound bombs, 564,969 1,000-pound bombs, 3,089,916 500-pound bombs, 1,055,289 250-pound bombs, 1,520,209 100-pound bombs, and 1,151,885 incendiary bombs in the war against Germany.[56]

What effect did 7,431,001 bombs dropped at a cost of $30 billion have on the German industrial web? Eighth Air Force high-altitude daylight precision strategic bombing, aimed by the Norden bombsight, averaged 31.8 percent of its bombs within 1,000 feet of the aiming point from an average altitude of 21,000 feet. Fifteenth Air Force averaged 30.78 percent from 500 feet lower altitude. A 20-foot crater from a 500-pound bomb was only overturned earth if no critical industrial tool or structure had formerly occupied its space. Even if American bombardiers had been able to hit their targets regularly, their bombs were too small to damage most of the industries at which they were aimed. The Army Air Forces chose smaller bombs because flooding the target area increased the chances of getting a hit. Ironically, wartime practice proved heavier bombs were more accurate.[57]

In prewar doctrinal development, the Air Corps Tactical School faculty was concerned with hitting the target and assumed the standard Air Corps bomb weighing 100 pounds would destroy it. Fortunately for the United States, at least the Army Air Forces adopted the 500-pound bomb as the standard weapon for World War II. The key construction materials of German industries were iron, steel, and concrete. Synthetic gasoline plants were built to withstand pressures up to 10,000 pounds per square inch and temperatures of several thousand degrees. Against such structures, only direct hits were effective. The doctrine of daylight precision strategic bombing assumed circular errors of several hundred feet, not direct hits.[58]

At the end of the war two people publicly questioned precision bombing and the Norden bombsight's contribution to it. Maj. Alexander P. de Seversky, the Army's post–World War I bombsight expert, claimed that he had evidence of the "gross exaggeration about the allegedly miraculous powers" of the Norden bombsight—a technology he described as barely advanced beyond bombsights built two decades earlier (presumably his own C-1). Improvements in accuracy, he said, were due to the skill of the aircrews flying the bombers. Sen. Elbert Thomas of Utah believed precision bombing to be "one of the outstanding hoaxes of military history." Germany had "a bombsight so much better than ours that it made their ordinary bombardiers as good as our experts."[59]

Privately many airmen also questioned precision bombing, but did their jobs regardless. Burrell Ellison of the 392nd Bomb Group claimed:

> We did more damage to German agriculture than we did to manufacturing. We did tear up a lot of fields and forests. I question now, as I questioned in 1943–44, if the bombing was worth the expense in time, money and life. But question or no question, we flew day in and day out and nobody expected to live through it. I know that the completion of tour of duty was a surprise to me. It was akin to being born again.[60]

Despite these doubts, American precision bombing was sufficiently accurate to cause shortages in products critical to the German war effort. Much of the effectiveness of an attack, whatever the accuracy, was dependent on the priority Germany assigned to repairing it. From July 1943 to February 1944 Eighth Air Force attacked the German aircraft assembly industry as a top priority, yet the Luftwaffe never suffered from aircraft shortages because of rapid repairs. A November 30, 1944, attack on the Friedrich-Alfred Hutte iron and steel plant, with a low priority for repair, dropped only three 500-pound bombs within 1,000 feet of the aiming point and eliminated all production for 83 days. The Maschinenfabrik at Augsburg on October 19, 1944, received 150 500-pound bombs within 1,000 feet of the aiming point and suffered a 27-day loss of production because of a high repair priority.[61]

The Air Corps Tactical School faculty and the AWPD/1 team had not anticipated the need for repeat missions to keep a bombed target destroyed. Albert Speer told his captors in 1945 that the reason strategic bombing failed to knock Germany out of the war was the failure to follow up initial bombings. Still, these bombings caused Germany to divert enormous resources from other vital areas to repair the damage of strategic bombing and to defend against it. Speer estimated Germany lost 10,000 heavy guns, 6,000 tanks, and 20,000 antiaircraft guns in 1943 because of the bombing campaign. It was, he said, Germany's "greatest lost battle."[62]

The bombing of the Regensburg-East marshalling yard on December 20, 1944, demonstrated the most serious weakness of daylight precision strategic bombing. Accuracy was excellent, but repair crews returned the yard to service in four days. Holding up 1,200 railroad cars every day was a creditable contribution to the Allied war effort, but repeating the attack every four days to insure the loss of this one marshalling yard, among hundreds, was beyond American capabilities.[63]

To suggest, as one observer did, that "there appears to be precious little in the conduct of the daylight bomber offensive against Germany through June 1944 that vindicate the theory of precision, industrial bombardment," is to set up a straw man that bombing had to destroy the German economy to be successful.[64] Accuracy lagged behind doctrine, but daylight precision strategic bombing forced the Luftwaffe into a battle of attrition that allowed Eighth Air Force to win air superiority over Europe for OVERLORD and the ground offensive that followed.[65] Germany could make substitutions and keep critical industries in operation through expensive repair efforts, but daylight precision strategic bombing forced a major diversion of German war-fighting capabilities away from its forces in the field to defend and repair industrial and transportation sites in Germany. Germany was able to increase its military production during the war, but daylight precision strategic bombing limited that expansion and made sure it would occur in areas that would not contribute to German military successes. Bombing stopped German oil production and destroyed 20 percent of German war production in the last 16 months of the war. These were worthy accomplishments.[66]

Bombing accuracy during the attack on the Augsburg Maschinenfabrik in October 1944 was only average, but was enough to cost Germany 644 tanks that might have turned the tide at the Battle of the Bulge. Any army corps would be proud to claim the destruction of 644 enemy tanks in one battle. Accuracy for the Fifteenth Air Force's May 31, 1944, attack on the Romano Americana Refinery at Ploesti was poor, but sufficient to cost Germany 38,550 metric tons of oil products that would have kept the German army mobile at many critical points in 1944. Strategic bombing was a vital, though not independent, component in the Allied war strategy.[67]

Ironically, the failure to achieve prewar hopes of precision during World War II spawned an unintended consequence. More precise bombing would still have destroyed the resources Germany required to wage war, but by its very preciseness would have failed to convince the German people that they were beaten. By not laying waste to thousands of acres of urban landscape, by not killing hundreds of thousands of civilians, and by not causing great amounts of collateral damage, true precision bombing would have eliminated much of the horror of war. The area or imprecise bombing of German cities failed to destroy the morale and will of the German people, but along with the ground invasion succeeded in convincing them that Germany had been both defeated and beaten. According to the Strategic Bombing Survey, the effort depressed morale, convinced 78 percent of the German people that the war had been a mistake, and "brought home to the German people the full impact of modern war." These attacks left the German people with a solid lesson in the disadvantages of war. There would be no "stab in the back" myths as after World War I.[68]

That strategic bombing failed to win the war independently is clear.[69] Doctrine called for bombing to "paralyze the nation's ability to wage war" and eliminate Germany's "capability of conducting military operations." Daylight precision strategic bombing did not deprive the German military of the weapons it needed to wage war, though bombing certainly deprived Germany of the weapons needed to wage war effectively. That daylight precision strategic bombing could not have won the war independently if given several more months is not clear.[70]

Accuracy was not good. Thousands of bombs fell so that a few could hit the target. Whatever precision bombing did to knock out vital industries was done by remarkably few bombs. If most bombing were as inaccurate as the bombing of the Leuna synthetic fuel plant, the Army Air Forces dropped nearly 1.5 million tons of bombs to get 50,000 tons to do any damage. Nevertheless, whether by several or by several hundred bombs, strategic bombing did destroy its targets. The campaign took longer than the six months AWPD/1 had foreseen, but still deprived Germany of critical capabilities. The driving force behind the pursuit of true precision bombing after World War II was the recognition that so few bombs could have such substantial effects in war—if accurately aimed.

America's high-altitude bombing technology in World War II was the best in the world, but inadequate for the objectives of daylight precision strategic bombing. No matter how sophisticated the aircraft, the bombsight, and the autopilot, no matter how well trained the bombardier and how brilliant the doctrine, once the bomb was released, daylight precision strategic bombing relied on the crudest of military technologies—simple explosives surrounded by a steel jacket. The bombardiers aiming their bomb loads at Germany's industrial infrastructure contributed mightily to victory at great cost,[71] but the doctrine that sent them to bomb Germany depended on hitting the nail on the head, not the broad side of the barn.

11

Japan's Congested and Highly Inflammable Cities

etween the world wars Army airmen looked at Japan and saw a fabric of packed cities, not industrial complexes. In his search for air-power targets, Billy Mitchell toured the Far East for six months in 1923–24. On record opposing the bombing of civilians, he believed the best means to defeat Japan would be attacks against her "congested and highly inflammable cities." The great Tokyo fire of 1923 had killed over 100,000 people—proof enough of Japan's vulnerability to fire. Mitchell told the General Board of the Navy that "Japan is more susceptible to attack by aircraft than any other country in the world," with cities "very easily destroyed."[1] The lure of Tokyo's paper and wood structures was a powerful force running counter to the convictions of daylight precision strategic bombing.

Japanese victories in World War II's early days forced the Americans to fight their way across the Pacific before Army Air Forces bombers could come into range of the Japanese home islands. Honolulu was 3,400 miles from Tokyo, Sydney 4,300, and Manila 1,800. Even Tinian, destined to become a major base for the air assault on Japan, was 1,500 miles away. For three years the U.S. Navy fought the Japanese navy to bring the new B-29 long-range bomber within reach.

Army bombers in these efforts continued to rely on high-altitude bombing aimed by Norden bombsights, though without notable success. The American people, shocked by the defeat at Pearl Harbor, read in earnest about the exploit of Capt. Colin P. Kelly Jr. News stories had Kelly's B-17 hitting a Japanese battleship with three well-aimed bombs before Kelly crashed his damaged aircraft into the ship. None of the bombs struck the Japanese vessel, which was a light cruiser. An explosion blew Kelly out of his damaged B-17, but his parachute failed to open.[2]

The Army claimed many successes in its attacks on Japanese shipping from high altitude with the Norden bombsight, though generally the claims could not be substantiated. What successes were documented came from below 4,000 feet. On July 30, 1942, for example, eight B-17s dropped sixty-four bombs from 1,500 feet on a transport, achieving seven hits. General Arnold explained that inadequate training and lack of opportunity caused the meager results against maneuvering targets. He told President Roosevelt that "the results obtained have not been due to any inherently defective characteristic of the fundamental theory." Arnold ballyhooed Army participation in the battle of Midway, claiming his airmen dropped 322 bombs and achieved twenty-two hits and forty-six near-misses on seven Japanese battleships or aircraft carriers and ten lesser ships. Japanese records captured after the war revealed no hits and no damage resulting from the high-altitude attacks. Bombs missed the Japanese carriers *Soryu* and *Hiryu* by 160 to 650 feet.[3]

During the war land-based aircraft sank five of the thirteen battleships sunk by all sides, twenty-two of the forty-four cruisers, 158 of the 209 destroyers, and four of the twenty aircraft carriers. Of the total, aircraft of all types accounted for 43 percent of ships sunk, surface vessels 23 percent, and submarines and mines the remainder. High-altitude bombings by strategic bombers in horizontal flight using the Norden bombsight were singularly ineffective in this role. The only major warship confirmed sunk by the Army Air Forces from high altitude during the war was the Japanese light cruiser *Abukuma*. PT boats had previously disabled the 5,170-ton ship during the Battle of Leyte Gulf, before forty-four B-24s and B-25s from the Fifth and Thirteenth Air Forces struck on October 27, 1944. Army aircraft employing tactics of strafing, skip-bombing, and low-level bombing tallied most of the Army's ship-sinking claims.[4]

The Navy gave up on high-altitude Norden bombing early in the war. Vice Adm. William F. Halsey Jr., then Commander of Air Forces, Pacific Fleet, wrote BuAer and BuOrd on September 26, 1942, recommending that the Norden bombsight and Norden stabilized bombing approach equipment (SBAE) be eliminated from naval aircraft because they served no function. Wartime experience, he claimed, showed that ships would "maneuver out from under bombs dropped at high altitude." Halsey allowed tactical commanders to remove bombsights from their aircraft in April 1943, violating BuOrd regulations.[5]

In August 1943 Undersecretary of the Navy James V. Forrestal requested an evaluation of the Norden's value. BuOrd, long the bombsight's advocate, concluded that it was of use to the Army but not the Navy. It remained opposed to eliminating stocks in case naval aircraft had to bomb the Japanese mainland from high altitudes. In January 1944 BuOrd stopped shipping Norden bombsights to the Pacific. Six months later the Pacific Fleet officially removed Norden bombsights from its torpedo bombers because "they are not used and are not wanted as there is no interest in high altitude horizontal bombing and it is doubtful if there are many personnel in the area qualified to do this type of bombing." Ironically, the chief of staff of Air Forces, Pacific Fleet, making this decision was Rear Adm. John J. Ballentine, who had supervised Norden development projects in the 1920s.[6]

Torpedo bombing proved nearly as ineffective as high-altitude horizontal bombing, though for a different reason. At Coral Sea, dive bombers wrecked the *Shoho*, but it took several torpedo hits before it sank. Although the torpedo bomber was still the best means of sinking a ship from the air, its vulnerability to antiaircraft fire limited its effectiveness. The Navy preserved its torpedo bomber capability through the war because dive bombers had proven unable to sink battleships. Most torpedo bombers, however, adopted the glide bombing technique, diving at a flatter angle of 40 or 50 degrees from high altitudes to minimize exposure to enemy fire. The Navy launched 1,287 aerial torpedoes during the war, achieving 514 hits (40%).[7]

The most famous test for naval aviation and dive bombing came at the Battle of Midway on June 4, 1942. Although naval tactics dictated a coordinated attack, circumstances brought the torpedo bombers of Rear Adm. Frank J. Fletcher to attack Vice Adm. Chuichi Nagumo's four aircraft carriers alone. In a confirmation of the vulnerability of the torpedo bomber, Japanese defenders downed thirty-six out of forty-two attacking TBD Devastators. Their sacrifice stood in stark contrast to their inability to achieve a single hit. Fifty SBD Dauntless dive bombers, however, made Midway the turning point in the Pacific War. Nine struck at the *Kaga*,

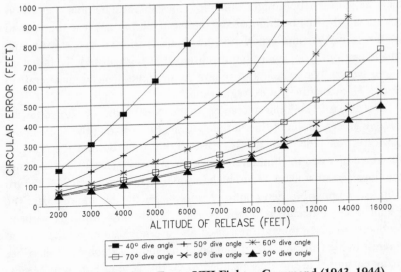

Figure 11.1. Dive-Bombing Error, VIII Fighter Command (1943–1944)

Source: VIII Figher Command Operational Research Section, "Errors in Dive Bombing," February 23, 1944, File 131.504C, Vol. 3, HRA.

achieving four hits (44.4%), two of three the *Akagi* (66.7%), three of eight the *Soryu* (37.5%), and four of seven the *Hiryu* (57.1%). Fourteen of the attacking dive bombers were lost.[8]

Antiaircraft gunfire improved during the war, forcing dive bombers into an increasingly dangerous environment, as predicted by the Army Air Corps before the war. Dive bombers escaped to higher altitudes and reduced accuracy, confirming the Army's experience that altitude was as much the enemy of bombing accuracy for dive bombing as for high-altitude horizontal bombing (see Figure 11.1). Naval aviators adopted the toss-bombing technique, where a bomber released its bomb during a dive at 6,000 feet. The added velocity of the bomb provided a trajectory closer to the line of sight, increasing accuracy, while the increased altitude limited exposure to defensive fire.[9]

Navy dive bombing pushed American air bases to within B-29 striking distance of Japan by July and August 1944. Unwilling to wait and trying to keep China in the war, Army Air Forces chief Henry Arnold pushed for early operations from bases in India and China. In November 1943 Arnold's Committee of Operations Analysts identified six target systems for the effort: merchant shipping, steel production, urban industrial areas, aircraft plants, antifriction bearings, and the electronics industry. Code-named MATTERHORN, the strategic bombing campaign of Brig. Gen. Kenneth B. Wolfe's XX Bomber Command, the operational organization of Twentieth Air Force, began on June 5, 1944, with a strike against Bangkok. Clouds forced radar bomb-aiming and only sixteen to eighteen bombs landed anywhere near the target area.[10]

XX Bomber Command's first target on the Japanese home islands was the Imperial Iron and Steel Works at Yawata on June 7, 1944. It was the perfect choke-point, producing 25 percent of Japan's steel. Flying at extreme range with small bomb loads at night produced miserable bombing accuracy—photographic intelligence revealed the nearest bomb crater was 3,700 feet from the target. The cost was seven of the sixty-eight B-29s launched.

Maj. Gen. Curtis E. LeMay replaced Wolfe in July, but results remained mixed. Night missions proved fruitless, while accuracy during the day made most missions futile. A radar run on the Pladjoe refinery at Palembang, Sumatra, produced one hit out of 156 bombs dropped. Another daylight raid on the Yawata Iron and Steel Works did no damage, but cost fourteen B-29s. Daylight precision strategic bombing was going nowhere in the war against Japan.

The one notable success during this early period was the raid on a Manchurian coke plant at Anshan on September 8, 1944. For the loss of four B-29s, ninety-one others knocked out six of sixteen coke batteries. Accuracy, however, was poor by European standards—fewer than 10 percent of the bombs landed within 1,000 feet of the assigned aiming point. LeMay instituted major changes to improve accuracy, based on his European experience. He formed the B-29s into tight twelve-aircraft combat boxes under the direction of a lead bombardier sighting for range and deflection and flying by the C-1 automatic flight control equipment (AFCE). Bombardiers adopted the synchronous bombing procedure by which both the optical Norden bombardier and radar operator controlled the bomb run.[11] Despite losses, XX Bomber Command became a daylight strike force because high-altitude precision bombing required daylight for accuracy.[12]

Three missions against the Rama VI railroad bridge at Bangkok typified the failures and successes of these early daylight precision strategic bombing missions. On December 14, 1944, thirty-three B-29s missed the 1,456-foot bridge. Three weeks later forty-four aircraft gained one hit on the bridge and did substantial damage to the approaches. In February 1945 another strike put four 1,000-pound bombs on the target.

Table 11.1. XX Bomber Command Operations (in tons, including mining operations)

Date	High Explosives	Incendiary	Mining	Total
June 1944	501	46	0	547
July 1944	209	0	0	209
August 1944	184	68	0	252
September 1944	521	0	0	521
October 1944	1,023	646	0	1,669
November 1944	1,415	215	0	1,630
December 1944	678	878	0	1,556
January 1945	1,584	422	233	2,239
February 1945	1,261	604	36	1,901
March 1945	1,019	417	259	1,695
Total	8,395	3,296	528	12,219

Source: Twentieth Air Force, "Statistical Operations," September 1945, File 760.308-1, HRA.

Also noteworthy as a portent of Japan's future was LeMay's December 15, 1944, mission against the dock area of Hankow, China. Using incendiaries, his B-29s destroyed nearly half the heavily populated target. The significance of this area fire bombing was not lost on LeMay.[13] XX Bomber Command's record was mixed, with the attack on Anshan its only notable success. Training and experience proved priceless. MATTERHORN units began moving to Guam and Tinian in the spring of 1945. In ten months XX Bomber Command dropped 11,244 tons of bombs, 29 percent of which were incendiaries (see Table 11.1).

The capture of Guam, Tinian, and Saipan in the summer of 1944 overcame the need for MATTERHORN. XXI Bomber Command began its strategic bombing of Japan from the Mariana Islands in November 1944. The Joint Chiefs of Staff ordered its commander, Brig. Gen. Haywood S. Hansell Jr., to "achieve the earliest possible progressive dislocation of the Japanese military, industrial, and economic systems and to undermine the morale of the Japanese people to a point where their capacity and will to wage war was decisively weakened." Targets were the aircraft industry, arsenals, electronic plants, oil refineries, and finished military goods. Hansell's orders also called for firebomb attacks on Japanese cities to test their vulnerability. Rather than an assault on the more basic elements in Japan's economy, as the Air Corps Tactical School would have had it, this was to be an attempt to weaken the ability of the Japanese to resist an invasion.[14]

Hansell was a key figure behind daylight precision strategic bombing both at the Air Corps Tactical School and as a member of the Air War Plans Division. He sent twenty-four B-29s after the Nakajima Musashino aircraft engine plant in Tokyo on November 24, 1944. Although skies were clear for this first mission, bombardiers discovered a force of nature that would make precision bombing from high altitudes nearly impossible. The jet stream, a weather phenomenon only revealed when B-29s flew above 30,000 feet, pushed the ground speed of B-29s to 445 MPH—too fast for the Norden bombsight. Musashino officials reported all bombs missed.[15]

Weather officers discovered that southeasterly trade winds collided with cold winds from the Asian continent and caused swirling layers of clouds to move toward Japan at different speeds and directions. Crews ran into winds of 200 MPH six miles up. Flying against the winds slowed aircraft and exposed them to enemy defenses. Flying at an angle to them caused so much drift that the Norden bombsight could not compensate. Flying with the winds occasionally pushed ground speeds above 500 MPH—too fast for Norden bombsight synchronization.[16] Against the jet stream B-29s did well to get 10 percent of their bombs within 1,000 feet of the assigned aiming point, compared to 42 percent at lower altitudes against Singapore, Rangoon, and Bangkok.[17]

H_2X radar, developed because Wright Field foresaw future aircraft would fly too fast for the Norden bombsight, proved equally ineffective. A mission to the Mitsubishi assembly plant at Nagoya under radar conditions left hundreds of craters 40 miles to the left and 30 miles short of the target.

A crisis in daylight precision strategic bombing was at hand. According to the Japanese, twenty-two missions against Japanese industries knocked out but one factory. In multiple raids against the Musashino Aircraft Factory, 835 B-29s dropping 2,300 tons of bombs damaged only 4 percent of the sprawling facility. The only obvious solutions to bombing inaccuracy were lower bombing altitudes or area incendiary bombing of Japan's tinderbox cities. Hansell, committed to Air Corps Tactical School doctrine, fought against both. Lower altitudes, he thought, would mean greater losses of the $509,000 B-29 and its crew of eleven to thirteen airmen. Area bombing would not destroy the Japanese capability for waging war. The Air Staff and Arnold pressed him to undertake incendiary missions to Tokyo on November 29, 1944, and to Nagoya on January 3, 1945, as tests, but from high altitude the results were limited. Many fires broke out, but they were widely separated and easily controlled.[18]

Hansell's XXI Bomber Command achieved only one successful precision attack, causing serious damage to the Kawasaki Aircraft Industries plant near Akashi on January 19, 1945—too late to save Hansell's job. The next day Arnold replaced Hansell with Curtis LeMay. In the words of Brig. Gen. Lauris Norstad, Twentieth Air Force chief of staff, "LeMay is an operator, the rest of us are planners." He had helped save daylight precision strategic bombing in Europe. He was the man to call when Arnold wanted a job done. LeMay had no misconceptions about what was expected of him: "If you don't get results, you'll be fired."[19]

LeMay's initial efforts were no more successful than Hansell's. Weather, high altitudes, and high winds made bombing ineffective, including a test incendiary attack on Kobe. On February 19, 1945, Norstad assigned incendiary test raids priority over aircraft assembly plants and LeMay responded with a maximum effort against Tokyo six days later. High altitude again limited its effectiveness, but 172 B-29s burned one square mile of built-up urban area to the ground. After four months the campaign against Japan's industrial web had not destroyed any of the nine top-priority targets. The Navy had done more damage to Musashino in one attack by dive bombers than 2,148 B-29 sorties and 5,398 tons of high-altitude bombs.[20]

The flammability of Japanese cities beckoned. Unable to destroy the machines of war, LeMay resolved to kill the human beings who operated the machines and to destroy the cities that housed the machines. Despite the Japanese civilians about to die, LeMay was still thinking as a graduate of the Air Corps Tactical School. Japanese industries were yet the target and he was going to keep them from operating even if in this roundabout fashion. In his memoirs he wrote:

No matter how you slice it, you're going to kill an awful lot of civilians. Thousands and thousands. But if you don't destroy the Japanese industry, we're going to have to invade Japan. And how many Americans will be killed in an invasion of Japan? Five hundred thousand seems to be the lowest estimate. Some say a million. . . . We're at war with Japan. We were attacked by Japan. Do you want to kill Japanese or would you rather have Americans killed?

The lessons of area-bombing Dresden, Germany, on February 13, 1945, were still fresh. American Marines were dying on Iwo Jima—6,821 of them—to support LeMay's bombers. The time for a radical change in strategy had come.[21]

The Air Staff pushed for a switch to incendiary area bombing, but LeMay believed high altitudes would limit effectiveness. Poor ballistics made the M-69 incendiary cluster unaimable from high altitudes. Conventional wisdom judged low-altitude missions too dangerous, but LeMay's intelligence sources told him that Japan had not deployed low-altitude antiaircraft artillery because of its experience against high-altitude B-29s. Area bombing did not need the precision of daylight, so the darkness of night and surprise made low altitudes safer. It was the greatest gamble of his career. Low altitudes, unhindered by the jet stream and heavy cloud formations, compensated for the lost accuracy of night bombing. The X-1 Reflex Sight Attachment with coated optics to increase light transmission made the Norden M-9 bombsight an acceptable aiming mechanism for night missions. Although not designed for this purpose, the APQ-13 H_2X radar worked well at low altitudes. Lower altitudes and stripping the big bombers of their defensive weapons reduced gas consumption and increased bomb loads.[22]

On March 9, 282 B-29s dropped 2,000 tons of M-69 jelled-gasoline incendiaries from 7,000 feet on Tokyo by intervalometers set at 50 feet. The aiming point was a large burning cross marked by pathfinder aircraft dropping M-47 napalm bombs across a three- by four-mile rectangle in the center of the city, inhabited by more than 1 million Japanese. Packed in 500-pound clusters,[23] the six-pound M-69 bomblets scattered over 15.8 square miles of Tokyo. Later crews aimed at unburned areas between fires. Fourteen aircraft went down, but high winds created a fire storm and at least 78,000 Japanese died. After the war LeMay explained his intentions: "I'll tell you what war is about—you've got to kill people, and when you've killed enough they stop fighting."[24]

XXI Bomber Command next struck against Nagoya on March 11. Planners increased intervalometer settings to 100 feet to get a larger path of destruction, but the decreased bombing density reduced the intensity of the fires. Next came Osaka, Kobe, and Nagoya with 50-foot intervalometer settings. Running short on M-69 clusters, LeMay's aircraft carried M-17 magnesium thermite bombs. Although less effective against urban areas, they kept the fire-bombing campaign going. LeMay's trail of fire left five of Japan's largest cities blackened ruins (see Table 11.2). Exhaustion, the depletion of incendiary bombs, and the diversion to support the Okinawa invasion halted the effort.

The Norden bombsight was of limited use during these raids. Altitudes were low and aiming points were huge bonfires. LeMay continued precision bombing raids, but without success. Night precision raids from low altitude using flares proved equally futile, though an April 12 strike against

Table 11.2. Twentieth Air Force Fire Raids (March 9, 1945–April 15, 1945)

Date	Target	Altitude (feet)	Destruction (square miles)
March 9, 1945	Tokyo	8,000	15.8
March 11, 1945	Nagoya	8,000	2.1
March 13, 1945	Osaka	8,000	8.1
March 16, 1945	Kobe	7,000	2.9
March 18, 1945	Nagoya	7,000	3.0
April 13, 1945	Kawasaki	8,000	10.7
April 15, 1945	Kawasaki	9,000	2.9
April 15, 1945	Tokyo	9,000	5.2

Source: XXI Bomber Command, "Graphic Summary of Operations," May 1, 1945, File 762.3011, HRA.

Musashino finally destroyed Hansell's old nemesis. This success spurred LeMay to launch dangerous daylight strikes against the Hitachi factory in Tokyo and the Kawanishi plant in Konan from low altitudes. The Norden proved its mettle and B-29s destroyed both targets.[25]

With bomb stocks replenished, LeMay returned to low-altitude night incendiary missions in April. Tokyo (four times), Kawasaki, Nagoya (twice), Yokohama, Osaka (twice), and Kobe burned before incendiary bomb-depletion again diverted LeMay to precision targets. Beginning on June 9, XXI Bomber Command would strike at precision targets when the weather permitted, but use area bombing when it did not. Incendiaries were ineffective against cities already burned and LeMay had to target smaller cities, including Hachioji with only 60,000 inhabitants. Typical was the July 6 strike against Chiba, Akashi, Shimizu, and Kofu. Thick undercast clouds forced the 570 B-29s to use radar, sufficiently accurate that day to burn 3.25 square miles of urban area.[26] Japan proved defenseless against these raids. To intensify the effect on morale, LeMay ordered Japanese cities notified by leaflets of their impending destruction.

In 10 months of operation, XXI Bomber Command dropped 167,736 tons of bombs, 61 percent incendiaries, at a cost of 414 B-29s. Precision bombing had not destroyed Japan's industrial web, but area bombing had burned over 150 square miles of Japanese cities and the industries within them. Despite the success of area bombing, 45.5 percent of all Twentieth Air Force sorties were for daylight precision strategic bombing. Area bombing accounted for 47.8 percent, though in the last five months of

Table 11.3. XXI Bomber Command Operations (in tons, including mining operations)

Date	High Explosives	Incendiary	Mining	Total
November 1944	343	232	0	575
December 1944	1,495	610	0	2,105
January 1945	927	477	0	1,404
February 1945	1,140	1,015	0	2,155
March 1945	3,086	10,761	1,070	14,917
April 1945	13,209	4,283	288	17,780
May 1945	6,937	17,348	2,617	26,902
June 1945	9,954	22,588	2,229	34,771
July 1945	9,388	33,163	2,390	44,941
August 1945	8,438	12,591	1,157	22,186
Total	54,917	103,068	9,751	167,736

Source: Twentieth Air Force, "Statistical Operations," September 1945, File 760.308-1, HRA; Twentieth Air Force Operations Analysis Section, "Bombing Accuracy Report No. BA-1," July 21, 1945, File 760.56-1, HRA; Twentieth Air Force Operations Analysis Section, "Report on Bombing Accuracy of Night Incendiary Missions," August 6, 1945, File 760.56-2, HRA.

the war 70 percent of the missions were area strikes. Accuracy on night incendiary missions remained poor—13 percent of incendiary bombs landing within 2,000 feet of the assigned point of impact. These were area bombing weapons, however, and considering the volatility of their targets, close was good enough.[27]

Despite the success of the area bombing campaign, the Army Air Forces continued to pursue precision. Four groups of Superfortresses of the 315th Wing carried AN/APQ-7 Eagle radar sets for precision radar bombing from above 30,000 feet. The higher frequency provided by the 18-foot airfoil-shaped antenna carried beneath the aircraft gave a clearer representation of ground features. The 315th used Eagle for attacks on oil targets, selected as choke-points because of guidance from the Strategic Bombing Survey in Germany. Electronically synchronized with the Norden bombsight, the Eagle was expected by developers to achieve near-visual accuracy. The Norden, without the visual input of a human bombardier, calculated the correct bomb-release time. With 1,095 sorties, the 315th averaged 13.5 percent of its bombs within 1,000 feet of the aiming point (see Table 11.3).

By August 1945 Twentieth Air Force and air-power advocates were in trouble. Ten months of pounding, including the destruction of its largest cities, had not knocked Japan out of the war. Wanting to avoid a ground invasion of the Japanese home islands, air planners turned to a solution that represented a bankruptcy of their strategy—more of the same, but with bigger bombs. On August 6 the United States sent the *Enola Gay* to Hiroshima, where bombardier Maj. Thomas W. Ferebee dropped the ultimate area weapon.[28] Ironically the aiming point that day was the Aioi Bridge over the Ota River, consistent with the doctrine of daylight precision strategic bombing. The Interim Committee, assigned the responsibility of planning for this new weapon, had recommended that it be aimed at a Japanese "war plant surrounded by workers' homes." The "Little Boy" atomic fission bomb killed 70,000 and destroyed 4.5 square miles of urban area.[29]

Japan did not surrender and Twentieth Air Force ordered 131 B-29s to bomb the Toyokawa naval arsenal the next day. On the eighth, 343 bombers firebombed Yawata and Fukuyama while sixty-nine more precision-bombed a Tokyo aircraft plant. With no word from Japan, 107 B-29s hit oil targets in Amagasaki while *Bock's Car* and Capt. Kermit K. Beahan dropped the "Fat Man" atomic bomb on Nagasaki. The Nagasaki target again complied with prewar doctrine—the Mitsubishi Steel and Arms Works. On August 9 25,000 died and 1.5 square miles of Nagasaki were leveled.

Still, there was no word from Tokyo. More B-29s dropped conventional bombs on the ninth and tenth, before Pres. Harry Truman ordered a bombing halt for surrender negotiations. Delays and mixed signals from Japan encouraged the president to order bombing resumed on the fourteenth. Five more targets experienced precision bombing by 584 B-29s and two cities area bombing by 186 B-29s before Truman announced Japan's unconditional surrender.

The United States dropped 160,800 tons of bombs on the Japanese home islands. Navy dive bombers operating from aircraft carriers accounted for 6,788 tons of these in sixteen strikes against precision targets from February to August 1945. When exposed to enemy land defenses and the weather difficulties of missions over Japan, naval dive bombing proved less accurate than at sea—an average circular error of 250 feet. In strikes against Japanese aircraft industries, the B-29s dropped 8 percent of their bombs on targeted structures and 8.4 percent within the open areas of the plants. Navy dive bombers averaged 14.9 percent hits on buildings and 21 percent within open areas. Army bombers missed with 83.6 percent of their bombs, the Navy with 64.1 percent.[30]

The Navy also used gunfire against strategic targets on the Japanese home islands, but its battleships and heavy cruisers did not fare so well. In July and August 1945 naval surface vessels fired on twenty-seven industrial targets, hitting twenty-two. One ship aimed at individual buildings of the Japan Musical Instrument Company at close range, but the average error in the mean point of impact was over 3,000 feet. Even with spotter aircraft, of 802 shells fired from 10.5 miles at the Kamaishi Japan Iron Works, a target covering 182 acres, only 29 percent landed within the compound. The ships averaged 25 percent hits, roughly comparable to the accuracy of heavy bombers flying four miles up.[31]

At a cost of $3–4 billion and 335 lost aircraft, B-29s accounted for 91 percent of the 160,800 tons of bombs dropped on Japan. Surprisingly, Twentieth Air Force achieved a day visual and radar precision bombing average of 31 percent within 1,000 feet of the aiming point during the war—a record similar to Eighth Air Force's 32 percent and Fifteenth Air Force's 31 percent. On Norden-aimed visual missions, the Twentieth's B-29s averaged 38 percent. The average altitude of daylight precision missions for the Twentieth Air Force was 4,500 feet lower than Eighth Air Force, which explained some of its success.[32] Bombardiers achieved this remarkable accuracy record despite the jet stream and missions covering 3,000 miles. With such accuracy and other advantages, why did the Army Air Forces give up on daylight precision strategic bombing against Japan so quickly in favor of area bombing?[33]

The fight-to-the-death nature of the Pacific war convinced Americans that only an extermination campaign could defeat the Japanese. On Tarawa seventeen Japanese soldiers survived the 4,500 who began the battle. The intensity of the fighting and the apparent willingness of the Japanese to fight to the death scared American leaders into a bombing strategy based on killing people rather than blowing up industries. An extermination campaign was the logical result. Japan's sneak attack on Pearl Harbor only served to vindicate this belief.[34]

LeMay claimed the switch to area bombing came because Japanese industries were closely integrated into the cities. These cities were the industries and the industries were the cities. Japan's economy, he argued, operated with many small shops built in the homes of urban workers. He saw drill presses still standing in the ruins of civilian homes after the fire raids. These cottage industries were too small to be targets of a strategic bombing campaign, but they were the choke-points in the Japanese industrial fabric. According to one Japanese author,

By the end of 1944, Japan was truly fully mobilized, and in the normal sense there were no more civilians in Japan. The government considered the civilian population to be just as much an element in the prosecution of the war as the soldiers at the front. There was no way by 1944 that civilians could be separated from the military in Japan.[35]

Japan's industrial output peaked in mid-1944 and began declining rapidly after that because of the Navy's blockade, not strategic bombing. Army Air Forces B-29s bombed factories already idled by the blockade. The Strategic Bombing Survey believed that the blockade defeated Japan, but failed to convince the Japanese leadership it had lost. B-29s were therefore left with a target the Air Corps Tactical School faculty had not considered. Strategic bombing had to persuade the Japanese government that it could not win, changing victory from "one of slow strangulation to a relatively quick knock-out."[36] LeMay's attacks on sixty-eight Japanese cities and towns destroyed 2,502,000 housing units and forced the Japanese government to tear down 614,000 more for firebreaks, leaving 30 percent of the population homeless. Government policies and the bombing forced 8.5 million civilians to flee the industrial cities. In nine months, bombing caused 806,000 civilian casualties. Night area and atomic bombing convinced the Japanese they had lost the war, just as the bludgeon of inaccurate daylight precision strategic bombing had done in Germany. By that it saved the hundreds of thousands of lives, American and Japanese, that would have come from an American invasion of Japan to force unconditional surrender.[37]

Many have emphasized the reasons behind the switch from precision to area bombing, including racism, vengeance for Pearl Harbor, the desire to impress the Soviets, and the Army Air Forces's quest for postwar independence. Ira Eaker had told Carl Spaatz "we should never allow the history of this war to convict us of throwing the strategic bomber at the man in the street." Later he admitted, however, that he had "always believed that civilians supporting national leaderships were equally responsible with the military. . . . The man who builds the weapon is as responsible as the man who carries it into battle." Killing "bad people to spare good people" was the proper function for strategic bombing, even if not complying with official doctrine. The Strategic Bombing Survey claimed the switch to area bombing occurred "because of the contributions in numerous ways of the civilian population to the fighting strength of the enemy, and to speed the securing of unconditional surrender."[38]

The most direct reason for the switch was the simplest and most pragmatic. From high altitudes, Twentieth Air Force bombardiers could not hit the nail on the head or the broad side of a barn. They aimed at what they could hit—cities.

Despite the inaccuracy of wartime bombing, American intent had generally been to destroy the machines of war. B-29s were the greatest and most expensive expressions of the doctrine of daylight precision strategic bombing. The ultimate irony was that these bombers would also come to represent the failure of that doctrine as leaders abandoned it and took up area bombing with the B-29 as the primary weapon for mass destruction. Doctrine makers of the 1930s looked to strategic bombing to avoid the horrors of World War I trench warfare. What they found in the skies over Japan avoided the trenches but was equally horrific.

Epilogue

The Norden M-9 remained the bombsight of the Army Air Forces and the U.S. Air Force into the nuclear age. It lost much of its secrecy when the *New York Times* revealed the United States had shipped it to the Soviets in the spring of 1944 to entice them into providing the Army Air Forces with shuttle bombing bases near Poltava.[1] The coming of jet bombers forced multiple modifications to the Norden design, but the basic system soldiered on. Attempts to achieve greater bombing precision through radio-controlled bombs still depended on the Norden bombsight for control and release. When the Navy needed an inexpensive, accurate, rugged device for dropping acoustic sensors along the Ho Chi Minh Trail during the Vietnam conflict, it brought the Norden bombsight out of mothballs.[2]

The C-1 autopilot also labored on after the war. The AFCE/SBAE (automatic flight control equipment/stabilized bombing approach equipment), still built by the Minneapolis-Honeywell Regulator Company, gave early Cold War pilots fingertip control over their jets, in addition to improving the accuracy of their bombsights. In the 1950s the Air Force and Navy replaced it with new Honeywell autopilots that worked much the same as the C-1, but relied on electromechanical and electronic components.[3]

Increasingly radar and electronics took over bomb-aiming responsibilities. The World War II engineering revolution bypassed Carl Norden, who refused to read the writings of other engineers and missed the switch to electronics. The Navy gave up on the Norden first, replacing it with the AN/ASB-1 radar bombing and navigation system, using both optical and radar sighting. The Air Force built on the wartime successes of NOSMO and NOSMEAGLE, pairing various radars and the Norden M-9B to overcome the weather limitations of optical sighting and the inherent inaccuracy of radar sighting.

In the 1950s Norden technology reached its limit. Bombers were becoming too fast for its mechanical components and the atomic and thermonuclear bombs had made pinpoint bombing unnecessary. *Dave's Dream*, a Norden-equipped B-29, aimed a Fat Man atomic bomb at the USS *Nevada* near the Bikini Atoll in July 1946 under perfect conditions from 29,000 feet. It missed by 2,130 feet, but 20,000 tons of TNT-equivalent atomic explosives still destroyed the target. A B-52 used radar from 40,000 feet in May 1956 to drop a thermonuclear bomb, but missed by 19,000 feet due to bombardier error. The inaccuracy was embarrassing, but a yield of 3.75 megatons made it hardly critical.[4]

New electronic devices with transistors made the gears, cogs, and discs of the Norden bombsight obsolescent. The B-50D, RB-36, and B-45 bombers used the AN/APQ-24 radar bombsight, which could achieve accuracies within 625 feet from an altitude of 25,000 feet under all weather conditions—close enough for nuclear weapons. The B-47 and B-52 bombers carried K-1 and K-2 bombing and navigational systems, combining the AN/APQ-31 bombing radar system, an electromechanical analog computer, and a Y-1 optical periscopic bombsight. Built by Sperry, the system weighed 1,700 pounds, had 79,000 parts, and used 410 vacuum tubes. Early electronics did not mean simplicity and reduced weight.[5]

On the horizon were various bombing and navigation systems based on ground radio transmissions, including SHORAN (*short-ra*nge *n*avigation) and LORAN (*long-ra*nge *n*avigation), and space-based GPS (*g*lobal *p*ositioning *s*ystems). By the 1980s and 1990s electro-optic targeting systems based on forward-looking infrared sensors with laser designators replaced bombsights. LANTIRNs (*low-a*ltitude *n*avigation and *t*argeting *i*nfra*r*ed for *n*ight), AN/AVQ-26 Pave Tacks, and Pave Pennys were the "Norden bombsights" of the 1991 Persian Gulf War, truly dropping pickles into pickle barrels. In principle these aiming systems were as simple as "X marks the spot."[6]

The company Carl Norden formed with Ted Barth also changed in the Cold War. In 1944 Carl L. Norden, Inc., formed a research and development subsidiary named Norden Laboratories, Inc., mainly to prepare for entering commercial fields after the war. When bombsight operations ended in November 1945, Carl L. Norden, Inc., and Norden Laboratories moved to White Plains, New York. The Veterans Administration took over Norden's two buildings in New York at 80 Lafayette Street and 50 Varick Street. Carl Norden retired and left these companies in the hands of Ted Barth, who soon retired to concentrate on philanthropic activities and politics.[7] The Barden Corporation maintained its precision ball-bearing plant at Danbury, Connecticut.[8] Norden Laboratories merged with the Ketay Instrument Company of New York in 1955 to become Norden-Ketay Corporation, purchased by United Aircraft Corporation on July 1, 1958, renamed the Norden Division. Under these names it produced a variety of precision instruments and systems in support of the Cold War, including digital converters, pressure transducers, airborne radar, bomber director and navigation systems, synchros, servomotors, potentiometers, amplifiers, flight instruments, television photo-reconnaissance systems for jet-powered aircraft, a terrain clearance radar for low-flying aircraft, optical systems for star tracker applications, and guidance and control systems for missiles. These represented a significant shift to electronics and alternating current from the mechanical engineering and direct current of Carl Lukas Norden, as well as a geographical shift from New York to Norwalk, Connecticut.

In 1966 Norden Division became a major military contractor when it won a contract to build the revolutionary heads-up vertical and integrated cockpit display for the F-111. The contract nearly destroyed the company. Norden bid $132 million for a project that cost $357 million. The U.S. Air Force reduced its order from 761 systems to 210 to stay within budget, but refused to pay Norden more than $245 million. The company absorbed the additional $112 million in cost overruns.[9]

As the Cold War wound down, military contracts ran out. One notable exception was the JSTARS battlefield surveillance system that, although rushed into battle with Norden technicians still manning the equipment, proved spectacularly successful in identifying the pell-mell Iraqi retreat from Kuwait along the "Highway of Death" during the Gulf War. In 1994

United Technologies sold its money-losing subdivision to Westinghouse. With few commercial applications, the future does not look promising for Norden's successor company.

Of Carl Norden, his bombsight brought sufficient wealth to separate him from postwar financial concerns. He never saw his bombsight as an instrument of destruction, but as a means for shortening wars and reducing casualties through the precision bombing of military and industrial targets. His wife occasionally chastised him for being a "merchant of death," but he never expressed any concern for financial profits (that was Barth's job) and always insisted he was trying to make war more humane. He fled into retirement in Switzerland after the war to escape the attention his bombsight brought him. It was a self-imposed exile because he wanted nothing to do with postwar weapons of mass destruction. According to his son, the inventor of the most precise optical bombsight ever developed never knew his device had been used to aim the bombs that destroyed Hiroshima and Nagasaki. Religiously, "it would have destroyed him."[10] He died on June 15, 1965, at age 85 in Zurich from tongue cancer, no doubt connected to his life-long cigar addiction.

Norden's bombsight was the key technology behind the development of daylight precision strategic bombing in the United States. It held out the prospect of winning wars quickly with minimized casualties. Although nuclear war was the antithesis of daylight precision strategic bombing, the memory of World War II was sufficient to delude millions of Americans into believing that the American way of war was the most humane on earth, attacking the machines of war rather than the human beings behind the machines of war. Strategic bombing combined the American love of technology with the American desire to keep losses on both sides, but especially on the American side, to a minimum. Although this was not his intention, Carl Norden had dehumanized war, making it impersonal and without guilt—waging war against nonliving, unfeeling, cold assemblages of metal and concrete. He had helped to make war more tolerable. Several decades of living under the threat of thermonuclear war and two large "brush-fire" wars in Asia made war less sufferable, at least until highly accurate television and laser-guided bombing again seemed to make war more tolerable. The Gulf War proved, however, as World War II had with the Norden bombsight, that clouds, smoke, dust, enemy defenses, the need for timely and accurate intelligence, expense, and chance remain constants in war. Coalition forces dropped 17,000 precision guided munitions into the "pickle barrel" in that war, but also 210,000 conventional "dumb" bombs missing by an average of over 300 feet. War remains war. Precision bombing of buildings and machines means fewer people will die, but people will still die.

Appendix A

United States Bombsight Acquisition, 1911–1945

Bombsight	Manufacturer	Remarks
Scott (1911)	Riley E. Scott	Experimental model for Army
Mark I Wimperis (WWI)	Edison Photograph/Pierce/Cotten/Gorham	12,000 manufactured for United States
Michelin (WWI)	Michelin (French)	
Mark III (1918)	International Register	3,500 ordered, 2,200 delivered
Type A-1 (1918)	Gorham	100 for Army
Type A-2 (1918)	Frederick Pierce	1,000 for Army
Type A-3 (1918)		Proposal
Sperry (1918)	Sperry Gyroscope	2 experimental models for Navy
Barr (c. 1919)		Proposal
Loring (c. 1919)		Proposal
Ford (c. 1919)		Proposal
Duff Double Drift (c. 1919)		Proposal
Hathaway-Loring (c. 1919)		Proposal
Milne-Loring (c. 1919)		Proposal
Goerz-Boykow (c. 1919)		Proposal

Bombsight	Manufacturer	Remarks
Meijer (c. 1919)		Proposal
Beggs (c. 1919)		Proposal
Miller (c. 1919)		Proposal
Riley-Scott (c. 1919)		10 for Army
Kimball (c. 1919)		Proposal
Hathaway (c. 1919)		Proposal
Hatchett (c. 1919)		Proposal
Improved Michelin (1920)	Michelin (French)	9 for experimental use by Army
Schmidt (1921)	Edmund Schmidt	Proposal
C-1 (1921)	Seversky through McCook Field	Experimental development for Army
Cope-Bagnell (1922)	Cope-Bagnell Company	Proposal
Mark IV (1922)	Norden through Witteman-Lewis Aircraft	300 for Navy and 141 for Army (Mark III plus Norden stabilizer)
D-1 (1922–25)	Estoppey through Eberhart Steel/Pioneer	Army procured 114 from Pioneer, Navy 14 from Eberhart, Army 2 from McCook Field
Mark X (1922)	Frankford Arsenal	1 experimental model for Army
C-2 (1923)	Seversky	Experimental development for Army
D-2 (1925)	Estoppey through Pioneer	3 experimental models for Army
D-3 (1925)	Estoppey through Sperry	2 experimental models for Army
D-4 (1926)	Estoppey through Gaertner	230 for Army, 40 for Navy
K-1 (1926)	Inglis through McCook Field	3 experimental models for Army
Mark XI (1926)	Norden	80 procured for Navy, 15 for Army, plus 5 experimental models
E-1 (1927)	Wright Field	Optical lens mounted in aircraft floor
F-1 (1927)	Wright Field	Experimental development for Army (Mark III with PDI and new stabilizer)
G-1 (1928)	Wright Field	Experimental development for Army (Mark I with PDI and new stabilizer)

Bombsight	Manufacturer	Remarks
Mark XIII (1928)	General Electric	1 experimental model for Navy
C-3 (1929)	Seversky through Sperry	25 experimental models for Army
D-5 (1929)	Estoppey through Sperry	1 experimental model for Army
Mark XV/15 (1929)	Norden	Navy designation, 2 experimental models, 1 production prototype, 89,893 all versions
Navy/Army Mod. 1/M-1, 2, 3 (1932)	Norden	179 for Navy, 100 for Army (new stabilizer housing)
Mod. 2/M-4 (1934)	Norden	72 for Navy, 81 for Army (new PDI, LABA, SBAE)
Mod. 3/M-5 (1936)	Norden	102 for Navy, 82 for Army (shielding and tachometer)
Mod. 4/M-6 (1938)	Norden	80 for Navy, 469 for Army (increased altitude and trail)
Mod. 5/M-7 (1942)	Norden	16,725 for Navy and Army (GBA, AES)
M-8 (1942)	Norden	Remove AES
M-9 (1942)	Norden	27,500 for Army (X-1 reflex optics)
M-9A (1943)	Norden	1,500 for Army (increased trail)
M-9B (1943)	Norden	43,000 for Army (increased altitude and trail)
C-4 (1932)	Sperry	3 procured experimentally, 28 in production contract for Army
L-1 (1932)	Inglis through Sperry	5 experimental models for Army
D-7 (1932)	Estoppey	Experimental development for Army
C-5 (1933)	Sperry	6 for Army testing, 1 for Navy
Mark I Dive Bombsight (1935)	Sperry	16 experimental models for Navy
Universal Sight/Mark XVII/17 (1937–postwar)	Norden/NDRC/Bell Telephone	Experimental development, optical/electronic (AN/APQ-31)

Bombsight	Manufacturer	Remarks
N-1 (1938)	Sperry	20 for Army
D-8 (1938–42)	Gaertner and NCR	80 by Gaertner, 10,000 by NCR for Army and Lend-Lease
O-1 (1939)	Sperry	600 for Army, to British in 1941
Richmond (1939)	B. O. Richmond	Proposal
Shapiro (1939)	Morrey H. Shapiro	Proposal
Hanes (1939)	Warner Hanes	Proposal
Pullin (1939)	William E. Pullin	Proposal
Cahoon (1939)	Donald M. Cahoon	Proposal
Brown (1939)	Richard Brown	Proposal
Mark II Dive Bombsight/ later the Mark 16 and 17 (1939)	Norden	4 experimental models for Army and Navy
Alkan Dive Bombsight (1940)	Specialties Company	French sight, proposal
S-1 (1940)	Sperry	5,140 for Army and Lend-Lease
Luther (1940)	Ruben Luther	Proposal
NOSMEAGLE (1941–postwar)	NDRC/Bell Telephone/ Norden	AN/APQ-7 radar with NOSMO (*Norden Sight Modification*) for Army
T-1/Mark XIV (1941)	Sperry/AC Spark Plug	23,000 produced for British
D-4B (1942)	Estoppey through National Cash Register	2,000 for Lend-Lease, 80 for Army
Pioneer Low Altitude (1942)	Pioneer Instrument Company	Experimental development for Navy
MAD Bombsight (1942)	NDRC	Magnetic Anomaly Detector with automatic bomb release
Bossi (1942)	Romeo A. Bossi	Proposal
Durgin (1942)	Franklin W. Durgin	Proposal
Orcutt (1942)	Lester Orcutt (Civil Air Patrol)	Local production
N-3A (1942)		Army N-3A gunsight with reflector and stabilizer
Lewis (1942)	Mitchum Tully and Company	Proposal
Houston (1942)	H. W. Houston	Proposal
Helicopter Bombsight (1942)	Frigidaire Division of General Motors	Army consideration
Greene (1942)	Norman Greene	Proposal

Bombsight	Manufacturer	Remarks
Calkins Night Sight (1942)	James M. Calkins	Proposal
Chaffin-McQuie-Hamilton (1942)		Proposal
Micro-H (Electronic—WWII)	Various	Ground beacons and receiver
H₂S/H₂X (Electronic—WWII)	Various	Airborne radar
Gee (Electronic—WWII)	Various	Ground beacons and receiver
Oboe (Electronic—WWII)	Various	Ground beacons, receivers, and transmitters
Gee-H (Electronic—WWII)	Various	*Gee* plus *Oboe* in reverse
Airship Bombsight (WWII)	Airship Patrol Squadron 12	Local production
Gale/Mark 21 (WWII)	Naval Air Station, San Diego	Local production
Keeney (1943)		Proposal
Fuller Minimum Altitude (1943)		Army testing
Mark 20 Low Altitude Anti-Submarine (1943)	NDRC	Navy order 1,000, none procured
U-1 (1943)	Frigidaire Division of General Motors	Experimental development for Army
Rochester Low-Level (1943)	Rochester Athenaeum and Mechanics Institute	Experimental development for Army
Mark 23 Low Altitude Anti-Submarine (1944)	NDRC/Kodak/American Cystoscope Makers	Navy order 1,000, none procured
LAB (1944)		Low-altitude radar (AN/APQ-5) and Norden bombsight
Igor (1944)		Proposal
Mark 24 (1945)	Franklin Institute	Experimental development for Navy
K-1, K-2, K-3, and Peanut Dive Bombsights (1945)	NDRC	Experimental
Integrator Toss Bombsight (1945)		Army testing (AN/ASG-10)
A-1 Davis-Draper Dive Bombsight (1945)		Army testing

$$H_2S/H_2X$$

Appendix B

Prime Contractors for the Norden Bombsighting System

American Thread Company, New York, N.Y.
Atlas Ball Bearing Company, SKF Industries, New York, N.Y.
Baker and Company, Newark, N.J.
Breeze Corporation, Newark, N.J.
Burroughs Adding Machine Company, Detroit
C & H Menzer Company, New York, N.Y.
Cannon Electric Development Company, Los Angeles
Cardanic Corporation, Easthampton, Mass.
Carl L. Norden, Inc., Brooklyn, N.Y.
Chase Brass and Copper Company, New York, N.Y.
Clarostat Manufacturing Company, Brooklyn, N.Y.
Conklin Brass and Copper Company, New York, N.Y.
Cornish Wire Company, New York, N.Y.
Dever and Edds, New York, N.Y.
Driver-Harris Company, Harrison, N.J.
Edgeworth Hardware and Supply Company, New York, N.Y.
General Electric Company, New York, N.Y.
General Electric Supply Company, New York, N.Y.
Guarantee Specialty Company, New York, N.Y.
Herzog Miniature Lamp Works, Long Island, N.Y.
International Projector Company, New York, N.Y.
James Goldmark Company, New York, N.Y.

Lukas-Harold, Indianapolis
Manufacturers Machine and Tool Company, Brooklyn, N.Y.
Minneapolis-Honeywell Regulator Company, Minneapolis
Mitchell-Rand Company, New York, N.Y.
National Carbon Company, Cleveland
National Screw and Manufacturing Company, Cleveland
New Departures Division, General Motors, Bristol, Conn.
P. R. Mallory and Company, New York, N.Y.
Patton MacGuyer Company, Providence, R.I.
Peter A. Frasse Company, New York, N.Y.
Remington-Rand, Elmira, N.Y.
Robbins and Myers, Springfield, Ohio
Strahs Aluminum Company, New York, N.Y.
Victor Adding Machine Company, Chicago
W. A. Moyer and Sons, Parkers Landing, Pa.
Waltham Screw Company, Waltham, Mass.
Westinghouse Electric Manufacturing Company, Pittsburgh, Pa.
Wisdenbach-Brown, New York, N.Y.

Bombsights and automatic pilots assembled by Carl L. Norden, Inc., were designated by an *N* in front of the serial number. Similarly, Victor-produced bombsights used a *V,* Cardanic a *C,* Minneapolis-Honeywell an *H,* Lukas-Harold an *L,* and Remington-Rand an *R.*

Appendix C

USAAF Bombardier Training (graduates)

Category	12-31-41	6-30-42	12-31-42	6-30-43
Bombardier instructor	—	—	—	152
Bombardier/Dead reckoning navigator instructor	—	—	—	—
Bombardier preflight	—	—	3,678	10,312
Bombardier-navigator preflight	—	2,796	4,553	—
Bombardier school	224	1,183	2,675	5,053
Precision bombardier for B-29	—	—	—	2,875
Bombardier prebasic training	—	—	—	—
Bombardier refresher	—	—	—	—
Bombardier-navigator	—	—	—	61
D-8 bombsight bombardier-navigator	—	—	666	225
Dead reckoning bombardier-navigator	—	—	—	—
Total	224	3,979	11,572	18,678

12-31-43	6-30-44	12-31-44	6-30-45	8-31-45	Total
988	936	1,174	1,716	470	5,436
84	22	—	—	—	106
7,366	10,448	8,916	—	—	40,720
—	163	29	—	—	7,541
—	—	—	—	—	9,135
6,178	391	—	—	—	9,444
—	—	—	584	893	1,477
—	—	—	3,572	774	4,346
231	1,186	71	662	335	2,546
—	—	—	—	—	891
1,475	7,116	10,388	5,049	909	24,937
16,322	20,262	20,578	11,583	3,381	106,579

Source: "History of Flying Training," July 1939–December 1946, File 134.71-101, HRA.

Appendix D

The Bombsighting Problem

If all bombs hit their targets, war would be much simpler. World wars could be fought more quickly, with less destruction, and at reduced cost.

Bombsights performed two basic functions for finding that one point in the sky from where a bomb, when dropped, would hit its target. First the sight had to allow the bomb-carrying aircraft to fly on a track so that when released the bomb landed on a line parallel to the track of the aircraft that intersected the target. This was the *deflection* problem. The difference between the longitudinal axis of the airplane and the actual track the aircraft followed on the ground, caused by wind, was called the *drift angle*. The ground distance between a point directly under the aircraft at the time that the bomb hit the ground to the point where the bomb lands because of cross winds and air resistance was *trail*. For a 500-pound bomb dropped from 20,000 feet by a bomber traveling at 160 MPH, the trail would be approximately 2,300 feet (with no wind). Adjusting the bombsight's drift vector solved the deflection problem. Successive observations of the target through the bombsight's telescope determined the drift angle. The aircraft then flew on a heading that insured the ground track would intersect the target. The bombsight computer also calculated the additional change in heading needed to compensate for the influence of the cross wind on the bombs as they dropped.

Second, the sight had to calculate the lead time necessary to allow the bomb to travel along the proper deflection track to the target. This was the *range* problem—the distance from the point where the aircraft dropped its bomb to the target. Determined mathematically, range was a calculation of the effect of gravity on a

Table D.1. Time of Bomb Fall (160 MPH release speed)

Altitude (feet)	600-pound bomb (in seconds)	1,100-pound bomb (in seconds)
2,000 feet	11.25	11.25
5,000 feet	18.00	18.00
10,000 feet	25.50	25.75
14,000 feet	30.50	30.75
18,000 feet	34.75	35.00
20,000 feet	36.75	37.25

bomb. This acceleration toward the ground varied as to geographical location, but was approximately 32 feet per second per second in a vacuum. The bombsight combined gravity and the aircraft's ground speed, determined by measuring the changes between the sighting angle to the target and a vertical line directly beneath the aircraft, to solve the range problem.

The vertical force of gravity added to the horizontal force of the releasing aircraft's forward motion determined the parabolic trajectory of the falling bomb. The resulting bomb range was the distance the bomb traveled from the point on the earth's surface directly beneath the point of release to the point where its parabolic arc intersected the earth's surface at the target. In a vacuum the only input needed for accurate bombing in range was the ground speed of the aircraft, the altitude, and some means for releasing the bomb at exactly the proper range from the target. For a B-17 cruising at 160 MPH at an altitude of 23,000 feet, the time of fall of a 600-pound M-32 bomb would be approximately 38 seconds, giving a bomb range of 8,875 feet. Already the inherent errors of the procedure should be clear— if the speed calculation was off by 2 MPH and the altitude by 25 feet, the bomb range differed by 115 feet (see Table D.1).

Altimeters were therefore critical to the achievement of accuracy in bombing. Initially these were inaccurate aneroid barometers, using scales marked in feet rather than in pounds of atmospheric pressure. A World War I altimeter at 30,000 feet could be off by as much as 3,500 feet. In 1923 the Air Service's Engineering Division at McCook Field designed a sensitive altimeter especially for bombsight use. The altimeter was not perfected until 1929, but Maj. Jimmy Doolittle used a Kollsman Instrument Company's altimeter in his pioneering blind instrument landing experiments at Mitchel Field, Garden City, New York.

Accurate bombing, however, demanded more sensitive and accurate altimeters. One major problem with the barometric pressure altimeter was that it provided the air pressure above sea level, while most Air Corps operations were over land. In the interwar period the Air Corps worked on sonic altimeters for judging altitude above land or sea, using whistles and timing the return of the echo. General Electric pursued its commercial applications, but the heavy devices were only useful up to about 1,300 feet. A better solution was the radio altimeter, developed by

General Electric beginning in 1928. By 1938 a production model was available, providing an instantaneous reading of 50 feet to 5,000 feet above the terrain below, unaffected by air pressure, temperature, humidity, or clouds. In the next year the Radio Corporation of America developed a radio altimeter effective up to 20,000 feet, with an error of plus or minus 200 feet. At $20,000 each, these radio altimeters were too much for military budgets of the 1930s. Available at the start of the war, the less expensive AN/ARN-1 was effective only to 400 feet and the AN/APN-1 only to 4,000. Not surprisingly, the Army Air Forces's Armament Laboratory at Wright Field concluded in 1941 that the "largest error in aerial bombing is due to errors in the determination of the altitude (absolute) of the airplane."

In 1941 Western Electric and General Electric perfected the SCR-518A pulse radar system for measuring altitude up to 20,000 feet. Although it was still heavy and expensive, the Army ordered 8,000 in 1941. By 1943 engineers had reduced the weight from 100 to 30 pounds using smaller, more powerful vacuum tubes. At the end of the war the SCR-718 series pulse radar altimeter could gauge accurate altitudes up to 50,000 feet.[1]

Bombsight designers knew bombs did not drop in a vacuum, as air resistance acted to slow the bomb, reducing range and increasing time of fall. Air resistance also depended on the temperature, humidity, local atmospheric pressure, speed of the falling bomb (resistance or drag increases relative to the speed of the object), and the ballistics of the bomb (shape, size, weight, and condition of the bomb's surface). The bomb range was less than in a vacuum and the difference between the two ranges (in a vacuum and in the atmosphere) was *trail*. Technicians determined trail by experimentation or trials. The Army used the Aberdeen Proving Ground in Maryland and the Navy the Dahlgren Naval Proving Ground in Virginia to drop bombs under different conditions, extrapolating common values to develop a bombing table that would provide the trail amount for a specific bomb, at a specific speed, under specific atmospheric conditions. Wind either directly into or directly behind the falling bomb was a range factor generally ignored, because the wind would have the same influence on the airplane. The calculation of the ground speed of the aircraft compensated for the influence of wind. This was why most early bombsights required a bomb run directly up- or downwind, translating the influences of the wind into a factor that could be negated with adjustments for aircraft ground speed (true air speed plus or minus the influence of wind).

For most bombsights, range was a matter of the *sighting angle*, or the angle formed by a vertical line from the aircraft to the ground, and the line of sight from the aircraft to the target. The bombsight determined the bombing range, which was the distance on the earth's surface from the line of sight to the vertical line from the aircraft to the ground, compensating for trail. This was the point of release.

The complexity of the bombsighting problem can best be seen in diagram form (see Figure D.1).

Indicative of the difficulty of the bombsighting problem is the theoretical error that individual factors contribute to the inaccuracy of a bombsighting operation (see Table D.2).

Inherent errors in bombsights and bombardiers increased with altitude. Billy Mitchell's bombers in the 1921 ship-bombing tests could depend on the odds in-

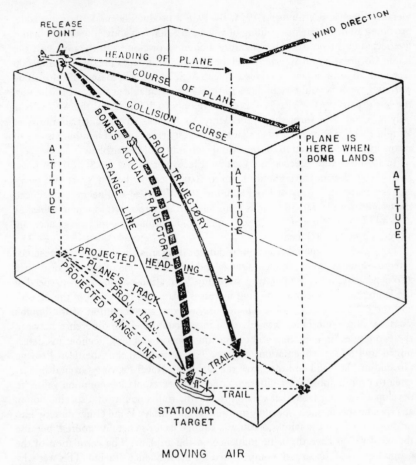

Figure D.1

suring at least several hits from below 2,500 feet. Air Corps strategists formulated plans for war based on bombing tests from 8,000 feet, but even at this altitude accuracy errors were expanding beyond the destructive powers of Air Corps bombs. A bomb depends on over-pressure, temperature, and fragmentation of the bomb casing (shrapnel) to damage or destroy a target. A cubic foot of TNT (trinitrotoluene) on explosion releases about 10,000 cubic feet of gas at a temperature of about 2,800°C. This gas expands at about 8,000 feet per second, achieving an over-pressure of 147,000 psi. This destructive force results in cratering when the bomb hits the earth and declines quickly because of the tamping effect of the soil (see Table D.3).

The fragmentation effect declines with distance (see Table D.4).

At 25,000 feet, errors made precision bombing a matter of luck and providence.

Table D.2. Theoretical Errors of Bombsighting Factors (in feet; ground speed of 300 MPH and 1,100-pound M-33 bomb)

	Altitude (feet)		
Cause of Error	2,500	8,000	25,000
Ground track off 1 degree	96	174	318
Ground speed off 3 MPH	51	100	182
Altitude off 250 feet	74	74	74
Time of fall off 1 second	440	440	440
True vertical off 2 mils	5	16	46
Cross hair width	1	4	10
Error in trail from error in ground speed of 2 MPH	1	6	26
Error in altitude with resultant error in time of fall and ground speed of 250 feet	280	162	100

Table D.3. Cratering Effect of Bombs in Sandy Loam

Bomb Size (pounds)	Fuze Type	Crater Depth (feet)	Crater Diameter (feet)
500	Delayed	5	20
500	Instant	2	9
1,000	Delayed	13	45
1,000	Instant	6	20
2,000	Delayed	17	50
2,000	Instant	7	22

Table D.4. Lethal Radiuses of Bombs

Bomb Size (pounds)	Lethal Radius (feet)
100	40–60
250	47–70
500	60–90
1,000	70–105
2,000	83–125

Perhaps in peacetime these errors could be reduced with proper training and maintenance, but in the fog of war, while under attack by enemy aircraft and antiaircraft artillery, with vision disrupted by clouds and smoke, such errors would be magnified, not reduced.

The biggest problem facing Army and Navy engineers was to develop a bombsight that was not too complex to render it useless under operational conditions. It would have to solve the above problems, while striking a compromise between accuracy and simplicity of operation. Initial World War I sights had been the essence of simplicity, relying mainly on luck for a hit. As surface defenses forced aircraft to drop bombs from greater altitudes, luck was not enough.

World War I research tried to determine the correct range setting for the time of drop using mechanical means. The critical component was determining the ground speed of the aircraft, using it to set the correct range angle or point of release. Bombardiers determined ground speed by "timing" the motion of the aircraft over the ground, by calculating the vector sums of the wind and the aircraft's air speed, or by "synchronizing" a moving component of the bombsight with the aircraft's motion over the ground. All three added significant complexity to the bombsight.

In the timing technique, the crew used a stopwatch or similar device to measure the time required to fly over a predetermined angle or distance on the ground. On a sight with a movable telescope, this meant measuring the time required to fly over the same object on the ground during the telescope's swing through a predetermined arc. On a sight with a fixed telescope, the bombardier measured the time required to fly over the same object on the ground from the point the object passed through the front cross wire until the object passed through the rear cross wire. A variation was to measure the time required to fly over a known distance on the ground. Because the distance measured on the ground varied as to altitude, tables or scales were required to transfer time into ground speed. Another variation was to fix the front cross wire on the target for a period equal to the number of seconds it would take for the bomb to fall from that altitude to the target. The operator moved the rear cross wire back an amount equal to the change in the distance between the front and rear cross wires during that period, which corresponded to trail. Sights using these techniques were called timing sights. The effect was to calculate an average speed over a time interval.

The second method for determining ground speed involved flying a straight course for a prolonged time to calculate the effects of wind on the flight of the aircraft. Because such smooth and level flights exposed the bomber to defensive fire for a time longer than the other two methods, airmen rarely used the drift method except in early bombsights. The technique was effective at low altitudes, where an approximation of the wind speed allowed quick ground speed calculations without a significant loss of accuracy.

The third means for determining ground speed was the synchronous method. Rather than measuring a fixed point's movement relative to the aircraft, it measured the movement of the aircraft relative to a fixed point on the ground. The bombardier carefully held the bombsight's cross hairs fixed on a point until the rotational speed of a wheel or gear in the sight's mechanism could be synchronized with the movement of the aircraft relative to the fixed point. Whereas the timing bombsight provided an average speed over a time interval, the synchronous sight matched the speed at the point of measurement and was updated continuously as long as the bombardier kept the cross hairs fixed on an object on the ground. Once synchronized, no other adjustments were necessary for the period of the bombing run.

The problem with the timing method was that it was an average determination of ground speed and required a long, level bomb run to achieve an accurate measurement. This exposed the aircraft and crew to enemy defensive fire for a prolonged period. Timing for several minutes was "too long for comfort, inviting poor concentrations on the process, and resulting in poor manipulation of an otherwise quite accurate instrument." It assumed a steady speed over the entire period of the measurement, when in fact that speed might vary. Getting an aircraft to fly straight, level, and at a constant speed under combat conditions was a frustrating challenge. The timing method relied on a simple mechanical device, but also on a human operator making simultaneous visual observations with manual manipulations of a timing device and therefore contained considerable errors.

The synchronous method was vulnerable to any slight oscillation of the telescope, which would affect the speed of the revolving mechanism, providing an erroneous ground speed. In the aircraft of the 1920s, weather and vibration created great obstacles to stabilization. A high degree of stabilization, either by gyroscope, pendulum, dash pot (shock absorber), or automatic pilot was essential to proper synchronization, while the timing method averaged out these oscillations. The synchronous method relied on a complicated mechanical device, but required the human operator to do no more than keep a cross wire fixed on a distant point for a brief time. The trade-off was mechanical complexity with human simplicity (the synchronous method) or mechanical simplicity with human complexity (the timing method). In precision bombing, the former was preferable to the latter, but required greater expense and a higher degree of manufacturing accuracy. Expense, manufacturing difficulties, and the problem of achieving the necessary degree of stabilization hindered the development of the synchronous sight, despite its theoretical advantages over the timing sight.

World War I bombsights generally used the vector-sum or timing methods. Bombsights of the 1920s, including the Estoppey D-1 through D-4 and the Norden Mark XI, employed the timing method. Both the Norden M-series and Sperry S-1 bombsights of World War II used the synchronous method.[2]

Appendix E

Operation of the Norden Mark 15/M-Series Bombsight

I. PREPARATION FOR BOMBING RUN—to be performed 30 to 45 minutes before the airplane is expected to reach the target area.

A. Check stabilizer gyro to insure that gyro is operating and has attained normal running speed before proceeding further.

B. Check torque motor to insure torque motor is operating.

C. Check PDI to insure PDI system is operating properly.

D. Turn on bombsight gyro by moving the bombsight toggle switch to the "ON" position.

E. Align bombsight clutch by aligning the course centering marks on the bombsight clutch connecting rod with the course centering pointer.

F. Make train bombing adjustment. If train bombing is to be used the sight should be adjusted to place the mean point of impact on the target. Loosen the knurled nut on the trail spotting arm, moving the trail arm to the correct mil value, and tightening the knurled nut on the trail spotting arm.

G. Compute true air speed and bombing altitude using the E-6B computer, or equivalent.

H. Set disc speed and trail from the bombing tables and set this data into the sight.

  1. Set the disc speed into the sight by turning the altitude knob in a clockwise direction. Make sure the "change speed" lever is in the correct position.

    a. Move the telescope motor toggle switch to the "ON" position and check disc speed with a type 43D-3 bombsight disc speed tachometer.

b. Adjust the altitude knob until the correct disc speed reading is obtained on the tachometer.

c. Continue checking and adjusting until the correct speed, within ½ RPM, is obtained on at least three checks.

d. Move the telescope motor toggle switch to the "OFF" position.

2. Set trail into the sight by loosening the knurled nut, moving the trail arm to the correct mil value as indicated by the scale on the trail plate and tightening the knurled knob to lock the trail arm at this setting.

I. Check reflex optics—on bombsights equipped with the type X-1 reflex sight, check this unit to make certain that its indicator is coincident with the telescope indicator.

1. If these indicators are not coincident, align them by moving the reflex optics clutch to its inoperative position, manually rotating the reflex optic head until its indicator is at the same angle as the bombsight telescopic indicator, and re-engaging the clutch.

2. Turn the rheostat which controls the light that illuminates the reticle of the reflex sight to provide the desired intensity of illumination of the cross hairs on the reflector plate.

J. Move the telescope motor drive clutch into engaged position and make sure the telescope sector indicator is positioned at, or near, the maximum sighting angle for convenience in picking up the target when it is first sighted.

K. Preset dropping angle from the automatic bombing computer, or from the E-6B, and use the rate knob to move the rate sector indicator to the proper setting on the tangent scale.

L. Adjust the B-7 bombsight mount to level the stabilizer. Use the leveling bubbles mounted on top of the bombsight gyro housing to judge the vertical. Make sure that the bombsight gyro is caged and that the airplane is flying straight and level before performing this operation. Care exercised in obtaining a good level will eliminate the necessity for making large corrections to level the bombsight gyro during the bombing run.

II. BOMBING RUN—the synchronous bombing run is started when the airplane reaches the initial point specified at the preliminary briefing. The bombardier should contact the pilot on the interphone at this point and coordinate the remainder of the run. The actual technique that will be employed will vary with the nature of the mission. In general, however, each of the following steps must be performed in much the same sequence as they are presented.

A. Switch on the bomb rack by moving the toggle switch or switches to "ON" position to select the desired bomb bay or rack.

B. Open bomb bay doors by moving the bomb bay door toggle switch to the "ON" position. When the doors are open the bomb bay door light will be on.

C. Uncage the bombsight gyro as soon as the airplane is flying straight and level.

D. Swing the sight onto the target, or if equipped with the type X-1 reflex optics, align the vertical cross hair with the target.

1. Grasp the directional arm jaws with the left hand, if flying on the autopilot,

and hold the autopilot clutch to avoid turning the airplane while lining the sight up with the target.

2. Grasp the turn and drift knobs with the right hand and swing the bombsight head into alignment with the target.

E. Use the search knob or displacement knob to swing the horizontal cross hair onto the target.

F. Move the telescope motor toggle switch to the "ON" position.

G. If evasive action is to be taken, disengage autopilot clutch to permit turning the airplane with the bombardier's turn knob.

H. Start evasive action, if these tactics are to be employed during the approach to the target. These maneuvers, when employed, will be limited to turns of from 5 degrees to 15 degrees and the time on each leg will be from 10 to 20 seconds. The bombardier will turn the airplane in these maneuvers by moving the bombardier's turn knob in the appropriate direction and amount. These turns should be planned so as to gradually work the airplane upwind so that the final turn onto the target can be made in a downwind direction.

1. Level the bombsight gyro, if necessary, by using the leveling knobs to center the bubbles in the spirit-type levels mounted on the gyro housing.

2. Hold the bombsight manually to keep the line of sight on the target until the bombsight clutch is engaged to stabilize the bombsight in azimuth.

3. Move the horizontal cross hair back on the target with the displacement knob.

4. Make a note of the sighting angle which will indicate the time to turn onto the target to complete a bombing run of the desired duration. This value can be obtained from the automatic bombing computer, or the bombing tables, for 30-second runs. For runs of longer or shorter duration the proper sighting angle will have been computed on the ground before takeoff.

5. Watch the telescope sector indicator for the time to turn on the target for the bombing run and plan the evasive action accordingly.

6. Stop evasive action and turn the airplane on the target for the bombing run when the telescope sector indicator reaches the sighting angle that signals the start of a bombing run of the desired duration.

I. Obtain drift angle from the automatic bombing computer, or from the E-6B computer, and turn the airplane, while holding the line of sight on the target, until the correct drift angle is indicated on the drift scale. Engage the bombsight clutch as soon as the drift has been preset.

J. Place the vertical cross hair on the target with the turn knob. Double grip the turn and drift knobs to stop relative motion between the cross hair and the target. Only very fine adjustments should be required, inasmuch as this operation will consist simply of refining the course that was established when the drift angle was preset.

K. Check level of bombsight gyro to make sure the airplane is flying straight and level.

L. Place the horizontal cross hair on the target with the displacement knob. Use the rate knob to stop relative motion between the cross hair and the target. Care should be exercised not to overcontrol at this point. Only very fine adjustments

of the rate knob should be required, inasmuch as this operation will consist simply of refining the rate that was established when the dropping angle was preset.
M. Move the release lever up to firing position and lock in firing position by moving the lever upward to the limit of its travel and pressing the small locking pin into the operative position.
N. Extreme caution must be taken not to overcontrol at this point. If the preceding operations have been carefully performed, a good course and a good rate have been established. Any adjustment made at this point should only be for the purpose of removing any very small errors still present. The gear ratios are such that any major adjustments at this time in course and/or rate may well result in much larger bombing errors than if the small remaining errors are accepted and the cross hairs moved back on the target by means of the turn and displacement knobs.
O. When the telescope sector indicator drives into coincidence with the rate sector indicator bombs are released automatically.
P. Notify the pilot that the bombs have been released.
Q. Prepare the equipment for possible violent evasive maneuvers.

1. Close bomb-bay doors.
2. Cage bombsight gyro.
3. Engage autopilot clutch and disengage bombsight clutch.
4. Turn off telescope motor.
5. Turn off bombsight gyro.
6. Latch release lever.
7. Turn off switches to bomb rack or racks.
8. Return altitude knob to minimum speed stop.
9. Return telescope sector indicator to maximum setting.
10. Return trail arm, and trail spotting arm if sight is so equipped, to zero.
11. Cover bombsight.[1]

Glossary

AES (*A*utomatic *E*rection *S*ystem) Modification of Norden bombsight to allow for automatic leveling of bombsight without resorting to manual adjustment based on spirit levels.

AFCE (*A*utomatic *F*light *C*ontrol *E*quipment) Air Corps term for gyroscopically stabilized automatic pilot designed to manipulate aircraft controls through the bombsight in order to maintain level flight during the bombing run. Different from Navy **SBAE** in serving as general aircraft automatic pilot in addition to bombing operations.

Altimeter Aircraft instrument used for determining vertical distance above sea level.

Area target In American usage, a precision target that required a distribution of bombs throughout the area of the target.

Automatic pilot Device designed to manipulate the control surfaces of an aircraft automatically to insure level flight free of yaw, pitch, or roll. Also autopilot.

Automatic release system Device on Norden bombsight allowing for automatic and instantaneous release of bombs when sighting angle and dropping angle indicators coincided.

Bomb run The brief part of a bombing mission immediately preceding bomb release. Also bombing approach.

CEP   (*C*ircular *E*rror *P*robable) Measure of accuracy and reliability of bombing. Expressed as radius of a circle within which at least 50 percent of bombs dropped will land.

Circular error   Distance from a given point of impact, or from the mean point of impact of a pattern of bombs, to the center of the target, measured as the radius of a circle around the point of impact, or the mean point of impact of a pattern of bombs. Often given as **circular error probable (CEP)**, which was .939 times the arithmetic mean circular error. Also equal to 1.746 multiplied by the square root of the product of the range error probable and the deflection error probable ($1.746 \sqrt{R_e \cdot D_e}$).

Crosstrail   Distance between the true course of the airplane and the collision course to the target or distance that ground track of aircraft must be aligned upwind.

Dead reckoning   Estimating an aircraft's position at a given time by calculating heading, time, speed, and wind from a known position. Used in bombing from or through clouds or overcast.

Deflection   Distance measured on the ground from the point directly under an aircraft on a track parallel to the target to the target.

Deflection error   The distance from a given point of impact, or from the mean point of impact of a bombing pattern, to the center of the target measured perpendicular to the direction of approach (normal to the ground track). Often given as deflection error probable (DEP), which was .845 times the arithmetic mean deflection error.

Dive bombing   Descending from high-altitude horizontal flight to low altitude at an angle of between 70 degrees and 90 degrees from the horizontal in Navy usage, or above 30 degrees from the horizontal in Army usage, releasing the bomb or bombs just prior to recovery from the dive.

Drift angle   Difference between the longitudinal axis of an airplane or heading and the actual track the aircraft followed on the ground.

Dropping angle   The angle between a vertical line from an aircraft's bombsight and the line of sight at the point of bomb release.

Fuze   Mechanical detonating device for setting off the bursting charge of a bomb. Delayed fuzes allowed penetration of the bomb before explosion to produce a greater mining and tamping effect.

GBA   (*G*lide *B*ombing *A*ttachment) Modification of Norden bombsight to allow bomb-aiming while in a glide or climb.

Glide bombing   Descending from higher altitude horizontal flight to lower altitude at an angle between 40 and 50 degrees from the horizontal in Navy usage and less than 30 degrees from the horizontal in Army usage, releasing the bomb or bombs just prior to recovery from the glide.

Gross error   Bombing errors of greater than 3,000 feet, not considered in Army Air Forces's accuracy calculations.

Ground speed   Velocity of an aircraft relative to ground.

Ground track   Track of an aircraft on the ground.

Gyroscope   Spinning flywheel revolving around an axis mounted to be free to rotate about one or both of two axes perpendicular to each other and to the axis of spin with a tendency to hold a fixed position in space.

Gyrostabilizer   Gyroscope-stabilized device for maintaining level flight.

Horizontal bombing   Releasing bomb or bombs in level, horizontal flight.

Industrial fabric   The interrelationship and interdependency between components of a nation's industries.

Initial point   Geographic point located approximately five minutes from a target to provide an exact orientation for the bombing run.

Intervalometer   An electromechanical device for dropping two or more bombs in succession to achieve a predetermined pattern of explosions on the ground. See **Train bombing.**

M-series bombsights   Army designation for Norden synchronous bombsights, series M-1 through M-9.

Mark XI bombsights   Navy designation for Norden timing bombsights.

Mark XV bombsights   Navy designation for Norden synchronous bombsights, Mod. 1 through Mod. 5, redesignated Mark 15 during World War II.

Mil   Navy method of measuring bombsight accuracy, in terms of angular measurement of errors, equal to a distance of one foot for each 1,000 feet of altitude. At 25,000 feet of altitude, an error of one mil would result in a ground error of 25 feet (*Ground Error* = mil × (alt/1,000).

Mining effect   Increase in destructive power of a bomb by burying in the earth prior to detonation, estimated at approximately 4½ times the power of a bomb's high explosive charge. Effect is achieved through **tamping.**

Morale bombing   (also spelled "moral" bombing) Attempting to destroy the will of an enemy people by the terror of direct bombing on that people.

MPI   (*M*ean *P*oint of *I*mpact) Center of impact of a pattern of bombs.

NOSMO   (*No*rden *S*ight *Mo*dification) Norden optical bombsights combined with H₂X airborne radar.

Overcast   Covering of clouds. Expressed in tenths (1/10th, 2/10ths, etc.) to represent the degree of vision blockage. Also undercast, referring more directly to a cloud layer below aircraft.

Pattern bombing   Dropping a number of bombs from a formation of bombers to achieve a relatively uniform distribution for the purpose of saturating a target to improve the probabilities of hitting the target. Also known as carpet bombing. See **Saturation bombing.**

Pitch   Movement of an airplane around its lateral axis (from wing tip to wing tip).

Precision target   Targets that, to be destroyed, require either a direct hit by a bomb of the proper size or a hit within a limited distance therefrom.

Radial error   Direct linear distance from the target to the point of bomb impact.

Range   Distance measured on the ground from the point directly under an aircraft to the target or point of bomb detonation along the proper deflection track.

Range angle   Angle formed by line of sight to target and vertical line from aircraft to ground at the time of bomb release.

Range error   The distance from a given point of impact, or from the mean point of impact of a pattern of bombs, to the center of the target, measured parallel to the direction of approach (along the ground track of the aircraft). Often given as range error probable (REP), which was .845 times the arithmetic mean range error.

Roll   Movement of an airplane around its longitudinal axis (from nose to tail).

S-1 bombsights   Army designation for Sperry synchronous bombsights.

Salvo   At the time of release, dropping all bombs instantaneously from an airplane.

Saturation bombing   Dropping a number of bombs from a formation of bombers to achieve a relatively uniform distribution for the purpose of saturating a target to improve the probabilities of achieving a hit. Also known as carpet bombing. See **Pattern bombing.**

SBAE   (*S*tabilized *B*ombing *A*pproach *E*quipment) Navy term for gyroscopically stabilized automatic pilot designed to manipulate aircraft controls through the bombsight in order to maintain level flight during the bombing run. See **AFCE.**

Sighting angle   The angle formed by the line of sight to target and a vertical line from the aircraft to the ground.

Slant range   Straight-line distance from aircraft to target.

Synchronous technique   Turning of a wheel or gear in a bombsight mechanism to match the movement of the aircraft over a fixed point on the ground. Measurement of the movement of an aircraft relative to a fixed point on the ground.

Tamping   Filling in above an explosive charge to increase its power. Achieved in **mining effect** when bombs are dropped from high altitude.

Time of fall   Time duration from bomb release to bomb impact, roughly equal to the square root of the altitude divided by 16.08 ($\sqrt{Alt}/16.08$).

Timing technique   Use of stopwatch to measure the time required to fly over the same object on the ground, measured during the swing of a bombsight's telescope through a predetermined arc or from the movement of the object from the front cross hair to the back cross hair in a bombsight's telescope, in order to determine ground speed. Measurement of a fixed point's movement relative to the aircraft.

Trail   Horizontal distance measured on the ground that a bomb lags behind the airplane that dropped it. Distance from the point of impact of a bomb to a point directly beneath the airplane that dropped it at the instant of bomb impact.

Train bombing   Dropping two or more bombs in succession at predetermined intervals (using an **intervalometer**) from the same airplane to achieve dispersal across an area target.

Trajectory   The path of a bomb through the air from the point of release to the point of impact.

True air speed   Velocity of aircraft through air, including influences of wind.

Water-hammer effect   Result of a bombing near-miss, wherein the weight of thousands of tons of water focus the force of the exploding bomb against the hull of a ship.

Yaw   Movement of an airplane around its vertical axis (from ventral to dorsal).

Abbreviations

ACTS	Air Corps Tactical School
AWPD/1	Air War Plans Division/1
BuAer	Bureau of Aeronautics
BuOrd	Bureau of Ordnance
HRA	U.S. Air Force Historical Research Agency, Maxwell Air Force Base, Montgomery, Ala.
NACA	National Advisory Committee for Aeronautics
OAFH	Office of Air Force History, Washington, D.C.
RG	Record Group
TR	War Department Training Regulation
USSBS	U.S. Strategic Bombing Survey

Notes

Major sources and references cited frequently appear in full in the bibliography.

Introduction

1. After the war the Victor Adding Machine Company acquired the *Enola Gay*'s Norden bombsight when the government declared it surplus property. In 1947 the company donated the sight to the Smithsonian Institution. It remains there today, awaiting the completion of the *Enola Gay* restoration project.

2. Ferebee's initial combat bombing mission was the first Army Air Forces B-17 mission of the war against German targets in France. His pilot, Paul Tibbets, and navigator, Dutch Van Kirk, were also aboard the *Enola Gay* over Hiroshima on August 6, 1945.

3. Cross, *The Bombers*, 181; Richard Rhodes, *The Making of the Atomic Bomb* (New York: Simon and Schuster, 1988), 705–11; interview of Paul W. Tibbets Jr., September 1966, File K239.0512–602, U.S. Air Force Historical Research Agency, Maxwell Air Force Base, Montgomery, Ala. (hereafter HRA); Thomas and Witts, *Enola Gay*; and U.S. Strategic Bombing Survey (hereafter USSBS), Report No. 3 (Pacific War), *The Effects of Atomic Bombs on Hiroshima and Nagasaki* (Washington, D.C.: Government Printing Office, 1946).

4. For an account of the Nagasaki mission, see Chinnock, *NAGASAKI*; and USSBS, *Effects of Atomic Bombs*.

5. Rhodes, *Making of the Atomic Bomb*, 733–44. The Manhattan Engineer District originally estimated 66,000 at Hiroshima and 39,000 at Nagasaki dead from the immediate effects

of the atomic blasts. See *Manhattan Project: Official History and Documents*, Reel 12, Pt. 5, p. 18, microfilm at Air University Library, Maxwell AFB, Montgomery, Ala.

6. E. J. Loring, "Bombing and Bombing Sights," *Scientific American* 126 (January 1922): 49; and Sherry, *The Rise of American Air Power*, xi.

7. Leonard Thompson, writing of Gallipoli, in Jay M. Shafritz, *Words on War* (New York: Prentice-Hall, 1990), 417.

8. Peter Vansittart, *Voices from the Great War* (New York: Franklin Watts, 1984), 97.

9. Walker and Wickam, *Huffman Prairie to the Moon*, 235.

10. Thomas and Witts, *Enola Gay*, 219.

11. Boynton L. Broun, who tested the Norden Mark XV for the Navy at Dahlgren Naval Proving Ground in 1934, said, "It was called the pickle-barrel sight because of its accuracy." See McCollum, ed., *Dahlgren*, 36. *Time* magazine wrote in 1939 that the Army Air Corps could "drop a bomb into a barrel from 18,000 feet." See "In the Air," *Time*, October 23, 1939, 33. Henry Arnold, commander of all army air units in World War II, wrote of airmen bragging about "tossing it right in the pickle barrel." See Arnold, *Global Mission*, 150. *Newsweek* in 1942 attributed the phrase to "a highly publicized Army test of the sight, in which Norden-equipped bombers laid their eggs smack on pickle barrels." See "Pickle Barrelers," *Newsweek*, April 20, 1942, 50–51. *Current Biography 1945* cited the phrase as "drop a dime into a pickle barrel at fifty thousand feet" (434). "Norden Bomb Sight" in *Science News Letter* 46 (December 9, 1944), identified the Norden as "the bombsight that helps Yank bombardiers hit a pickle-barrel with a blockbuster" (382). Most probably the origins of the "pickle barrel" are apocryphal, lost in the mists of American folklore. One of its most vivacious popularizers was Theodore "Ted" Barth, in the 1930s president of Carl L. Norden, Inc., which manufactured the bombsight. Barth was a genius at public relations and a guess that Barth coined the phrase would not be without foundation.

12. Hughes Rudd, "Maytag Messerschmitt," in Stuart Leuthner and Oliver Jensen, *High Honor* (Washington, D.C.: Smithsonian Institution Press, 1989), 380.

13. Foulois to Deputy Chief of Staff, November 23, 1934, Air Technical Service Command Historical Office, "Case History of Norden Bombsight and C-1 Automatic Pilot," January 1945, File 202.2-35, HRA.

14. See, for example, Watts, *The Foundations of U.S. Air Doctrine*.

15. "As of December 31, 1946, the net allotment to the Manhattan Project totaled two-billion-three-hundred and eleven million dollars." See *Manhattan Project: Official History and Documents*, Reel 2, Pt. 7, Vol. 5, p. 2.6. Leslie Groves, director of the project, recorded that only $2.191 billion of the $2.3-billion allocation was actually spent, making the costs of the Norden project equal to 68 percent of the Manhattan Project. See Leslie R. Groves, *Now It Can Be Told: The Story of the Manhattan Project* (New York: Da Capo, 1962), 360.

16. The Army Air Forces procured 81,537 Norden bombsights, models M-1 through M-9B, the Navy 8,353. A 1942 contract for the bombsights called for a unit price of $8,500. Each bombsight also needed an autopilot/bombing approach apparatus ($5,000), a glide bombing attachment on some versions ($3,300), stabilizers, disc speed tachometers, rotor speed tachometers, pilot direction indicators, reflex sight attachments, low-altitude attachments, tangent scale kits, steering motors, formation sticks, rate end computers, spare parts, and so on. For the entire project, $1.5 billion, including government funds to expand production, is a conservative estimate. See Production Section to Colonel Shepard, July 20, 1945, File 471.63, Folder—Bombsights—"M" Series—Norden, Box 3381, RD-3047, Record Group 342, Records of the Engineering Division, Central Decimal Correspondence File, Material Command, Wright Field, 1917–51, Suitland National Records Center (hereafter RG342); Robert V. Brown, "The Navy's Mark 15 (Norden) Bombsight: Its Development and Procurement, 1920–1945," Office of the General Counsel, Department of the Navy, 1946, 320; and BuOrd

to Chief of Air Corps, January 28, 1942, File 471.63, Folder—Bombsight—Navy, Box 3903, RD-3851, RG342.

17. Although subject to criticism, the USSBS calculated just after the war that strategic bombing killed 300,000 Germans and 330,000 Japanese during the war. It was impossible to divide British- from American-caused bombing casualties in Germany, but all bombs dropped on Japan came from American aircraft and nearly all were aimed with Norden bombsights. See USSBS, Report No. 1, *Summary Report (European War)* (Washington, D.C.: Government Printing Office, 1945), 1; and USSBS, Report No. 1 (Pacific War), *Summary Report (Pacific War)* (Washington, D.C.: Government Printing Office, 1945), 20. Max Hastings, *Bomber Command: The Myths and Reality of the Strategic Bombing Offensive, 1939–1945* (New York: Dial, 1979), 352, records German figures for deaths from Allied bombing as 593,000.

18. Coffey, *Decision over Schweinfurt*, v–vi; Ronald Fernandez, *Excess Profits: The Rise of United Technologies* (Reading, Mass.: Addison-Wesley, 1983), 206; Loyd Searle, "The Bombsight War: Norden vs. Sperry," *IEEE Spectrum* (September 1989): 60–64; Chinnock, *NAGASAKI*, 66; and *Atlanta Journal and Constitution*, November 19, 1990, p. A7. Military files from World War II are full of letters from women willing to sacrifice their long hair in the interests of the national defense. Late in the war, after much of the secrecy associated with the Norden had been peeled away, the Army notified prospective sources of human hair that "although a cross-hair design is produced in Army Air Forces' bombsights, it is not made by using either spider webs or blond hair as is often believed." See, for example, ACAS/Materiel, Maintenance and Distribution to Mrs. Elliott Dexter, May 1, 1944, File 452.26, Box 1277, Central Decimal Files, Oct. 1942–44, Textual Records of the Army Air Forces, Record Group 18, National Archives (hereafter RG18). Evidently the confusion was tied to the unfortunate terminology of "cross *hairs.*" If the synonym "cross *wires*" had been used, most people would have assumed metal wires were used. The pieces of glass were heat-fused and human hair or spider silk would not have survived the heat of the fusing process.

19. LeMay and Kantor, *Mission with LeMay*, 265.

Chapter 1. Means for Dropping Projectiles from Aerial Crafts

1. See appendix D for a more detailed explanation of the bombsighting problem.

2. Air Service Engineering Division, "Report on Bomb Sights," September 1, 1925, File 216.2101–34, HRA.

3. See appendix D for a more detailed explanation of the timing method of bombsighting.

4. Arnold, *Global Mission*, 34.

5. Riley Estel Scott, "Means for Dropping Projectiles from Aerial Crafts," U.S. Patent Office, No. 991,378 (filed May 4, 1910, awarded May 2, 1911); Juliette A. Hennessy, *The United States Army Air Arm, April 1861 to April 1917* (Washington, D.C.: USAF Historical Division, 1958; rpt., Washington, D.C.: OAFH, 1985), 45–46, 53–54, and 174; and "Hearings on the Act to Increase the Efficiency in the Air Service," 1913, in Maurer Maurer, ed., *The U.S. Air Service in World War I*, Vol. 2, *Early Concepts of Military Aviation* (Washington, D.C.: OAFH, 1978), 3–17. Arnold recorded that Scott dropped twelve bombs out of fifteen within a 60-foot square and that the Michelin Prize was $5,000. Before Congress, Scott testified to the accuracy and prize money as given above. Lt. John H. Towers initiated U.S. Navy involvement with bombsights on February 8, 1913, when he began experiments in level bombing at Guantanamo Bay, getting "fairly accurate results . . . using fairly simple device gotten up by one of the men." See U.S. Office of Naval Operations, *United States Naval Aviation, 1910–1970*, 7 (hereafter U.S. Naval Operations, *Naval Aviation*).

6. Trail is also the horizontal distance measured on the ground that a bomb lags behind

the airplane that dropped it—the distance from the point of impact of a bomb to a point directly beneath the airplane that dropped it at the instant of bomb impact.

7. Gill Robb Wilson, "Technique in Dying," in *Leaves from an Old Log* (Washington, D.C.: American Aviation Associates, n.d.), 81–82. Gill flew with the Lafayette Escadrille during World War I.

8. Maurer, ed., *Air Service in World War I*, Vol. 1, *The Final Report and A Tactical History* (Washington, D.C.: OAFH, 1978), 108; Army Air Service, "Bombardment from Aeroplanes: Instruction and Shooting Methods and Instruments," n.d. (1918?), File 167.4726–1, HRA; and *Ellington, 1918* (Ellington Field, Tex.: n.p, n.d.).

9. Geoffrey L. Rossano, ed., *The Price of Honor: The World War One Letters of Naval Aviator Kenneth MacLeish* (Annapolis, Md.: Naval Institute Press, 1991), 209.

10. U.S. Naval Operations, *Naval Aviation*, 10, contains the story of a bombardier from 1914 whose accuracy had been impaired by the inability to "disengage my fingers from the wind-wheel sooner."

11. Hal Boyle interview for Associated Press, December 11, 1943, in 2nd Bombardment Group History, 1918, File GP-2-HI (Bomb), HRA.

12. Such altitudes required the use of a three-foot telescope for bombsighting, a stopwatch for timing the movement of the target across a scale in the telescope, and a chart for determining bomb time of fall.

13. Maurer, *Early Concepts of Military Aviation*, 61, 50–51.

14. "Notes on British Bombsights and Bombing Tactics," July 10, 1941, File 248.222-51, HRA; and "British Bombsights," 1941, File 248.222–50, HRA.

15. War Department Training Regulation 440-96, "Bomb Ballistics and Bomb Sights," December 12, 1927, File 248.222-38, HRA; and Brown, "Navy's Mark 15 (Norden) Bombsight," 10–12.

16. "Annual Report of the Director of Air Service, 1919," File 167.4011, HRA; "Bomb Sight Production," n.d. (1918?), Folder—Bombing Equipment for DH-4, File 471.63, Box 40, RD-3093, RG342; Virginia G. Toole, Air Technical Service Command, "The Development of Bombing Equipment in the Army Air Forces," May 1945, File 201-13, HRA; Benedict Crowell, *America's Munitions, 1917–1918* (Washington, D.C.: Government Printing Office, 1919), 302–3; and Maurer, ed., *Air Service in World War I*, Vol. 4, *Postwar Review* (Washington, D.C.: OAFH, 1978), 541.

17. Army Air Service, "Bombardment from Aeroplanes"; Air Service Engineering Division, "Report on Bomb Sights"; Folder—Bomb Sights—General, File 471.63, Box 872, RD-3312, RG342; and "Brief History of Bombsight Development by the Army," October 22, 1943, File 452.26-F, Box 764, Central Decimal Files, Oct. 1942–44, RG18.

18. Hughes, *Sperry*, 261; and National Advisory Committee for Aeronautics, "The Chief Causes of Error in Bomb Dropping from Aeroplanes," January 1918, File 248.222-38, HRA.

19. Sperry to Engineering Bureau, Office of the Chief of Ordnance, March 13, 1918, and Trench Warfare Section of the Engineering Bureau, Office of the Chief of Ordnance, to Sperry, March 21, 1918, Folder—Visual Stabilization 1915–24, Box 29, Series V, Accession 1893, Elmer Ambrose Sperry Papers, Hagley Museum and Library (hereafter Elmer Sperry Papers).

20. These bombsights were also designated the Type B-1 (Mark III).

21. Sperry to Naval Observatory, September 16, 1915, Office of Naval Aeronautics to Bureau of Navigation, January 5, 1916, BuOrd to Bureau of Navigation, January 26, 1916, BuOrd to Sperry, May 18 and June 7, 1916, and Sperry to BuOrd, June 3, 1916, Folder—Visual Stabilization 1915–24, Box 29, Series V, Elmer Sperry Papers.

22. U.S. Naval Operations, *Naval Aviation*, 13; Hughes, *Sperry*, 237; Roscoe, *On the Seas*, 45; and Brown, "Navy's Mark 15 (Norden) Bombsight," 13–14.

23. "The Sperry Automatic Pilot," n.d. (1916?), Folder 42, Box 1, Series V, Public Relations Department Literature File, Sperry Gyroscope Company Records, Hagley Museum and Library (hereafter Sperry Gyroscope Records).

24. Léon Foucault discovered the gyroscope while trying to demonstrate the rotation of the earth in 1851. Although others had worked with gyroscopes before, Sperry's 1907 patent was for a gyroscope mounted on pivots instead of a fixed mount, incorporating the principle of precession into an active rather than passive device.

25. Elmer A. Sperry, "The Electrically-Driven Gyroscope and Its Uses," 1915–16, Folder 17, and "The Gyroscope and How to Demonstrate Many of Its Uses," n.d., Folder 18, Box 1, Series V, Public Relations Department Literature File, Sperry Gyroscope Records.

26. Lawrence Sperry called his device a mechanical pilot, while others preferred gyropilot or aeroplane stabilizer. After Sperry won the French award, the French press first used the term "automatic pilot." See Charles L. Keller, "Automatic Pilot, 1913 Version," *Sperry Engineering Review* 13 (October 1960): 20.

27. "The Sperry Automatic Pilot," Sperry Gyroscope Records; "Result of First Contest for Safety in Aeroplanes, in France," *Scientific American Supplement*, August 15, 1914, 108–9; "Installation of the Sperry Stabilizer on a Curtiss Flying Boat," *Aerial Age* 1 (June 14, 1915): 303; "The Sperry Gyroscopic Stabilizer," *Flight* 7 (January 29, 1915): 74–76; "Sperry Gyroscopic Stabilizer," *Flying* 3 (January 1915): 360–61; "The Sperry Gyroscopic Stabilizer," *Flying* 3 (August 1914): 196–200; and "The Sperry Gyroscopic Stabilizer in France," *Scientific American* 111 (July 11, 1914): 30.

28. Lawrence Sperry to Executive Committee, Sperry Gyroscope Company, March 1915, Folder—Airplane Stabilizer, Box 30, Series V, Elmer Sperry Papers; and "Sperry Aircraft Control Apparatus," n.d. (1920?), Folder—Public Relations Department—Sperry Aircraft Control Apparatus, Box 2, Series V, Public Relations Department Literature Files, Sperry Gyroscope Papers.

29. Although not known at the time, this "creep" was the product of aircraft acceleration and electrical brushes affecting the movement of the directional gyroscope, thereby altering its frame of reference.

30. D. S. Fahrney, "The History of Pilotless Aircraft and Guided Missiles," 1958, Chapter 3, "The U.S. Army and U.S. Navy Development of the Flying Directed Missile," in Box "Printed Material, Probably Duplication," Accession 1970, Elmer Sperry Papers (uncatalogued); Hughes, *Sperry*, 258–59, 263–64, 267; U.S. Naval Operations, *Naval Aviation*, 34, 36; Sperry to Hewitt, July 26, 1916, Sperry to Signal Corps, August 17, 1916, Sperry to Naval Bureau of Operations, May 19, 1917, McCormick to BuOrd, n.d. (August 1917), and Bane to Sperry, January 12, 1920, Folder—Aerial Torpedo, Box 29, Series V, Elmer Sperry Papers; and Charles L. Keller, "The First Guided Missile Program: The Aerial Torpedo," *Sperry Engineering Review* 14 (March 1961): 11–18.

31. According to Henry Arnold's memoir, the "Bug" could carry 300 pounds of explosives. See Arnold, *Global Mission*, 74.

32. Fahrney, "Development of the Flying Directed Missile," chap. 3 of "The History of Pilotless Aircraft and Guided Missiles." Orville Wright designed the aircraft, C. H. Wills of the Ford Motor Company the engine, and the Dayton Metal Products Company the controls.

33. Contract 242, April 14, 1920, Folder—Lawrence Sperry Papers, Box 1, Lawrence Sperry Aircraft Company Papers, Hagley Museum and Library (hereafter Lawrence Sperry Papers).

34. Alfred V. Verville of McCook's Engineering Division designed the "Messenger" airframe for Sperry's aerial torpedo.

35. Contract, November 16, 1922, Folder—Lawrence Sperry 1922—Correspondence, Box 1, Lawrence Sperry Papers. The Lawrence Sperry Aircraft Company spent $75,169.20

on the aerial torpedo project and received $94,702.08 from the Army; a profit of $19,532.88 for three years of work.

36. Army Air Corps Board Study No. 9, "Radio Controlled Aircraft," October 25, 1935, File 167.5-9, HRA; Kenneth P. Werrell, *The Evolution of the Cruise Missile* (Maxwell AFB, Ala.: Air University Press, 1985), 12–14, 21; Hughes, *Sperry*, 271–73; and Bill Gunston, *The Illustrated Encyclopedia of the World's Rockets and Missiles* (New York: Crescent Books, 1979), 31.

37. Lawrence Sperry to Engineering Division, November 14, 1921, Folder—Lawrence Sperry 1920–21—Engineering Division 1921, "Report of Work Carried on between May 15, 1922 and July 8, 1922," "Report of Board of Arbitration," July 22, 1922, Lawrence Sperry to Mitchell, November 8, 1922, and Contract, November 16, 1922, Folder—Lawrence Sperry 1922—Correspondence 1922, Box 1, Lawrence Sperry Papers.

38. I. B. Holley, *Ideas and Weapons* (New Haven: Yale University Press, 1953; rpt., Washington, D.C.: OAFH, 1983), 135.

39. Army Air Service, "Bombardment from Aeroplanes."

40. Maurer, ed., *Final Report*, 48.

41. Gorrell's plan called for 2,000 DH-4 bombers.

42. Col. E. S. Gorrell, "History of the Strategical Section, Air Service, American Expeditionary," February 1, 1919, File 167.4017-1, HRA; Greer, *The Development of Air Doctrine in the Army Air Arm, 1917–1941*, 10–13; Marvin L. Skelton, "Colonel Gorrell and His Nearly Forgotten Records," *Over the Front* 5 (Spring 1990): 56–71; and Maurer, *Early Concepts of Military Aviation*, 141–57, 192. Gorrell's plan called for the destruction of industries around the cities of Dusseldorf, Cologne, Mannhein, and the Saar Valley.

43. "History of the 96th Aero Squadron," August 20, 1917–18, File SQ-Bomb-96-HI, HRA; Maurer, *Early Concepts of Military Aviation*, 234–53, 376; and "When the Air War Was Young," 1917–19, File SQ-Bomb-96-HI, HRA.

44. Maurer, *Early Concepts of Military Aviation*, 376; and Miller, *History of the First Day Bombardment Group*, 9. Also see C. G. Barth, *History of the Twentieth Aero Squadron* (Winona, Minn.: Winona Labor News, n.d.).

45. Army Air Service, "Bombardment from Aeroplanes"; "Bomb Sight Development," n.d. (1918?), Folder—Bomb Sights—General, File 471.63, Box 872, RD-3312, RG342; "Brief History of Bombsight Development by the Army"; and Gordon T. Gould, "Trends in Bombing Sighting Equipment," Air War College thesis, 1954, 22.

Chapter 2. The Army's Pursuit of Precision Bombing

1. James Lea Cate and Wesley Frank Craven, "The Army Air Arm between Two Wars, 1918–39," in Craven and Cate, eds., *The Army Air Forces in World War II*, Vol. 1, *Plans and Early Operations, January 1939–August 1942* (Chicago: University of Chicago Press, 1948), 43.

2. TR440-95, "Bombardment Aviation," 1923, File 248.222-39, HRA; and USAF Historical Division, *The Employment of Strategic Bombers in a Tactical Role, 1941–1951*, USAF Historical Studies, No. 88 (Maxwell AFB, Ala.: Air University, 1954), 12. For a detailed account of battlefield interdiction and close air support, see Richard P. Hallion, *Strike from the Sky: The History of Battlefield Air Attack, 1911–1945* (Washington, D.C.: Smithsonian Institution Press, 1989).

3. Futrell, *Ideas, Concepts, Doctrine*, 1:39–52; and Greer, *Development of Air Doctrine*, 14–39.

4. "Report of President's Aircraft Board," November 30, 1925, File 167.48-1, HRA.

5. Air Service Tactical School, "Bombardment," 1924–25, File 248.101-9, HRA.

6. Brown, "Navy's Mark 15 (Norden) Bombsight," 19–20; National Advisory Committee

for Aeronautics (F. A. Lindemann), "The Chief Causes of Error in Bomb Dropping from Aeroplanes," January 1918, File 248.222-38, HRA; "The Oscillations of an Aeroplane in Flight and Their Effect on the Accuracy of Bombing Dropping," 1916, File 248.222-39A, HRA; Charles A. Ravenstein, *The Organization and Lineage of the United States Air Force* (Washington, D.C.: OAFH, 1986); and Walker and Wickam, *Huffman Prairie to the Moon.* The 1919 Bomb Board report also recommended the development of pilot direction indicators, sight illumination for night use, an aiming optical telescope, a stabilizer, and tests to determine whether the timing or synchronization methods of bomb sighting were superior.

7. Toole, "Development of Bombing Equipment"; and Doran to Sperry, June 23, 1921, Folder—Charles S. Doran Correspondence, 1918–28, Box 24, Series V, Elmer Sperry Papers.

8. Sperry to Engineering Division, May 19, June 11 and 23, July 9 and 12, 1921, and Engineering Division to Sperry, July 15, 1921, Folder—Visual Stabilization 1915–24, Box 29, Series V, Elmer Sperry Papers.

9. Supply Officer to Officer in Charge of Property, June 22, 1922, File 471.63, Folder—Bomb Sights General, Box 872, RD-3312, RG342; and Wimperis to Chief of Air Service, n.d. (June 1923), and Engineering Division to Chief of Air Service, June 15, 1923, File 471.63, Folder—Bomb Sights, Box 168, RD-3128, RG342.

10. Lawrence Sperry to Mitchell, March 9, 1921, and Mitchell to Lawrence Sperry, March 9, 1921, Folder—Lawrence Sperry 1920–21—U.S. War Department Air Service 1921–22, Box 1, Lawrence Sperry Papers; and Sperry to Engineering Division, April 13 and 21, 1921, and Engineering Division to Sperry, April 23, 1921, Folder—Seversky Bomb Sight 1921–24, Box 29, Series V, Elmer Sperry Papers.

11. Sperry to Engineering Division, May 12, 1922, and Engineering Division to Sperry, May 17, 1922, Folder—Seversky Bomb Sight 1921–24, Box 29, Series V, Elmer Sperry Papers.

12. Sperry to Engineering Division, April 25, May 18, and June 2, 1921, and Engineering Division memo, July 19, 1922, in ibid.

13. Engineering Division to Sperry, July 11 and September 6, 1921, Patrick to Sperry, December 27, 1924, and Sperry to Patrick, December 30, 1924, in ibid.

14. Armament Branch to Experimental Engineering Section, November 30, 1927, and MacDill to Armament Branch, December 7, 1927, File 471.63, Folder—Bomb Sights, Box 321, RD-3167, RG342. The C-2 was a simplified C-1.

15. Estoppey also modified his basic D-1 design into the D-1A for dirigibles, the D-1B for low altitudes, and the D-1C with gyroscopic stabilization.

16. Olmstead to Strauss, August 12, 1922, and Assistant Chief of Materiel Division to Chief of Contract Station, June 1, 1922, File 471.63, Folder—Bomb Sight Estoppey, Box 2323, RD-2644, RG342; Armament Section to Chief Engineer, April 3, 1923, File 471.63, Folder—Bomb Sights, Box 168, RD-3128, RG342; and Commander Aircraft Squadrons Battle Fleet to BuAer, November 23, 1925, File F41-8, Vol. 1, Box 709, Records of the Naval Bureau of Aeronautics, Confidential Correspondence, 1922–44, Record Group 72, National Archives (hereafter RG72). The Martin bomber used at Aberdeen to evaluate the D-1 was piloted by Lt. Harold George, a decade later to be one of the primary figures behind the development of the doctrine of daylight strategic precision bombing. Henry Inglis, Estoppey's colleague and competitor, operated the D-1 in the tests.

17. Engineering Division Memo, June 24, 1922, and Olmstead to Strauss, August 12, 1922, File 471.63, Folder—Bomb Sight Estoppey, Box 2323, RD-2644, RG342; Armament Section to Chief of Division, May 11, 1923, File 471.63, Folder—Bomb Sights, Box 168, RD-3128, RG342; TR440-96, "Bomb Ballistics and Bomb Sights"; 49th Bombardment Squadron to Commanding Officer Phillips Field, September 21, 1923, and Armament Sec-

tion to Chief of Division, May 11, 1923, File 471.63, Folder—Bomb Sights, Box 168, RD-3128, RG342; and Commander Aircraft Squadrons Battle Fleet to BuAer, November 23, 1925, File F41-8, Vol. 1, Box 709, BuAer Confidential Correspondence, 1922–44, RG72.

18. Pioneer to Engineering Division, February 20, 1925, File 471.63, Folder—Bomb Sight Estoppey, Box 2323, RD-2644, RG342; Inspector of Naval Aircraft at McCook Field to BuOrd, March 4, 1925, File F41–8, Vol. 1, Box 2278, BuAer General Correspondence, 1925–42, RG72; and Armament Section to Procurement Section, March 26, 1925, File 471.63, Folder—Bomb Sights, Box 244, RD-3149, RG342.

19. Inglis to Sperry, February 3, 1925, Sperry to Engineering Division, February 11, 1925, and "Report of Inglis on Initial Service Tests of Bomb Sight Type D-3," October 13, 1926, File 471.63, Folder—Bomb Sight Estoppey, Box 2323, RD-2644, RG342; and Armament Section to Procurement Section, March 26, 1925, File 471.63, Folder—Bomb Sights, Box 244, RD-3149, RG342.

20. Armament Section to Chief Engineer, April 3, 1923, File 471.63, Folder—Bomb Sights, Box 168, RD-3128, RG342; Materiel Division, "Air Corps Technical Report on Tests of Modified Air Corps Bombsight, Type D-4," November 7, 1931, File 216.2101-24, HRA; BuAer to BuOrd, July 26, 1934, and "D-4 Manual," File F41-8, Vol. 2, Box 2279, BuAer General Correspondence, 1925–42, RG72; Technical Control Branch to Central District Supervisor, January 13, 1942, File 471.63, Folder—Bomb Sights, Box 2893, RD-2885, RG342; and Materiel Division to Estoppey, July 2, 1932, File 471.63, Folder—Bomb Sights, Box 531, RD-3222, RG342.

21. "Report on Laboratory and Flight Tests of the D-5 Bombsight," June 29, 1928, File 471.63, Folder—Bomb Sights, Box 355, RD-3176, RG342; "Experimental Test Requirements and Manual on D-5—First Model Bomb Sight—Langley Field," December 1, 1928, and Wolfe to Chief of Materiel Division, March 11, 1929, File 471.63, Folder—Bomb Sights, Box 397, RD-8186, RG342.

22. There was no D-6 designation assigned.

23. Isbell to BuOrd, February 18, 1932, File F41-8, Folder—Aircraft Ordnance 151-200, Box 1474, Records of the Naval Bureau of Ordnance, General Correspondence, Record Group 74, Suitland (hereafter RG74).

24. Estoppey to Engineering Division, August 30, 1924, File 471.63, Folder—Bomb Sights, Box 205, RD-3139, RG342; Legal Section to Estoppey, February 20, 1923, File 471.63, Folder—Bomb Sights, Box 168, RD-3128, RG342; Patrick to Engineering Division and attachments, January 7, 1926, Estoppey to Engineering Division, September 7, 1926, Engineering Division to Estoppey, September 10, 1926, Estoppey to Materiel Division, February 5, 1927, Legal Office to Estoppey, February 11, 1927, Estoppey to McCook Field, February 28, 1927, Contracting Officer to Estoppey, December 12, 1927, Materiel Division memo, May 29, 1930, Estoppey to Materiel Division, January 14, 1931, Engineering Section to Estoppey, January 22, 1931, and Chief of Armament Branch to Chief of Engineering Division, January 19, 1932, File 471.63, Folder—Bomb Sight Estoppey, Box 2323, RD-2644, RG342; Secretary of Navy to Estoppey, August 17, 1932, and General Inspector of Naval Aircraft to BuOrd, March 11, 1932, File F41-8, Folder—Aircraft Ordnance, Box 1474, BuOrd General Correspondence, RG74; and Rose to Hackett, September 9, 1932, File 471.63, Folder—Bomb Sights, Box 531, RD-3222, RG342.

25. Estoppey to Secretary of Navy, January 29, 1932, Secretary of Navy to Estoppey, August 17, 1932, and BuOrd to Judge Advocate General, May 11, 1932, File F41-8, Folder—Aircraft Ordnance, Box 1474, BuOrd General Correspondence, RG74.

26. Chief of Engineering Section to Estoppey, November 15, 1933, Chief of Engineering Section to Gaertner, August 24, 1934, Chief of Materiel Division to Estoppey, October 11, 1935, Estoppey to Secretary of War, January 15, 1936, Chief of Materiel Division to Estop-

pey, January 31, 1936, Materiel Division to Estoppey, July 30, 1936, Estoppey to Woodruff, October 22, 1936, and Woodruff to Estoppey, December 19, 1936, File 471.63, Folder—Bomb Sight Estoppey, Box 2323, RD-2644, RG342.

27. "Report of Inglis on Initial Service Tests of Bomb Sight Type D-3," RG342.

28. The "revolving door" worked both ways. While an assistant vice-president for Sperry, Harris B. Hull personally promoted the sale of a book, *Winged Warfare*, authored by Henry Arnold, chief of the Air Corps, and Ira Eaker, who would lead Eighth Air Force in Europe during World War II. When Eaker went to England to set up Eighth Air Force he took then Lt. Harris B. Hull along as his A-2 (intelligence) officer. Eaker also took Capt. Frederick W. Castle, an officer in the Sperry Company before the war, to serve on his staff. Another officer serving with Eaker was Hugh Knerr, who had resigned from the Air Corps in 1939 to go to work for the Sperry Company. The Navy forced Sperry to fire Knerr in 1942 as a result of a series of articles he wrote for *American Mercury* in support of strategic bombing and critical of the Navy. Recalled to active duty in the Army Air Forces, Knerr went to England and took command of the Air Service Command in Europe, responsible for maintenance and supply, including bombsights, in Eaker's Eighth Air Force. See Murray Green, "Hugh J. Knerr: The Pen and the Sword," in Frisbee, ed., *Makers of the United States Air Force*, 99–126; Knerr papers, File 168.7028–1, HRA; and Parton, *"Air Force Spoken Here,"* 111, 120, 131–32. With this Sperry connection, it is testimony to the integrity of these men that none intervened in favor of the Sperry bombsight during the war.

29. Experimental Engineering Section to Sperry, February 3, 1929, File 471.63, Folder—Bomb Sights, Box 397, RD-8186, RG342.

30. By way of comparison, in June 1929 the Navy completed Contract Nos-12919 with the Norden Company to construct two new bombsights for $20,500. These bombsights became the Mark XV—the Norden bombsight.

31. Isbell to BuOrd, February 17, 1932, File F41-8, Folder—Aircraft Ordnance 151-200, Box 1474, BuOrd General Correspondence, RG74.

32. The decision not to purchase the Sperry L-1 bombsight was made by Maj. Hugh J. Knerr, chief of the Field Service Section of the Materiel Division. Six years later Knerr became vice-president of the Sperry Company. See Knerr to March Field Commanding Officer, April 5, 1934, File 471.63, Folder—Bomb Sights General, Box 872, RD-3312, RG342. Inglis eventually received patents for his L-1 bombsight, nos. 2105147 and 2105148. For the results of the Langley and March tests, see Materiel Division, "Air Corps Technical Report on Comparative Tests of Types L-1, Mark XI and D-7 Bombsights," February 4, 1932, File 216.2101-27A, HRA; and Materiel Division, "Air Corps Technical Report on Tests on L-1 Bombsight," May 10, 1932, File 216.2101–27, HRA.

33. Materiel Division, "Air Corps Technical Report on Test of the C-4 Bombsight Mock-Up," November 11, 1930, File 216.2101-20, HRA; 2nd Bombardment Group to Materiel Division, December 16, 1932, and "Progress of C-4 Bombsight Tests," December 23, 1932, File 471.63, Folder—Bomb Sights, Box 531, RD-3222, RG342; and Isbell to BuOrd, February 16, 1932, File F41-8, Folder—Aircraft Ordnance 151-200, Box 1474, BuOrd General Correspondence, RG74.

34. Barth to Sherman, n.d. (April 1935?), in Brown, "Navy's Mark 15 (Norden) Bombsight," 118–19.

35. National Advisory Committee for Aeronautics (F. A. Lindemann), "The Chief Causes of Error in Bomb Dropping from Aeroplanes"; and Toole, "Development of Bombing Equipment."

36. Copp, *A Few Great Captains*, 275.

37. "Air Corps Technical Report on Investigation and Possible Development of an Alignment and Computing Mechanism," December 7, 1932, File F41-8, Box 46, BuAer General

Correspondence, 1939–42, RG72; Isbell to BuOrd, February 12, 1932, Schoeffel to BuOrd, February 18, 1932, File 471.63, Folder—Bomb Sights, Box 531, RD-3222, RG342; and Isbell to BuOrd, February 15, 1932, File F41-8, Folder—Aircraft Ordnance 151–200, Box 1474, BuOrd General Correspondence, RG74.

38. USAF Bombardment School, "M-Series Bombsight: Student Study Guide," January 1951, File K221.712A-16, HRA; and Brown, "Navy's Mark 15 (Norden) Bombsight," appendix A2.

39. Experimental Engineering Section to General Inspector of Naval Aircraft, December 15, 1927, General Electric to Howard, September 17, 1928, and Brower to Experimental Engineering Section, June 3, 1929, File 452.7, Folder—Automatic Steering Device, Box 570, RD-3232, RG342.

40. Robins to Materiel Division, December 14, 1931, "Automatic Steering Device," June 14, 1932, and Engineering Section Memo, December 12, 1933, File 452.7, Folder—Automatic Steering Device, Box 570, RD-3232, RG342.

41. Elmer A. Sperry Jr. told his audience at the Fifth Lester D. Gardner Lecture, May 1, 1963, that Hugh Knerr was responsible for the Air Corps' decision to build an autopilot, based on his argument that a lightweight autopilot would eliminate the need for one member of a bomber crew, thereby making room for more bombs. See transcript, Folder—Automatic Airplane Pilot, Box 30, Series V, Elmer Sperry Papers.

42. Sperry and the Army had discussed autopilot development since 1922. The Army unofficially encouraged Sperry to seek foreign sales to pay for development. See Gearhart to Sperry, February 10, 1922, Folder—Lawrence Sperry 1920–21—U.S. War Department Air Service 1921–22, Box 1, Lawrence Sperry Papers.

43. Elmer A. Sperry, assignor to Sperry Gyroscope Company, "Automatic Pilot," U.S. Patent Office, No. 1,818,103 (filed April 3, 1926, awarded August 11, 1931); Elmer A. Sperry Jr., assignor to Sperry Gyroscope Company, "Automatic Pilot," U.S. Patent Office, No. 1,779,991 (filed April 26, 1927, awarded August 12, 1930); Elmer A. Sperry Jr., assignor to Sperry Gyroscope Company, "Automatic Pilot," U.S. Patent Office, No. 1,779,991 (filed August 8, 1927, awarded October 28, 1930); and Elmer A. Sperry Jr., assignor to Sperry Gyroscope Company, U.S. Patent Office, "Automatic Pilot," Patent 1,725,599 (filed May 6, 1926, awarded August 20, 1929).

44. The three years of testing and modification produced two patents for Sperry. See Elmer A. Sperry Jr., assignor to Sperry Gyroscope Company, "Automatic Pilot," U.S. Patent Office, No. 1,725,600 (filed April 26, 1927, awarded August 20, 1929), and "Course-Maintaining Means for Automatic Pilots," U.S. Patent Office, No. 1,730,952 (filed June 9, 1927, awarded October 8, 1929).

45. Elmer A. Sperry Jr., to his wife, October 4, 1928, Folder—Automatic Airplane Pilot, Box 30, Series V, Elmer Sperry Papers. The crew included W. B. Mayo (head of Stout), H. A. Hicks (head of Stout's engineering department), Leroy S. Manning (test pilot for Stout), and Elmer A. Sperry Jr. See Sperry to Sperry Gyroscope, October 4, 1928, Folder—Automatic Airplane Pilot, Box 30, Series V, Elmer Sperry Papers.

46. Sperry to Engineering Division, March 12, 1925, Contracting Officer to Sperry Gyroscope, October 28, 1929, and Sperry to Materiel Division, November 23, 1929, File 452.7, Folder—Automatic Pilot, Box 630, RD-3250, RG342; and Elmer A. Sperry Jr., assignor to Sperry Gyroscope Company, "Automatic Control of Aircraft," U.S. Patent Office, No. 1,859,752 (filed June 29, 1928, awarded May 24, 1932). The Boeing 247 was the first commercial aircraft equipped with the Sperry automatic pilot. See M. Gould Beard and Percy Halpert, "Automatic Flight Control in Air Transportation," *Sperry Engineering Review* 8 (May–June 1955): 2–9.

47. Armament Branch to Equipment Branch, November 1, 1929, and Samuel Mills,

"Sperry Company and Air Corps Engineers Develop and Test Successful Airplane Controlling Device," n.d., File 452.7, Folder—Automatic Pilot, Box 630, RD-3250, RG342. In a private correspondence, Foulois stated the following reasons for developing the autopilot: navigation aid, pilot relief, fog flying, aerial mapping, aerial torpedo control, and bombing, intending for the autopilot to be connected directly to the bombsight to eliminate the need for pilot direction indicators. See Foulois to Gillmore, January 25, 1930, File 452.7, Folder—Automatic Pilot, Box 630, RD-3250, RG342.

48. A critical technology of the A-1 was Sperry's development of an air-stabilized gyroscope. Acceleration of the aircraft and bearing friction tended to make the gyroscope precess in a direction at right angles to the force of the acceleration or friction. This caused the autopilot to engage and apply correcting action when not necessary. Sperry directed an air stream at pendulum vanes covering four exhaust ports in the shaft space at the bottom of the gyroscope. When acceleration or friction caused gyroscopic precession, the gyroscope followed the vertical seeking pendulums, compensating and maintaining the true vertical. See "Sperry Automatic Pilot for Airplanes," n.d. (1932?), Folder 106, Box 2, Series V, Public Relations Department Literature File, Sperry Gyroscope Records.

49. Mills, "Sperry Company and Air Corps Engineers"; and Army Air Corps Board Study No. 9, "Radio Controlled Aircraft," HRA.

50. Sperry to Mayo, April 1, 1929, Folder—Automatic Airplane Pilot, Box 30, Series V, Elmer Sperry Papers.

51. "The Automatic Pilot for Aircraft," n.d. (1933?), Folder 127, Box 2, "The Sperry Pilot for Automatic Flying," n.d. (1933?), Folder 183, Box 3, and Thompson to General Manager, March 16, 1933, Folder 127, Box 2, Series V, Public Relations Department Literature File, Sperry Gyroscope Records.

52. Sperry Gyroscope Company, "The Sperry Pilot for Automatic Flying," December 1934, Folder 208, Box 3, Series V, Public Relations Department Literature File, Sperry Gyroscope Papers; and Wiley Post, "Destination—New York," *Sperryscope* 7 (October 1933): 7–10. The quotation is from "Song of Elmer . . . the Pilot Who Never Gets Tired," *Sperryscope* 10 (October 1943): 20. In British use crews called the A-2 "George."

53. Seversky to Armament Section, August 2, 1926, and MacDill to Seversky, September 22, 1926, File 471.63, Folder—Bomb Sights, Box 321, RD-3167, RG342.

54. Mortimer F. Bates, assignor to Sperry Gyroscope Company, "Bomb Sight Alignment and Rudder Control," U.S. Patent Office, No. 1,880,671 (filed October 18, 1929, awarded October 4, 1932).

55. "Bombing Record Plot of 1,100 lb. T.N.T. Bombs dropped at Pee Dee River Bridge," December 23–24, 1927, and "Results of Bombing of Pee Dee River Bridge," December 19–28, 1927, File 248.222-39, HRA; and Robert I. Curtis, John Mitchell, and Martin Copp, *Langley Field, the Early Years, 1916–1946* (Langley AFB, Va.: Office of History, 1977), 77.

56. "Results of Bombing of Pee Dee River Bridge"; and Maurer, *Aviation in the United States Army*, 225–26. Ironically, the accuracy of the Norden bombsight made this type of salvo bombing, dropping on the leader, unnecessary in the 1930s, but wartime experience forced a return to Duncan's tactic in 1943.

57. TR440-96, "Bomb Ballistics and Bomb Sights."

58. Chief of the Air Corps to Chief of Materiel Division, January 6, 1928, File 471.63, Folder—Bomb Sights, Box 355, RD-3176, RG342.

59. Chief of Materiel Division to Chief of Air Corps, January 19, 1926, in ibid.

60. Chief of Air Corps to Materiel Division, January 20, 1928, in ibid.

61. "Report of the Bombardment Board," February 7, 1928, in ibid.

62. Seversky's "large cash payments and royalties" turned out to be $86,250 for three experimental bombsights.

63. Chief of Air Corps to Materiel Command, March 7, 1928, Seversky to Chief of Air Corps, April 20, 1928, MacDill to Seversky, March 16 and April 10, 1928, Seversky to Chief of Experimental Engineering Section, April 3, 1928, Inglis to Chief of Experimental Engineering Section, May 3, 1928, Zettel to Contracting Officer, May 10, 1928, Zettel to Experimental Engineering Section, September 18, 1928, and Chief of Air Corps to Materiel Division, November 20, 1928, File 471.63, Folder—Bomb Sights, Box 355, RD-3176, RG342.

64. The *Shasta* was part of the World War I Emergency Fleet, originally known as the *Sagaland*. It was 400 feet long with a beam of 52 feet, a double bottom hull, and two watertight bulkheads.

65. In 1932 Air Corps bombers were more successful when they attempted to "sink" a sunken ship, the *Haines*, that was a navigation obstacle. The average radial error of the bombs was only 25 feet. See Maurer, *Aviation in the United States Army*, 227–29; Murray Green, "The *Shasta* Disaster: Forgotten Lessons in Interservice Relations," *Air University Review* 30 (March–April 1978): 68–74; *New York Times*, August 10, 1931, 8:3, August 12, 1931, 39:1, August 13, 1931, 24:6, August 14, 1931, 1:5, and August 15, 1931, 3:3; and "Bombing of Mount Shasta," August 11, 1931, File 248.222-29A, HRA. In 1937 the Army also bombed a harbor boat, the *Morgan Lewis*, in Panama. Three B-10s dropped fourteen 300-pound bombs in formation from 6,000 feet under clear skies. All bombs either hit on or near the 150-foot long vessel, sinking it in 12 minutes. See Commanding Officer, Albrook Field, to Adjutant General, U.S. Army, September 16, 1937, File 248.222-35, HRA.

66. "Armament Representative's Tour in Interest of Bombsight Development," February 5, 1932, File 471.63, Folder—Bomb Sights, Box 531, RD-3222, RG342.

67. Schoeffel to BuOrd, February 18, 1932, in ibid.

68. Armament Branch to Engineering Section, October 5, 1932, in ibid.

69. Armament Branch to Engineering Section, June 13, 1932, Materiel Division to Chief of Air Corps, September 24, 1932, and Armament Branch to Engineering Section, October 5, 1932, in ibid. The bomb aiming device for pursuit-fighter aircraft consisted of nothing more than a piece of optic glass mounted in the floor of the aircraft through which pilots could see the ground.

70. The Materiel Division had planned to use the $325,000 to purchase fifteen Navy Mark XIs, twenty-five Navy Mark XVs, and thirty D-7s.

71. Materiel Division to Chief of Air Corps, February 6, 1932, and Chief of Air Corps to Materiel Division, March 8, 1932, File 471.63, Folder—Bomb Sights, Box 531, RD-3222, RG342.

72. Field Service Section to Experimental Engineering Section, October 28, 1930, and Armament Branch to Engineering Section, June 1, 1931, File 471.63, Folder—Bomb Sights General, Box 872, RD-3312, RG342; and Robins to Chief of Air Corps, October 31, 1932, File 471.63, Folder—Bomb Sights, Box 531, RD-3222, RG342. Because they were taking up valuable storage space, the Engineering Section agreed in August 1931 to allow the disposal of all but 2,000 of the Mark I-As, valued at $41.83 each.

73. Arnold to Chief of Air Corps, January 25, 1934, File 471.63, Folder—Bomb Sights General, Box 872, RD-3312, RG342.

Chapter 3. To Sink Ships

1. Russell F. Weigley, *The American Way of War: A History of United States Military Strategy and Policy* (New York: Macmillan, 1973), 173–82, 191; Alfred T. Mahan, *The Influence of Sea Power upon History, 1660–1783* (Boston: Little, Brown, 1918); and "Hearings Before the General Board of the Navy," September 30–December 4, 1924 Meetings, Final Report, January

17, 1925, Reel 6, 1:9, 14. Mahan more directly viewed the enemy fleet as the Navy's prime objective (*guerre d'escadre*), not the enemy's commerce (*guerre de course*).

2. Hattendorf, Simpson, and Wadleigh, *Sailors and Scholars*, 143–44; and Ronald Spector, *Professors of War: The Naval War College and the Development of the Naval Profession* (Newport, R.I.: Naval War College, 1977), 147–48.

3. The tests began on October 3, 1920, against the USS *Indiana* and continued until November 1924 against the uncompleted USS *Washington*. See Turnbull and Lord, *History of United States Naval Aviation*, 193–204, for a detailed record of the Navy's side of the ship-bombing tests.

4. The United States was the only country to carry out comprehensive bombing tests against warships in the interwar period. The British used German warships turned over to them after World War I for testing new naval armor-piercing shells. The RAF dropped dummy bombs against the radio-controlled *Agamemnon* with DH-9As from 6,000 to 14,000 feet in 1923. Dropping one bomb at a time, airmen achieved only 10 hits out of 223 bombs dropped. In July 1924 they failed to hit the ship with 114 bombs. The only live bombs used were against the HMS *Monarch*, but were placed against the hull and on the deck, not dropped. See Stephen Roskill, *Naval Policy between the Wars*, Vol. 1, *The Period of Anglo-American Antagonism, 1919–1929* (London: Collins, 1968), 248–49.

5. The first target was the war prize German submarine *U-117* on June 21, 1921, 50 miles off Cape Charles. Twelve 163-pound bombs with two to four direct hits sent it to the bottom in only 16 minutes. The second test was a tougher nut—the ex-USS *Iowa*. This radio-controlled battleship withstood two direct hits by 520-pound bombs out of 80 dropped. This test helped to convince the Navy that greater bombing accuracy was needed. The tests accelerated with attacks on a surrendered German destroyer, *G-102*, sunk on July 13, 1921. A rain of 25-pound bombs had little effect, but seven hits by 300-pounders did. Again, accuracy was wanting—seven hits out of forty-four bombs dropped. The German cruiser *Frankfurt* on July 18 was next. Mitchell's aircraft dropped forty-four bombs and got four hits, the Navy seven of thirty-one.

6. The Army tried to begin a new round of ship-bombing tests in 1925, but the Navy claimed there were no surplus ships available. See Secretary of the Navy to Secretary of War, August 12, 1925, File 168.6502-19, HRA.

7. "Report of the Joint Board on Results of Aviation and Ordnance Tests Held during June and July 1921, and Conclusions Reached," April–August 1921, File 248.222-69, HRA. For a popular version of the Navy's reactions to the tests, see Graser Schornstheimer, "Airplane Bomb vs. Battleship," *New York Times Current History Magazine* 14 (September 1921): 923–27. Schornstheimer concluded that aircraft could not hit and damage maneuvering ships equipped with adequate underwater protection and damage control teams. For Mitchell's version of the tests, see Mitchell, *Winged Defense*, 41–76.

8. W. W. Warlick, *Naval Aviation* (Annapolis, Md.: U.S. Naval Institute, 1925), 97–99; and "Problem in Probability," August 18, 1925, File 471.63, Folder Bombs—General, Box 243, RD-3148, RG342.

9. Roscoe, *On the Seas*, recorded that Mitchell used a "new automatic bombsight designed for Sperry by Seversky" (159). Thomas G. Foxworth, *The Speed Seekers* (New York: Doubleday, 1976), wrote that Mitchell used "the earliest successful gyroscope-stabilized automatic bombsight" of Seversky in the tests (13). The Seversky C-series bombsights were just beginning research and development and were neither available nor successful at the time of the ship-bombing tests. The Sperry Company had begun its research on a stabilized bombsight in 1920, but had no sight ready for the Mitchell tests. Sperry's only involvement with Mitchell's first tests was an attempt by the Army to use a Sperry gyroscope to stabilize the Navy's Mark III bombsight. The Air Service worked to find twenty Michelin sights to equip Mitch-

ell's bombers. Some had to be retrieved from the Gallaudet Aircraft Corporation and the Glenn Martin Company. See Davidson to Supply Officer (McCook Field), February 26, 1921, and Davidson to Commanding Officer, Langley Field, March 21, 1921, File 471.63, Folder—Bomb Sights—Michelin, Box 168, RD-3128, RG342. Mitchell, in *Winged Defense*, recorded that he used "crude bomb sights" for the tests and a Sperry gyroscope to maintain level flight during bomb runs (50).

10. "Report of Operations of 1st Air Brigade in Naval Ordnance Tests," April–August 1921, File 248.222-69, HRA.

11. Brown, "Navy's Mark 15 (Norden) Bombsight," 16–17.

12. Ibid., 26–27.

13. Ibid., 27–34.

14. Norton to Commanding Officer, First Aviation Group, October 27, 1925, File F41-8, Vol. 1, Box 2278, BuAer General Correspondence, 1925–42, RG72; and Brown, "Navy's Mark 15 (Norden) Bombsight," 21–22, 39–40.

15. This description of Carl L. Norden is based on interviews with his son, Carl F. Norden, on December 9, 1989, and April 22, 1990; letter from Frank S. Preston, March 31, 1990; interview with Ned Lawrence, March 13, 1990; interview with James E. Taylor, March 29, 1990; interview with Richard S. Baldwin, April 3, 1990; "Obituary: Carl Lukas Norden," *New York Times*, June 16, 1965, 43:1; John G. Fitzgerald, "Norden," *Beehive* (Fall 1958): 13–17; "The Beginning Was 2 Men, $12,000 and 1 Floor in New York," *Norden Times*, May 1978, 4–5; "Norden Described as Artist by His Son," *Norden Times*, April 1978, 4–5; "Pickle Barrel Club: Respite from the War," *Norden Times*, August 1978, 4–5; and *Current Biography 1945*, 432–34.

16. Hughes, *Sperry*, 158.

17. Preston, letter to author.

18. Hough to Lane, June 22, 1925, File QM (27), Box 1318, BuAer Confidential Correspondence, 1922–44, RG72.

19. Arnold to Towers, November 16, 1939, and Hoover to Kirk, May 7, 1941, File QM (27), Box 1318, BuAer Confidential Correspondence, 1922–44, RG 72.

20. Brown, "Navy's Mark 15 (Norden) Bombsight," 43.

21. Ibid., 45.

22. Norden to BuAer, August 3, 1925, File QM (27), Folder—Bomb Sights, Vol. 1, Box 4363, BuAer General Correspondence, 1925–42, RG72; and Barth to Dargue, April 24, 1935, File 168.7119-49, HRA.

23. "The Beginning Was 2 Men," 4–5.

24. Interview with Ned M. Lawrence, October 9, 1991.

25. "Pickle Barrel Club," 4–5; and interviews with Carl F. Norden.

26. Brown, "Navy's Mark 15 (Norden) Bombsight," 47.

27. *Hearing Before the President's Aircraft Board* (Washington, D.C.: Government Printing Office, 1925), 233.

28. Brown, "Navy's Mark 15 (Norden) Bombsight," 50–53.

29. General Inspector of Naval Aircraft (Wright Field) to BuAer, September 2, 1927, and Leahy to Battle Fleet, May 3, 1928, File F41-8, Vol. 1, Box 2278, BuAer General Correspondence, 1925–42, RG72.

30. Inspector of Ordnance (Dahlgren) to BuOrd, October 14, 1927, File F41-8, Vol. 1, Box 709, BuAer Confidential Correspondence, 1922–44, RG72; and Brown, "Navy's Mark 15 (Norden) Bombsight," 58–65.

31. In 1928 Hayden-Stone and Company of New York sought to develop the Mark XI for commercial purposes, but Barth rejected its offer in keeping with his Navy contract. See

Memo of Conference, May 29, 1928, File F41-8, Vol. 1, Box 2278, BuAer General Correspondence, 1925–42, RG72.

32. Carl L. Norden and Theodore H. Barth, assignors to United States of America, as represented by the Secretary of the Navy, U.S. Patent Office, No. 2,428,678 (filed May 27, 1930, awarded October 7, 1947); Brown, "Navy's Mark 15 (Norden) Bombsight," 65–69; and Norden to BuAer, May 13, 1931, File F41-8, Vol. 1, Box 2278, BuAer General Correspondence, 1925–42, RG72.

33. For the $1 claim, see Fitzgerald, "Norden," 15. For the Navy record, see Brown, "Navy's Mark 15 (Norden) Bombsight," 94, 98.

34. The Hallenback-Hungerford Building at 80 Lafayette Street in New York City was perfectly suited for bombsight manufacture. The railroad industry constructed the building as a printing facility, equipping it to withstand heavy floor loads and freight elevator capacities, ideal for the heavy machine tools Norden would install there. Today the building serves as the office of New York City's Consumer Protection Agency. See letter from Ned M. Lawrence to author, March 9, 1990.

35. Stetson Conn, gen. ed., *The United States Army in World War II*, Special Studies, *Buying Aircraft: Matériel Procurement for the Army Air Forces*, by Irving Brinton Holley Jr. (Washington, D.C.: Office of the Chief of Military History, 1964), 80–84.

36. Barth to BuOrd, February 9, 1934, in Brown, "Navy's Mark 15 (Norden) Bombsight," 66–69.

37. Jacob A. Vander Meulen, *The Politics of Aircraft: Building an American Military Industry* (Lawrence: University Press of Kansas, 1991), 42.

38. Holley, *Buying Aircraft*, 80–84.

39. *The Statutes at Large of the United States of America from December, 1925, to March, 1927*, vol. 44, pt. 2 (Washington, D.C.: Government Printing Office, 1927), 787; and Holley, *Buying Aircraft*, 89–93.

40. Interview of Carl F. Norden, December 9, 1989; and Brown, "Navy's Mark 15 (Norden) Bombsight," 38.

41. Chief BuAer to Manager of NAF, March 31, 1931, and Commander VT-2B to Chief BuOrd, December 4, 1930, F41-8, Vol. 1, Box 2278, BuAer General Correspondence, 1925–42, RG72; Commander VP-4B to BuAer, September 8, 1931, and BuOrd to Commander Aircraft Scouting Force, May 12, 1932, File F41-8, Vol. 2, Box 2279, BuAer General Correspondence, 1925–42, RG72; and Jacobs, *A Scientist and His Experiences with Corruption and Treason in the U.S. Military-Industrial Establishment*, 165.

42. General Electric to Inspector of Naval Material, October 30, 1932, File F41-8, Folder—General Electric, Box 1474, BuOrd General Correspondence, RG74.

43. BuOrd to General Inspector of Naval Aircraft, January 5, 1928, and BuOrd to CNO, February 12, 1930, F41-8 (Mk XI/34), Vol. 1, Box 709, BuAer Confidential Correspondence, 1922–44, RG72; and Brown, "Navy's Mark 15 (Norden) Bombsight," 71–74.

44. Leahy to General Inspector of Naval Aircraft (Wright Field), January 5, 1928, F41-8 (Mk XI/34), Vol. 1, Box 709, BuAer Confidential Correspondence, 1922–44, RG72; "Air Corps Technical Report on Bombsight, Type Mark XI," January 20, 1931, File F41-8, Box 46, BuAer General Correspondence, 1939–42, RG72; Armament Branch to Experimental Engineering Section, February 23, 1928, File 471.63, Folder—Bomb Sights, Box 355, RD-3176, RG342; and Armament Branch to Experimental Engineering Section, July 25, 1929, File 471.63, Folder—Bomb Sights, Box 397, RD-8186, RG342. The Army acquired its first Mark XI bombsight in June 1929. See Leahy to Bureau of Supplies and Accounts, June 29, 1929, File F41-8, Vol. 1, Box 2278, BuAer General Correspondence, 1925–42, RG72.

45. BuOrd to Inspector of Naval Ordnance (Dahlgren), January 8, 1929, F41-8 (Mk XI), Vol. 1, Box 709, BuAer Confidential Correspondence, 1922–44, RG72.

46. BuOrd to BuAer, March 11, 1929, and BuOrd to General Inspector of Naval Aircraft, Wright Field, September 13, 1932, File F41-8, Vol. 1, Box 709, BuAer Confidential Correspondence, 1922–44, RG72.

47. Flight Commander Edmonds of the HMS *Ben-My-Chree*, a seaplane carrier, dropped an 800-pound torpedo from his Short Type 184 aircraft at a 5,000-ton Turkish supply ship in August 1915—the first "kill" for an aerial torpedo. Ironically, a British submarine had already sunk the Turkish ship; Edmonds sank a ship beached by its crew.

48. Wagner, *American Combat Planes*, 107–16, 348–50.

49. Turnbull and Lord, *Naval Aviation*, 213; Wagner, *American Combat Planes*, 350; and Norman Friedman, *U.S. Naval Weapons* (Annapolis, Md.: Naval Institute Press, 1982), 116–17, 268.

50. U.S. Navy Department Bureau of Ordnance, *United States Navy Bureau of Ordnance in World War II*, 359.

51. Sherrod, *History of Marine Corps Aviation in World War II*, 23; Turnbull and Lord, *Naval Aviation*, 216; E. L. Jones, "Dive Bombing—Evolution, 1911–1943," File 168.2-18, HRA; and Peter C. Smith, *The History of Dive Bombing* (Annapolis, Md.: Nautical and Aviation Publishing, 1981), 23.

52. Sherrod, *Marine Corps Aviation*, 25, cites the date as July 16, 1927.

53. Neill Macaulay, *The Sandino Affair* (Chicago: Quadrangle, 1967), 80–81; U.S. Naval Operations, *Naval Aviation*, 61; Chief of Air Corps to Commanders of All Air Corps Activities, "Marine Activity in Nicaragua," April 23, 1928, File 248.12605, HRA; Hallion, *Strike from the Sky*, 72–74; Sherrod, *Marine Corps Aviation*, 23–25; and Ross E. Rowell, "Aircraft in Bush Warfare," *Marine Corps Gazette* 14 (September 1929): 180–203.

54. Macaulay, *Sandino*, 80–81, 88–90, 163, 137, 146–47, 159, 176, and 367. Also see Sergio Ramirez, ed., *Sandino: The Testimony of a Nicaraguan Patriot 1921–1934* (Princeton: Princeton University Press, 1990). Upon return to the United States, these marine aviators demonstrated their bombing technique at aerial exhibitions in Montreal, New York, Chicago, Miami, and Cleveland. At the Cleveland air show, dive bombing impressed Ernst Udet, in charge of the technical development of the Luftwaffe, who incorporated dive bombing into Germany's blitzkrieg strategy. See Sherrod, *Marine Corps Aviation*, 25; and Hallion, *Strike from the Sky*, 72–74.

55. Turnbull and Lord, *Naval Aviation*, 217–18.

56. U.S. Naval Operations, *Naval Aviation*, 60.

57. Ibid., 60–61; and BuAer Service Technical Note No. 6, Series of 1930, "High Speed Diving," January 8, 1932, File 248.211-36P, HRA.

58. U.S. Fleet Problem No. 2, December 6, 1923, and Joint Army-Navy Problem No. 2, January 14–19, 1924, File A16-3, Vol. 1, Box 198, BuAer Confidential Correspondence, 1922–44, RG72.

59. Joint Army-Navy Problem No. 3, October 2, 1926, File A16-3, Vol. 1, Box 198, BuAer Confidential Correspondence, 1922–44, RG72; Commander-in-Chief Battle Fleet to Battle Fleet, November 7 and 28, 1928, File A16-3, Vol. 1, Box 199, BuAer Confidential Correspondence, 1922–44, RG72. Professor William F. Trimble of Auburn University provided the information about the Taylor Board.

60. Foxworth, *Speed Seekers*, 57–88; Dubuque and Gleckner, *The Development of the Heavy Bomber, 1918–1944*; Miller and Sawers, *The Technical Development of Modern Aviation*; and E. P. Warner, *Technical Development and Its Effect on Air Transportation* (Norwich, Vt.: Norwich University Press, 1938).

61. Jones, "Dive Bombing—Evolution, 1911–1943," HRA; and Wagner, *American Combat*

Planes, 114–28, 183–84, 354–61. The Martin XT5M-1 and Naval Aircraft Factory XT2N-1, the first dive bombers designed to carry a 1,000-pound bomb, were available for Navy testing in 1930.

Chapter 4. The Norden Bombsight and Precision Bombing Doctrine

1. Picking to BuOrd, April 16, 1929, File F41-8, Vol. 1, Box 2278, BuAer General Correspondence, 1925–42, RG72; Brown, "Navy's Mark 15 (Norden) Bombsight," 75–77; Barth to Picking, April 22, 1929, File F41-8, Folder—Aircraft Ordnance, Box 1474, BuOrd General Correspondence, 1926–39, RG74; and BuOrd to BuAer, May 20, 1929, File F41-8, Folder—1-220, Box 174, BuOrd General Correspondence Confidential, 1926–39, RG74.

2. The most succinct explanation of the methods for determining ground speed can be found in Henry B. Inglis, "Bomb Sight and Pilot Director," U.S. Patent Office, No. 2,105,147 (filed February 8, 1930, renewed June 15, 1936, awarded January 11, 1938), 3.

3. Georges Estoppey, "Bomb Sight," U.S. Patent Office, No. 1,804,679 (filed January 7, 1925, awarded May 12, 1932); Estoppey, "Aerial Navigation Equipment," U.S. Patent Office, No. 1,784,929 (filed April 1, 1926, awarded December 16, 1930); Mortimer F. Bates, assignor to Sperry Gyroscope Company, "Bomb Sight," U.S. Patent Office, No. 1,783,769 (filed June 1, 1926, awarded December 2, 1930); and General Electric to Inspector of Naval Material, October 30, 1932, File F41-8, Folder—General Electric, Box 1474, BuOrd General Correspondence, RG74.

4. Brown, "Navy's Mark 15 (Norden) Bombsight," 86.

5. BuOrd to Commander Carrier Division, December 23, 1930, File F41-8, Vol. 1, Box 2278, BuAer General Correspondence, 1925–42, RG72; Inspector of Naval Aircraft (Wright Field) to BuAer, February 8, 1938, File F41-8, Vol. 3, Box 2279, BuAer General Correspondence, 1925–42, RG72; and BuOrd to Judge Advocate General, May 11, 1932, File F41-8, Folder—Aircraft Ordnance, Box 1474, BuOrd General Correspondence, RG74.

6. The Navy measured the accuracy of its bombsights in mils, not feet or circular error. The number of mils of error was the bombing error on the ground, measured in feet, divided by one one-thousandth of the altitude. For consistency, the author has presented all accuracy measurements converted to feet of error, not mils. The mils method can be misleading. The accuracy of a bombsight in mils does not change as the altitude increases. According to the Navy system, a bombsight with an accuracy of 10 mils would always be accurate to 10 mils regardless of altitude, which provides a false sense of precision. At 5,000 feet this bombsight would have a circular error of 50 feet, while at 20,000 feet the circular error would be 200 feet.

7. Brown, "Navy's Mark 15 (Norden) Bombsight," 86–89.

8. James B. Sykes to Capt. Arthur B. Cook, August 2, 1933, File F41-8, Vol. 2, Box 2279, BuAer General Correspondence, 1925–42, RG72; Inspector of Ordnance in Charge to BuOrd, October 27, 1932, File F41-8, Folder—MK XV 1-75, Box 171, BuOrd General Correspondence Confidential, 1926–39, RG74; and Brown, "Navy's Mark 15 Bombsight," 97–99.

9. Known as "gross bombing errors," both the Army and Navy, in peace and war, routinely excluded bomb drops over a certain distance from the target from their accuracy calculations. Two hundred bombs landing 100 feet from a target would give an average circular error of 100 feet. Ten more landing two miles away because of a navigational error would give an overall average circular error of 598 feet if not excluded.

10. McCollum, ed., *Dahlgren*, 19, 71, 79; and Jacobs, *Scientist and His Experiences*, 76–83, 165–67, 170. Jacobs also claimed that after the war BuOrd contracted with Norden Laboratories to design the AN/ASB-1 bombsight, which he described as terribly inaccurate. This Norden bombsight received the approval of the Naval Ordnance Test Station at Inyokern,

California, under the direction of Dr. L. T. E. Thompson. BuOrd's chief negotiator for the AN/ASB-1 was Robert Adams, brother of Paul Adams, who had just purchased Norden Laboratories. After the Navy had contracted to buy the new bombsight, Thompson and Robert Adams went to work for Norden Laboratories.

11. Barth to Howard, July 28, 1931, and Howard to Barth, July 30, 1931, File 471.63, Folder—Bomb Sights—General, Box 872, RD-3312, RG342.

12. U.S. Naval Operations, *Naval Aviation*, 79; and Chief of Air Corps to Chief of BuAer, October 5, 1931, File F41-8, Vol. 2, Box 2279, BuAer General Correspondence, 1925–42, RG72.

13. Foulois to Deputy Chief of Staff, November 23, 1934, and Foulois to Chief of Materiel Division, March 30, 1933, File 202.2-35, HRA; "Relationship of the Development of the AAF Bombing Doctrine to the Development of the Modern Bombsight," n.d., File K110.7017-2, HRA; Brown, "Navy's Mark 15 (Norden) Bombsight," 92–93; and U.S. Naval Operations, *Naval Aviation*, 79. Although the Army wished to buy twenty-five, it had funds for only twenty-three.

14. In 1919, as a result of Norden successes with ship stabilizers, Sperry threatened Norden with a lawsuit over "alleged secrets he is now making use of . . . discovered while in our employ." The primary issue was a gyroscopic stabilizer patent Norden applied for on April 15, 1916, while still on Sperry's payroll as a consulting engineer. See Thompson to Sperry, September 27, October 10, and October 14, 1919, Folder—Administrative Records A. Norden, Box 24, Series V, Elmer Sperry Papers.

15. BuOrd to General Inspector of Naval Aircraft (Wright Field), September 13, 1932, File F41-8, Vol. 1, Box 709, BuAer Confidential Correspondence, 1922–44, RG72; Brown, "Navy's Mark 15 (Norden) Bombsight," 98; and Theodore H. Barth, assignor to United States of America as represented by the Secretary of the Navy, "Synchronizing Bomb Sight," U.S. Patent Office, No. 2,438,532 (filed September 28, 1932, awarded March 30, 1948). Carl L. Norden's name does not appear in the twenty schematic illustrations or in the twenty columns of text of the patent.

16. According to his son, Norden became enraged if anyone spoke of him having "invented" a bombsight, for he argued only God could invent. Mere mortals only discovered God's creations. Interview with Carl F. Norden, December 9, 1989, and April 22, 1990.

17. In the early versions the telescope turned to establish synchronization with the ground. The M-6 and later versions rotated the mirror.

18. The speed of the disc was a constant 5,300 revolutions per minute, but its point of contact with a roller changed. If the roller moved toward the outside of the disc, its speed increased. If moved toward the center, its speed decreased.

19. The rate knob controlled the location of the roller's contact with the disc, thereby controlling the speed of the mirror's rotation.

20. Eighth Air Force, "Report on Bombing Accuracy, 1 September 1944–31 December 1944," File 520.56A, HRA; "Handbook of Instruction for Bombsight Type M-9," June 5, 1945, File 168.69-30, HRA; "Norden Bombsight—Magician and Mathematician: Solved 2 Concurrent Trigonometry Problems," *Norden Times*, July 1978, 4–5; USAF Bombardment School, "M-Series Bombsight: Student Study Guide," HRA; "The Bombsight," *Flying* 35 (July 1945): 28–30, 124–26; and Ayling, *Bombardment Aviation*, 37–39.

21. Greer, *Development of Air Doctrine*, 19; and Mitchell, *Our Air Force*, xix.

22. Mitchell, *Memoirs of World War I;* Mitchell, *Winged Defense*, 16; Mitchell, *Skyways*, 253, 255–56, 262–63; Mitchell, *Our Air Force*, xxii–xxiii, 41, 55–56; Mitchell, "Notes on the Multi-Motored Bombardment Group Day and Night," n.d. (1923), File 248.222-57, HRA; Sherry, *Rise of American Air Power*, 29–30; Cate and Craven, "Army Air Arm between Two Wars," 38–39; and Hurley, *Billy Mitchell*, 111–35, 168–69.

23. Mitchell, "Notes on the Multi-Motored Bombardment Group Day and Night," HRA; and Mitchell, *Our Air Force*, 41, 55–56. Mitchell advocated the targeting of cities in case of war against Japan, because Japanese cities were congested and flammable. See Hurley, *Billy Mitchell*, 87.

24. Mitchell, *Our Air Force*, 57–58.

25. Douhet, *The Command of the Air*, 146–52.

26. *Command of the Air, 1927*, 117–20, and *The War of 19—*, 298–348, both in ibid.

27. Douhet based his calculations on 100 kilograms of explosives destroying a circle 25 meters in radius. Ten tons of explosives, poison gas, and incendiaries carried by ten bombers would therefore destroy an area 500 meters in diameter. He concluded that 1,000 bombers could destroy 50 population centers per day. See Douhet, *Command of the Air*, 20–22, 49.

28. Ibid., 19–20.

29. Edward Warner, "Douhet, Mitchell, Seversky: Theories of Air Warfare," in *Makers of Modern Strategy: Military Thought from Machiavelli to Hitler*, ed. Edward Mead Earle (Princeton: Princeton University Press, 1944), 495; and Bernard Brodie, "The Heritage of Douhet," *Air University Quarterly Review* 6 (Summer 1953): 126. For Douhet's views on the capabilities of bombing, see Douhet, *Command of the Air*, 7, 20.

30. Greer, *Development of Air Doctrine*, 19; and *Parliamentary Debates: Official Report*, House of Commons, 5th ser., vol. 270, col. 632.

31. Smith, *British Air Strategy between the Wars*, 46, 57; and Webster and Frankland, *The Strategic Air Offensive against Germany, 1939–1945*, vol. 1, *Preparation*, 46, 60, 64.

32. Spaight, *Air Power and the Cities*, 3–5, 150, 152, 160–61, 177, 193, 196, 231.

33. Prewar British "Western" air plans called for strikes against ball bearings, aluminum, components, electricity, general products, rail lines, and bridges. See Smith, *British Air Strategy*, 287, 291, 295–96.

34. Webster and Frankland, *Strategic Air Offensive*, vol. 4, *Annexes and Appendices*, 71–76, 119, 135; Smith, *British Air Strategy*, 280; and Hastings, *Bomber Command*, 45–47.

35. Cross, *Bombers*, 81; and "The Planning and Development of Bombs for the German Air Force, 1925–1945," 1956, File K113.107-192, HRA.

36. Dargue to Sherman, March 26, 1936, File 168.7119-47, HRA.

37. Hurley, *Billy Mitchell*, 37. Weigley, *American Way of War*, 236, citing Harvey A. DeWeerd, *President Wilson Fights His War: The American Military Experience in World War I* (New York: Macmillan, 1968), xx, identifies Pres. Woodrow Wilson as the author of this quotation.

38. Greer, *Development of Air Doctrine*, 14–15.

39. Cited in Sherry, *Rise of American Air Power*, 32, and Spaight, *Air Power*, 8–10.

40. James Lea Cate, "Plans, Policies, and Organization," in Craven and Cate, eds., *Plans and Early Operations*, 597; and James Warner Bellah, "Bombing Cities Won't Win the War," *Harper's Magazine* 179 (November 1939): 658–63.

41. Gerald E. Wheeler, *Admiral William Veazie Pratt, U.S. Navy: A Sailor's Life* (Washington, D.C.: Naval Historical Division, 1974), 357.

42. "Report of President's Aircraft Board," HRA.

43. Air Service Tactical School, "Bombardment," 1924–25, File 248.101-9, HRA. The 1926 version of the text made no significant changes in the course material. See ACTS, "Bombardment," 1926, File 248.101-9, HRA.

44. "Bombardment," November 5, 1942–October 29, 1943, File 245.34, Vol. 1, HRA; and "Commandants of the Air Corps Tactical School, 1920–1942," File K110.612-2, HRA.

45. Greer, *Development of Air Doctrine*, 48.

46. Walker biography, File K110.7004-39, HRA; and Lt. K. N. Walker, "Bombardment

Aviation: Bombing Probable Errors; Theory, Establishment and Use," 1931, File 248.222-39, HRA. Walker's formula for circular error probable (CEP) was 1.746 times the square root of the range error times the deflection error, or CEP = $1.746\sqrt{R_e \cdot D_e}$.

47. Hofstetter to Walker, December 23, 1929, File 248.222-42, HRA.

48. Royce to Walker, December 11, 1929, and Commander, Bombardment Section, Air Corps Advanced Flying School, Kelly Field, to Walker, January 20, 1930, File 248.222-42, HRA.

49. Fairchild to Walker, December 14, 1929, Todd to Walker, January 2, 1930, Valentine to Walker, February 4, 1930, and Jouett to Walker, December 4, 1929, File 248.222-42, HRA.

50. "Aberdeen Proving Ground Test," November 24, 1931, File 248.222-42, HRA; and Ley, *Bombs and Bombing*, 85–92.

51. TR440-96, "Bomb Ballistics and Bomb Sights"; and ACTS, "Bombardment Aviation," 1931, File 248.222-42, HRA.

52. ACTS, "The Power and Effect of Demolition Bombs," 1939–40, File 248.2209A-2, HRA.

53. "Results of Bombing of Pee Dee River Bridge" and "Bombing Record Plot of 1,100 lb. T.N.T. Bombs dropped at Pee Dee River Bridge," HRA. Germany ran similar bombing tests in the prewar era, though typical of Hitler's flair for the grandiose, the Luftwaffe built its own testing ground at Fassberg in late 1935, including full-sized steel-reinforced concrete and steel truss bridges. Bombing experiments convinced the Luftwaffe that delayed fuzes were best against concrete targets, while instantaneous fuzes were best for steel targets. See "Military Attaché Report," January 15, 1936, File 248.222-45, HRA.

54. ACTS, "Bombardment Aviation," HRA; and K. N. Walker, "Bombardment Aviation—Bulwark of National Defense," *U.S. Air Services* 18 (August 1933): 15–19.

Chapter 5. The Air Corps Adopts a Bombing Strategy for World War II

1. Antoine Henri Jomini (1779–1869) wrote *Summary of the Art of War* to synthesize the lessons of the Napoleonic Wars.

2. The Lassiter Board called for the development of a strategic bomber force in 1923, reinforcing the more highly publicized efforts of Gen. Billy Mitchell, but to no end.

3. Sherman, *Air Warfare*, 210–18.

4. Interview of Laurence S. Kuter, 1974, File K239.0512-810, HRA; "Relationship of the Development of the AAF Bombing Doctrine to the Development of the Modern Bombsight," HRA; interview of Donald Wilson, 1975, File K239.0512-878, HRA; Haywood S. Hansell Jr., interview with author, September 11, 1987; and Arnold to Chief of Air Corps, December 23, 1935, File 248.222–42, HRA.

5. Parton, *"Air Force Spoken Here,"* 108–9, claims that Hugh Knerr was primarily responsible for the development of this doctrine. Knerr was not at the ACTS during the years of doctrinal formation. Knerr's outspoken support for the bomber and the resulting reaction led him to retire from the Air Corps in 1939, when he went to work for the Sperry Gyroscope Company.

6. Herbert A. Dargue Papers, File 168.7119-2, HRA; Laurence S. Kuter, "Maj. Gen. H. A. Bert Dargue: A Lesson in Leadership," *Air Force Magazine* 62 (February 1979): 80–82; and H. A. Dargue, "Bombardment Aviation and Its Relation to Antiaircraft Defense," *Coast Artillery Journal* 77 (September–October 1934): 333–35. Dargue's relationship with Barth went back to World War I, where Dargue served as a flight instructor in France, while Barth commanded the Army's gas mask production program. Through the 1920s and 1930s Dargue and his family vacationed regularly with Barth, including a number of camping trips to Maine.

Barth's apartment became a hotel for the Dargue family whenever they visited New York. Dargue was Barth's primary source for tickets to the annual Army-Navy football game. Had he survived a plane crash near Bishop, California, on December 12, 1941, on his way to investigate the fiasco at Pearl Harbor, Dargue certainly would have been one of the key leaders of the air war.

7. "A Study of Prepared Air Corps Doctrine," January 31, 1935, File 248.211-65, HRA.

8. Donald Wilson, "Origin of a Theory for Air Strategy," *Aerospace Historian* 18 (Spring 1971): 21–22; and interview of Wilson, HRA.

9. Another instructor at ACTS, Maj. Muir S. Fairchild, preferred to call this target the "National Economic Structure." See Greer, *Development of Air Doctrine*, 115. According to Charles W. McArthur, *Operations Analysis in the U.S. Army Eighth Air Force in World War II*, 8, Fairchild initiated the idea of bottlenecks in an industrial economy in 1932 while an instructor at ACTS.

10. The doctrine of daylight strategic precision bombing is summarized in Cate and Craven, "Army Air Arm between Two Wars," 51–52.

11. Interview of Wilson, HRA.

12. Wilson, "Origin of a Theory for Air Strategy," 19–25; and Donald Wilson, *Wooing Peponi: My Odyssey thru Many Years* (Monterey, Calif.: Angel Press, 1973), 236–39.

13. ACTS, "The Air Force," 1931, File 248.1011-189, HRA; and ACTS, "Bombardment Aviation," February 1, 1931, File 248.101-9, HRA. This edition of the basic school text, authored by Walker, was the most precise and informative of all the ACTS texts covering two decades. Most were masterpieces of generality and abstraction. Walker's text discussed the capabilities of bombsights and identified the types of bombs to be used against different targets. It explained the damages wrought by aerial bombs, the degree of cratering resulting from delayed fuzes, the danger zones for bomb fragmentation, and the mathematical probabilities of hitting a target based on the results of the Langley Annual Bombing and Machine Gun Matches. It was here that Walker wrote for a generation of Air Corps leaders that low-altitude bombing was more accurate than high, but was less effective because bombs rolled when dropped from low altitudes and failed to achieve penetration and the mining effect.

14. Instructors at ACTS at the time included lieutenant colonels Donald Wilson and Edgar Sorenson; Maj. Muir Fairchild; captains Ralph Snavely, Laurence Kuter, and Hoyt Vandenberg; and first lieutenants Haywood Hansell Jr. and Leonard Harman.

15. Greer, *Development of Air Doctrine*, 48; ACTS, "Bombardment Aviation," 1936, File 248.101-9, HRA; James J. Truscott, "The Doctrine of the Tactical School," Air Command and Staff College thesis, 1965, 19–21; and ACTS, "Bombardment Aviation," 1939, File 248.101-9, HRA.

16. ACTS, "Bombardment Aviation Problems," 1931–38, File 248.101-9A, HRA; ACTS, loose classroom materials, 1936, File 248.222-40, HRA; and Hansell, *The Strategic Air War against Germany and Japan*, 12–14.

17. FM 1-10, "Tactics and Techniques of the Air Attack," 1932, File 248.211-13, HRA; and Maurer, *Aviation in the United States Army*, 388.

18. The only challenge from within the ACTS came from Maj. Claire Chennault, who criticized the planners for their conviction that large bombers would always get through. Chennault did not criticize, however, the underlying industrial fabric concept.

19. "The Probable Error of Bombing," October 8, 1924, File 248.222-39, HRA; and ACTS, "Bombing Accuracy—Original Analysis of Annual Matches Prior to 1932," n.d. (1932?), File 248.222-39, HRA. The average radial error in this case has been determined by Kenneth Walker's formula: 1.746 multiplied by the square root of the range error multiplied by the deflection error or CEP = $1.746\sqrt{R_e \cdot D_e}$.

20. *New York Times*, July 11, 1926, 1:6, 7, 8, July 12, 1926, 1:4, 5, 6, 7, 8, and July 13, 1926, 1:6, 7, 8; and ACTS, "The Power and Effect of Demolition Bombs," HRA. The 500-pound bomb actually weighed 496 pounds, with the TNT (trinitrotoluene) filling accounting for 266 pounds. One reason for the overestimation of its destructive power was tests indicating that tamping resulting from high-altitude drops increased the explosive effect of the bomb by 4.5 times.

21. ACTS, "Bombardment Aviation Problems," HRA.

22. ACTS, "Practical Bombing Probabilities—Conclusion," 1938–39, File 248.2208A-7, pt. 4, HRA; Air Corps Board, Study No. 45, "Study of Bombing Accuracy," 1939–40, File 248.2209A-5, HRA; and interview of Kuter, HRA.

23. *Parliamentary Debates*, 5th ser., vol. 270, col. 632; and Cate and Craven, "Army Air Arm between Two Wars," 65.

24. Copp, *Few Great Captains*, 331.

25. Ibid., 103–4; Maurer, *Aviation in the United States Army*, 392–93; and Robert Olds biography, File K110.7004-34, HRA. Arnold did not attend ACTS. Olds attended in 1928. Olds died of an illness in 1943 and did not participate in the great bombing campaigns of World War II.

26. Training Manual (TM) 1-250, October 1944, Folder—Bombing Accuracy Analytical Studies I, Box 76, Subject File, Carl Spaatz Papers, Manuscript Division, Library of Congress; and Army Air Forces Board, "Study of Bombing Accuracy," Report No. 45, June 8, 1942, File 167.5-45, HRA. Probability studies prepared earlier for the doctrine makers indicated that it took first-class bombardiers 1.5 aircraft, each dropping one bomb, to get a 70 percent assurance of a hit on a 100- by 600-foot target from 12,000 feet. With second-class bombardiers it required 2.5 aircraft. With third-class bombardiers four aircraft were required. The training group with the best bombing record in 1941, the 4th Composite Group, required six aircraft to achieve a 70 percent assurance of at least one hit. An average group such as the 11th required ten and the lowest ranking group, the 12th, required thirty.

27. "Air Corps Tentative Training Manual 2170-105," 1939, Files 145.91-522 and 145.91-523, HRA.

28. Army Air Forces Board, "Study of Bombing Accuracy," Report No. 45, November 16, 1942, and May 15, 1943, HRA.

29. Air Corps Board Study No. 58, "Comparison of Glide and Low Altitude Bombing with High Altitude Bombing," December 7, 1940, File 167.5-58, HRA.

30. "Memorandum for Commander Aircraft, Base Force," August 16, 1937, BuAer to CNO, November 24, 1937, File A16-3, Vol. 4, Box 200, BuAer Confidential Correspondence, 1922–44, RG72; and "Direct Hits and Near Misses on Utah, Joint Exercises No. 4," 1938, File 168.7012-23, HRA. Copp, *Few Great Captains*, 397, writes that Maj. Gen. Frank M. Andrews, commanding general of GHQAF, requested the effort on August 14, 1937, because the Navy dismissed the Air Corps' success on the thirteenth. LeMay and Kantor, *Mission with LeMay*, 142–52, record the Navy demanding the effort of August 14 in order to prove that Navy ships could escape high-altitude bombing through evasive maneuvers.

31. USAF Historical Division, *Strategic Bombers in a Tactical Role*, 17–18; Greer, *Development of Air Doctrine*, 111–14; TR440-15, "Employment of the Air Forces of the Army," 1935, and Air Corps Board Study No. 31, "The Functions of the Army Air Forces," October 29, 1936, in Cate and Craven, "Army Air Arm between Two Wars," 48; FM 1-5, "Employment of Aviation of the Army," April 15, 1940, File 170.121001-5, HRA; and FM 1-10, "Tactics and Techniques of Air Attack," November 20, 1940, File 170.121001-10, HRA.

32. Air Corps Board Study No. 44, "Air Corps Mission Under the Monroe Doctrine,"

October 17, 1938, in Cate and Craven, "Army Air Arm between Two Wars," 50; Air Corps Board Study No. 58, "Comparison of Glide and Low Altitude Bombing with High Altitude Bombing," HRA; and Barth to Dargue, February 7, 1940, File 168.7119-49, HRA.

33. Capt. Ralph Snavely told his students at ACTS that the best evidence of the correctness of the doctrine of daylight precision strategic bombing was Hitler using the mere threat of bombing to win all of his territorial objectives short of war. See ACTS, "Introduction to Bombing Course," 1938–39, File 248.2208A-1, HRA.

34. Greer, *Development of Air Doctrine*, 101; *Foreign Relations of the United States, 1939* (Washington, D.C.: Government Printing Office, 1956), 1:541–42; and James Lea Cate and E. Kathleen Williams, "The Air Corps Prepares for War, 1939–41," in Craven and Cate, *Plans and Early Operations*, 136.

35. George was chief of the ACTS Bombardment Section from 1931 to 1934 and director of the Department of Air Tactics and Strategy from 1934 to 1935. Hansell, Kuter, and Walker were instructors, respectively, from 1935 to 1938, from 1935 to 1938, and from 1929 to 1933. The other key individual in the inception of the doctrine of daylight strategic precision bombing at ACTS, Donald Wilson, was at the time of AWPD/1 one of two Army Air Forces's representatives in the Plans Division of the War Department General Staff. The Air War Plans Division, a separate agency under the Army Air Forces, developed air plans for World War II, but submitted them for approval and incorporation into the Plans Division's overall plans for the war. Wilson was therefore indirectly an author of AWPD/1. His connection to ACTS was as the chief of the Air Force Section from 1931 to 1934 and as director of the Department of Air Tactics and Strategy from 1936 to 1941. According to Richard D'O. Hughes, the air plan for defeating Germany was primarily the work of George, because he was the only planner able to write in shorthand. No secretaries were allowed in the planning room for security purposes. See Hughes to Laidlaw, September 5, 1958, File 168.7264-7, HRA.

36. Gaston, *Planning the American Air War*, 56; Hansell, *The Air Plan that Defeated Hitler*, 86; and AWPD/1, "Munitions Requirements of the Army Air Forces," August 12, 1941, File 145.82-1, HRA.

37. Hughes memoir, 1955–57, File 520.056-234, HRA.

38. Ibid.

39. Air War Plans Division, AWPD/1, "Munitions Requirements of the Army Air Forces to Defeat Our Potential Enemies," 1941, Folder—Air War Plans-AWPD #1, Box 65, Subject File, Spaatz Papers; and "A Study of Proposed Air Corps Doctrine by the Air Corps Tactical School, Based on Information Furnished by the War Plans Division, General Staff, in Memorandum Dated December 21, 1934," 1935, File 248.211-65, HRA.

Chapter 6. The Navy Adopts Dive Bombing for World War II

1. Kraus to Naval Aircraft Factory, May 31, 1938, File Aer-E-32-LID, F41-8, Box 710, BuAer Confidential Correspondence, RG72; Materiel Division, "Report on Conference with Navy on Bombsight Problem," November 21, 1942, File 471.63, Folder—Bomb Sights, Box 2893, RD-2885, RG342; and Butts to Chiefs of BuAer and BuOrd, May 24, 1934, File F41-8, Vol. 1, Box 709, BuAer Confidential Correspondence, 1922–44, RG72.

2. Chief BuOrd to Chief BuAer, May 3, 1935, and Chief BuOrd to Commander Aircraft Battle Force, May 6, 1935, File F41-8, Vol. 2, Box 709, BuAer Confidential Correspondence, 1922–44, RG 72.

3. BuOrd to Commander Aircraft Battle Force, August 14, 1937, File F41-8, Vol. 3, Box

710, BuAer Confidential Correspondence, 1922–44, RG72; and Bombing Squadron Four to BuOrd, June 5, 1939, Commander-in-Chief U.S. Fleet to BuOrd, August 14, 1939, and BuOrd to Commander-in-Chief U.S. Fleet, August 30, 1939, File F41-8/NOs 42552, Folder— 39771, Box 168, BuOrd General Correspondence Confidential, 1926–39, RG74.

4. BuAer to BuOrd, April 16, 1941, File F41-8, Vol. 5, Box 711, BuAer Confidential Correspondence, 1922–44, RG72.

5. Chief BuOrd to Commander Aircraft Battle Force, May 6, 1935, and Acting Chief BuOrd to BuAer, October 15, 1936, File F41-8, Vol. 2, Box 709, BuAer Confidential Correspondence, 1922–44, RG72; and Brown, "Navy's Mark 15 (Norden) Bombsight," 104–6.

6. Report of conference, May 17, 1938, File 471.63, Box 1893, RD-2451, RG342; and Engineering Section Memo, May 31, 1938, File 471.63, Folder—Aiming Angle Bombsight, Box 978, RD-3339, RG342.

7. Inspector of Ordnance (Dahlgren) to BuOrd, September 19, 1939, File F41-8, Vol. 5, Box 711, BuAer Confidential Correspondence, 1922–44, RG72; and BuOrd to Norden, April 11, 1942, File F41-8, Vol. 6, Box 711, BuAer Confidential Correspondence, 1922–44, RG72. The Army developed three dive-bombing sights for its own use during World War II under the pressure of field units clamoring for anything to improve bombing accuracy: the K-2 "Peanut," the AN/ASG-10 "Integrator," and the A-1 Davis-Draper. None were available until late in the war and the Army Air Forces judged them inaccurate and impracticable. In World War II the Navy used Arabic numbers to designate equipment formerly assigned Roman numerals. The Navy also redesignated the Norden Mark 2 Aiming Angle Sight the Mark 16 and began a simplified Mark 17 version in April 1942.

8. U.S. Navy Bureau of Ordnance, *Navy Bureau of Ordnance*, 360; Friedman, *U.S. Naval Weapons*, 189; and Bulky Files, October 1942–44, Box 724, File 452.26, RG18.

9. Commander Battle Force to Battle Force, May 16, 1931, Commander Aircraft Battle Force to Aircraft Battle Force, June 12, 1931, Commander Battle Force to Battle Force, June 24, 1931, Commander Aircraft Battle Force to Units Concerned, February 17, 1932, Commander-in-Chief U.S. Fleet to Fleet, November 28, 1933, and Commander-in-Chief U.S. Fleet to Chief BuAer, December 26, 1933, File A16-3, Vol. 1, Box 199, BuAer Confidential Correspondence, 1922–44, RG72; and Lyon to BuOrd, March 26, 1932, and BuAer to BuOrd, April 20, 1932, File F41-8, Vol. 2, Box 2279, BuAer General Correspondence, 1925–42, RG72.

10. "Instructions for Cruising Exercises United States Fleet," March 14, 1934, File A16-3, Vol. 2, Box 199, BuAer Confidential Correspondence, 1922–44, RG72; and Commander-in-Chief U.S. Fleet to Fleet, January 17, 1934, File A16-3, Vol. 1, Box 199, BuAer Confidential Correspondence, 1922–44, RG72.

11. The duties included gunnery observation, the destruction of enemy aircraft, protection for spotter aircraft, tactical scouting, smoke laying, illumination, torpedo attack, and dive-bomber attack to "break up enemy force attacks, hinder enemy fire control, and for destruction of enemy capital ships."

12. Commander-in-Chief U.S. Fleet to BuAer, June 6, 1936, File A16-3, Vol. 3, Box 199, BuAer Confidential Correspondence, 1922–44, RG72.

13. Commander-in-Chief U.S. Fleet to Fleet, April 27, 1938, File A16-3, Vol. 4, Box 200, BuAer Confidential Correspondence, 1922–44, RG72.

14. Brown, "Navy's Mark 15 (Norden) Bombsight," 232–34.

15. Ibid., 244–49; Johnson, *Fly Navy*, 138; Belote and Belote, *Titans of the Seas*, 16; Melhorn, *Two-Block Fox*, 114–15; U.S. Naval Operations, *Naval Aviation*, 63–64; and Wheeler, Pratt, 274–75, 368. The quotation is from U.S. Bureau of Ordnance, *Navy Bureau of Ordnance*, 359–60.

Chapter 7. Preparation for War

1. Foulois to Deputy Chief of Staff, November 23, 1934, File 202.2-35, HRA; and Isbell to BuOrd, April 3, 1933, File F41-8, Folder—MK XV 1-75, Box 171, BuOrd General Correspondence Confidential, 1926–39, RG74. Foulois left no record of his visit to Barth, but Lt. Arnold J. Isbell of BuOrd stumbled upon Foulois and Maj. Herbert Dargue in Barth's apartment while in New York to pick up a completed Mark XV bombsight. Isbell dutifully reported what transpired.

2. "Story of Norden Bombsight Released," *Norden Insight*, December 1944, 54.

3. Chief BuOrd to General Inspector of Naval Aircraft, Wright Field, September 13, 1932, and Assistant Chief BuAer to Chief BuAer, May 26, 1933, File F41-8 (Mk XV/4), Vol. 1, Box 709, BuAer Confidential Correspondence, 1922–44, RG72; "Confidential Correspondence Concerning Bomb Sights," 1935, File 170.1-55, HRA; Acting Director of Naval Intelligence to North American Aviation and Airplane Development Corporation, n.d., File F41-8, Vol. 2, Box 709, RG72; and Chief BuOrd to Chief BuAer, October 16, 1931, File F41-8, Vol. 2, Box 2279, BuAer General Correspondence, 1925–42, RG72. The chief of BuAer forwarded Admiral Larimer's letter to Air Corps Chief Foulois on October 22, 1931.

4. Foulois to Deputy Chief of Staff, November 23, 1934, and Stark to Chief of Air Corps, May 16, 1935, File 202.2-35, HRA; and Chief of Air Corps to Chief of Materiel Division, April 17, 1935, File 471.63, Folder—Bombsight Navy, Box 3903, RD-3851, RG342. The Air Corps lowered the security classification of the M-series bombsight from secret to confidential on June 4, 1935.

5. Materiel Division memo, August 10, 1937, File 202.2-14, HRA.

6. Intelligence Section Memo, January 13, 1931, File 471.6-D, Box 299, Central Decimal Files, 1939–42, Series II, RG18; and Dargue to Sherman, March 26, 1936, File 168.7119-47, HRA.

7. Schoeffel to BuOrd, July 31, 1937, File F31-1 (10), Vol. 1, Box 636, BuAer Confidential Correspondence, 1922–44, RG72; FBI memo, May 6, 1940, File 65-10347-10X, FBI Records; and Carl F. Norden, interview with author, October 22, 1990.

8. Chief BuOrd to CNO, November 6, 1939, File F41-8, Vol. 4, Box 710, BuAer, RG72; and Glassman to Plans Division, December 6, 1939, File F41-8, Vol. 5, Box 711, BuAer, RG72. The letter from the chief of BuOrd to the CNO contained copies of the offending articles from *Time*, October 9, 1939, 34, and *Collier's*, October 14, 1939, 64–65.

9. Hoover to McCabe, January 17, 1940, File 471.6-B, Box 300, Central Decimal Files, 1939–42, Series II, RG18.

10. Foxworth to Hoover, May 8, 1940, File 65-10347-4, and FBI memo, May 9, 1940, File 65-10347-10XI, FBI Records.

11. Foxworth to Hoover, June 4, 1940, File 65-10347-17, FBI Records.

12. Assistant Director to Hoover, July 30, 1941, File 65-10347-77, Sackett to Hoover, June 22, 1940, File 65-10347-18X, and September 25, 1940, File 65-10347-42, Hoover to Sackett, May 8, 1941, File 65-10347-74, and Sackett to Hoover, March 13, 1944, File 65-10347-66, FBI Records. The FBI censored the identity of this undercover agent in all documents acquired from the FBI under the Freedom of Information Act. File 65-10347 is replete with the reports of the undercover agent, but devoid of evidence linking anyone at Norden to unlawful or traitorous activity, despite the agent's attempts to entrap his fellow workers.

13. Hoover to Berle, July 10, 1940, File 65-10347-19, memo, July 14, 1940, File 65-10347-22, and Connelley to Hoover, August 5, 1940, File 65-10347- (blank), FBI Records;

and *New York Times,* July 1, 1941, 1:1 and 22:2; July 24, 1941, 19:3; and September 4, 1941, 12:3.

14. *New York Times,* September 9, 1941, 1:3; September 10, 1941, 1:2; September 24, 1941, 6:6; September 25, 1941, 27:8; and October 3, 1941, 12:3.

15. "Pickle Barrelers," 50–51; and *New York Times,* January 3, 1942, 1:2. David Kahn, *Hitler's Spies: German Military Intelligence in World War II* (New York: Macmillan, 1978), 328–33, and Ladislas Farago, *The Game of the Foxes: The Untold Story of German Espionage in the United States and Great Britain during World War II* (New York: David McKay, 1971), 45–56, have published accounts of the Lang affair.

16. Arnold to Marshall, September 13, 1940, File 471.6-D, Box 299, Central Decimal Files, 1939–42, Series II, RG18; and *New York Times,* December 16, 1948, 1:6.

17. *The Statutes at Large of the United States of America from December, 1925, to March, 1927,* vol. 44, pt. 2 (Washington, D.C.: Government Printing Office, 1927), 787; Schoeffel to Bu-Ord, July 31, 1937, File F31-1 (10), Vol. 1, Box 636, BuAer Confidential Correspondence, 1922–44, RG72; and Dargue to Chief of Army Air Forces, July 3, 1941, Lovett to Forrestal, July 24, 1941, and Forrestal to Lovett, August 11, 1941, File 471.6-F, Box 299, Central Decimal Files, 1939–42, Series II, RG18. In late June 1941 Chief of the Inspector Division of the Army Air Forces Herbert A. Dargue visited his old friend Ted Barth at Carl L. Norden, Inc., to discover the reason for the slow delivery of bombsights. Barth blamed BuOrd for all problems, feeling direct negotiations between the Army and Norden were the only solution. Dargue duly reported Barth's recommendation to Arnold and in late July 1941 Assistant Secretary of War for Air Robert A. Lovett asked Undersecretary of the Navy James V. Forrestal to allow such direct negotiations. Forrestal denied the request, citing the need to control Norden bombsight production because it was of "greatest usefulness against moving targets [and was] of vital importance to the Navy." See Chief of Inspection Division to Chief of AAF, July 3, 1941, Lovett to Forrestal, July 24, 1941, and Forrestal to Lovett, August 11, 1941, File 202.2-35, HRA.

18. Materiel Division to Chief of Air Corps, January 7, 1932, File 452.7, Folder—Automatic Steering Device, Box 570, RD-3232, RG342; Materiel Division memo, n.d., File 452.7, Folder—Automatic Pilot—Sperry, Box 1383, RD-3459, RG342; and Kahn, *Hitler's Spies,* 86. In the language of Wright Field's engineers, the A-2's momentary lag was a "slight oscillatory hunting." In a licensing agreement with the German firm of Askania Werke A.G., Sperry supplied Germany and its air force with a much-needed, efficient autopilot.

19. Materiel Division Routing and Record Sheet, August 31, 1939, and Administrative Branch to Air Corps Eastern District Supervisor, July 19, 1940, File 452.19, Folder—Automatic Pilot Type A-3, Box 4064, RD-3895, RG342. Sperry, AC Spark Plug, Electric Autolite, Addressograph Multigraph, and Jack and Heintz mass-produced over 4,000 A-3s a month during the war for installation in a wide variety of aircraft: C-47, C-54, C-60, C-53, C-56, C-57, A-29, B-25C, B-25D, B-34, AT-18, AT-7, and P-61 with mechanical bypasses, and AT-7, C-46, C-69, and F-5 with hydraulic bypasses.

20. Mortimer F. Bates, assignor to Sperry Gyroscope Company, "Bomb Sight," U.S. Patent Office, No. 1,783,769 (filed June 1, 1926, awarded December 2, 1930), and Bates, "Bombsight Alignment and Rudder Control."

21. One year earlier BuAer had asked BuOrd to link the Norden Mark XI bombsight to an "automatic steering device" in response to requests from aircraft commanders aboard the Battle Fleet. BuAer did not have in mind an SBAE or an autopilot, but was only reporting what pilots found obvious—the Mark XI was too complex to allow the pilot to maintain a precise bombing run. Nothing came of the request, however, because BuOrd was busy perfecting the new Mark XV bombsight and testing the Sperry autopilot—as separate items.

Internal memorandum, BuAer, April 20, 1931, File F41-8, Vol. 1, Box 2278, BuAer General Correspondence, 1925–42, RG72.

22. Isbell to BuOrd, February 16, 1932, File F41-8, Folder—Aircraft Ordnance, Box 1474, BuOrd General Correspondence Confidential, RG74; and "The Beginning Was 2 Men," 4–5.

23. Plans Division to Chief of BuAer, July 31, 1936, File F31-1 (10), Vol. 2, Box 2100, BuAer General Correspondence, 1925–42, RG72; and Brown, "Navy's Mark 15 (Norden) Bombsight," 112–13.

24. Barth to Dargue, March 15, 1934, File 168.7119-49, HRA.

25. Norden to BuOrd, February 6, 1935, cited in Brown, "Navy's Mark 15 (Norden) Bombsight," 115–16.

26. Chief BuOrd to Chief BuAer, February 21, 1935, File F41-8, Vol. 2, Box 709, BuAer Confidential Correspondence, 1922–44, RG72; and Brown, "Navy's Mark 15 (Norden) Bombsight," 115–16.

27. Inspector of Ordnance in Charge (Dahlgren) to BuOrd, May 28, 1935, File F31-1 (10), Vol. 1, Box 636, BuAer Confidential Correspondence, 1922–44, RG72; Naval Inspector of Ordnance (Dahlgren) to BuOrd, August 6, 1935, File F41-8, Vol. 2, Box 709, BuAer Confidential Correspondence, 1922–44, RG72; and Naval Inspector of Ordnance (Dahlgren) to BuAer, July 14, 1936, File F31-1 (10), Vol. 2, Box 2100, BuAer General Correspondence, 1925–42, RG72.

28. Inspector of Ordnance in Charge (Dahlgren) to BuOrd, March 24, 1936, File F31-1 (10), Vol. 1, Box 636, BuAer Confidential Correspondence, 1922–44, RG72; and Theodore H. Barth, assignor to the United States of America as represented by the Secretary of the Navy, "Aircraft Control System," U.S. Patent Office, No. 2,485,953 (filed April 24, 1940, awarded October 25, 1949).

29. Brown, "Navy's Mark 15 (Norden) Bombsight," 120–22, 124–26.

30. Ibid., 126.

31. BuOrd to Chief of Air Corps, December 15, 1937, File F41-8, Vol. 3, Box 710, BuAer Confidential Correspondence, 1922–44, RG72; and BuOrd to Chief of Air Corps, April 29, 1944, File F41-8, Vol. 5, Box 711, BuAer Confidential Correspondence, 1922–44, RG72.

32. Knerr to Materiel Division, September 3, 1936, File 452.7, Folder—Automatic Pilot—Sperry, Box 1383, RD-3459, RG342.

33. The Norden SBAE weighed 150 pounds, but when installed with the Sperry autopilot it used several of the same components, saving 24 pounds.

34. Patrol Squadron 7 to BuAer, April 12, 1935, Patrol Squadron 8 to BuAer, May 22, 1939, Patrol Squadron 43 to BuOrd, October 29, 1940, Inspector of Ordnance in Charge (Dahlgren) to BuOrd, January 7, 1941, Patrol Wing Two to BuAer, July 12, 1939, Commander Aircraft Scouting Force to BuAer, June 30, 1939, BuAer memo, July 26, 1939, and Patrol Wing One to BuAer, October 27, 1939, File F31-1 (10), Vol. 1, Box 636, BuAer Confidential Correspondence, 1922–44, RG72.

35. BuAer to Commander Aircraft Scouting Force, December 4, 1939, File F31-1 (10), Vol. 1, Box 636, BuAer Confidential Correspondence, 1922–44, RG72; and Brown, "Navy's Mark 15 (Norden) Bombsight," 133–41.

36. Experimental Engineering Section memo, September 15, 1941, File 202.2-35, HRA. The Dahlgren Proving Ground asked for the suspension of all SBAE production until problems with Norden's bombing system were corrected, but BuOrd overruled it on the grounds that no other alternative was available. See Brown, "Navy's Mark 15 (Norden) Bombsight," 141.

37. Boeing to Materiel Division, August 18, 1941, and Experimental Engineering, "Flight

Control Cable Tensions," November 5, 1941, File 452.19, Folder—SBAE-AFCE Unsatisfactory Reports, Box 1383, RD-3459, RG342.

38. Materiel Center to BuAer, January 6, 1940, Contract Section, Materiel Center to Pioneer Instrument Division, March 4, 1940, and Air Materiel Command memo, November 21, 1943, File 452.19, Folder—Pilot Automatic Type A-5, Box 2243, RD-2626, RG342. The Sperry Gyroscope Company began the A-5 project in March 1940, completing an experimental model in February 1941. Refinements took another year, but developers were unable to tie the A-5 to the Norden bombsight. It would not replace the Norden SBAE, though the Air Materiel Command attached the A-5 as an AFCE to the Sperry S-1 bombsight for use in B-24 Liberator bombers. AC Spark Plug and Autolite of Toledo, Ohio, produced the A-5 during the war.

39. BuAer to NAF, December 20, 1940, and NAF to BuAer, January 9, 1941, File F41-8, Vol. 5, Box 711, BuAer Confidential Correspondence, 1922–44, RG72.

40. BuOrd to BuAer, April 1, 1941, File F41-8, Vol. 5, Box 711, BuAer Confidential Correspondence, 1922–44, RG72; Brown, "Navy's Mark 15 (Norden) Bombsight," 144–45; BuOrd to Chief of Air Corps, June 16, 1941, Naval Inspector of Ordnance (Dahlgren) to BuOrd and BuAer, August 25, 1941, and BuOrd to BuAer, September 10, 1941, File F41-8, Vol. 6, Box 711, BuAer Confidential Correspondence, RG72; BuOrd to Chief of Air Corps, June 16, 1941, File 471.6-E, Box 299, Central Decimal Files, 1939–42, Series II, RG18; NAF to BuAer, August 27, 1941, and April 17, 1941, File F31-1 (10), Vol. 1, Box 636, BuAer Confidential Correspondence, 1922–44, RG72; and Memo to Chief of Experimental Engineering Section, August 28, 1941, File 471.63, Folder—Norden, Box 1893, RD-2451, RG342.

41. BuAer to Commander Patrol Wing, Support Force, May 23, 1941, File F31-1 (10), Vol. 1, Box 636, BuAer Confidential Correspondence, 1922–44, RG72; BuAer to CNO, January 14, 1942, Bureau of Supplies and Accounts to Norden, May 28, 1942, File F41-8, Vol. 6, Box 711, BuAer Confidential Correspondence, 1922–44, RG72; and BuOrd to CNO, February 5, 1942, File F41-8, Vol. 4, Box 2279, BuAer General Correspondence, 1925–42, RG72. The new SBAE/AFCE had servomotors located near the control surfaces to defeat the cable tension problem, a pilot's control panel to eliminate the need to have adjustments made through the pilot direction indicator, "covered and protected potentiometers and wiper brushes" to replace the Norden's contact brushes, a sealed flight gyroscope, and shock mountings for the flight gyroscope to reduce the possibility of damage to the bearings.

42. The director of military requirements at Headquarters, Army Air Forces, designated the Minneapolis-Honeywell device the A-6 and redesignated the Norden SBAE the A-3, causing confusion with the various Sperry autopilots. The assistant chief of the Materiel Division changed the designations to B-1 for the 12-volt Minneapolis-Honeywell AFCE and C-1 for the 24-volt Minneapolis-Honeywell AFCE. See Director of Military Requirements, Headquarters AAF, "Military Requirement Policy No. 18," May 24, 1942, File 452.7, Folder—Automatic Pilot—Minneapolis-Honeywell, Box 1817, RD-2438, RG342.

43. In operation the bombsight stabilizer and vertical flight gyroscope of the autopilot detected deviations from straight and level flight. The directional panel of the autopilot measured and seven vacuum tubes amplified these deviations electrically and sent them to servomotors located near the control surfaces. Power came from a rotary inverter, which generated alternating current for the amplifier from the direct current of the aircraft power supply. The three 23-pound servomotors operated from the 24-volt direct current of the aircraft's power supply. In operation the bombardier turned the bombsight course knobs to control the autopilot. The pilot also had a control panel and a formation stick ("pilot's controller") for flying through the power-assisted autopilot system. This latter device was similar to the "high-tech" joystick controls of modern aircraft. See "Handbook, Operation and Service Instructions,

Type C-1 Automatic Pilot (Minneapolis-Honeywell)," Technical Order 5A1-2-5-1, June 25, 1943.

44. "The Beginning Was 2 Men," 4–5; memo to Chief Materiel Division, September 23, 1941, File 452.19, Folder—Automatic Pilot Minneapolis-Honeywell, Box 2785, RD-2857, RG342; *New York Times*, September 21, 1943, 25:5; Experimental Engineering Section memo, September 15, 1941, File 202.2-35, HRA; Director of Military Requirements, Headquarters AAF, "Military Requirement Policy No. 18," May 24, 1942, File 452.7, Folder—Automatic Pilot Minneapolis-Honeywell, Box 1817, RD-2438, RG342; BuOrd to Commanding General, Army Air Forces, n.d. (June 1942?), File 452.19, Folder—C-1 Automatic Pilot, Box 2244, RD-2626, RG342; Chief Aircraft Laboratory from Experimental Engineering Section, March 14, 1942, Chief Aircraft Laboratory from Experimental Engineering Section, April 13, 1942, Chief Aircraft Laboratory from Experimental Engineering Section, May 25, 1942, File 452.19, Folder—AFCE—Cable Travel, Box 2780, RD-2856, RG342; and Newby, *Target Ploesti*, 124.

45. Teletype from Armament Section to Production Engineering Section, July 20, 1942, and Chief of Experimental Engineering to Chief of Production Division, July 20, 1942, File 452.19, Folder—C-1 Automatic Pilot, Box 2244, RD-2626, RG342.

46. Assistant Chief of Air Staff, Intelligence, "Interview with Lt. Col. John B. Montgomery," April 13, 1943, and Anderson to Fairchild and Giles, May 4, 1943, Folder—Bombing Accuracy, Box 76, Subject File, Spaatz Papers.

47. Brown, "Navy's Mark 15 (Norden) Bombsight," 175–78. The Air Corps wanted to switch from 12-volt to 24-volt because certain aircraft equipment, such as power turrets, required 24 volts. Navy aircraft worked on 12-volt power. The Air Corps wanted the switch from direct current to alternating current because AC did not require complex and costly commutators and transformers and because it was easier to switch AC to DC using a rectifier than to switch from DC to AC.

48. Jamison to Materiel Division, April 25, 1941, File 471.63, Folder—Attachment-Glide Angle, Box 3381, RD-3047, RG342; and Brown, "Navy's Mark 15 (Norden) Bombsight," Appendix C7. The Navy admitted later that the attachments were possible "without interference with bombsight deliveries."

49. Bell Telephone Laboratories and the National Defense Research Committee completed a Universal Sight in February 1945, capable of both optical and radar bombsighting. Only an experimental device, the Universal Sight, consisting of a Norden bombsight combined with an AN/APQ-31 radar unit, required years of research and development after the war before it reached the production stage. See Secretary of Navy to Commander-in-Chief of U.S. Fleet, February 10, 1945, File F41-8, Vol. 4, Box 174, RG72; and Col. William M. Garland, "The Bombing Problem and the New Universal Sight," Air War College thesis, February 1948.

50. Memo of meeting, October 21, 1937, File F41-8, Vol. 3, Box 710, BuAer Confidential Correspondence, 1922–44, RG72.

51. Simple adjustments to the Norden bombsight allowed it to be used at low altitudes, but lowering its minimum altitude by 200 feet also caused the sight to lose 1,000 feet from its maximum altitude, making the LABA necessary.

52. Brown, "Navy's Mark 15 (Norden) Bombsight," 151–68. At 1,800 feet, Navy crews missed their targets by an average 250 feet sighting through the Norden bombsight with the LABA, but only 150 feet through the bombsight without the LABA.

53. Materiel Division to Director of Bombardment, September 29, 1942, File 471.63, Folder Attachment—Glide Angle, Box 3381, RD-3047, RG342; and Brown, "Navy's Mark 15 (Norden) Bombsight," 151–68. Carl L. Norden, Inc., claimed the cancellation cost the company $228,748.34.

54. BuOrd to Commander Aircraft Pacific Fleet, April 14, 1942, File F41-8, Vol. 6, Box 711, BuAer Confidential Correspondence, 1922–44, RG72; and "Service Test Requirements and Manual on Automatic Gyro Leveling System for M-Series Bombsights," April 2, 1943, File 471.63, Folder—Norden M-Series Bombsights, Box 2323, RD-2644, RG342.

55. Armament Laboratory to Air Service Command, April 24, 1943, File 471.63, Folder—Automatic Gyro Leveling Device, Box 120, RD-4043, RG342; Army Air Forces Board, "Mercury Erection System on M-Series Sights," October 8, 1943, Arnold to Materiel Division, August 12, 1943, and "Service Test Requirements and Manual on Automatic Gyro Leveling System for M-Series Bombsights," April 2, 1943, File 471.63, Folder—Norden M-Series Bombsights, Box 2323, RD-2644; ACAS/MMD to ACAS/OCR, December 18, 1943, Deputy ACAS/OCR to Second Air Force, February 23, 1944, and Ninth Bombardment Group to Materiel Division, August 26, 1943, File 452.26-G, Box 764, Central Decimal Files, Oct. 1942–44, RG18; and Langley Field to 2nd Bombardment Wing, April 2, 1941, and Giles to Lovett, July 12, 1944, File 471.6-F, Box 299, Central Decimal Files, 1939–42, Series II, RG18.

56. HQ GHQAF to Chief of Air Corps, December 23, 1937, Experimental Engineering Section to Field Service Section, March 24, 1941, Norden to Naval Inspector of Ordnance at Norden, Inc., December 10, 1941, and Materiel Division to BuOrd, August 31, 1942, File 471.63, Folder—Attachment Glide Angle, Box 3381, RD-3047, RG342; BuOrd to BuAer, February 24, 1944, File F41-8, Vol. 2, Box 712, BuAer Confidential Correspondence, 1922–44, RG72; "Glide Bombing Attachment Mark Two," n.d., File 248.232-3, HRA; and AAF School of Applied Tactics to Materiel Command, October 16, 1943, Materiel Division to BuOrd, January 7, 1944, File 452.26-G, Box 764, Central Decimal Files, Oct. 1942–44, RG18.

57. The GBA consisted of a barometer measuring changes in altitude while an analog computer adjusted the bombsight's disc speed to compensate for the changes. See "Final Report on Test of Glide Bombing Attachment," October 16, 1943, Arnold to Materiel Command, January 11 and March 13, 1944, and Memo of Conference with Navy, January 29, 1944, File 471.63, Folder—Attachment Glide Angle, Box 3381, RD-3047, RG342; and BuAer to CNO, April 24, 1944, File F41-8, Vol. 2, Box 712, BuAer Confidential Correspondence, 1922–44, RG72.

58. "Report of Conference of C. L. Norden Company, Navy and Materiel Division Personnel on M-Series Bombsights," August 6, 1941, Folder—Norden, File 471.63, Box 1893, RD-2451, RG342; BuOrd to BuAer, September 13, 1942, File F41-8, Vol. 4, Box 2279, RG72; and File 471.63, Folder—Bombsight Anti-Glare Equipment for "M" Series, Box 2894, RD-2885, RG342.

59. "Report of Conference of C. L. Norden Company," RG342; Materiel Division, "Report on Conference with Navy on Bombsight Problem," RG342; Production Section to Colonel Shepard, July 20, 1945, File 471.63, Folder Bombsights—"M" Series—Norden, Box 3381, RD-3047, RG342; and AAF Proving Ground Command, "Final Report on Test of Reflex Sight for M-Series Bomb Sight," July 2, 1942, File 471.6-J, Box 299, Central Decimal Files, 1939–42, Series II, RG18.

60. Commanding General of Air Corps to Chief of Air Staff, January 21, 1936, File 201-13, HRA; and Chief of Materiel Division to Acting Chief of Air Corps, January 18, 1936, and Chief of Materiel Division to Acting Chief of Air Corps, April 8, 1937, File 202.2-35, HRA.

61. FBI memo, May 6, 1940, File 65-10347-10X, FBI Records.

62. See Sackett to Hoover, December 5, 1940, February 19 and 12, 1941, Files 65-10347-49, 65-10347-61, and 65-10347-57, FBI Records.

63. Chief of Materiel Division to Chief of Air Corps, January 18, 1936, File 202.2-35, HRA.

64. Sperry sold an early model of its bombsight to the Japanese in the mid-1930s. See Air Staff Post-Hostilities Intelligence Requirements in the Far East, "Japanese Bombsights and Bombing Equipment," December 1945, File 720.6191-162, HRA.

65. Memo of meeting, August 10, 1937, File 202.2-35, HRA; and Schoeffel to BuOrd, July 31, 1937, File F31-1 (10), Vol. 1, Box 636, BuAer Confidential Correspondence, 1922–44, RG72.

66. Arnold to Chief of Materiel Division, January 28, 1936, File 202.2-35, HRA.

67. Brown, "Navy's Mark 15 (Norden) Bombsight," 256.

68. Ibid., 257–60.

69. Memorandum, August 28, 1940, File F41-8, Folder 24, Box 1632, BuOrd General Correspondence, Confidential, 1939–42, RG74; BuOrd to Chief of Air Corps, July 15, 1941, File 471.6-E, Box 299, Central Decimal Files, 1939–42, Series II, RG18; and Brown, "Navy's Mark 15 (Norden) Bombsight," 265–67.

70. Bowles, *History of Lukas-Harold*; "Production of Sights at Elmira Ends Oct. 1," *Norden Insight* 2 (July 1944): 3; Norden to BuOrd, October 3, 1939, File F41-8, Folder NOs58954, Box 170, BuOrd General Correspondence Confidential, 1926–39, RG74; and Brown, "Navy's Mark 15 (Norden) Bombsight," 320.

Chapter 8. Procurement for War

1. Kenney to Weaver, January 7, 1942, Folder—Norden, File 471.63, Box 1893, RD-2451, RG342; and AAF to BuOrd, February 16, 1942, File 471.6-H, Box 299, Central Decimal Files, 1939–42, Series II, RG18.

2. Materiel Command memo, October 9 and 27, 1942, Chief of Resources Control Section to Chief of Production Engineering, May 19, 1944, and Acting Chief of Resources to Midcentral District Depot, August 1, 1944, File 471.63, Folder—Bombsights—Type D-8, Box 3902, RD-3851, RG342; Technical Control Branch to Central District Supervisor, January 13, 1942, Chief Materiel Division memo, January 31, 1942, and Experimental Engineering memo, March 4, 1942, File 471.63, Folder—Bomb Sights, Box 2893, RD-2885, RG342; and Inspector of Ordnance in Charge to BuOrd, March 15, 1943, File F41-8, Vol. 8, Box 712, BuAer Confidential Correspondence, 1922–44, RG72. See Air Service Command, "Technical Order—Instructions for D-8 Bombsight," July 25, 1942, File 218.16-1, HRA, for a detailed description of and instructions in the use of the D-8. After the war Georges Estoppey unsuccessfully sued the United States for recovery of royalties on the D-8. See 83 Federal Supplement 840, Case No. 46698, and 113 Court of Claims 294.

3. Webster and Frankland, *Annexes and Appendices*, 37–38; Hill to Office of Chief of Air Corps, October 13, 1941, File 471.63, Folder—Bombsight—Mark XIV, Box 2451, RD-2451, RG342; *New York Times*, July 20, 1944, 5:3; "Notes on British Bombsights and Bombing Tactics," July 10, 1941, File 248.222-51, HRA; "British Bombsights," 1941, File 248.222-50, HRA; "Bombsight T-1," August 1943, File 234.779–104, HRA; Cross, *Bombers*, 17, 53, 59, 74, and 121; "T-1 Production," April 16, 1945, File 168.7252-32, HRA; Smye to Wright, October 8, 1942, File F41–8, Vol. 4, Box 2279, RG72; and British Air Commission to Commanding General Army Air Corps, File 471.63, Folder—Bombsight—T-1, Box 3903, RD-3851, RG342. A continuously set vector sight, the Mark XIV had cross wires that showed the bombardier where the bombs would fall at any particular instant.

4. Memo, January 8, 1942, and Knox to Stimson, January 18, 1942, File 202.2-35, HRA; BuOrd to Chief of Air Corps, February 24, 1942, File 471.6-H, Box 299, Central Decimal Files, 1939–42, Series II, RG18; and Technical Control Branch memo, February 28, 1942, Record of Meeting on Norden Bombsight, February 27, 1942, and Arnold to Office of Chief

of Air Corps, February 23, 1942, File 471.63, Folder—Bomb Sights, Box 2893, RD-2885, RG342.

5. Materiel Center to Cardanic Corporation, April 29, 1942, File 471.63, Folder—Cardanic Company, Box 2323, RD-2644, RG342; and Chief of Production Engineering to Burroughs Adding Machine Company, January 31, 1942, Burroughs to Chief of Production Engineering, February 21, 1942, Burroughs to Air Materiel Division, March 11, 1942, Knudsen to Air Materiel Center, July 18, 1942, and memo to Production Division, July 24, 1942, File 471.63, Folder—Norden M-Series Bombsights, Box 2323, RD-2644, RG342.

6. War Production Board memo, April 22, 1943, File 471.63, Folder—Cardanic Company, Box 2323, RD-2644, RG342; and BuOrd to Commanding General AAF, April 22, 1943, File 452.26-D, Box 27, Office of Assistant Chief of Air Staff (Materiel and Services, Research and Development Branch), RG18.

7. Production Division memo, October 27, 1942, and Production Division to Arnold, May 29, 1943, File 471.63, Folder—Cardanic Company, Box 2323, RD-2644, RG342; and Materiel Division to Materiel Command, May 31, 1943, File 471.63, Folder—Attachment Glide Angle, Box 3381, RD-3047, RG342.

8. The four companies were Electric Autolite of Toledo, Ohio, Moto-Meter Gauge and Equipment of LaCrosse, Wis., Mills Novelty Company of Chicago, and the Conn Instrument Company of Elkhart, Ind.

9. Sennett to Production Engineering, January 27, 1942, Folder—Norden, File 471.63, Box 1893, RD-2451, RG342.

10. "BuOrd Circular Letter No. V 49-42," December 29, 1942, File F41-8, Vol. 4, Box 2279, BuAer General Correspondence, 1925–42, RG72; Experimental Engineering Section memo, September 15, 1941, File 202.2-35, HRA; and teletype from Armament Section to Production Engineering Section, July 20, 1942, File 452.19, Folder—C-1 Automatic Pilot Folder, Box 2244, RD-2626, RG342.

11. See appendix B for a list of firms involved in wartime Norden bombsight production.

12. Brown, "Navy's Mark 15 (Norden) Bombsight," appendix C9; and Production Division memo, November 11, 1942, File 471.63, Folder—Norden Bomb Sight, Box 3379, RD-3054, RG342.

13. King to Marshall, November 29, 1942, Stimson to Knox, n.d. (November 30, 1942), and Marshall to King, December 7, 1942, File 202.2-35, HRA.

14. Arnold to McCain, September 28, 1943, File 452.26-F, Box 764, Central Decimal Files, Oct. 1942–44, RG18; and Giles to Assistant Chief of Air Staff (Materiel, Maintenance, and Distribution), August 26, 1943, Echols to Giles, August 26, 1943, and McCain to Arnold, October 2, 1943, File 202.2-35, HRA.

15. BuOrd to Army and Navy Munitions Board, March 20, 1943, File F41-8, Vol. 8, Box 712, RG72, BuAer.

16. According to his son, Carl Norden selected the town personally because the workers there had no experience in ball bearings, which would allow the elder Norden to train them properly without having to counter the knowledge of the wrong way to build bearings. Carl F. Norden, interview with author, December 9, 1989. The Barden Company still produces precision ball bearings in Danbury, Connecticut.

17. New Departure Division of General Motors to Air Service Command, June 15, 1942, Production Engineering Section to Commanding General AAF Materiel Command, July 1, 1942, and Air Materiel Center memos, August 26 and 29, 1942, Folder—Norden, File 471.63, Box 1893, RD-2451, RG342; Report of Conference, March 10, 1943, Folder—Norden M-Series Bombsights, File 471.63, Box 2323, RD-2644, RG342; and BuAer to BuOrd, April 29, 1943, File F41-8, Vol. 8, Box 712, RG72, BuAer. The services set up a joint Army-

Navy Bombsight Bearings Committee in April 1943 to coordinate solutions to the ball-bearings problem.

18. "Schedule of Bombsight Procurement," January 30, 1943, Commanding General GHQAF to Chief of Air Corps, January 21, 1936, Materiel Division to Chief of Air Corps, April 8, 1937, File 202.2-35, HRA; Robins to Chief of Air Corps, April 8, 1937, in "Relationship of the Development of the AAF Bombing Doctrine to the Development of the Modern Bombsight," n.d., File K110.7017-2, HRA; and Westover to Andrews, January 24, 1936, File 202.2-14, HRA.

19. Barth to Dargue, April 27, 1937, File 168.7119-49, HRA.

20. Chief of Production Engineering Section, Materiel Command, memo, May 7, 1941, File 202.2-35, HRA.

21. The Army Air Corps purchased twenty Sperry N-1s in 1938 for $320,000. Coupled with the A-2 automatic pilot, the N-1 became the O-1 in 1939. To keep the Sperry program alive, the Air Corps purchased 600 O-1s, but they were cumbersome and difficult to operate, and in 1941 the Air Corps turned them over to the British. See Toole, "Development of Bombing Equipment"; and Chief of Materiel Division to Chief of Air Corps, April 8, 1937, in "Relationship of the Development of the AAF Bombing Doctrine to the Development of the Modern Bombsight," HRA.

22. Eastern Procurement District to ACAS/Materiel Maintenance and Distribution, February 16, 1944, and IBM to Materiel Division, February 28, 1944, File 452.26, Box 1277, RG18.

23. "Service Test Requirements and Manual on Automatic Gyro Leveling System for M-Series Bombsights," April 2, 1943, File 471.63, Folder—Norden M-Series Bombsights, Box 2323, RD-2644.

24. Report of Board, September 15, 1943, File 471.63, Folder—Norden M-Series Bombsights, Box 2323, RD-2644; Toole, "Development of Bombing Equipment," 73; and Production Division to Arnold, December 9, 1943, File 471.63, Folder—Norden M-Series Bombsights, Box 2323, RD-2644.

25. Loyd Searle ("The Bombsight War: Norden vs. Sperry") has suggested the S-1 was superior to the Norden and that the decision to cancel the S-1 was the result of a conspiracy. The entire Army Air Forces, not just a Board of Officers, assembled a truly impressive amount of data proving the opposite. The S-1 used a circle aiming point in its optics rather than the cross hairs of the Norden, resulting in a 30 to 40 percent decrease in efficiency and the obscuring of targets at high altitude. Combat crews recorded hundreds of malfunctions with the S-1/A-5 due to voltage problems resulting from crews turning on their radios or turrets. Second Air Force dropped 170,096 practice bombs with the Norden bombsight, achieving an average circular error of 278 feet, compared to 328 feet for the S-1 based on 71,143 bombs. See memo for Perrin, October 25, 1943, and Commanding General Second Air Force to Commanding General Army Air Forces, August 21, 1943, File 452.26, Box 763, Central Decimal Files, Oct. 1942–44, RG18. Eighth Air Force reported that it took 28 man-hours to repair a Norden bombsight and 12 hours for a C-1 autopilot, compared to 34 hours for an S-1 and 14 hours for an A-5 autopilot. See Eighth Air Force Service Command memo, n.d. (1944?), File 519.8724-1, HRA. Brig. Gen. E. S. Perrin, Deputy Chief of Staff, ordered schools to stop training bombardiers in the S-1 in September 1943 because of a general "lack of confidence in the operational value of the Sperry sight." See AAF Historical Study No. 5, "Individual Training of Bombardiers," May 1944, File 101-5, HRA.

26. Chief of Procurement Division memo, March 17, 1945, File 202.2-35, HRA; and Engineering Division memo, December 29, 1943, Folder—Norden M-Series Bombsights, File 471.63, Box 2323, RD-2644, RG243.

27. Materiel Division memo, August 25, 1944, File 202.2-35, HRA.

28. Developmental Engineering Branch to Chidlaw, April 14, 1944, File 452.26-H, Box 764, Central Decimal Files, Oct. 1942–44, RG18; and Eighth Air Force Service Command memo, n.d. (April 1944?), File 519.8724-1, HRA. Eighth Air Force's goal was to have sixty-four Norden or Sperry S-1 bombsights per heavy bombardment group, depending on whether the group used B-24s or B-17s. By March 1944 it was 1,351 bombsights above this goal.

29. Brown, "Navy's Mark 15 (Norden) Bombsight," 205–6; BuAer to Secretary of the Navy, December 2, 1941, File F41-8, Folder—Mark 15, Box 1280, BuOrd General Correspondence, Confidential, 1939–42, RG74; Chief Materiel Division to Wright Field, January 15, 1942, File 471.63, Folder—Norden M-Series, Box 1893, RD-2451, RG342; and Secretary of Navy to Director of Materials Division, March 2, 1942, File 202.2-35, HRA.

The U.S. Navy trained 140 Soviet airmen in the operation of the Norden bombsight at the Elizabeth City, N.C., naval air station beginning in April 1944. In November 1944 an American mission traveled to the Soviet Union to teach a number of engineering officers to maintain the Norden bombsight. The training was part of a $100-million lend-lease program, code-named "Zebra" under Lt. Cdr. Stanley Chernack, to send 188 patrol bombers to the Soviet Union, including 100 Nordens. The Army Air Forces also decided in May 1944 to begin shipping Norden-equipped B-25s to the Soviet Union, although the actual transfer did not begin until late 1944. See Williams to Engineering Division, November 4, 1944, File 471.63, Folder—Bomb Sights and Racks–Russia, Box 2894, RD-2885, RG342; and *New York Times*, September 27, 1946, 1:2–3.

30. Deputy Chief of Staff to Production Division, June 26, 1944, File 202.2-35, HRA; Materiel Division to Materiel Command, June 19, 1944, File 452.26-H, Box 764, Central Decimal Files, Oct. 1942–44, RG18; and Chief of Materiel Division to Commanding General of Materiel Command, August 7, 1943, File 471.63, Folder—Norden M-Series Bombsights, Box 2323, RD-2644, RG342.

31. The "N" Division Plant of Remington Rand was the most controversial of all plants producing Norden bombsights during the war. Production lagged and the quality was so poor that Carl L. Norden, Inc., had to remanufacture most Remington Rand sights. BuOrd investigated and blamed "poor management." In November 1943 President Roosevelt issued an executive order seizing the plant, which BuOrd turned over to Norden.

A CIO union, the United Electrical Workers, complained to the Office of War Mobilization that Norden had caused the problem at Elmira, evidently in retaliation for union attempts to make Norden a union shop. BuOrd production specialist Cdr. John D. Corrigan investigated and exonerated Norden. Barth then hired Corrigan's former firm, for which Corrigan secretly still worked, as engineering advisors for $104,000. On the basis of Senate War Investigating Committee (the Truman Committee) hearings, a federal grand jury in Manhattan in December 1944 charged Barth, Norden vice-president Ward B. Marvelle, and two engineers, Corrigan and Robert H. Wells, of the firm of Corrigan, Osbourne and Wells, with blocking production at Remington Rand. Corrigan and Wells went to trial twice, the first resulting in a hung jury, the second in a guilty verdict. U.S. Assistant Attorney General G. Osmond Hyde dropped the case against Barth because of a lack of evidence and against Marvelle because of his death. In May 1948 the Second Circuit Court of Appeals reversed the decision against Corrigan and Wells because the government had used "incompetent, prejudicial evidence." The government chose not to prosecute the case further. See "The True Facts about the Charges against Carl L. Norden, Inc.," 1944, Carl L. Norden, Inc.; "A Bomb on Norden," *Time*, January 1, 1945, 55; *New York Times*, June 12, 1943, 7:4, November 30, 1943, 24:3, July 28, 1944, 10:3, December 20, 1944, 1:1, June 1, 1945, 10:4, November 27, 1945, 25:6, June 10, 1947, 9:5, and September 26, 1947, 9:5; Jacobs, *A Scientist and His*

Experiences, 84–85; Federal Reporter 2nd Series 168, p. 641, Docket 20876; O'Donnell to FBI Special Agent, May 29, 1944, Gordon to FBI Special Agent, June 19, 1947, and office memo, December 2, 1947, File 46-7753-65, FBI Records.

32. Conference memo, October 7, 1944, and Production Engineering Section to BuOrd, November 4, 1943, File 202.2-35, HRA.

33. Commander Air Force Pacific Fleet to BuOrd, July 13, 1944, File F41-8, Vol. 3, Box 712, BuAer Confidential Correspondence, 1922–44, RG72; CNO to Commander-in-Chief Pacific Fleet, March 29, 1945, File F41-8, Vol. 4, Box 174, BuAer Confidential Correspondence, RG72; and BuOrd to BuAer, March 16, 1945, File F41-8, Vol. 1, Box 1737, BuAer General Correspondence, 1942–45, RG72.

34. Brown, "Navy's Mark 15 (Norden) Bombsight," 317–19.

35. Engineering Section to Materiel Division, April 3, 1944, File 202.2-35, HRA; U.S. Bureau of Ordnance, *Navy Bureau of Ordnance,* 354–55; and Production Division memo, November 11, 1942, File 471.63, Folder—Norden Bomb Sight, Box 3379, RD-3054, RG342.

Chapter 9. The Young Men behind Plexiglas

1. LeMay and Kantor, *Mission with LeMay,* 136–37; "Interview of Bombardier Instructors," 1943, File 221.051-1, HRA; and Maurer, *Aviation in the United States Army,* 229.

2. 2nd Bombardment Group, "Training Program for the Period September 14, 1931 to March 26, 1932," File 248.222-31, HRA; TR440-40, March 11, 1929, and November 26, 1935, File 248.222-31, HRA; and 7th Bombardment Group, "Training Reports," March 1937, File 248.222-31, HRA.

3. Edward H. Kemp and A. Pemberton Johnson, eds., "Psychological Research on Bombardier Training," 1947, File 141.28-9, HRA.

4. AAF Historical Study No. 5, "Individual Training of Bombardiers."

5. Kemp and Johnson, eds., "Psychological Research on Bombardier Training."

6. AAF Historical Study No. 5, "Individual Training of Bombardiers." Bombardier-navigator training was performed at Santa Ana, California.

7. AAF Training Command, "Report of Bombardier Conference," January 5–7, 1944, File 220.7193-6, Vol. 4, HRA; AAF Historical Study No. 5, "Individual Training of Bombardiers"; and Kemp and Johnson, eds., "Psychological Research on Bombardier Training."

8. In April 1943 the Army Air Forces cut flight training to six weeks for good candidates and eliminated it altogether if the candidate was a washout from any other advanced school. Flying training included instruction in code, physics, math, map reading, aircraft identification, chemical warfare defense, physical education, and formation drill. See AAF Historical Study No. 5, "Individual Training of Bombardiers."

9. TM 1-250 called for 300 bomb releases under a variety of conditions, from altitudes of 1,000 to 20,000 feet. In wartime the need to get as many bombardiers trained as fast as possible cut training to less than 160 bomb releases, none from altitudes above 11,000 feet. In early 1943 a bomb shortage reduced releases to 125. See TM 1-250, October 1944, Folder—Bombing Accuracy Analytical Studies I, Box 76, Subject File, Spaatz Papers.

10. Kemp and Johnson, eds., "Psychological Research on Bombardier Training."

11. AAF Historical Study No. 5, "Individual Training of Bombardiers"; Steinbeck, *Bombs Away,* 47–66; "Norden Bombsight," *Science News Letter* 46 (December 9, 1944): 382; Midland AAF Field Bombardier School to Commanding General AAF, June 15, 1944, File 220.7193-6, Vol. 4, HRA; and Kemp and Johnson, eds., "Psychological Research on Bombardier Training."

12. Ayling, *Bombardment Aviation,* 41; and Thomas H. Greer, "Individual Training of Fly-

ing Personnel," in Craven and Cate, eds., *The Army Air Forces in World War II*, vol. 6, *Men and Planes* (Chicago: University of Chicago Press, 1955), 559–60.

13. Commanding Officer Childress Army Air Field to Commanding Officer, 5th Statistical Control Unit, Flight Training Command, February 19, 1944, File 168.271-49, HRA; Eagle Pass Army Air Field to CG AAF Director of Personnel, April 22, 1943, File 168.271-50, HRA; and AAF Historical Study No. 5, "Individual Training of Bombardiers."

14. Brendan Gill, "Young Man behind Plexiglass," *New Yorker*, August 12, 1944, 29. During the war, bombardiers experienced 17.6 percent of bomber crew casualties, the tail gunner 12.5 percent, the navigator 12.2 percent, the waist gunners 10.45 percent, the pilot 7.4 percent, and the copilot 6.6 percent. See Martin J. Miller, "The Armored Airmen: World War II, U.S. Army Air Force Body Armor Program," *Aerospace Historian* 32 (Spring/March 1985): 27–32.

15. Gill, "Young Man behind Plexiglass," 26–37.

16. John W. Corrington, *The Bombardier* (New York: Putnam's, 1970), 66–68.

17. "Policy Governing M-Series and S-Series Bombsights and Automatic Flight Control Equipment," July 1, 1942, File 471.63, Folder—Bombsight Policy Letter, Box 2324, RD-2644, RG342.

18. "Bombardier Oath," *Norden Insight* 1 (September 1942): 7. Col. John P. Kenny, commandant of the AAF Bombardier School at Midland, Texas, told *Newsweek* in April 1943 that the bombardier oath was superfluous because the normal military oath required soldiers to destroy equipment about to fall into enemy hands. Kenny claimed the oath had been the invention of a public relations officer at Midland. See "End of a Secret," *Newsweek*, April 26, 1943, 29–30.

19. Arnold circular letter, August 29, 1942, Folder—Norden, File 471.63, Box 1893, RD-2451, RG342; and Elmer Bendiner, *The Fall of Fortresses: A Personal Account of the Most Daring—and Deadly—Air Battles of World War II* (New York: Putnam's, 1980), 66.

20. Chief of Air Staff to All Units, May 1, 1943, File 519.8724-1, HRA; BuOrd Circular Letter FV3-44, December 6, 1944, File F41-8, Vol. 1, Box 1737, RG72; General Inspector of Naval Aircraft, Wright Field, to BuOrd, December 13, 1940, File F41-8, Vol. 5, Box 711, RG72; and "Policy Governing M-Series and S-Series Bombsights," RG342.

21. Steinbeck, *Bombs Away*, 47–66; and Lent, *Bombardier*, 32.

22. Stanley Johnstone, "Bombers and Bomb Sights," *Science Digest* 10 (January 1945): 52–55, a reprint from the *Chicago Sunday Tribune* of July 27, 1941; and "Pickle Barrelers," 50–51.

23. Perhaps because of poor communication or in response to several security lapses in the 1930s, the Army Air Forces did not downgrade its bombsights and the associated AFCE until June 1943. See "Policy Governing M-Series, S-Series and T-Series Bombsights and Automatic Flight Control Equipment," June 15, 1943, File 452.26-H, Box 764, Central Decimal Files, Oct. 1942–44, RG18.

24. BuOrd Circular Letter No. V 29-42, October 24, 1942, in BuOrd to Vice CNO, October 20, 1942, File F41-8, Vol. 4, Box 2279, RG72; and Cable, Tanger to Director of War Organization and Movement, March 5, 1943, File 452.26, Box 763, Central Decimal Files, Oct. 1942–44, RG18. When Lt. Col. James H. Doolittle led his B-25 formation to Tokyo on April 18, 1942, the Norden bombsights had been removed and replaced with sights costing "only a few cents" designed by Capt. Charles R. Greening. From a bombing altitude of 1,500 feet and considering the objectives of Doolittle's Raid, great precision was not needed. See "Doolittle Raiders Reunion," 1955, File 168.309-6, HRA.

25. "End of a Secret," 29–30; "Bombsight No Longer Mystery," *Stars and Stripes*, April 16, 1943; "What Bombardier Needs," *Science News Letter* 43 (April 24, 1943): 260; Kurt Rand,

"The Norden Bombsight," *Flying* 33 (July 1943): 37–38, 148; "The Bombsight," *Flying* 33 (October 1943): 103–7, 342–44; and Ayling, *Bombardment Aviation*, 37, 79.

26. BuOrd Circular Letter No. FV1-47, May 5, 1947, File 471.63, Folder—Bombsight—Navy, Box 3903, RD-3851, RG342.

27. *Bombardiers' Information File*, 1945.

28. From November 1940 to October 1943 the Air Corps/Army Air Forces trained 17,925 precision bombardiers, 1,133 precision bombardiers–celestial navigators, 1,543 bombardier-navigators, 666 D-8 bombardier-gunners, and 225 D-8 bombardier-navigators. See AAF Historical Study No. 5, "Individual Training of Bombardiers."

29. AAF Historical Study No. 5, "Individual Training of Bombardiers"; Training Division to Air Service Command, December 19, 1941, and February 16, 1942, File 471.6-H, Box 299, Central Decimal Files, 1939–42, Series II, RG18; and Dorsey to Commanding General Army Air Forces, November 11, 1943, File 452.26-G, Box 764, Central Decimal Files, Oct. 1942–44, RG18. The Army Air Forces Training Command reported 243 Norden M-1 through M-5 models, 374 M-6 models, and 1,336 M-7 and M-9 models (1,002 in aircraft, 514 in ground trainers, and 437 for other uses), and 917 Sperry S-1 bombsights (447 in aircraft, 224 in ground trainers, and 246 for other uses) in its October 1943 inventory.

30. File 471.63, Folder—Bombing Teacher, Box 872, RD-3312, RG342; "How the Link Bombing Trainer Works," *Norden Insight* 2 (May 1944): 5; Volta Torrey, "How the Norden Bombsight Does Its Job," *Popular Science* 146 (June 1945): 70–73, 220, 224, 228, 232; and *New York Times*, December 21, 1944, 11:6.

31. Thomas H. Greer, "Combat Crew and Unit Training," in Craven and Cate, eds., *Men and Planes*, 605; AAF Board, "Study of Bombing Accuracy," Report No. 45, November 16, 1942, and May 15, 1943, HRA; and "AAF Bombing Accuracy," Report No. 1, April 11, 1945, File 134.71-83, HRA.

32. AAF Historical Study No. 8, "Bombsight Maintenance Training in the AAF," June 1944, File 101-8, HRA.

33. "Aeronautical Instrument and Gyropilot School Syllabus of Instruction," July 1–August 31, 1944, File 234.779, Vol. 2, HRA; "A-3 Automatic Pilot Syllabi," January 25, 1945, File 234.779-100, Vol. 12, HRA; and "History of Training Detachment Sperry Gyroscope," May 15–December 31, 1942, File 234.779, HRA.

34. The Army Air Forces closed the University of Minnesota program in March 1943 and transferred the C-1 school to Lowry Field. The instructors went to England to help Eighth Air Force with its C-1 problems. See "History of AAF TD Minneapolis-Honeywell Regulator Company," July 27, 1942–July 10, 1943, File 234.539, HRA.

35. TM 1-250, Spaatz Papers.

36. LeMay and Kantor, *Mission with LeMay*, 258–59.

Chapter 10. Daylight Precision Strategic Bombing against Germany

1. Webster and Frankland, *Annexes and Appendices*, 49–50, 112–19, 124–27.

2. "Report by Mr. Butt to Bomber Command on his Examination of Night Photographs, 18 August 1941," in Webster and Frankland, *Annexes and Appendices*, 205–13; and Webster and Frankland, *Preparation*, 169. Bomber Command achieved its best night accuracy from May to August 1944, when circular error averaged 4,380 feet. Late in the war Bomber Command launched sixteen daylight attacks, achieving a circular error of 2,484 feet. See USSBS, Report No. 64, *Description of RAF Bombing* (Washington, D.C.: Government Printing Office, 1947), Exhibit G.

3. Webster and Frankland, *Preparation*, 99, 182, 322–24, and Webster and Frankland, *Strategic Air Offensive*, vol. 3, *Victory*, 44; Hastings, *Bomber Command*, 132; Beck, *Under the Bombs*, 2; and Arthur T. Harris, *Bomber Offensive* (New York: Macmillan, 1947), 147.

4. An analysis of 3,399 reported problems leading to gross bombing errors from May 1, 1944, to March 31, 1945, identified smoke as the leading cause (498), followed by improper bombardier procedures (327), clouds (317), enemy defenses (269), misidentification of the target (254), and bombsight malfunctions (65). See "Visual Bombing Difficulties," June 27, 1945, Folder—Bombing Accuracy Analytical Studies II, Box 77, Subject File, Spaatz Papers.

5. Eaker to Spaatz, August 27, 1942, Folder—Bombing Accuracy, Box 76, Subject File, Spaatz Papers.

6. Guido R. Perera, "Memoirs, Washington and War Years, 1936–1960," 1973, File 168.7042, HRA; Zilbert, *Albert Speer*, 36; and Arthur B. Ferguson, "The Daylight Bombing Experiment," in Craven and Cate, eds., *Army Air Forces in World War II*, vol. 3, *Europe: ARGUMENT to V-E Day, January 1944 to May 1945* (Chicago: University of Chicago Press, 1951), 733.

7. "History of the Organization and Operations of the Committee of Operations Analysts," 1942–44, File 118.01, HRA; W. W. Rostow, *Pre-Invasion Bombing Strategy: General Eisenhower's Decision of March 25, 1944* (Austin: University of Texas Press, 1981), 17; and W. W. Rostow, "The London Operation: Recollections of an Economist," unpublished manuscript.

8. VIII Bomber Command, "Preliminary Report on Bombing Accuracy," January 4, 1943, Folder—Bombing Accuracy Analytical Study I, Box 76, Subject File, Spaatz Papers; and Arthur B. Ferguson, "The War against the Sub Pens," in Craven and Cate, eds., *Army Air Forces in World War II*, vol. 2, *Europe: TORCH to POINTBLANK, August 1942 to December 1943* (Chicago: University of Chicago Press, 1949), 270.

9. "Final Report of Bombing Board," January 2, 1943, File 145.96-142, HRA; and McArthur, *Operations Analysis*, 28.

10. Superior students averaged a circular error of 200 feet in stateside training during the war. See Deming AAF Field Bombardier School to Commanding General AAF Training Command, June 9, 1944, File 220.7193-6, Vol. 4, HRA.

11. Eighth Air Force Operational Analysis Section, "Report for Colonel W. B. Leach on the History and Development of the Bombs and Fuzes Subsection," April 10, 1945, File 520.3033, HRA; and McArthur, *Operations Analysis*, 40, 65–67.

12. The 500-pound bomb had a lethal fragmentation radius of 60 to 90 feet. This figure did not enter into Eighth Air Force calculations because humans were not the targets of American bombs. See 2nd and 3rd Operations Analysis Sections, Far Eastern Air Forces, "Number of Aircraft Necessary for Proposed Military Operation," August 15, 1944, File 131.504C, Vol. 3, HRA.

13. Hughes Memoirs, 1955–57, File 520.056-234, HRA.

14. LeMay and Kantor, *Mission with LeMay*, 231, 237–38; Parton, "*Air Force Spoken Here*," 235–36; and Headquarters AAF Operations Analysis, "The Causes of Bombing Errors as Based on Eighth Air Force Combat Operations," July 15, 1947, File 143.504-3, HRA. The C-1 AFCE allowed a bombardier to take two or three evasive maneuvers during the bomb run, except the last 10 or 15 seconds, but the need to fly in formation prevented such actions.

15. Before the war the Air Corps developed yellow warning and blue drop lights for use by the leader, but they were not used in combat during the war. See 7th Bombardment Group memo, October 2, 1936, File 471.62, Folder—Bombing Methods and Bomb Sight Development, Box 2891, RD-2884, RG342. In 1943 the Army Air Forces also developed a technique for dropping a group's bombs on signal from the ground. Eureka ground beacons (AN/PPN-1) signaled the proper release point through Rebecca radio receivers (AN/APN-2) on board

the bombers. In testing, circular errors as small as 45 feet became common, though associated problems prevented field deployment. See AAF Board Project No. (T-5) 35 (H2567), "Rebecca-Eureka Bombing," August 9, 1943, File 245.621, HRA. An alternate plan to use the radio equipment of the AZON guided bomb to achieve an automatic release of a formation's bombs was subject to enemy jamming and was therefore dropped. See AAF Board Project No. (M-2) 68, "Test of Simultaneous Radio Bomb Release Equipment Unit," May 13, 1944, File 245.621, HRA; Eighth Air Force Commanding General to Eighth Air Force Service Command Commanding General, "Radio Bomb Release—Marker Receiver Type," April 14, 1945, File 452.26, Folder—Bombsights, Box 232, RD-3690, RG342; and "Report on Azon Radio Bomb Release," August 25, 1944, File 452.26, Bulky Files, Oct. 1942–1944, Box 724, RG18. A similar plan to use a ground-based inverted Norden bombsight and telescope to spot the correct release point in the sky was also stillborn. See First Bombardment Division to Commanding General Eighth Air Force, August 7, 1944, File 452.26, Folder—Bombsights, Box 232, RD-3690, RG342.

16. "Report on Procedures," May 17, 1943, and December 31, 1943, File WG-1-HI, HRA.

17. Eighth Air Force Operational Research Section, "Effect of Ground Speed and Size of Formations on Range Errors in B-17 and B-24 Bombing Formations," July 3, 1944, Folder—Bombing Accuracy Analytical Studies I, Box 76, Subject File, Spaatz Papers; and USSBS, *Summary Report (European War)*, 4. On B-17s the salvo switch was mounted on the bombardier's control panel, allowing easy access. On some B-24s the salvo switch was on a separate panel behind the bombardier. When even a second's delay could cause a bombing error of several hundred feet, such a problem increased inaccuracy. This factor alone could explain why B-17s were more accurate than B-24s during the war. In 1944 the average percent within 1,000 feet for B-17 groups was 36.3, but only 27.5 for B-24 groups. See "AAF Bombing Accuracy," July 1944–45, Report No. 2, File 134.71-83, HRA. The USSBS concluded that the B-17 was a more efficient combat aircraft because it was more accurate, more durable, flew higher, and had more defensive machine guns. See USSBS, Report No. 63, *Bombing Accuracy, USAAF Heavy and Medium Bombers in the ETO* (Washington, D.C.: Government Printing Office, 1947), 1, 10–11.

18. "Report on Survey of Aircrew Personnel in the Eighth, Ninth, Twelfth, and Fifteenth Air Forces," April 1944, File 141.28B, HRA; LeMay and Kantor, *Mission with LeMay*, 256; VIII Bomber Command Operational Research Section, "Concerning a New Method for Analyzing Bombing Accuracy and Probabilities under Combat Conditions," January 30, 1943, and "Analysis of VIII Bomber Command Operations from the Point of View of Bombing Accuracy," October 31, 1943, File 131.504C, Vol. 1, HRA; and Fifteenth Air Force, "Bombing Accuracy Studies," 1944–1945, File 670.56-2, HRA.

19. Eighth Air Force Commanding General to Eighth Air Force Service Command Commanding General, March 31, 1944, and July 17, 1944, File 452.26, Folder—Bombsights, RD-3690, RG342.

20. Operation Research Section to Commanding General Eighth Air Force, June 13, 1944, Folder—Bombing Accuracy, Box 76, Subject File, Spaatz Papers; and USSBS, *Bombing Accuracy*, 8. The Eighth Air Force Operational Research Section reasoned the intervalometer scattered "bombs so widely that the number of bombs hitting the target is serious diminished." From 22,000 feet using a 50-foot intervalometer setting meant a "decrease in number of hits by ratio of 137 to 100, but a gain in efficiency from 75% with Salvo to 85 or 90% with intervalometer. *The loss is much greater than the gain.*" See Eighth Air Force Operational Research Section, "Memorandum on Salvo and Intervalometer Releases," September 16, 1944, File 520.547B, HRA. Fifteenth Air Force preferred the intervalometer release over the salvo release.

21. VIII Bomber Command Operational Research Section, "Analysis of VIII Bomber Command Operations from the Point of View of Bombing Accuracy," HRA; USSBS, *Bombing Accuracy*, 2; and McArthur, *Operations Analysis*, 31–33.

22. Operation Research Section to Eighth Air Force Commanding General, June 13, 1944, Folder—Bombing Accuracy, Box 76, Subject File, Spaatz Papers.

23. USSBS, *Bombing Accuracy*, Exhibit C; VIII Bomber Command Operational Research Section, "Effect of Spacing between Combat Wings on Bombing Accuracy," September 11, 1943, and "Memorandum on the Desirability of Using a Single MPI in Most Instances," September 4, 1943, Folder—Bombing Accuracy, Box 76, Subject File, Spaatz Papers; Eighth Air Force Operational Analysis Section, "Report on Bombing Accuracy, 1 September 1944 to 31 December 1944," April 20, 1945, Folder—Bombing Accuracy Analytical Studies II, Box 77, Subject File, Spaatz Papers; and VIII Bomber Command Operational Research Section, "Analysis of VIII Bomber Command Operations from the Point of View of Bombing Accuracy," HRA.

24. USSBS, Report No. 128, *Huels Synthetic Rubber Plant*; and Bendiner, *Fall of Fortresses*, 112.

25. Roger A. Freeman, *Mighty Eighth War Diary* (London: Jane's, 1981), 126. The Air Corps had based its doctrine of daylight precision strategic bombing on the TNT-filled high-explosive bomb. Maj. Gen. Fred Anderson, commanding officer of VIII Bomber Command, made the 100-pound M-47 napalm bomb a standard weapon in Eighth Air Force bomb loads in 1943 because of British successes and studies done by his Operational Research Section. See McArthur, *Operations Analysis*, 65.

26. Eighth Air Force Operational Research Section, "Memorandum on Salvo and Inter-valometer Releases," September 16, 1944, File 520.547B, HRA; USSBS, Report No. 53, *The German Anti-Friction Bearing's Industry* (Washington, D.C.: Government Printing Office, 1947), 35; and Coffey, *Decision over Schweinfurt*, 60, 325.

27. Doolittle to Ronald Schaffer, August 24, 1979, File 168.7126-20, HRA.

28. Eighth Air Force Operational Research Section, "Report of Bombing Accuracy for the Month of February," March 15, 1945, File 520.547A, HRA.

29. USAF Historical Division, *Strategic Bombers in a Tactical Role*, 49, 60–61, 77–79.

30. Ibid., 83–85; John J. Sullivan, "The Botched Air Support of Operation *Cobra*," *Parameters* 18 (March 1988): 97–110; Hallion, *Strike from the Sky*, 206–14; and Stephen D. Borows, "Cobra: The Normandy Breakout," *Armor* 93 (September–October 1984): 24–29.

31. USSBS Oil Division, "Weapons Effectiveness and Bombing Techniques," n.d., File 248.222-15, HRA.

32. USSBS, Report No. 115, *Ammoniakwerke Merseburg GmbH, Leuna, Germany* (Washington, D.C.: Government Printing Office, 1947).

33. Eighth Air Force Operational Analysis Section, "Report on Bombing Accuracy 1 September 1944–31 December 1944," April 20, 1945, File 131.504C, Vol. 1, HRA; "Report on Survey of Aircrew Personnel in the Eighth, Ninth, Twelfth, and Fifteenth Air Forces," HRA; and Ronald Schaffer, *Wings of Judgment: American Bombing in World War II* (New York: Oxford University Press, 1985), 63.

34. Fifteenth Air Force Operations Analysis Section, "PFF Bombing Accuracy September and October 1944," November 8, 1944, File 670.310-5, HRA.

35. Hugh Odishaw (Radiation Laboratory of MIT), "Radar Bombing in the Eighth Air Force," 1946, Box 80, Subject File, Spaatz Papers; "GEE-H Instructional Manual," January 1945, File 168.6005-73B, HRA; Webster and Frankland, *Annexes and Appendices*, 4–17; and Eighth Air Force Operational Research Section, "Memorandum on Operational Accuracy of GEE-H Bombing of 2nd Bombardment Division," April 17, 1944, Folder—Bombing Accuracy Analytical Studies I, Box 76, Subject File, Spaatz Papers. *Gee-H* provided two means for

bombing. The first was a timed run from a precomputed point called the "Warning Point Technique." The second was called the "Bombsight Technique," using checkpoints from the *Gee-H* navigator for synchronizing the Norden bombsight.

36. Odishaw, "Radar Bombing"; and "Introduction to Micro-H Bombing for Aircrews," August 29, 1944, File 168.6005-73C, HRA. At the end of the war the Army Air Forces deployed the SHORAN (short-range navigation) system, like *Gee-H*, but providing continuous information to the pilot direction indicator to allow the operator to concentrate on synchronizing rate. Shoran did not use the Norden bombsight, but a separate computer utilizing the radar's rate and altitude information to determine the bomb release point.

37. An executive order of June 29, 1941, established the Office of Scientific Research and Development to assure "adequate provision for research on scientific and medical problems relating to the national defense." Within the OSRD the NDRC recommended contracts with "universities, research institutions, and industrial laboratories for research and development on instrumentalities of warfare." Division 14 dealt with radar. See U.S. National Archives, *Federal Records of World War II* (Washington, D.C.: Government Printing Office, 1950), 207–9, 212–15. The Navy pursued a radar bombsight through Carl L. Norden, Inc. Bell Telephone Laboratories informed BuOrd of its progress on radar research in December 1941. BuOrd contacted Norden and brought the two companies together on May 11, 1942. BuOrd won commitments from Norden to design the stabilizer and bombing computer and from Bell Telephone Laboratories to design a three-centimeter radar system, capable of bombing from 250 feet up to 30,000 feet. See BuOrd to Naval Inspector of Ordnance (Norden), December 18, 1941, and Minutes of Conference, May 14, 1942, File F41-8, Vol. 6, Box 711, BuAer Confidential Correspondence, 1922–44, RG72.

38. Toole, "Development of Bombing Equipment," 108–10.

39. The England-based Eighth Air Force called such bombing "H₂X with visual assistance." The Italy-based Fifteenth Air Force called it "synchronous bombing" or "PFF-synchronous bombing." PFF stood for pathfinder force. See 1st Operations Analysis Section, "PFF-Synchronous Bombing—Fifteenth Air Force," September 20, 1944, and Fifteenth Air Force Operations Analysis Section, "Development of Radar Bombing—Fifteenth Air Force," January 18, 1945, File 131.504C, Vol. 4, HRA. For an explanation of how the Norden bombsight worked with radar, see AAF Board, "Tactical Evaluation of the AN/APQ-5B Bombing Computer used with AN/APS-15A Radar," May 14, 1945, File 245.64, HRA.

40. Odishaw, "Radar Bombing"; Eighth Air Force, "Report of Bombing Accuracy," September 1, 1944–December 31, 1944, File 520.56A, HRA; Eighth Air Force Operational Analysis Section, "Report on Bombing Accuracy 1 September 1944–31 December 1944," HRA; "Navigator's Training Manual, Operation of An/APS-15," July 1943, File 168.6005-73A, HRA; and Webster and Frankland, *Annexes and Appendices*, 11–15. In radar bombing training the Army Air Forces developed a unique use for the Norden bombsight. Wright Field modified an SCR-584 antiaircraft gun fire control radar to track the training aircraft. The radar determined the aircraft's position and transferred information on heading, altitude, and speed to a Norden bombsight mounted to project a light beam onto a map. A radio link determined the point of bomb release.

41. School of Applied Tactics, "Radar Bombing," 1942–45, File 248.231-140, and "Bombing Errors," n.d., File 248.222-47, HRA.

42. School of Applied Tactics, "Radar Bombing," HRA.

43. Army Air Forces Board, "Tactical Evaluation of the AN/APQ-7A (NOSMEAGLE)," Report No. 4148B413.44, December 7, 1945, File 245.64, HRA; Engineering Division memo, October 14, 1944, File 202.2-35, HRA; and Toole, "Development of Bombing Equipment," 123, HRA. Ironically Wright Field developed the NOSMEAGLE system not for improved accuracy, but because dramatically increased trail values resulting from the antici-

pated higher speeds of jet aircraft were beyond the capabilities of the Norden bombsight. Higher speeds meant bomb runs of shorter duration, limiting the usefulness of visual observation. See Armament Laboratory to Engineering Division, May 1, 1944, and June 21, 1944, File 202.2-35, HRA. The Eagle's accuracy was based on a 16-foot antenna hung in an 18-foot airfoil beneath the aircraft. See Engineering Branch to Materiel Command, January 5, 1944, File 452.26-G, Box 764, Central Decimal Files, Oct. 1942–1944, RG18. For an explanation of how the Norden bombsight worked when connected to the NOSMEAGLE system, see AAF Board, "Tactical Evaluation of the AN/APQ-7A (NOSMEAGLE)," December 7, 1945, File 245.64, HRA.

44. Eighth Air Force Operational Analysis Section, "Report on Bombing Accuracy 1 September 1944–31 December 1944," HRA.

45. Hudson to Laidlaw, April 11, 1960, File 520.056-263, HRA; Ardery, *Bomber Pilot*, 173–74; and Jeffrey Ethell and Alfred Price, *Target Berlin: Mission 250, 6 March 1944* (London: Jane's, 1981), 143–44.

46. Eighth Air Force, "Attack of Secondary and Last Resort Targets," October 29, 1944, File 519.5991-1, HRA; and Doolittle to Spaatz, January 30, 1945, File 520.422, HRA.

47. David J. C. Irving, *The Destruction of Dresden* (London: W. Kimber, 1963), 96.

48. Eighth Air Force Operational Analysis Section, "Report on Bombing Accuracy on Berlin Operations of 18 March 1945," April 1, 1945, File 131.504C, Vol. 1, HRA; and Eighth Air Force Operational Research Section, "Bombing Techniques—General," 1945, File 520.547A, HRA.

49. *Army Air Forces Statistical Digest, World War II* (Washington, D.C.: Office of Statistical Control, 1945), 242. Combined with the British bombing campaign, less than 14 percent of Allied bombs fell on the industrial fabric of Germany, 32 percent on transportation targets, 24 percent on "industrial areas" (city bombing), and 11 percent in support of armies in the field. See USSBS, Report No. 2, *Overall Report (European War)*, 8.

50. AAF Operations Analysis, "The Causes of Bombing Errors as Based on Eighth Air Force Combat Operations," July 15, 1947, File 143.504-3, HRA. This postwar evaluation determined that an average of 39.7 percent of bombing error came from antiaircraft artillery, 21.7 percent from altitude, and 11.8 percent from smoke and haze.

51. School of Applied Tactics, "Radar Bombing," HRA. One possible cause for error not presented here was a casual procedure followed by every bombardier during the war. Lt. Col. Paul W. Tibbets, commander of the 509th Composite Group, assigned responsibility for dropping the atomic bombs on Hiroshima and Nagasaki, became frustrated at his bombardier's lack of accuracy in testing at a bombing range in California. Close observation revealed that Maj. Thomas Ferebee did his preliminary adjustments and calculations on the Norden bombsight while seated. As he prepared to fix the sight on his aiming point, however, perhaps as a result of the increased tension of the moment, Ferebee and presumably tens of thousands of other American bombardiers lifted themselves slightly off their seats at the last few seconds while positioning the aiming point squarely in the center of the bombsight's telescope. This changed their viewing angle ever so slightly—a change of a nearly minuscule angle that would be amplified to an error of several hundred feet on the ground. See Thomas and Witts, *Enola Gay*, 68–69. Additionally, Harvard University researchers discovered close to the end of the war that each bombardier's lens, pupils, and retinal images differed when focusing on objects at various distances—a problem magnified by the bombsight telescope. Such factors only multiplied inherent bombing inaccuracies. See Boyce, *New Weapons for Air Warfare*, 85.

52. Materiel Division to Commanding General Materiel Command, August 25, 1944, File 202.2-35, HRA.

53. See, for example, Allen Raymond, "How Our Bombsight Solves Problems," *Popular Science* 143 (December 1943): 116–19, 212, 214, who notes the "technical miracle of precision

bombing . . . the bomb, which started out as a monster of terror and destruction, is to become an instrument of mercy, like a surgeon's scalpel."

54. Greenfield, *American Strategy in World War II*, 120–21. At peak strength, the American strategic forces arrayed against Germany included 7,177 heavy bombers, supported by 619,020 personnel. See USSBS, *Overall Report (European War)*, Table 1.

55. The Air Corps Tactical School faculty wrote just before the war that "we believe—if 227 bombs must be dropped to get one in an area bigger than a baseball diamond—it may be better to employ bombardment to augment the artillery than against small vital objectives." See ACTS, "Practical Bombing Probabilities—Conclusion," 1938–39, File 248.2208A-7, Pt. 4, HRA.

56. *AAF Statistical Digest*, 237.

57. USSBS, "Daylight Bombing Accuracy of the 8th, 9th and 15th Air Forces," August 24, 1945, File 137.306-6, HRA. The average circular error for different bombs in Europe was 2,694 feet (100-pound bomb), 2,978 feet (250-pound bomb), 1,673 feet (500-pound bomb), 1,308 feet (1,000-pound bomb), and 571 feet (2,000-pound bomb). See AAF Operations Analysis, "The Causes of Bombing Errors as Based on Eighth Air Force Combat Operations," HRA.

58. Only just prior to the war did the Air Corps begin to doubt the effectiveness of the 100-pound bomb and to consider larger bombs. See ACTS, "Practical Bombing Probabilities—Conclusion," HRA; ACTS, "Analysis and Development of Fragmentation Bombs," HRA; and ACTS, "The Power and Effect of the Demolition Bomb," 1938–39, File 248.2208A-3, HRA. FM 1-110, "Selection of Bombs and Fuzes for Destruction of Various Targets," April 9, 1945, File 170.121001-110, HRA, instructed planners to use "the smallest bomb which will effectively damage or destroy the individual target," claiming a single 500-pound bomb could "irreparably" damage 75 percent of the lathes, drills, planers, and other tools in a 60- by 180-foot building.

59. *New York Times*, September 28, 1944, 12:2; and Sen. Elbert D. Thomas (Utah), "Sitting Ducks in Our Air Force," *American Magazine* 141 (April 1946): 122.

60. Burrell Ellison, letter to author, August 24, 1993.

61. Purdue University Statistical Laboratory, "Bomb Effectiveness Analysis: Final Report," April 1, 1952, File K168.8-9, Vols. 1–3, HRA.

62. Webster and Frankland, *Annexes and Appendices*, 371–95; and Albert Speer, *Spandau: The Secret Diaries*, trans. Richard and Clara Winston (New York: Macmillan, 1976), 339–40. The USSBS concluded that "no indispensable industry was permanently put out of commission by a single attack" during the war. See USSBS, *Summary Report (European War)*, 16. Speer claimed that the German response to the bomber offensive required 33 percent of the output of the German optics industry, 50 to 55 percent of the electrotechnical industry, and 30 percent of the artillery. See Webster and Frankland, *Annexes and Appendices*, 371–95.

63. Statistical Laboratory, Purdue University, "Bomb Effectiveness Analysis," HRA.

64. Watts, *Foundations of U.S. Air Doctrine*, 85. J. F. C. Fuller, *The Second World War, 1939–1945* (New York: Duell, Sloan, and Pearce, 1949), 231, claimed "the strategic bombing of Germany up to the spring of 1944 was an extravagant failure. Instead of shortening the war, its cost in raw materials and industrial man-power, prolonged it." Greenfield, *American Strategy*, 120–21, argued that "the dream and ultimate goal of air war is to produce surrender by air power with only incidental help from other forces."

65. See Stephen L. McFarland and Wesley Phillips Newton, *To Command the Sky: The Battle for Air Superiority over Germany, 1942–1944* (Washington, D.C.: Smithsonian Institution Press, 1991).

66. Kenneth P. Werrell, "The Strategic Bombing of Germany in World War II: Costs and Accomplishments," *Journal of American History* 73 (December 1986): 705. According to

Minister of Armaments Albert Speer, the American bombing attacks of 1944 caused a 30 to 40 percent drop in the projected output of German industries. See Webster and Frankland, *Annexes and Appendices*, 371–95.

67. Statistical Laboratory, Purdue University, "Bomb Effectiveness Analysis: Final Report," HRA.

68. USSBS, Report No. 64b, *The Effects of Strategic Bombing on German Morale* (Washington, D.C.: Government Printing Office, 1947), 1:12–13, 7; and USSBS, *Summary Report (European War)*, 16, 4. The USSBS claimed bombing caused "defeatism, fear, hopelessness, fatalism, and apathy." These were the products of the bombing: 305,000 dead, 780,000 wounded, 1.865 million homes destroyed, the forced evacuation of 4.885 million, and the deprivation of utilities to 20 million Germans. The Federal Statistical Office in Wiesbaden, Germany, claimed that bombing killed 593,000 German civilians and destroyed 3.37 million dwellings. See Hastings, *Bomber Command*, 352.

69. There are some who argue strategic bombing did win the war. Immediately after the war, Bernard Brodie argued that strategic bombing knocked the German war economy "flat on its back," though too late to affect the outcome on the battlefield. See Bernard Brodie, "Strategic Bombing: What It Can Do," *Reporter*, August 15, 1950, 28–31. In a 1988 book, Alfred C. Mierzejewski argued that the Army Air Forces's campaign against the German transportation network after the summer of 1944 effectively destroyed the German industrial war effort by interdicting the critical choke-point in the German economy—coal. He documented the surplus capacity in that economy in defense of the length of time required for the collapse. The collapse did not come until the last six months of the war, however, by which time Allied armies were inside Germany's borders. Additionally, Mierzejewski saw war as a strictly economic issue—stop the shipment of coal and you destroy the economy and defeat Germany. Despite this collapse, the German military fought on. The synthetic oil industry produced fuel almost exclusively for the military. The oil campaign therefore struck primarily against the armed forces and led more directly to the defeat of the German military. Germany would be defeated only when Allied ground armies occupied its territory. See Mierzejewski, *The Collapse of the German War Economy*.

70. "A Study of Prepared Air Corps Doctrine," HRA; Wilson, "Theory for Air Strategy," 19–25; and Wilson, *Wooing Peponi*, 236–39. The most telling data supporting the conclusion that several more months of bombing would have destroyed the German industrial capability to wage war comes from the Strategic Bombing Survey. See also Table 10.4.

71. Eighth and Fifteenth Air Forces lost 8,325 bombers and 67,646 personnel killed or missing in action during the course of the strategic bombing campaign against Germany. See USSBS, *Appendix*, 2.

Chapter 11. Japan's Congested and Highly Inflammable Cities

1. Hurley, *Billy Mitchell*, 87; and Hearings Before the General Board of the Navy, 1917–1950, Roll 6, 1925, Eberle Board, p. 1327.

2. Martin Caidin, *The Ragged, Rugged Warriors* (New York: Dutton, 1966), 185–96. Ironically, it was the Navy that credited Kelly with sinking the battleship *Haruna*. See *New York Times*, April 11, 1942, 7:7.

3. Current Intelligence Section, "Synopsis of U.S. Army Aircraft Horizontal Bombing Attacks," 1942, and Joint Chiefs of Staff, "Employment of High and Medium Altitude Bombing against Maneuvering Surface Targets," JCS 181, December 28, 1942, Folder—Bombing Methods, Box 79, Subject File, Spaatz Papers; Office of Naval Intelligence, *The Japanese Story*

Table 10.4. German Armaments Production (January/February 1942 = 100)

Month	1942	1943	1944	1945
January	103	182	241	227
February	97	207	231	175
March	129	216	270	145
April	133	215	274	
May	135	232	285	
June	144	226	297	
July	153	229	322	
August	153	224	297	
September	155	234	301	
October	154	273	273	
November	165	268	268	
December	181	263	263	

Source: USSBS, Report No. 2a, *Statistical Summary (Appendix)* (Washington, D.C.: Government Printing Office, 1945), Chart No. 15, p. 113.

of the Battle of Midway (Washington, D.C.: Government Printing Office, 1947); and Gordon W. Prange, Donald M. Goldstein, and Katherine V. Dillon, *Miracle at Midway* (New York: McGraw-Hill, 1982). In 1943 the Army Air Forces Board carried out extensive studies of the capabilities of the Norden bombsight in B-17s from various altitudes. Against a small boat at rest the circular error was between 80 and 180 feet. Against a maneuvering boat, 1,119 bombs achieved a circular error of 646 feet and a 3 percent hit rate from 20,000 feet. See AAF Board, "Tactics and Technique of High Altitude Attack on Maneuvering Targets," April 4, 1943, File 245.64, HRA; and USAF Historical Division, *Strategic Bombers in a Tactical Role*, 108.

4. "A Study of Major Combatant Ships Sunk as a Direct Result of Air Attack," September 26, 1949, File 168.15-25, Vol. 9, HRA; and Wilson, *Wooing Peponi*, 266–67.

5. Halsey to BuOrd, September 26, 1942, File F41-8, Vol. 8, Box 712, BuAer Confidential Correspondence, 1922–44, RG72; and Brown, "Navy's Mark 15 (Norden) Bombsight," 302.

6. Brown, "Navy's Mark 15 (Norden) Bombsight," 297–98, 308.

7. "Sea Targets," March 1944, File 248.222-35, HRA; and Friedman, *U.S. Naval Weapons*, 190–91, 117.

8. Naval Intelligence, *Japanese Story;* and Prange et al., *Miracle at Midway.*

9. Fourteenth Air Force Operations Analysis Section, "Types of Bombing," April 14, 1945, File 131.504C, Vol. 3, HRA; and Friedman, *U.S. Naval Weapons*, 191.

10. James L. Cate, "XX Bomber Command against Japan," in Craven and Cate, eds., *Army Air Forces in World War II*, vol. 5, *The Pacific: MATTERHORN to Nagasaki, June 1944 to August 1945* (Chicago: University of Chicago Press, 1953), 96–98.

11. Boeing constructed the B-29 to use either the Sperry S-1 or Norden M-series bombsights. The bombsight of choice was the Norden.

12. "AAF Bombing Accuracy," Report No. 1, April 11, 1945, File 134.71-83, HRA; AAF Tactical Center, "Tactical Doctrine, Very Heavy Aircraft," November 20, 1944, File 248.232-11, HRA; and Cate, "XX Bomber Command," 116.

13. LeMay agreed to area bombing only after Maj. Gen. Albert C. Wedemeyer, commander of U.S. Forces in the China Theater, asked for Joint Chiefs of Staff intercession.

14. USSBS, *Summary Report (Pacific War)*, 16; USSBS, Report No. 66 (Pacific War), *The Strategic Air Operations of Very Heavy Bombardment in the War against Japan (Twentieth Air Force)* (Washington, D.C.: Government Printing Office, 1946), 2; and Rhodes, *Making of the Atomic Bomb*, 588.

15. Edoin, *The Night Tokyo Burned*, 14–15.

16. Carl Norden designed the M-9 bombsight for a maximum speed of 400 MPH. The highest recorded ground speed for a B-29 over Japan was 535 MPH.

17. "AAF Bombing Accuracy," Report No. 1, April 11, 1945, File 134.71-83, HRA.

18. Edoin, *Night Tokyo Burned*, 14–15. The National Defense Research Committee concluded in October 1942 that the firebombing of Japanese cities was feasible, but remained opposed to killing civilians. See National Defense Research Committee, "Incendiary Bombing," October 9, 1942, File 248.222-35, HRA.

19. Hansell to Boyle, December 1964, File 168.7004-64, HRA; and LeMay and Kantor, *Mission with LeMay*, 347. Hansell blamed poor training, inadequate radar, B-29 engine problems, inadequate supplies, Army and Navy pressure for him to fail, enemy defenses, extreme range, and weather for the failure of daylight precision strategic bombing against Japan.

20. James L. Cate and James C. Olson, "Precision Bombardment Campaign," in Craven and Cate, eds., *Pacific*, 573–74.

21. LeMay and Kantor, *Mission with LeMay*, 342–52, 373–74; and Schaffer, *Wings of Judgment*, 151.

22. LeMay to Arnold, March 22, 1945, File 762.1623-1, HRA.

23. The AN-M13 cluster consisted of sixty M-69s and weighed 417 pounds. The AN-M18 cluster carried thirty-eight M-69s and weighed 350 pounds. An explosive charge propelled the 2.8 pounds of burning oil of each M-69 over a radius of 75 yards, to burn for four or five minutes. See FM 1-110, "Selection of Bombs and Fuzes for Destruction of Various Targets," HRA.

24. LeMay quoted in Rhodes, *Making of the Atomic Bomb*, 586.

25. In April Twentieth Air Force launched twelve precision bombing missions, including four against industrial targets and eight against the Kyushu Airfield, averaging 29 percent of its bombs within 1,000 feet of the aiming point. Strike altitudes were from 8,000 to 16,000 feet. See XXI Bomber Command, "Graphic Summary of Operations," May 1, 1945, File 762.3011, HRA.

26. XXI Bomber Command, "Mission Report for Missions 251–255," July 6, 1945, File 762.331, HRA.

27. James L. Cate and James C. Olson, "The All-Out B-29 Attack," in Craven and Cate, eds., *Pacific*, 661.

28. In the war against Japan, a B-29 with conventional weapons could destroy 0.01 square miles of urban area. With atomic weapons, it could destroy 2.78 square miles of urban area. See Twentieth Air Force, "Summary of Combat Operations," August 2–9, 1945, File 760.308-3, HRA.

29. Rhodes, *Making of the Atomic Bomb*, 651.

30. Twentieth Air Force, "Statistical Operations," File 760.308-1, and "Summary of Combat Operations," June 5, 1944–August 15, 1945, File 760.308-2, HRA; USSBS, *Summary Report (Pacific War)*, 17; and USSBS, Report No. 15 (Pacific War), *The Japanese Aircraft Industry* (Washington, D.C.: Government Printing Office, 1947), 116.

31. USSBS, Report No. 88 (Pacific War), *Report of Ships Bombardment Survey Party (Enclosure J), Comments and Data on Accuracy of Firing*.

32. From high altitude Twentieth Air Force averaged 12 percent of its bombs within 1,000 feet of the aiming point. From medium altitude, in small formations dropping-on-the-leader, it averaged 37 percent. See USSBS, *Very Heavy Bombardment*, 15.

33. Twentieth Air Force Operations Analysis Section, "Bombing Accuracy Report No. BA-1," July 21, 1945, File 760.56-1, HRA. Weather forced XXI Bomber Command to drop 70 percent of all incendiaries and 43.3 percent of all high-explosive bombs in 1945 by radar. See "AAF Bombing Accuracy," July 1944-1945, Report No. 2, File 134.71-83, HRA.

34. Rhodes, *Making of the Atomic Bomb*, 517-20, 556.

35. Edoin, *Night Tokyo Burned*, 114.

36. The USSBS concluded that "by August 1945, even without direct air attack on her cities and industries, the over-all level of Japanese war production would have declined below the peak levels of 1944 by 40 or 50 percent solely as a result of the interdiction of overseas imports." See USSBS, *Summary Report (Pacific War)*, 15; and USSBS, Report No. 53 (Pacific War), *The Effects of Strategic Bombing on Japan's War Economy* (Washington, D.C.: Government Printing Office, 1946), 2.

37. USSBS, *Summary Report (Pacific War)*, 11, 17-18, 20-21, 26; Jerome B. Cohen, *Japan's Economy in War and Reconstruction* (Minneapolis: University of Minnesota Press, 1949), 58, 107-14, 406-7; and USSBS, *Effects of Strategic Bombing*, 3.

38. Ferguson, "Daylight Bombing Experiment," 733; Ira Eaker to Ronald Schaffer, January 11, 1979, File 168.7126-20, HRA; USSBS, Report No. 14 (Pacific War), *The Effects of Strategic Bombing on Japanese Morale* (Washington, D.C.: Government Printing Office, 1947), 1; Gar Alperovitz, *Atomic Diplomacy: Hiroshima and Potsdam; The Use of the Atomic Bomb and the American Confrontation with Soviet Power* (New York: Simon and Schuster, 1965); Sherry, *Rise of American Air Power*, 256-73; and Schaffer, *Wings of Judgment*, 107-27.

Epilogue

1. *New York Times*, August 14, 1945, 9:4-8. This project, code-named Operation Zebra, was kept a secret at the request of the Soviet Union. The Navy secretly trained 140 Soviet airmen in Elizabeth City, North Carolina, as part of a $100-million lend-lease deal that provided the Soviets with 188 navy patrol bombers, 100 of which were equipped with Norden bombsights. See *New York Times*, September 27, 1945, 1:2-3.

2. Letter from Carroll J. Watkins to author, March 15, 1991; and Albert L. Partini, "Navy Used Norden Sight in Vietnam," *Crosshairs* 5 (September 1990): 32.

3. USAF Bombardment School, Mather AFB, "C-1 Autopilot Student Study Guide," January 1951, File K221.712A-17, HRA.

4. Chuck Hansen, *U.S. Nuclear Weapons: The Secret History* (Arlington, Tex.: Aerofax, 1988), 31, 73; and Group History, 509th Bombardment Group, 1946, File GP-509-SU-PE, HRA.

5. Mark H. Smith and Robert L. Wendt, "A Bombing System Reliability Program," *Sperry Engineering Review* 9 (May-June 1956): 14-19.

6. Lt. Col. John W. Skelton, "Current and Future Bombsighting Equipment," from "Armament Notes: Conference at Air Proving Grounds," June 8-9, 1949, File 240.151-5, HRA.

7. In 1950 Barth retired to Wareham, Massachusetts, where he funded the Tobey Hospital through his Barth Foundation, which still operates in New York. In 1959 he served as the first vice-president of the National Republican Club.

8. *New York Times*, November 12, 1945, 28:3, and May 24, 1946, 32:1.

9. Fernandez, *Excess Profits*, 206, 225.

10. Interviews with Carl F. Norden, December 9, 1989, and April 22, 1990.

Appendix D. The Bombsighting Problem

1. "Handbook for Radio Altimeters," November 4, 1944, File 168.69-25, HRA.

2. Sources for this appendix include TR 440-96, "Bomb Ballistics and Bomb Sights," HRA; Air Corps Tactical School, "Bomb Ballistics," 1936, File 248.222-36, HRA; "Handbook for Radio Altimeters," HRA; Midland AAF Field, "Bombs and Fuses," July 1943, File 286.391-19, HRA; 2nd and 3rd Operations Analysis Sections, Far Eastern Air Forces, "Number of Aircraft Necessary for Proposed Military Operation," HRA; and Air Service Engineering Division, "Report on Bomb Sights," HRA.

Appendix E. Operation of the Norden Mark 15/M-Series Bombsight

1. "Handbook of Instructions for Bombsight Type M-9," June 5, 1945, File 168.69-30, HRA.

Select Bibliography

Documentary Collections

Hagley Museum and Library, Wilmington, Del.
Elmer Ambrose Sperry Papers
Lawrence Sperry Aircraft Corporation Papers
Records of the Sperry Gyroscope Company, Public Relations Department Literature Files

Library of Congress, Washington, D.C.
Curtis LeMay Papers, Manuscript Division
Carl Spaatz Papers, Manuscript Division

National Archives
RG 18, Textual Records of the U.S. Army Air Forces
RG 72, Records of the U.S. Navy Bureau of Aeronautics
RG 74, Records of the U.S. Navy Bureau of Ordnance

U.S. Air Force Historical Research Agency, Maxwell Air Force Base, Ala.
Records of the U.S. Air Force

U.S. Department of Justice, Washington, D.C.
Records of the Federal Bureau of Investigation

Washington National Records Center, Suitland, Md.
RG 342, Records of U.S. Air Force Commands, Activities, and Organizations; Records of the Engineering Division, Materiel Command, Wright Field

Interviews

Richard S. Baldwin
Elizabeth Bayley
Howard T. Bjork
William Colbourn
Earl B. Gross
Haywood S. Hansell Jr.
Quitman C. Hurdle
Paul Lang
Ned Lawrence
Robert C. Lory
Carl F. Norden
Richard O'brien
Alfred M. Oppenheim
Frank S. Preston
James E. Taylor
Carroll J. Watkins
Joe Whittaker

Books

Ardery, Philip. *Bomber Pilot: A Memoir of World War II.* Lexington: University of Kentucky Press, 1978.
Arnold, H. H. *Global Mission.* New York: Harper, 1949.
Arnold, H. H., and Ira C. Eaker. *Winged Warfare.* New York: Harper, 1941.
Ayling, Keith. *Bombardment Aviation.* Harrisburg, Pa.: Military Service Publishing Co., 1944.
Beck, Earl R. *Under the Bombs: The German Home Front, 1942–1945.* Lexington: University Press of Kentucky, 1986.
Belote, James H., and William M. Belote. *Titans of the Seas.* New York: Harper and Row, 1975.
Bowles, Gene. *History of Lukas-Harold.* N.p.: Pioneer Printing Services, 1980.
Boyce, Joseph C. *New Weapons for Air Warfare: Fire-Control Equipment, Proximity Fuzes, and Guided Missiles.* Boston: Little, Brown, 1947.
Boyle, Andrew. *Trenchard.* London: Collins, 1962.

British Bombing Survey Unit. *The Strategic Air War against Germany, 1939–1945.* London: His Majesty's Stationery Office, n.d.

Brittain, Vera Mary. *Seed of Chaos: What Mass Bombing Really Means.* London: New Vision, 1944.

Caldwell, Cyril C. *Air Power and Total War.* New York: Coward-McCann, 1943.

Charlton, Lionel E. O. *War from the Air: Past, Present, Future.* London: T. Nelson and Sons, 1935.

Chinnock, Frank W. *NAGASAKI: The Forgotten Bomb.* New York: New American Library, 1969.

Coffey, Thomas M. *Decision over Schweinfurt: The U.S. 8th Air Force Battle for Daylight Bombing.* New York: McKay, 1977.

———. *Iron Eagle: The Turbulent Life of General Curtis LeMay.* New York: Crown, 1986.

Cohen, Jerome B. *Japan's Economy in War and Reconstruction.* Minneapolis: University of Minnesota Press, 1949.

Conn, Stetson, gen. ed. *The United States Army in World War II.* Vol. 8, pt. 7, *Buying Aircraft: Matériel Procurement for the Army Air Forces,* by Irving B. Holley, Jr. Washington, D.C.: Office of the Chief of Military History, 1964.

Cooke, Ronald C., and Roy C. Nesbit. *Target, Hitler's Oil: Allied Attacks on German Oil Supplies, 1935–45.* London: Kimber, 1985.

Copp, DeWitt S. *A Few Great Captains: The Men and Events that Shaped the Development of U.S. Air Power.* Garden City, N.Y.: Doubleday, 1980.

———. *Forged in Fire: Strategy and Decisions in the Air War over Europe, 1940–1945.* Garden City, N.Y.: Doubleday, 1982.

Craven, Wesley Frank, and James Lea Cate, eds. *The Army Air Forces in World War II.* Vol. 1, *Plans and Early Operations, January 1939–August 1942.* Chicago: University of Chicago Press, 1948. Vol. 2, *Europe: TORCH to POINT-BLANK, August 1942 to December 1943.* Chicago: University of Chicago Press, 1949. Vol. 3, *Europe: ARGUMENT to V-E Day, January 1944 to May 1945.* Chicago: University of Chicago Press, 1951. Vol. 5, *The Pacific: MATTER-HORN to Nagasaki, June 1944 to August 1945.* Chicago: University of Chicago Press, 1953. Vol. 6, *Men and Planes.* Chicago: University of Chicago Press, 1955.

Cross, Robin. *The Bombers: The Illustrated Story of Offensive Strategy and Tactics in the Twentieth Century.* New York: Macmillan, 1987.

Davenport, William W. *Gyro! The Life and Times of Lawrence Sperry.* New York: Scribner's, 1978.

De Seversky, Alexander P. *Victory through Air Power.* New York: Simon and Schuster, 1942.

Dickens, Gerald. *Bombing and Strategy: The Fallacy of Total War.* London: Sampson Low, Marston, n.d.

Douhet, Giulio. *The Command of the Air.* Edited by Richard H. Kohn and Joseph P. Harahan, translated by Dino Ferrari. New York: Coward McCann, 1942; rpt., Washington, D.C.: Office of Air Force History, 1983.

Drake, Francis Vivian. *Vertical Warfare.* Garden City, N.Y.: Doubleday, 1943.

Dubuque, Jean H., and Robert F. Gleckner. *The Development of the Heavy Bomber, 1918–1944.* Maxwell AFB, Ala.: USAF Historical Division, 1951.

Edoin, Hoito. *The Night Tokyo Burned.* New York: St. Martin's, 1987.

Eliot, George F. *Bombs Bursting in Air: The Influence of Air Power on International Relations.* New York: Reynal and Hitchcock, 1939.

Fabyanic, Thomas A. *Strategic Air Attack in the United States Air Force: A Case Study.* Manhattan, Kan.: Military Affairs/Aerospace Historian, 1976.

Finney, Robert T. *History of the Air Corps Tactical School, 1920–1940.* USAF Historical Studies, no. 100. Maxwell AFB, Ala.: Air University, 1955.

Fletcher, Eugene. *Fletcher's Gang: A B-17 Crew in Europe, 1944–45.* Seattle: University of Washington Press, 1988.

Freeman, Roger A. *The Mighty Eighth: Units, Men and Machines. A History of the U.S. 8th Air Force.* London: Jane's, 1986.

Frisbee, John L., ed. *Makers of the United States Air Force.* Washington, D.C.: Office of Air Force History, 1987.

Futrell, Robert Frank. *Ideas, Concepts, Doctrine: A History of Basic Thinking in the United States Air Force, 1907–1964.* Maxwell AFB, Ala.: Air University Aerospace Studies Institute, 1971.

Gaston, James C. *Planning the American Air War: Four Men and Nine Days in 1941.* Washington, D.C.: National Defense University Press, 1982.

Greenfield, Kent Roberts. *American Strategy in World War II: A Reconsideration.* Baltimore: Johns Hopkins University Press, 1970.

Greer, Thomas H. *The Development of Air Doctrine in the Army Air Arm, 1917–1941.* USAF Historical Studies, no. 89. Maxwell AFB, Ala.: Air University, 1955; rpt., Washington, D.C.: Office of Air Force History, 1985.

Hansell, Haywood S., Jr. *The Air Plan that Defeated Hitler.* Atlanta: Higgins-McArthur/Logino and Porter, 1972.

———. *The Strategic Air War against Germany and Japan.* Washington, D.C.: Office of Air Force History, 1986.

Hattendorf, John B., B. Mitchell Simpson, and John R. Wadleigh. *Sailors and Scholars: The Centennial History of the U.S. Naval War College.* Newport, R.I.: Naval War College, 1984.

Hayes, Thomas J. *Elements of Ordnance: A Textbook for Use of Cadets of the United States Military Academy.* New York: John Wiley and Sons, 1938.

Hughes, Thomas P. *Elmer Sperry: Inventor and Engineer.* Baltimore: Johns Hopkins University Press, 1971.

Hurley, Alfred F. *Billy Mitchell: Crusader for Air Power.* New York: Franklin Watts, 1964.

Jablonski, Edward. *Flying Fortress: The Illustrated Biography of the B-17s and the Men Who Flew Them.* Garden City, N.Y.: Doubleday, 1965.

Jacobs, Donald H. *A Scientist and His Experiences with Corruption and Treason in the U.S. Military-Industrial Establishment.* Victoria, B.C.: Jacobs Instrument Co., 1969.

Johnson, Brian. *Fly Navy: The History of Naval Aviation.* New York: William Morrow, 1981.

Jones, H. A. *The War in the Air.* Oxford: Clarendon, 1937.

Kennett, Lee. *A History of Strategic Bombing*. New York: Scribner's, 1982.

Kerr, E. Bartlett. *Flames over Tokyo: The U.S. Army Air Forces' Incendiary Campaign against Japan, 1944–1945*. New York: Donald I. Fine, 1991.

Kohn, Richard H., and Joseph P. Harahan, eds. *Strategic Air Warfare: An Interview with Generals Curtis E. LeMay, Leon W. Johnson, David A. Burchinal, and Jack J. Catton*. Washington, D.C.: Office of Air Force History, 1988.

LeMay, Curtis E., and MacKinlay Kantor. *Mission with LeMay: My Story*. Garden City, N.Y.: Doubleday, 1965.

LeMay, Curtis E., and Bill Yenne. *Superfortress: The Story of the B-29 and American Air Power*. New York: McGraw-Hill, 1988.

Lent, Henry B. *Bombardier: Tom Dixon Wins His Wings with the Bomber Command*. New York: Macmillan, 1944.

Ley, Willy. *Bombs and Bombing*. New York: Modern Age, 1941.

McArthur, Charles W. *Operations Analysis in the U.S. Army Eighth Air Force in World War II*. Providence, R.I.: American Mathematical Society, 1990.

McCollum, Kenneth G., ed. *Dahlgren*. Dahlgren, Va.: Naval Surface Weapons Center, 1977.

MacIsaac, David. *Strategic Bombing in World War Two: The Story of the United States Strategic Bombing Survey*. New York: Garland, 1976.

Maurer, Maurer. *Aviation in the United States Army, 1919–1939*. Washington, D.C.: Office of Air Force History, 1987.

Melhorn, Charles M. *Two-Block Fox: The Rise of the Aircraft Carrier, 1911–1929*. Annapolis, Md.: Naval Institute Press, 1974.

Middlebrook, Martin. *The Schweinfurt-Regensburg Mission*. New York: Scribner's, 1983.

Miller, Ronald, and David Sawers. *The Technical Development of Modern Aviation*. London: Routledge and Kegan Paul, 1968.

Mitchell, William. *Memoirs of World War I: "From Start to Finish of Our Greatest War."* New York: Random House, 1960.

———. *Our Air Force: The Keystone of National Defense*. New York: Dutton, 1921.

———. *Skyways: A Book on Modern Aeronautics*. Philadelphia: Lippincott, 1930.

———. *Winged Defense: The Development and Possibilities of Modern Air Power—Economic and Military*. New York: Putnam's, 1925.

Mierzejewski, Alfred C. *The Collapse of the German War Economy, 1944–1945: Allied Air Power and the German National Railway*. Chapel Hill, N.C.: University of North Carolina Press, 1988.

Miller, Thomas G., Jr. *History of the First Day Bombardment Group*. West Roxbury, Mass.: World War I Aero Publishers, n.d.

Morrison, Wilbur H. *Fortress without a Roof: The Allied Bombing of the Third Reich*. New York: St. Martin's, 1982.

———. *The Incredible 305th: The "Can Do" Bombers of World War II*. New York: Duell, Sloan, and Pearce, 1962.

———. *Point of No Return—The Story of the Twentieth Air Force*. New York: Time Books, 1979.

Newby, Leroy W. *Target Ploesti: View from a Bombsight*. Novato, Calif.: Presidio, 1983.

Parton, James. *"Air Force Spoken Here": General Ira Eaker and the Command of the Air.* Bethesda, Md.: Adler and Adler, 1986.

Roscoe, Theodore. *On the Seas and in the Skies: A History of the U.S. Navy's Air Power.* New York: Hawthorn, 1970.

Saundby, Sir Robert H.M.S. *Air Bombardment: The Story of Its Development.* New York: Harper, 1961.

Savage, Mark. *How Planes Fight and Bomb.* New York: Watts, 1943.

Saward, Dudley. *The Bombers' Eye.* London: Cassell, 1959.

———. *Victory Denied: The Rise of Air Power and the Defeat of Germany, 1920–45.* New York: Watts, 1987.

Sherman, William C. *Air Warfare.* New York: Ronald Press, 1926.

Sherrod, Robert. *History of Marine Corps Aviation in World War II.* Washington, D.C.: Combat Forces Press, 1952.

Sherry, Michael S. *The Rise of American Air Power: The Creation of Armageddon.* New Haven: Yale University Press, 1987.

Smith, Malcolm. *British Air Strategy between the Wars.* Oxford: Oxford University Press, 1984.

Smith, Peter C. *Vengeance!: The Vultee Vengeance Dive Bomber.* Shrewsbury, England: Airlife, 1986.

Spaight, J. M. *Bombing Vindicated.* London: Geoffrey Bles, 1944.

Spaight, James M. *Air Power and the Cities.* London: Longmans, 1930.

Steinbeck, John. *Bombs Away: The Story of a Bomber Team.* New York: Viking, 1942.

Thomas, Gordon, and Max Morgan Witts. *Enola Gay.* New York: Stein and Day, 1977.

Turnbull, Archibald D., and Clifford L. Lord. *History of United States Naval Aviation.* New Haven: Yale University Press, 1949; rpt., New York: Arno Press, 1972.

U.S. Navy Department Bureau of Ordnance. *United States Navy Bureau of Ordnance in World War II.* Washington, D.C.: Government Printing Office, 1953.

U.S. Office of Naval Operations. *United States Naval Aviation, 1910–1970.* Washington, D.C.: Government Printing Office, 1970.

U.S. Strategic Bombing Survey. Report No. 1. *Summary Report (European War).* Washington, D.C.: Government Printing Office, 1945.

———. Report No. 2. *Overall Report (European War).* Washington, D.C.: Government Printing Office, 1945.

———. Report No. 62. *Weather Factors in Combat Bombardment Operations in the European Theater.* Washington, D.C.: Government Printing Office, 1947.

———. Report No. 63. *Bombing Accuracy, USAAF Heavy and Medium Bombers in the ETO.* Washington, D.C.: Government Printing Office, 1947.

———. Report No. 109. *Oil Division, Final Report.* Washington, D.C.: Government Printing Office, 1947.

———. Report No. 115. *Ammoniakwerke Merseburg GmbH, Leuna, Germany.* Washington, D.C.: Government Printing Office, 1947.

———. Report No. 128. *Huels Synthetic Rubber Plant.* Washington, D.C.: Government Printing Office, 1947.

———. Report No. 1 (Pacific War). *Summary Report (Pacific War).* Washington, D.C.: Government Printing Office, 1946.

———. Report No. 66 (Pacific War). *The Strategic Air Operations of Very Heavy Bombardment in the War against Japan (Twentieth Air Force).* Washington, D.C.: Government Printing Office, 1946.

———. Report No. 88 (Pacific War). *Report of Ships Bombardment Survey Party (Enclosure J), Comments and Data on Accuracy of Firing.* Washington, D.C.: Government Printing Office, 1946.

———. Report No. 90 (Pacific War). *Effect of the Incendiary Bomb Attacks on Japan (Report on Eight Cities).* Washington, D.C.: Government Printing Office, 1947.

Verrier, Anthony. *The Bomber Offensive.* New York: Macmillan, 1968.

Wagner, Ray. *American Combat Planes.* Garden City, N.Y.: Doubleday, 1982.

Walker, Lois E., and Shelby E. Wickam. *From Huffman Prairie to the Moon: The History of Wright-Patterson Air Force Base.* Wright-Patterson AFB, Ohio: Air Force Logistics Command, n.d.

Watts, Barry D. *The Foundations of U.S. Air Doctrine: The Problem of Friction in War.* Maxwell AFB, Ala.: Air University Press, 1984.

Webster, Charles, and Noble Frankland. *The Strategic Air Offensive against Germany, 1939–1945.* Vol. 1, *Preparation.* Vol. 2, *Endeavour.* Vol. 3, *Victory.* Vol. 4, *Annexes and Appendices.* London: Her Majesty's Stationery Office, 1961.

Werrell, Kenneth P. *Eighth Air Force Bibliography: An Extended Essay and Listing of Published and Unpublished Materials.* Manhattan, Kan.: Sunflower University Press, 1981.

Wheeler, Keith. *Bombers over Japan.* Alexandria, Va.: Time-Life Books, 1982.

Williams, Al. *Airpower.* New York: Coward-McCann, 1940.

Wilson, Donald. *Wooing Peponi: My Odyssey thru Many Years.* Monterey, Calif.: Angel Press, 1973.

Winston, Robert A. *Dive Bomber.* New York: Holiday House, 1941.

Zilbert, Edward R. *Albert Speer and the Nazi Ministry of Arms: Economic Institutions and Industrial Production in the German War Economy.* London: Associated University Presses, 1981.

Articles and Reports

A., R. "Bomb Dropping." *Flight* 4 (February 3, 1912): 116.

"Aerial Bombs and Projectiles." *Aeronautics* 15 (September 1914): 94.

"Aerial Bomb Sights." *Engineer* 128 (August 29, 1919): 211–13.

"Aerial Torpedo Latest in Aero Warfare." *Aeronautics* 5 (October 1909): 160.

"Aircraft Bombing Trials Off Portsmouth." *Flight* 15 (August 16, 1923): 499–500.

"Airplane Bombing." *Journal of the Society of Automotive Engineers* 3 (November 1918): 323–24.

"Airplane versus Battleship." *Review of Reviews* 64 (October 1921): 429–30.

"Air Torpedo Tested." *Aerial Age* 14 (November 14, 1921): 221.

Atkinson, J. L. Boone. "Italian Influence on the Origins of the American Concept of Strategic Bombardment." *Air Power Historian* 4 (July 1957): 141–49.

"An Automatic Pilot." *Aerial Age* 13 (March 28, 1921): 62.

"An Automatic Pilot." *Aeronautics* 20 (February 1921): 77.

"The Automatic Pilot." *Scientific American Monthly* 3 (April 1921): 359–60.

"Automatic Pilot Installation in Twin-Motored Hydroaeroplane." *Aerial Age Weekly* 4 (January 1, 1917): 409, 418.

"Automatic Stability." *Aviation* 1 (October 1911): 16.

"Automatic Stability in Aeroplanes." *Engineering* 90 (1910): 505–6.

"Automatic Stability, Method of Obtaining, Invented by Mr. Cody." *Aero* 6 (October 1912): 284.

"Automatic Stability Problem Solved." *Aeronautics* 7 (July 1910): 36.

"The Aveline Automatic Airplane Control." *Aviation* 10 (March 1921): 363–64.

"The Aveline Automatic Pilot." *Aerial Age* 12 (March 7, 1921): 656–58, 667.

"The Aveline Automatic Pilot." *Flight* 13 (February 3, 1921): 73–75.

"The Aviation Lessons Taught by the Tripolitan and Balkan Campaigns." *Scientific American* 109 (September 13, 1913): 206.

"Backbone of the Fleet." *Scientific American* 125 (September 3, 1921): 158.

Baldwin, Hanson. "Blueprint for Victory." *Life*, August 4, 1941, 40.

Barth, Alan. "Strategic Bombing—An Autopsy." *Nation* 161 (November 24, 1945): 546–48.

Barth, Theodore H., assignor to the United States of America as represented by the Secretary of the Navy. "Aircraft Control System." U.S. Patent Office, No. 2,485,953 (filed April 24, 1940, awarded October 25, 1949).

———. "Synchronizing Bomb Sight." U.S. Patent Office, No. 2,438,532 (filed September 28, 1932, awarded March 30, 1948).

Barton, F. Alexander. "Bombs for Aerial Purposes." *Aeronautics* 5 (March 1912): 83.

Bates, M. F. "The Automatic Airplane Pilot: How Flying May Be Controlled." *Sperryscope* 2 (June 1920): 7, 14–16.

Bates, Mortimer F., assignor to Sperry Gyroscope Company. "Bomb Sight." U.S. Patent Office, No. 1,783,769 (filed June 1, 1926, awarded December 2, 1930).

———. "Bomb Sight Alignment and Rudder Control." U.S. Patent Office, No. 1,880,671 (filed October 18, 1929, awarded October 4, 1932).

Beard, M. Gould, and Percy Halpert. "Automatic Flight Control in Air Transportation." *Sperry Engineering Review* 8 (May–June 1955): 2–9.

"The Beginning Was 2 Men, $12,000 and 1 Floor in New York." *Norden Times*, May 1978, 4–5.

Bellah, James Warner. "Bombing Cities Won't Win the War." *Harper's Magazine* 179 (November 1939): 658–63.

Benjamin, Park. "The Fiske Torpedo-Launching Seaplane." *Flying* 4 (June 1915): 540–41.

Berthelot, Daniel. "New Bomb Device." *Aeronautics* 12 (March 1913): 102.

Blackburn. "The Blackburn Automatic Stability Device." *Flight* 2 (June 4, 1910): 429.

Blériot, Louis. "To Teach Aerial Bomb Dropping." *Aero and Hydro* 8 (September 5, 1914): 283.

"Bomb-dropping from Aeroplanes." *Flight* 6 (December 18, 1914): 1213–14.

"Bomb-Dropping in Mexico." *Aeronautics* 14 (February 1914): 60.

"Bomb Dropping in the Balkans." *Scientific American* 109 (October 11, 1913): 278.

"Bomb Dropping with Carranza." *Aeronautics* 9 (December 1915): 364–65.

"Bombing and Getting Bombed." *Scientific American* 118 (March 9, 1918): 209.

"Bombing Planes and Their Targets." *Scientific American* 119 (July 6, 1918): 86, 96, 97.

"Bombing Tests and Our Naval Policy." *Scientific American* 125 (August 6, 1921): 90.

"Bombing the Old Battleship Indiana." *Scientific American* 123 (December 4, 1920): 575.

"A Bomb on Norden." *Time*, January 1, 1945, 55.

"Bombs or Torpedoes." *Aviation* 11 (August 29, 1921): 256.

"The Bombsight." *Flying* 33 (October 1943): 103–7, 342–44.

"The Bombsight." *Flying* 35 (July 1945): 28–30, 124–26.

"Bombsight Announced: T-1." *Science News Letter* 46 (July 29, 1944): 67.

"A Bomb-Sighting Device." *Flight* 6 (April 4, 1914): 369.

"Bomb Throwing from Aircraft." *Aerial Age Weekly* 4 (October 9, 1916): 98, 106.

"Bomb Throwing from Aircraft." *Journal of the U.S. Artillery* 46 (July–August 1916): 102–6.

Bonnet, Henry. "A Prize for Stabilizers." *Aeronautics* 13 (September 1913): 94.

Bowers, Ray L. "The Energetic Sperrys." *Aerospace Historian* 14 (Summer 1967): 93–95, 98–101.

Brandrick, W. J. "Gyroscopic Stabilizers." *Flight* 2 (November 19, 1910): 961.

Brodie, Bernard. "The Heritage of Douhet." *Air University Quarterly Review* 6 (Summer 1953): 64–69, 121–27.

———. "Strategic Bombing: What It Can Do." *Reporter*, August 15, 1950, 28–31.

Bryan, George Hartley. "A Danger of So-Called Automatic Stability." *Nature* 91 (1913): 556–57.

"Building Aerial Torpedoes." *Aerial Age* 3 (April 24, 1916): 191.

Bumpus, F. A. "The Development of Torpedo-Carrying Aircraft." *Journal of the Royal Aeronautical Society* 32 (March 1928): 206–26.

Carollin, Norbert. "Captain Carollin on Bombing." *Aviation* 19 (November 9, 1925): 672–73.

Clarke, T. W. K. "Pendulum Stability." *Flight* 3 (March 18, 1911): 235.

"The Converse Automatic Stabilizer." *Aeronautics* 15 (August 1914): 39.

Conway, Arlington B. "Death from the Sky." *American Mercury*, February 1932, 167.

Cornelisse, Diana G. "Remarkable Journey." *Air Power History* 37 (Winter 1990): 7–14.

Crane, Conrad C. "Evolution of U.S. Strategic Bombing of Urban Areas." *The Historian* 50 (November 1987): 14–39.

Dargue, H. A. "Bombardment Aviation and Its Relation to Antiaircraft Defense." *Coast Artillery Journal* 77 (September–October 1934): 333–35.

Davis, Richard G. "Bombing Strategy Shifts, 1944–45." *Air Power History* 36 (Winter 1989): 33–45.

"Depth-Bombing from the Air." *Scientific American* 125 (July 2, 1921): 4–5.

"Details of a German Bomb Sight." *Scientific American* 164 (May 1941): 261–62.

"Details of Scott's Winning." *Aeronautics* 11 (October 1912): 118–19.

Eiani, H. O. "Automatic Stability Experiments." *Aero* 3 (December 9, 1911): 199.

"The Elements of Bomb-Dropping." *Air Service Journal* 1 (November 22, 1917): 629–30.

"The Elements of Bomb-Dropping." *Flying* 2 (October 10, 1917): 179–81.

Emme, Eugene M. "Some Fallacies Concerning Air Power." *Air Power Historian* 4 (July 1957): 127–40.

"End of a Secret." *Newsweek*, April 26, 1943, 29–30.

Estoppey, Georges. "Bombing Moving Ships." *U.S. Air Service* 8 (May 1923): 45–49.

———. "Bomb Sight." U.S. Patent Office, No. 1,804,679 (filed January 7, 1925, awarded May 12, 1932).

———. "Bomb Sighting Device." U.S. Patent Office, No. 2,118,041 (filed September 5, 1930, awarded May 24, 1938).

Fitzgerald, John G. "Norden." *Beehive* (Fall 1958): 13–17.

Flugel, Raymond R. "United States Air Doctrine: A Study of the Influence of William Mitchell and Giulio Douhet at the Air Corps Tactical School, 1921–1935." Ph.D. diss., University of Oklahoma, 1965.

"Former Lieut. Scott Wins Two Michelin Prizes." *Fly* 4 (September 1912): 8.

"Frankford Arsenal Aerial Torpedo." *Aviation and Aeronautical Engineering* 1 (November 1, 1916): 222.

Futrell, Robert E. "Airpower Lessons of World War II." *Air Force and Space Digest* 48 (September 1965): 42–53.

Gill, Brendan. "Young Man behind Plexiglas." *New Yorker*, August 12, 1944, 26–37.

Girardville, Lucas. "The Stability of Aeroplanes by Means of the Gyroscope." *Aeronautics* 4 (May 1911): 51–52.

Glines, C. V. "The Blue Ox." *Air Force Magazine* 75 (August 1992): 72–75.

Goldman, L. Beauclerc. "Automatic Versus Inherent Stability." *Flight* 4 (August 10 and December 28, 1912): 738, 1233–34.

"Government Buys Bomb-Dropping Device." *Aerial Age* 3 (April 24, 1916): 177.

Gradenwitz, Alfred. "Device for the Automatic Control of Airplanes." National Advisory Committee for Aeronautics, Technical Memorandums No. 495, January 10, 1929.

Graham, Vickie. "Brother Bombardiers: Putting a Pickle in a Barrel." *Airman* 31 (September 1987): 12–13.

Green, Murray. "The *Shasta* Disaster: Forgotten Lessons in Interservice Relations." *Air University Review* 30 (March–April 1978): 68–74.

Guidoni, Alessandro. "Early Experiments at Launching Torpedoes from an Aeroplane." *Flying* 4 (June 1915): 539–40.

"Gyropilot for Automatic Flying." *Sperryscope* 7 (September 1936): 7–10.

Hall, John V. "Inventions: The Automatic Balance of Aeroplanes." *Aero* 1 (September 14, 1909): 282.

Hansell, Haywood S., Jr. "General Laurence S. Kuter, 1905–1979." *Aerospace Historian* 27 (June 1980): 81.

Harlan. "The Harlan Bomb Dropper." *Aeronautics* 12 (April 1913): 140.

Herring, A. M. "Aeroplane with Gyroscopic Control." *Aero* 2 (January 11, 1910): 35.

Hobart, D. R. "The Eteve Automatic Stabilizer." *Aeronautics* 7 (November 1910): 151.

Hopper, Bruce C. "American Day Bombardment in World War I." *Air Power Historian* 4 (April 1957): 87–97.

Hubbarb, Thomas O'Brien. "The Dunne Automatic Stability System." *Aeronautics* 8 (March 1911): 81–83.

Huggins, Marion. "Gyropilot Goes Cross-Country." *Aero Digest* 17 (July 1930): 51–52.

"If Philadelphia Had Been Bombed." *Literary Digest* 81 (May 31, 1924): 24.

Inglis, H. B. "Bombing." *U.S. Air Services* 10 (October 1925): 31–35.

Inglis, Henry B. "Bomb Sight and Pilot Director." U.S. Patent Office, No. 2,105,147 (filed February 8, 1930, renewed June 15, 1936, awarded January 11, 1938).

"Installation of the Sperry Stabilizer on a Curtiss Flying Boat." *Aerial Age* 1 (June 14, 1915): 303.

"Inventions for Obtaining Perfect Automatic Stability." *Aero* 1 (September 28, 1909): 312–13.

Jacobs, W. A. "Strategic Bombing and American National Strategy, 1941–1943." *Military Affairs* 50 (July 1986): 133–39.

Johnson, C. Langley. "Gyroscopic Control." *Flight* 3 (March 25, 1911): 267.

Johnson, Valentine Edward. "Automatic Stability." *Flight* 1 (July 17, 1909): 434.

Johnstone, Stanley. "Bombers and Bomb Sights." *Science Digest* 10 (January 1945): 52–55.

Kamp, Walter V. "Kamp's Automatic Stability." *Aeronautics* 14 (March 1914): 87.

Kelham, Thomas. "Pendulum Stability." *Flight* 2 (November 19, 1910): 961.

Keller, Charles L. "The First Guided Missile Program: The Aerial Torpedo." *Sperry Engineering Review* 14 (March 1961): 11–18.

Kingsley-Field, C. "Gyroscopes as Stabilisers." *Flight* 4 (November 30, 1912): 1126.

Krauskopf, Robert W. "The Army and the Strategic Bomber." *Military Affairs* 22 (Summer 1958): 83–94.

Kuter, Laurence S. "Maj. Gen. H. A. Bert Dargue: A Lesson in Leadership." *Air Force Magazine* 62 (February 1979): 80–82.

"Limitations of Aerial Bombing." *Scientific American* 125 (July 2, 1921): 2.

Loening, Grover Cleveland. "Automatic Stability in Aeroplanes: Comments on Some American Patents." *Scientific American* 104 (May 13, 1911): 470–71, 488.

———. "The Wright Automatic Stabilizer." *Flying* 2 (January 1914): 29.

Loring, E. J. "Bombing and Bombing Sights." *Scientific American* 126 (January 1922): 49–51.

Lytton, Henry D. "Bombing Policy in the Rome and Pre-Normandy Invasion Aerial Campaigns of World War II: Bridge-Bombing Strategy Vindicated and Railyard Bombing Strategy Invalidated." *Military Affairs* 47 (April 1983): 53–58.

M., S. H. S. "Bomb Dropping." *Flight* 4 (February 10, 1912): 134.

——. "Rough Designs for a Bomb and Sight." *Flight* 4 (January 27, 1912): 78–79.

Macfie, R. F. "Automatic Stability from a New Standpoint." *Aeronautics* 4 (July 1911): 98–99.

MacLeod, A. Gordon. "Automatic Stability." *Aero* 1 (September 28, 1909): 314–15.

"Maintaining the Stability of Aeroplanes by Means of Gyroscopes." *Scientific American* 105 (July 22, 1911): 82.

Mallock, Henry R. A. "Reflections on Aerial Flight. With a Note on the Fallacy of Pendulum Stabilizers." *Scientific American Supplement*, December 20, 1913, 398–400.

Marmonnier, Louis. "The Gyroscopic Balancing of Aeroplanes." *Flight* 1 (December 25, 1909): 833.

"Mechanical Brains of the Air Forces." *Life*, January 24, 1944, 66–67.

"Michelin Bomb Dropping Contest." *Aero* 6 (September 1912): 265.

"Michelin Bomb-Dropping Prize." *Aero* 6 (March 1912): 62–63.

Milling, T. de Witt. "The R. E. Scott Projectile-Dropping Device." *Aero Club of America Bulletin* 1 (February–March 1912): 11–12.

"Modern Aircraft Bombs and Their Use." *Aviation* 16 (April 14, 1924): 390–93.

"Modern Torpedo Plane Has Early Ancestor." *Aviation* 18 (February 23, 1925): 215.

Moore, Willard G. "A Time Controlled Aerial Torpedo." *Aviation and Aeronautical Engineering* 1 (December 15, 1916): 322–23.

Murrelle, J. H. "Recent Bombing Operations." *Scientific American* 125 (August 20, 1921): 133.

Nealey, J. B. "Integration of the Automatic Pilot System and the Norden Bombsight." *Aero Digest* (June 1, 1945): 16–18.

"New Automatic Stabilizer." *Aviation* 18 (January 5, 1925): 20.

"New Bombsight." *Business Weekly*, November 6, 1943, 66.

"New Bomb Sight Invented." *Science News Letter* 42 (October 17, 1942): 248.

"A New Plea for Automatic Stability. A Reply to Some Criticisms." *Aero* 1 (September 28, 1909): 307.

Nickerson, Hoffman. "The Folly of Strategic Bombing: An Analysis of Maj. Gen. J. F. C. Fuller's New Book." *Ordnance* 33 (January–February 1949): 245–47.

Nisos, Michael J. "The Bombardier and His Bombsight." *Air Force Magazine* 64 (September 1981): 106–13.

"Norden Bombsight." *Science News Letter* 46 (December 9, 1944): 382.

"Norden Bombsight Is Really Master Robot." *Science News Letter* 47 (June 9, 1945): 361.

"Norden Bombsight—Magician and Mathematician: Solved 2 Concurrent Trigonometry Problems." *Norden Times*, July 1978, 4–5.

Norden, Carl L., and Barth, Theodore H., assignors to the United States of America. "Bomb Sight." U.S. Patent Office, No. 2,428,678 (filed May 27, 1930, awarded October 7, 1947).

"Norden, Carl Lukas." *Current Biography*, January 1945.

"Norden Secrets Out." *Scholastic* 42 (May 3, 1943): 13.

"Not by a Bombsight." *Newsweek*, January 1, 1945, 50.

Nunn, H. Lawrence. "Automatic Stability Device." *Flight* 2 (July 23, 1910): 587.

"Open Secret." *Time*, December 4, 1944, 50.

"Out of the Clouds." *Business Week*, December 2, 1944, 32.

Overy, R. J. "Hitler's War and the German Economy: A Reinterpretation." *Economic History Review* 35 (May 1982): 272–91.

P., N. S. "Bomb-Dropping from Aircraft." *Aeronautics* 7 (October 1914): 269–70.

Parker, Steven A. "Targeting for Victory: The Rationale behind Strategic Bombing Objectives in America's First Air War Plan." *Airpower Journal* 3 (Summer 1989): 58–70.

"Pendulum Stability." *Flight* 2 (December 3, 1910): 1000–1001.

"Pickle Barrel Club: Respite from the War." *Norden Times*, August 1978, 4–5.

"Pickle Barrelers." *Newsweek*, April 20, 1942, 50–51.

Postlethwaite, F. "Notes on Enemy Bombsights." *Aircraft Engineering* 14 (September 1942): 244–47, 250; and 14 (October 1942): 276–80.

"Precision Bombing and the Automatic Pilot." *Aero Digest* (October 1943): 116–17, 232.

"Profits and Secrets." *Time*, September 4, 1939, 44, 46.

"Radio-Controlled Torpedo Wins Favor of Navy and Army Experts." *Aerial Age* 3 (September 4, 1916): 744.

Rand, Kurt. "The Norden Bombsight." *Flying* 33 (July 1943): 37–38, 148.

Raymond, Allen. "How Our Bombsight Solves Problems." *Popular Science* 143 (December 1943): 116–19, 212, 214.

Rees, Joscelyne. "Precision Bombing—Fact or Fiction." *Military Technology* 11 (April 1987): 54–56.

"Result of First Contest for Safety in Aeroplanes, in France." *Scientific American Supplement*, August 15, 1914, 108–9.

Roland. "The Roland Bomb-Dropping Apparatus." *Flight* 6 (December 4, 1914): 1173.

Rowell, Ross E. "Aircraft in Bush Warfare." *Marine Corps Gazette* 14 (September 1929): 180–203.

Samson, Jack. "Nitemare's Secret Score." *Air Force Magazine* 73 (April 1990): 102–5.

Schornstheimer, Graser. "Airplane Bomb vs. Battleship." *New York Times Current History Magazine* 14 (September 1921): 923–27.

"Scientific Bomb Dropping." *Scientific American Supplement*, April 22, 1916, 260.

"Scientific Device for Bomb-Dropping from Aeroplanes." *Aeronautics* 9 (August 1911): 39–40.

"Scott Bomb Dropper Trials." *Aeronautics* 9 (November 1911): 179–80.

Scott, Riley E. "Dropping Bombs from Flying Machines." *Scientific American* 105 (October 28, 1911): 388–89.

——. "Means for Dropping Projectiles from Aerial Crafts." U.S. Patent Office, No. 991,378 (filed May 4, 1910, awarded May 2, 1911).

Scott, William B. "Electro-Optic Targeting Tools Bolster Bombing Accuracy of Allied Aircraft." *Aviation Week and Space Technology* 134 (January 28, 1991): 25.

"Scott Wins Michelin $5,000." *Aeronautics* 11 (September 1912): 94.

Searle, Loyd. "The Bombsight War: Norden vs. Sperry." *IEEE Spectrum* (September 1989): 60–64.

Simpson, B. W. "Bombing Accuracy." *Aviation* 19 (September 28, 1925): 393–96.

Skerrett, Robert G. "Making the Aeroplane Safe by the Gyroscopic Stabilizer." *Scientific American* 107 (June 7, 1913): 511–12.

Slavin, J. J. "Automatic Stability." *Aviation* 1 (March 1911): 31.

Smith, Harold. "Gyroscopic Control." *Flight* 3 (February 4, 1911): 102–3.

Smith, Mark H., and Robert L. Wendt. "A Bombing System Reliability Program." *Sperry Engineering Review* 9 (May–June 1956): 14–19.

Smith, Melden E., Jr. "The Strategic Bombing Debate: The Second World War and Vietnam." *Journal of Contemporary History* 12 (1977): 175–91.

"The Sperry Automatic Control." *Aeronautics* 11 (September 1916): 175.

"Sperry Automatic Pilot." *Aero Digest* 15 (December 1929): 166.

"The Sperry Automatic Pilot." *Flying* 5 (September 1916): 344–46.

Sperry, Elmer Ambrose. "What the Virginia Capes Aircraft Bombings Show." *Mechanical Engineering* 43 (September 1921): 624.

Sperry, Elmer Ambrose, Jr., assignor to Sperry Gyroscope Company. "Automatic Control of Aircraft." U.S. Patent Office, No. 1,859,752 (filed June 29, 1928, awarded May 24, 1932).

Sperry, Lawrence B., assignor to Sperry Gyroscope Company. "Mechanical Pilot for Aeroplanes." U.S. Patent Office, No. 1,324,134 (filed April 24, 1916, awarded December 9, 1919).

Sperry, Lawrence B. "Criticism of Albert Adams Merrill's Theories." *Aircraft* 4 (December 1913): 223, 231.

"The Sperry Gyroscopic Stabilizer." *Aeronautics* 14 (February 1914): 37, 39.

"The Sperry Gyroscopic Stabilizer." *Flight* 7 (January 29, 1915): 74–76.

"Sperry Gyroscopic Stabilizer." *Flying* 3 (January 1915): 360–61.

"The Sperry Gyroscopic Stabilizer." *Flying* 3 (August 1914): 196–200.

"The Sperry Gyroscopic Stabilizer in France." *Scientific American* 111 (July 11, 1914): 30.

"Sperry Stabilizer Meets with Success in European War." *Aerial Age* 1 (July 5, 1915): 367–68.

"Sperry Wins Stability Prize." *Aeronautics* 15 (July 1914): 12.

"Spider Silk for Bomb Sights." *Flying* 31 (July 1942): 62.

"Stability in Flying Machines." *Aeronautics* 13 (December 1913): 210–11.

Steel, George H. "Testing Aircraft Armament: Results of Army Air Corps and Ordnance Department Cooperation." *Army Ordnance* 7 (January–February 1928): 229–32.

"Success of the Sperry Gyroscope." *Flying* 3 (July 1914): 189.

"Super-Bombsight Used to Train Bombing Crews." *Science News Letter* 46 (September 16, 1944): 184.

"Testing the Sperry-Curtiss Stabilizer." *Flight* 6 (July 3, 1914): 712.

"Torpedo Attack from the Air." *Scientific American* 11 (December 26, 1914): 517, 523.

"Torpedo Controlled by Aircraft." *Aeronautics* 10 (February 1916): 98.

Torrey, Volta. "How the Norden Bombsight Does Its Job." *Popular Science* 146 (June 1945): 70–73, 220, 224, 228, 232.

Townesend, D. "Automatic Stability." *Flight* 4 (January 27, 1912): 95.

Tribken, E. Robert. "All-Attitude Automatic Pilots." *Sperry Engineering Review* 11 (June 1958): 27–32.

"Trying a Gyroscope Stabilizer." *Aeronautics* 13 (November 1913): 182.

"24 Hours of a Bomber Pilot." *Harper's Magazine* 189 (August 1944): 283–90.

"U-Boats Fear His 10-Cent Bombsight." *American Magazine* 134 (December 1942): 84.

"United States Aerial Bombing Tests on Battleships." *Flight* 15 (October 25, 1923): 657.

"U.S. President and Bomb-Dropping on Open Towns." *Flight* 6 (December 4, 1914): 1176.

Van Auken, Howard C., and Gerald N. Hanson, assignors to Sperry Gyroscope Company. "Bomb Sight." U.S. Patent Office, No. 2,409,648 (filed January 25, 1941, awarded October 22, 1946).

Vernham, Noel M. H. "Automatic Stability." *Aero* 6 (February 1912): 43.

———. "An Automatic Stabilizer." *Aero* 5 (October 1911): 200.

———. "The Vernham Stabiliser." *Aero* 5 (December 1911): 256.

Walden, Henry W. "Lateral Automatic Stability Device." *Aeronautics* 5 (October 1909): 128.

Walker, K. N. "Bombardment Aviation—Bulwark of National Defense." *U.S. Air Services* 18 (August 1933): 15–19.

Werrell, Kenneth P. "The Strategic Bombing of Germany in World War II: Costs and Accomplishments." *Journal of American History* 73 (December 1986): 702–13.

"What Bombardier Needs." *Science News Letter* 43 (April 24, 1943): 260.

"What Makes Our Bombsight So Deadly." *Popular Science* 143 (August 1943): 92–93.

Wheeler, Gerald E. "Mitchell, Moffett, and Air Power." *Aerospace Historian* 8 (April 1961): 79–87.

Whittaker, Wayne. "The Bombsight That Thinks." *Popular Mechanics* 83 (February 1945): 7–10, 160, 162.

Wilson, Donald. "Origin of a Theory for Air Strategy." *Aerospace Historian* 18 (Spring 1971): 19–25.

"Wright Automatic Stability System." *Aeronautics* 13 (October 1913): 138–39, 142.

"The Wright Automatic Stabilizer." *Aeronautics* 14 (January 1914): 3–4.

"Wrights' Automatic Stability." *Aeronautics* 5 (September 1909): 90–91.

Index

ABC-1, 101
Aberdeen Proving Ground, 30–31, 85–87
Abukuma, 192
Abwehr, 117
Accuracy: and blind bombing, 96; causes of inaccuracy, 185–86; and dive bombing, 202; and Eighth/Fifteenth Air Forces, 167–69, 171–76, 179, 184–86; in Gulf War, 209; of Mark III, 61; of Mark XI, 61, 71–72; of Mark XV, 71–72; and Mitchell ship-bombing tests, 47; in 1930s Army, 95, 97; in 1930s Navy, 110; nuclear, 2–3; and radar, 180–84, 201, 203, 207; and scoring techniques, 84, 172–73; and ship bombing, 99; and training, 159–60; and Twentieth Air Force, 197–98, 201, 203; and XX Bomber Command, 195–96; in World War I, 14, 18
AC Spark Plug Division, 137, 144
Adams, Charles F., 73
Aerial torpedo, 21–22, 48, 62–63
AFCE (automatic flight control equipment), 122–26, 195
Air Corps Act, 59–60
Air Corps Tactical School, 27, 83, 90–101, 184–85, 187–88, 204

Aircraft
—American: 247D, 39; A-20, 137; AT-11, 158, 163; B-2, 85–86; B-3A, 83; B-5, 85–86; B-9, 66, 96; B-10, 66, 96, 98, 130; B-12, 44; B-17, 4, 7, 39, 66, 96, 98, 100, 130, 137, 173; B-18, 123; B-24, 4, 130, 137, 144, 156, 173, 192; B-25, 137, 192; B-26, 137, 146; B-29, 1–2, 4, 130, 194–205, 207; B-34, 158; B-45, 207; B-47, 207; B-50, 207; B-52, 207; BF2C, 66; BM-1, 66; BM-2, 66; BT-1, 66; C-9, 37; C-45, 158; DH-4, 15, 63–64; DT-2, 63; F-111, 208; F4F, 110; F6C-2, 65; Keystone, 66, 96, 98; LB-5, 40; MBT, 63; N-9, 21; O2B, 64; PB4Y, 147; PBY, 137; PT-1, 63; PT-2, 63; RB-36, 207; SB2U, 110; SBD, 66, 110, 193–94; SC-1, 63; SC-2, 63; T2D-1, 63; T3M-1, 63; T4M-1, 63; TBD, 63, 110, 193; TG-2, 63; TM-1, 63
—British (Halifax; Lancaster; Mosquito; Wellington), 137
—French: Breguet 14 B-2, 24
—German: Do 17, 80; Do 19, 80; Gotha, 14; He 111, 80; Ju 87, 80; Ju 89, 80
Airfields. *See specific field*